I Aim to Be That Man

How God Used the Ordinary Life
of Avery Willis Jr.

Dear Tom,
    Thank you for the deep impact
you have had on our family—
as my parents' pastor, dad's best
friend, and the discipling you
taught to all of us. We so
appreciate you!
        Sherrie Willis Brown
            2018

Sherrie Willis Brown

ISBN 978-1-64299-852-8 (paperback)
ISBN 978-1-64299-853-5 (digital)

Christian Faith Publishing, Inc.
832 Park Avenue
Meadville, PA 16335
www.christianfaithpublishing.com

Cover photos courtesy of International Mission Board

Printed in the United States of America

Contents

Foreword

"Tom, I want you to preach the message at my funeral." Avery's request left me stunned. It was his admission that his death was not only inevitable but that it would occur sooner rather than later. Even as I agreed to his request, everything within me was shouting, "No!"

"I'll do it, but I don't want to talk about it," was the best I could muster at the moment. I don't remember much of the discussion that followed before we ended our phone conversation.

It was not that one couldn't see the ravages his illness had worked upon him. His weakened body bore the evidence of the battle. The years of incessant travel had taken their toll.

Avery's cheerfulness a few weeks earlier when accepting an award from Oklahoma Baptist University, his alma mater, could not disguise the weariness in his eyes. From there he had attempted to attend a farewell party for IMB president Dr. Jerry Rankin, but had spent the days in a hospital room instead. The following weeks found him again in the hospital, before returning home shortly before his graduation to glory.

But Avery's indomitable spirit had overcome numerous challenges, no matter the arena. To me, Avery Willis was larger than life. I'd often heard that *what* a person learns is not nearly as significant as the person *under* whom he learns. With Avery, you were always learning—from his lips *and* his life. He was the master teacher.

Master teacher. From my earliest association with Avery, three things gripped my attention. First, here was a man who was dead set on being a *student* of God's Word and communicating it with others by the most effective means possible. Home from the field, Avery was soon given an office next to mine in the church I pastored. Out of that office he began to put to paper and practice the course that ultimately became *MasterLife.*

What separated Avery from most, however, was that his insatiable desire to *learn* was matched by his fervent determination to *do* what he learned. Avery was both a *disciple* and a *disciple-maker.* This second characteristic gave Avery a genuine credibility that few possess. Every principle he taught was firmly ingrained in his life.

Then there was Avery's *vision*! If you had a thought, Avery had an idea. If you had an idea, Avery had a vision. If you had a vision, Avery had a dream—larger, grander, and more encompassing than any you'd heard before.

"*'Here comes that dreamer,'* they said to one another" (Gen 37:19). It was those words, spoken by Joseph's jealous brothers, that I took as the text for Avery's funeral service. Seated before me were Avery's wife, Shirley, his children, and other family members. The church, nestled in the hills of Northwest Arkansas, where Avery and Shirley had come to retire, was filled with people who had traveled from distant corners around the world—people who, like me, could each speak of the impact of Avery's life on our own.

Throughout the day, adjectives tumbled from our hearts and mouths in an attempt to describe him. Incessant student, master teacher, missionary, revivalist, leader, soul winner, innovator, visionary, caring husband, loving father and grandfather, author, encourager, and, oh yes—dreamer!

And from heaven's galleries behind which stands the King of kings, it seemed as if we could hear the voices in hushed reverence, saying, *"Here comes that dreamer!"*

Now, meet my friend, the dreamer!

Tom Elliff
Former President of the International Mission Board
Southern Baptist Convention

Note from the Author

My dad preached at his own funeral. I wish he would have written this book while he was at it!

Writing a memoir posthumously is tricky. It is usually the subjects of the study who decide which moments stand out in their life and what they learned from them. They also have the opportunity to choose what is written. In this instance, I had to make those choices.

After Dad's death, my mom sent me home with four large boxes—an entire filing cabinet worth—of Dad's journals. Hours were spent reading and selecting entries that best represented his thinking and his journey with the Lord. I have attempted to relay the events Dad would note as his spiritual markers—the times when God adjusted Dad's direction to follow Him into a new adventure.

In hindsight, it is easy to see how God built Dad's ministry one layer upon another, each building a foundation for the next. But he was not privileged with that perspective as we are. As a reader, you may sometimes want to know how events played out, but I moved you on with Dad to his next undertaking. I couldn't tell it all—sometimes for space, and sometimes because I didn't know since I walked the journey through his journals. When he turned a corner, so did I.

As often as possible, the story is told in his own words as excerpts from his journals, newsletters or sermons, portions taken from his own books, and stories told from family members, friends, and colaborers in the ministry. Seeking clues to the story he would want told, I imagined myself sitting with him, perusing with him what I had written, and what his responses would be.

Some of it is raw, and not what the public knew, but is the reality of Dad living out his obedience to his Lord. I hope I have not included more than he would have wanted, but sometimes we learn more from the weaknesses in our heroes than from their finest moments. I know Dad would not want any glory to go to himself, but only to God.

So my first acknowledgement is to the Holy God and Heavenly Father of all mankind, who is the source of all love, light, and power. The story is really His. It was God's powerful hand in the ordinary skin of a man that touched lives all over the world.

Secondly, my gratitude belongs to Avery T. Willis Jr., my earthly father, for the life he lived before me. He was the one who personally discipled me and with whom I became as much a friend as a daughter. Before delving into this venture, I knew Dad was highly respected. I did not realize that he was such a pioneer. Modern readers may see his actions and choices as standard mission practices, but at the time Dad was living them out, they were innovative—even radical—especially for Baptists bound by tradition. I knew he was gifted as an evangelist and pastor. I did not realize that, at different points in his life, God also granted him the spiritual gifts of teacher, apostle, and prophet. I knew he was driven, but I didn't fully understand the depth of his passion and commitment to get the gospel of Jesus to the *whole world*.

I must also thank Ron Owens, friend and neighbor to my parents, who took on the initial task of this book. He conducted interviews and collected information from many of the great men with whom Dad worked at LifeWay and at the International Mission Board in the last decades of his life. I learned how to turn journal entries into narration from Ron and to believe such a story is worth the time to tell. Some of these words are his.

My older brother, Randy, edited and rewrote to make the story clearer. Mom proofread and corrected facts. They helped me discern chunks of material I could leave out. They, and my husband, Steve, continually encouraged me to complete the project.

Finding time to write while teaching school full-time was difficult and extended the process longer than any of us expected. But the story was bigger than I knew, and Dad was more multifaceted in his talents than I realized. I was discipled again as I eavesdropped on his conversations with God.

Thank You, God, and thank you, family, for allowing me to speak for all of you. And now I leave to the Holy Spirit to accomplish what He will through this book. Be forewarned: in the reading of his life, Avery may yet serve as a disciple-maker in your life.

Sherrie Willis Brown

Introduction

Born in Lepanto, Arkansas, and buried less than three hundred miles away in Bella Vista, Arkansas, seventy-six years later, one might think Avery Willis Jr. was a simple man who lived his life, never venturing far from home.

Nothing could be further from the truth.

"It would be impossible to comprehend this side of heaven the extent of global evangelization that will continue to sweep the world because of Avery's witness, leadership, and influence among Southern Baptists, national Baptist conventions around the world, and other Great Commission partners," said Jerry Rankin, then president of the Southern Baptist International Mission Board. "His walk with the Lord was authentic. His faith was contagious. His vision unlimited. To participate in a strategy session with Avery was to be challenged beyond the ordinary and to catch a vision of possibilities characterized by the power and providence of God."[1]

You may choose to read this book because you knew Avery Willis personally and shared a part of his life. If so, then you know the breakthroughs he made and the legacy and vision he left on this earth, which will echo through generations and into eternity.

Perhaps you never met him, but his message or his ministry had a personal impact on your life. You may have participated in a *MasterLife* discipleship group, heard him preach, or been moved by his passion that every people group on the earth would have the opportunity to hear and know the name of Jesus.

Maybe you enjoy reading stories of "spiritual giants of the faith" because they encourage you to greater faith and obedience. If you are interested in missionary life, church planting, prayer, revival, disciple-making, or global missions, you can learn from Avery's life.

This account is less about giving tribute to a man or even recounting his most remarkable achievements, because those will be determined by the Eternal Judge. This is the human story of the life circumstances and the daily choices made by a man who sought to be an obedient disciple and who, in that process, became a disciple-maker of countless others.

One of Avery's favorite quotes was that of Dwight L. Moody, who, when challenged that "the world has yet to see what God can do with a man fully consecrated to him," responded with, "By God's help, I aim to be that man." Avery sought to do the same.

His definition of discipleship was refined from years of living it:

Discipleship is developing a personal, obedient, life-long relationship with Jesus Christ in which He transforms your character into Christlikeness, changes your values into Kingdom values, and involves you in His mission in the home, the church, and the world.[2]

A definition can be formed by carefully crafting words, but living it is something entirely different. Walking with God means daily talking to Him, seeking to understand both His will and His ways, having the faith to obey when it is easy and when it hurts, walking in humility even while being applauded and promoted, and being "very careful, then, how you live—not as unwise but as wise, making the most of every opportunity, because the days are evil" (Ephesians 5:15 NIV).

These are the daily habits of a true disciple—and the story of Avery Willis's life.

Prelude
What Does It Mean to Love?

From Avery's journal, January 30, 1968, written in free-flowing hand:

How do I love without reserve, that is, completely, when need overwhelms me? Can an ordinary person with social, family, and personal obligations even do it?

"Oh yes, we must love everyone as God has loved us," you answer.

But I say, it's impossible, because we are not God. We may try to imitate His love and seek to let Him love through us—but we have limitations, even as others demand our love.

Love would have me sit with a slightly handicapped man who comes to my home because no one else pays attention to him, and yet in the hour he takes (or more), a hundred other demands for that hour go unheeded. It isn't as if I can save him from drowning in five minutes and then plunge in for others. The time he demands seals the doom of others, and yet he is only "saved' temporarily because tomorrow he wants another hour.

Love would demand I give the shirt off my back, but in a land of millions of people who would consider beggars in America as rich people, they could take all my clothes, my family's clothes, and everything I own quicker than it takes me to write this.

Love demands our death, but our death to those drinking at the fountain of our souls is not more than a drop, soon evaporated by their burning need.

Love can be given, and I do not mind giving it, even if it costs my life, but can I do it and still be the steward of my life before God? And while others make demands on my conscience, the cries of my own "flesh and blood," my children, that I caused to be born, echo in my ears. They, too, need love that is spelled T-I-M-E. Their mother too, needs a husband.

Oh, this is the tension, the dissatisfaction of love. It can only be enjoyed by giving freely—yet it is so quickly diminished!

Perhaps greater than the audible cries of the beggars, the maimed in mind and body, the hawkers looking for a soft touch, or the others who just look at me, hoping they'll find the answer, are those I know whose hearts are breaking, whose lives are shattered, whose hopes are dimming, whose way grows devious—those I know I could help if I had the time, but alas, time is gone to the seller of houses, the demander of reports and up-to-date books, the friends and relatives who want me to drop them a line. Even as I'm working, I am constantly asking—"Am I getting the job done?"

You answer, "Well, you can only do so much."

That's what I've been saying—I can't love without reserve. I must reserve my health, home, sanity, contacts, reputation, etc.

What scares me is that my love will become just a series of prescribed actions—a pat on the back, a smile, a tip, until I don't see the problems anymore. Yet if I really do look at the problems of those who need me, it scares me to death. I can't even help all the surface ones, or the ones called to my attention, let alone those just below the surface that my good will has brought to the surface. Oh God, only You can love. We can only dimly reflect it."

I heard that at the funeral of M. Theron Rankin [former executive secretary of the Foreign Mission Board], *Bobbye Rankin said: "He was an ordinary man with the world in his heart." If she said it, it was because he was not an ordinary man. Most of us do not really even have the people on our block in our hearts, let alone the world. It is the care, the love that sets a man apart. This is the mark of a disciple—but we don't dare to care.*

These words poured out from a heart just completing four years on the mission field, observing material poverty and spiritual destitution beyond his previous imagination, and feeling stretched to his limits with the immensity of the task before him: that 105 million Indonesian people might die without knowing Jesus the Christ. He had lived through an attempted coup d'état and threat to his own family, learned to live and preach in another language, and undergone a radical rethinking of his own mission philosophy.

Through it all, the questions came faster than answers.

How can an ordinary man be like Jesus?
How do you experience the full power of God?
Where is the line between love and responsible
stewardship?

How do you know where and when God wants you to move?
How do you obey a new direction from God
when it seems counter to everything you have been doing?
How do you bring the kingdom of God to every culture?

In his struggle, Avery earnestly sought the wisdom and face of God.
Hear his words and wonderings,
prayers and prophecies,
cries and commitments,
grief and growth,
failures and faith.
Hear his heart.

*A spiritual marker identifies a time of transition,
decision or direction when I clearly know
God has guided me.*

—Henry Blackaby[1]

SECTION 1
Developing as a Disciple

Spiritual Marker #1

Avery was greatly influenced by his parents,
but he made his own commitment to follow Christ.

*Repent and be baptized,
every one of you in the name of Jesus Christ
for the forgiveness of your sins.*

Spiritual Marker #2

Avery's spiritual life, preaching, and witnessing
were transformed when he was filled with the Holy Spirit.

And you will receive the gift of the Holy Spirit.
—Acts 2:38 NIV

CHAPTER 1
Legacy

Sons are a heritage from the Lord,
children a reward from Him.
—Psalm 127:3 (NIV)

Heritage

From before his birth, Avery Thomas Willis Jr. had been dedicated to the Lord. Cold air seeped through cracks of the parsonage as Avery Jr. was born to evangelist and church-planter Avery Thomas (A.T.) Willis and Grace Carver Willis on a snowy February 21, 1934. The legacy into which he was born cannot be underestimated. He held a ringside seat to the faith walk of his parents. Their journey taught him to trust God, to obey, and to keep the kingdom of God uppermost.

His mother cooked three hot meals a day, and at least twice a day, the family sat down to eat together. Scripture verses propped in a plastic loaf of bread, signifying "daily bread," held a prominent place in the center of the breakfast table. Bible reading, family "devotions," and Scripture memory were part of the daily routine. Even the grandchildren remember that when Granddaddy came in and said, "Turn off the TV, let's have devotions," the expectation was immediate compliance, even if only five minutes remained in a show.

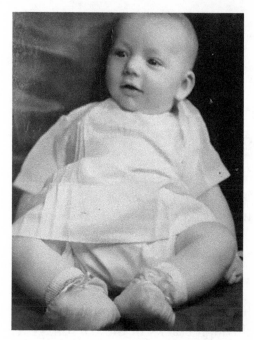 

Avery, six weeks, 1934   Avery, Jr. age 2, 1936

As a result, Avery Jr. learned the Scriptures from an early age. While in first grade, he responded to an appeal to read the whole Bible within a year. Even with the daily help of his mother, he did not finish in a year, but he did not quit until he read the Bible through. By his seventh birthday, Avery Jr. knew numerous Bible stories and could quote Psalm 1, Psalm 23, and John 3:16.

The Willis home, full of love and respect, was also strict. Negative talk or gossip about others was not allowed. Right and wrong were not up for debate. The Scripture to "avoid all appearance of evil" was upheld. Whatever might be considered a step toward compromising with "worldly sins" did not enter the home; movies, dancing—even playing cards and dice games—were not allowed.

A.T., Grace, Avery Jr., Norma, and Betty Willis

Avery wrote of his parents:

Reflections on Dad's and Mom's roles in discipling me:

1. *He intensely taught me the Word (doctrine)*
2. *He was aggressive in morality and holy living (ethics)*
3. *He was adamant about the church (Body life)*
4. *He was committed to personal and family devotions (worship)*
5. *He was fervent in soul-winning and involving me (witness)*

He deposited these truths in me. They have been multiplied as "investments." Mom supported and taught grace with this. Therefore, they really did disciple me. [1]

The parallel between Avery Jr.'s and his father's passion for those without Christ, their struggle to understand God's will, and their surrender to ministry—even how they wrote in their journals—was

19

almost uncanny. AT relayed three life-changing experiences with God—his dramatic call to preach, the empowering of the Spirit, and his surrender to the will of God for his life direction—in "an open letter to friends, schoolmates, and fellow Christian workers." To more fully understand Avery Jr., hear his father's story, the most influential person in his life.

A.T. Willis's Story

I am giving you three of the most sacred experiences in my life. Each one marks a transition period, an epoch in the course of my life. The sacred vows we make to God are not easily forgotten, but are rather written upon our memory and engraved upon our hearts. They serve as beacon lights to the Christian traveler. They hold our lives above the world as a telephone post does the wires over which a message can be clearly delivered and over which power is transmitted. Let us break these agreements and forget our promises to Him, and we experience the loss of power, happiness, and usefulness.

AT's father died when he was eleven months old, leaving his mother to raise four children. AT quit school in the seventh grade and went to work for the railroad. Later, he returned home to help out on his stepfather's farm. He knew God wanted him to preach but believed he couldn't do so because he only had a sixth-grade education.

One day, at the age of eighteen, AT was out plowing. He felt the Lord calling him to preach but argued, "You can strike me dead or anything else, but I cannot preach because I don't have enough education to preach the gospel." At that point, he collapsed to the ground and rolled across three rows of corn struggling to get up. He could not get his breath and believed he would die right there.

The Lord said, "You can get up when you will preach."

When a man tells me that he does not believe in a call to preach, I don't argue with him but I know one thing: that he did not receive the same call that I did in the same manner. If he had, he could not have slept through it so easily. What troubled me was I knew too well what God was saying to me.

As Jacob wrestled with the angel at Jabbok ford, I met the Lord in a special way while plowing the field near Kizy Creek in Haywood County, Tennessee.

For a long time, I had known what He wanted me to do but had refused to do it or let anyone know that I was called to it. The Lord seemed to let me know that this was my last day of opportunity to give Him my decision. Surely never a more pungent question confronted a worldly youth of eighteen than that of preaching the gospel. God placed before me two ways: one of life, and one of death. He showed me two worlds—this one and the one to come. He let me see two wills, my stubborn and rebellious will, and His Most Holy and Sovereign Will.

In an unquestionable manner He gave me the understanding that His Will was to be done. This resulted in a total surrender on my part for the first time of my life. It was there, without an elementary education, I closed the contract with God that if He would give me the words, I would preach in New York or anywhere else.

AT crossed the Mississippi River into neighboring Blytheville, Arkansas, to return to school. Although he was nineteen years old, he returned to the seventh grade. When the teacher asked him why, he said, "This is where I left off, so this is where I should start." The teacher graciously promoted him to ninth grade so he wouldn't be in class with twelve-year-olds. He finished school and then attended Jonesboro College.

Strange to say, that Satan did not agree to leave me alone after such complete surrender. About five years later while in Jonesboro Baptist College, I found myself completely in doubt of God, the Bible, Christ, Christian experience, and everything else sacred. Could a full-time pastor afford to tell such a condition to relatives, professors, or friends?

With such indescribable burden, I walked into my room, locked the door, and as an honest doubter, called upon God to reveal Himself or I would be forced to resign my church work and cast aside my Bible as I could not afford to be a hypocrite. At two in the morning, the floodgates of heaven were opened. God in His gracious, loving, and personal way turned loose every ray of sunlight or assurance upon my benighted soul of doubt. He drove away every darkened spot of gloom and fear. There, with joyful heart, I renewed my covenant of five years ago to live or die for Him and to close my heart against the devil with his cunning deception.

AT's personality was daring, bold, and frank, and he voiced his convictions with the directness of a prophet. He met Grace while preaching revival services in her home church. He had promised the Lord he would not date while he was preaching, so he waited until the end of the final night's service to invite her out. She declined, but the pastor's wife invited them all over for watermelon. By evening's end, Grace agreed to go out with AT.

Six months later, they sat in the car on a Wednesday evening, and AT asked Grace to marry him. He asserted, "I don't want to wait around either. Marry me tomorrow or don't marry me at all." At ten the next morning, allowing Grace time to go to town to buy a dress, they were married. Her stunned sister stood up with her.

Life for AT and Grace was not easy. As an evangelist, their sole income was freewill offerings from churches in which AT ministered, made doubly difficult by the hardships of the Depression and World War II. AT's journals record his struggles to serve God with all his might and to trust God when he didn't have the money to pay the rent or utilities. God always provided, but the family lived frugally. Avery Jr. remembered that being given money for a one-cent Tootsie Roll was a rare treat. At one point, he saved every teaspoon of his war ration of sugar until he had enough for his mother to make his favorite lemon icebox pie, which he savored all by himself.

Serving as evangelist and church planter also meant the family moved frequently. A few months after Avery Jr. was born, the family moved back to Jackson, Tennessee, and AT became pastor of Grace's home church, North Jackson Baptist Church.

Two years later, the family moved to Ft. Worth, Texas, for AT to attend Southwestern Baptist Seminary. While there, he pastored and began an evangelistic ministry. During this time, Norma Sue, the sister his parents claimed that Avery Jr. prayed for, was born.

While hard at work in a full-time church and carrying a full course in college and doing evangelistic work all summer, God spoke to me about evangelistic work through various means. But as I had more years of preparation ahead of me, I would postpone the decision for a while.

After receiving my degree from Union University and enrolling in seminary, my call became more definite and more pressing. It seemed God demanded a decision from me.

Once again my heart began its long habit of rebellion against God and His Will. My wife and children loomed up before me. My home became more attractive. The pastorate, with the parsonage, set salary, and wonderful fellowship of the brethren became more appealing than ever. As Jacob of old, I tried to drive a sharp bargain with God and compromise the question by being an "evangelistic pastor" as many of my friends advised me to do. This resulted in powerless preaching with only a few conversions and a personal life of misery.

I roved the open fields around old Seminary Hill, pleading with God, trying to get Him to accept my will and bless me with happiness and peace, irrespective of His Will. One day after studying Isaiah 6:1, I went into the prayer room almost beside myself with the weight of this decision. While walking up and down the room alone with God, I settled this question, which was no less soul-rendering than the last two.

What a day! It was almost like being converted again. Thank God, I could say again "Not my will but Thine be done." Whether I succeed or fail, have little or plenty, be counted wise or foolish, I became willing to follow the leadership of the Holy Spirit as I discerned it.

Following this decision, Christ led me to confess my decision in public. So on April 11, 1937, in the morning service of Gambrell Street Baptist Church, Fort Worth, Texas, at the call of God and the wooing of the Holy Spirit, I promised God before that church that I would unreservedly surrender my life and give all of my time exclusively to evangelistic work.

The things that I feel God has promised me and that I am trusting Him for are:

1. *The salvation of my soul and that of my family.*
2. *The words that I should speak on every occasion are to be given to me by the Holy Spirit.*

3.   *That He will open the doors that He wants me to go through; that is, I am not to worry; I am to preach. The Holy Spirit will select the places where I am to conduct meetings and I am not to go unless He does.*
4.   *I am trusting Him to sustain me and my family—physically, financially, and spiritually; that is, I am not to work schemes for money or talk money for myself but rather leave that to the Holy Spirit, who is God, and is present to take care of my needs. The finances and the success of every meeting I leave with him.*
5.   *That God will have fellowship with me in a special, personal way as I spend at least one hour alone with Him each day. There I am to receive my instructions and nowhere else. Lord, keep me from selfishness, lust, vain pride, and worldly glory.*

Upon graduation from Southwestern Baptist Seminary, AT pastored in the oil field country of Forsan, Texas, for a year, and then became a full-time evangelist for three years. He bought a large tent and preached revivals in towns from Texas to Tennessee. While he traveled, Grace and the children returned to live in Ft. Worth.

It was during that period that the Holy Spirit took hold of Avery Jr.'s heart, and his need for Jesus became very personal. Avery Jr. tells how his faith became his own.

Avery's Story: Personal Commitment

When I was six years old, I made my profession of faith in Christ. My father was preaching a revival service in a local mission in Fort Worth, and he invited me to accompany him. That night, the message seemed to come alive to me and I became keenly aware of my sinfulness. After an inward struggle, I dashed toward my father to tell him I wanted to be saved. I remember a feeling of total dependence on God to forgive me of my sins and take me to heaven. After giving my life to Christ, I felt that a burden had been lifted from me.

Because I was only six, my parents thoroughly questioned me as to my belief and reasons for making this decision. The next morning at breakfast, I asked when I was to be baptized. To test me, I suppose, my father asked, "Well, why should you be baptized?"

"Well, Dad, I was saved last night. Didn't you know?" I answered quickly.

He smiled at my reminder, not realizing how many more he would receive that day. As he walked out of the house that morning, Mrs. Boyd, our next-door neighbor, called out, "I heard Avery Jr. was saved last night!" When he walked into the barbershop, the barber, Denny Moore, said, "I'm glad to hear your son was saved last night." Puzzled, my dad asked how he knew that. "Why, he was over here this morning telling me all about it!"

Later, as Dad walked across campus, a friend of his, Bertis Fair, said, "So good to hear about Avery Jr." A few hours later, he saw Dr. Lee Scarborough, the president of the seminary, and was greeted with, "Well, Brother Willis, I'm glad to know Avery Jr. accepted Christ." Everywhere he went, I had already been. And everywhere I had been, I had told everyone I knew what had happened to me.

So Dad baptized me in the Gambrell Street Baptist Church, where we attended.[2]

Early Years

After his conversion, Avery Jr. immediately attempted to preach, Bible in hand. Though it may have seemed merely an imitation of his father, Avery believed differently.

At that early age, I became aware of a compelling conviction that God had made me and saved me because He wanted me to preach His good news. Standing on the fencepost of my grandmother's fence, my first sermon to anyone who would listen was "Christ for the Whole World" from John 3:16. My public decision of my "call" to preach when I was sixteen was only the expression of this abiding awareness of the purpose of God for my life. As I grew older and more self-conscious, I ceased preaching to my friends and relatives, but always knew that it was for a season. God had laid his hand on me.

In the midst of Avery Jr.'s second-grade year, the family moved to Memphis, Tennessee, for three months while AT was establishing a church in Dyersburg. AT had prayed for this town while in seminary, and the Lord directed him to be a pastor there. AT conducted an eleven-week tent revival from which grew the Second Baptist Church, later named Hillcrest. During the revival, Betty, his youngest daughter, was born in Memphis.

As the family settled in Dyersburg, the church first met in the Circuit Court Room of the courthouse. When the basement foundation of the future church building was completed, the church met there for three years. They were known in town as "the church in the hole in the ground." Grace played the piano in gloves because it was so cold. AT continued to construct the church building by hand, removing the nails from used lumber he collected from the Air Force base.

Vacation Bible School, Dyersburg, TN,
Can you find the pastor's son?

A Sneeze a Day
(Told by Avery's Sister, Betty)

Avery Jr.'s personality was usually calm, serious, and determined, but he also liked to have fun. He enjoyed practical jokes and magic tricks.

He and his younger sister, Betty, inherited beautiful singing voices from their mother. One Sunday, they were all sitting in the choir loft as their father, AT Willis, was preaching enthusiastically. Suddenly, a member of the choir began to sneeze. This was followed by another person's sneeze, and then another, until most of the choir members were sneezing in concert! AT turned around, confused.

Avery Jr. had placed sneezing powder into a folded piece of paper and then asked that the "note" be passed to another member at the end of the row. Betty recounts, "It is the only thing we ever did that Daddy didn't catch us!"

Avery Jr. in Junior High school (ca 1948)

Avery Jr. attended school in Dyersburg until the middle of his sophomore year of high school. He made respectable grades without needing to study much. He had average athletic skills, but displayed qualities that would later become defining characteristics. In his words, "The one quality I did possess was determination and endurance. I would play till I dropped."

During Avery Jr.'s sophomore year, AT resigned from Hillcrest Baptist Church to become the Superintendent of Missions and Evangelism in Huntsville, Alabama. Although Avery Jr. hated leaving friends of nearly eight years, this move instilled a greater level of self-confidence. He made new friends easily, got involved in school clubs, and convinced his parents to let him play football.

In 1950, AT stepped down from his superintendent position to pastor Southside Baptist Church, which had been organized under his direction.

He bought a new car, the first new car he had ever owned. His pride in this earthly treasure was short-lived, however. Before AT had made a single payment on it, Avery Jr. borrowed it to take his girlfriend on a date. Unfortunately, the date ended prematurely when Avery Jr. hit a tree, totaling the car.

As a result, Avery Jr. spent the summer helping erect the church building to pay for the car. In doing so, he learned carpentry skills, but he also learned that for the remainder of his life, he would prefer to hire out such work!

A New Calling

That summer, during a youth rally at a nearby church, Avery felt God directing him to be a missionary. When he got to the altar to make his decision public, he only mentioned he had surrendered to preach. A call to preach was not new, since that decision had been settled in his heart long before. But Avery recognized this as the beginning of his "missionary calling."

As a training opportunity, his father gave him the chance to conduct the prayer meeting in a small church struggling to revive. Avery recounted, *I nearly killed it! After studying for three weeks and reading many commentaries on prayer, I exhausted my knowledge in less than five minutes and was scared to death. I didn't try to lead a service again for six months!*

Senior year brought popularity. Avery was the starting guard on the varsity football team and also played baseball. He joined the Dramatics Club and, although he had never acted before, got the lead role in the senior play. He was a member of the National Honor Society, football editor of the yearbook, and chaplain of Hi-Y club. He was elected "friendliest boy in school."

Avery playing varsity baseball Huntsville, Alabama

Avery (#63 in center) on high school varsity football team, 1952

Avery preached his first official sermon when he was nearly eighteen at a youth rally in Monrovia, Alabama. He preached a thirty-minute message to about 250 people and knew the Lord had blessed it. He preached twice more before graduating from high school three months later.

He had initially planned to go to Samford University in Birmingham, Alabama, to be nearer to family in Huntsville. However, when his dad accepted a call to pastor Hillcrest Baptist Church in Tulsa, Oklahoma, Avery's plans changed. The family moved the day after Avery graduated from high school in 1952, and he immediately registered for summer school at Oklahoma Baptist University (OBU).

Once there, the realization that he was now responsible for his own future gave Avery initiative in his studies, work, and preaching. His freshman year of college became a turning point in his life.

CHAPTER 2
Finding the Power

Obedience is the secret to having God reveal Himself to you.
—Avery

A very had a close group of friends and roommates at Oklahoma Baptist University—friendships that would continue long after they graduated: Tal Bonham, Jack Edmonds, Bill Crews, Bill Richardson, Jack Wilson, Harold Hendricks, and Earl Bengs. Their shared passion to preach and serve God drew them together.

But they were not always serious. When not studying, they made time for pranks. One such event started simply enough with a wastebasket filled with water propped against a door and a friendly knock. In retaliation, Paul Sanders and Bill Richardson got a larger wastebasket, leaned it on someone else's door, and knocked. The water fights continued and escalated until water began to flood the rooms on the lower floors. The freshmen who lived in the basement suffered the brunt of it.[1]

On another occasion, several of the young men moved street barricades so that all of the highway traffic was directed through the circular driveway of the OBU president's house.

In the midst of fun, friendship, and studies, Avery was still listening closely to his Lord. His life would pivot in a watershed moment.

Abandoning Mediocrity

I spent the first semester of my freshman year having a good time. For the first time in my life I was responsible for my own decisions without my parents telling me what to do. But God began to get my attention. He spoke to me about my choices and who I really was. He said, "You are a nominal Christian."

"But, Lord," I said, "I am doing everything my church has asked me to do. I attend Sunday school, worship services twice on Sunday, church training classes, and even prayer meetings on Wednesday night. I tithe and help around the church."

"You are not a disciple who denies himself, takes up his cross daily, and follows Me."

I knew God was right. He kept pushing me to surrender my life to him. I waffled. I spent many nights walking through the fields around campus, talking to God, pondering what it meant to be a disciple. I knew I was at a crossroads. I sensed that I would either make the decision to become a true disciple of Christ or remain a mediocre Christian for the rest of my life.

I Aim to Be that Man

I told God that I was not a leader and that I could not do what He was asking me to do. He showed me 2 Chronicles 16:9," For the eyes of the Lord range throughout the earth to strengthen those whose hearts are fully committed to Him." God showed me that He was looking for someone—anyone—who would love Him with all their heart, soul, and strength, and obediently do whatever He asked.

He reminded me of D.L. Moody to whom Henry Varley said, "The world has yet to see what God will do with a man fully consecrated to Him." Moody had been struck to his soul and when the words would not leave him, responded, "By God's help, I aim to be that man."[2]

I replied, "Lord, I want to be like that—to have a heart fully committed to You. I am such an ordinary person that if You do anything with my life, everyone will know that You did it." I committed myself to be a disciple, deny myself, take up my cross daily, and follow Him. That decision changed the course of my life.[3]

My struggle with the "mission call" increased in intensity throughout my freshman year. I had heard of others who said that when they "surrendered to be a missionary," they didn't "have to" go. I decided this applied to me, even though I omitted the "surrendering" step.

It still nagged at me. I bargained with God that if I married a girl who was going to be a missionary, I would be one, too. I tried giving more money to missions. None of it brought me peace.

I decided I must settle the matter. I told God that I would go anywhere in the world I could reach the most people for Him. I was picturing myself in Africa, when a voice, almost audible, said, "Be an evangelist." I thought my mind was playing tricks on me because that was what I had been claiming to be.

Again it came. And suddenly, I <u>wanted</u> to go to the mission field—I begged God to let me go. "What about all those lost people over there—can't I go preach to them?" But the voice said, "Be an evangelist now. You will go." I learned that if I was not an evangelist where I was, going overseas would not make me into one.⁴

Avery began to experience an overwhelming desire to witness for Christ. Multiple times a week, he went to the Main Street Rescue Mission in Shawnee, a preaching mission for the homeless, or preached on the street. He led services at the tuberculosis sanatorium near Shawnee. He made friends with a Native American who invited him to preach to his fellow Native Americans. He would sometimes conduct a weekend retreat, preaching all day long. He studied books on soul-winning, memorized Scripture, and prayed—but he was not seeing much response to his witnessing. He knew in his heart that something was missing.

Filled with the Holy Spirit

Then, in February, 1953, I received a booklet that told of great men of God like Billy Graham, D.L. Moody, R.A. Torrey, and Billy Sunday whose lives and ministries had been transformed when they had been filled with the Holy Spirit. I wanted that, too, but I was unsure how to go about receiving it and didn't know anyone who could lead me through such an experience. So I found an empty classroom in a nearby church and committed to stay there and pray until I was filled with the Holy Spirit.

For two hours, I prayed, cried, and sought God to be filled, but nothing happened.

I went in search of a book that a friend had recommended, The Holy Spirit: Who He Is and What He Does *by R.A. Torrey. Through that book, I learned that the Holy Spirit was a Person, not just a power, influence, or attitude to possess. The book also included instructions to being filled:*

1. *Confess your sins, disobedience, emptiness and need for God's forgiveness.*
2. *Yield every part of yourself (body, mind, will, and emotions) to Christ.*
3. *Ask God to fill, control, and empower you, believing in faith that He will answer your prayer.*

So I began confessing every sin I could think of. As I did so, I began to experience how much the Holy Spirit loved me and how grieved the Holy Spirit was when I ignored him. I fully surrendered again to be used by God in any way He chose, and then I told the Lord, "I will accept the fact that I am filled with the Spirit on the basis of faith in Your Word, no matter what happens." I immediately sensed a deep awareness of the Spirit's love.

The intense awareness of the presence of the Holy Spirit was so strong that the next morning on my way to class, I realized I had stepped to one side of the sidewalk so that the Lord could walk beside me.

That evening, I witnessed to a boy on the street who accepted Christ as his Savior. Two nights later, two teenage boys accepted Christ. The next night, another man did. Expressing my excitement, I told a friend, "I don't see how this can continue. Every time I go out to witness, someone accepts Christ!"

That night, no one did.

I realized I needed to confess a sin of pride for thinking I had been responsible for those results. I confessed my pride, yielded, and asked the Holy Spirit to fill me anew. Once again, people to whom I witnessed came to Christ. Over thirty people became Christians through my personal witness over the next three months.

Through this, I learned that this filling of the Spirit was to be a daily, even moment-by-moment experience of receiving the Holy Spirit's conviction, confessing sin, and opening myself to the leadership and power of the Holy Spirit, relying on God to produce the results.[5]

The Holy Spirit's Power

About a month later, I met a man named Curly Clark in the Mission. During the invitation time, I asked him if he wanted to become a Christian, and he said that was why he had come. We went back to the counseling room, and he told me that he had been working as a roustabout on an oil rig. Then he said the Lord has been working on him for 17 days and he knew he needed to come to Christ. "But," he said, "I can't be saved. I was a member of Pretty Boy Floyd's gang and I have killed so many people, both in the war and as a member of this gang, that I am not even sure how many I have killed. In fact, I've been on death row three times. Each time the governor has pardoned me for different reasons so I've not been executed. But I know I can't be saved because I've killed all those people."

I shared with him that the apostle Paul had killed people and that God had forgiven him. Curly then prayed to give his life to Christ. He was so thrilled his sins had been forgiven that he wanted to tell the world. He said we could even call the police and he would tell them. Then he looked up and said, "Hey, I want you to pray for my arm! I hurt it on the oil rig, and I'm not able to lift it. Pray that it will be healed!"

I stuttered around and assured him that we would pray but that I was not sure what God would do about it. By that time, some others had joined us in the prayer room. While one of them was praying for him, Curly began to move his arm around, saying," Hey, I'm healed!" (It was surely not my faith that had healed him!)

"Oh," he said, "I need to tell my mother. She has prayed for me for so long." Since she lived only ten miles away, we offered to drive him there. On the way, Curly wanted to stop at one of the creeks by the road so we could baptize him, but we assured him he could wait until a church could baptize him.

It was quite late at night when we arrived and knocked on the farmhouse door. His mother's weak, plaintive voice said, "Oh, Curly." It was evident he had come home many times before drunk and in trouble. When she came to the door, he said, "Mom, I've been saved!" She began praising God, and heaven came down to that little house as we rejoiced.

We were so moved by the experience that four of us stayed up all night praying. God's presence was so powerful that we agreed to pray again the next night. As we did so, another student came in and asked what we were doing. When we shared how God was leading us to pray and confess our sins and seek the filling of the Spirit, the student wanted the same experience in his own life. This was repeated night after night until we had about 30 students gathering in our small dorm room, without our inviting any of them. This started a revival on campus, and several of those young men became pastors, ministry leaders, and missionaries.[6]

During his sophomore year at OBU, Avery became the student director of the Rescue Mission. He trained students whom he invited to speak, resulting in dramatic growth in their lives. Avery preached his first revival in the spring of his sophomore year, during which, nineteen people gave their lives to Christ.

He was called to his first pastorate at Center Point Baptist Church in Wilburton, Oklahoma, during the spring of 1954. Barely twenty years old, he drove each weekend from Shawnee to Wilburton, about 125 miles each way, and stayed with church members. His salary was $35 per week. The oldest deacon quadrupled his age, but Avery tackled the job with humility. Though he had been informed when he came that there were "no prospects in the community," the church led the association in baptisms and increased their mission giving from 10 percent to 15 percent during the next year and to 20 percent the following year.

Center Point Baptist Church (Avery's first pastorate), 1954

About this time, Avery decided he should start looking for a long-term relationship. Although his friend Earl had been dating Sherry for a month or so, Avery asked her for a date. He really enjoyed being with her and invited her out several more times. When Earl asked Sherry to go steady with him, she was undecided as to her answer. On the following Tuesday, she and Avery had planned to talk more about their relationship. But as Avery prayed, he felt led of the Spirit not to pursue dating her. When they got together, he chose to speak first and told her that if he was hindering her making a decision, he would remove himself as an obstacle.

After I had said my piece she said that she had told Earl that she wouldn't go steady with him. Boy, how ignorant can I get! Well, that's that. I hope God's will has been done but I wonder now if it has.

Avery turned his attention to other girls, and an entry in his journal two months later stated:

Earl and Sherry are engaged! I guess it was the Lord's will that I didn't go out with her. Good thing I listened and obeyed!

Six weeks before the end of his junior year, he asked the slim, blond Shirley Morris for a date.

SECTION 2
Pastoring in the United States

Spiritual Marker #3

God led Avery to a wife that would be his partner
in ministry, missions, and life.

He who finds a wife finds what is good and receives favor from the Lord.
—Proverbs 18:22 (NIV)

Spiritual Marker #4

God used Avery to develop small mission churches
into thriving, vibrant churches.

And the Lord added to their number daily those who were being saved.
—Acts 2:47 (NIV)

CHAPTER 3
First Loves

*Someone before you captured my heart and will always be my first love.
You will always be second.*

—Avery

As Avery considered his dating options on campus, he was attracted to two girls: Shirley and Frances. Avery began dating both of them, until a friend informed him that they worked together in the same tiny office. He reconsidered and made his choice.

Shirley

Shirley Jean Morris, daughter of a carpenter and a schoolteacher, was born and raised in Nowata, Oklahoma. She had committed her life to Christ near the age of ten. She later realized a need for a deeper, more personal relationship with God and chose to be baptized as a public demonstration of that decision.

She won state level in the Junior Bible Memory Work contest, which paid her first year to a ten-day summer camp at Falls Creek Baptist Assembly. She returned every summer for the next five years.

When she was fourteen, Shirley first felt God calling her to be a missionary. During the response time at one of the Falls Creek meetings, she felt a great deal of concern for the girl next to her, who was not a Christian. She began to pray that the girl would come to know Christ. The Lord spoke to Shirley's heart, saying, "How can you expect her to do what you want her to do when you are not willing to do what I want you to do?"

Surprised, as this was the first time Shirley remembered feeling a "call," she made a decision that night to obey whatever God asked of her. Returning to her cabin that night, Shirley learned that the girl for whom she had been praying had followed her to the altar and had surrendered her life to Christ. Shirley did not receive a clear direction from the Lord as to how missions would come about, but she had a sense that she would marry a preacher and they would hear from the Lord together.

Becoming Acquainted

Avery had been elected as vice president of the Ministerial Alliance and president of the Life Service Band, on-campus organizations for persons who intended to serve in a Christian vocation. These organizations sponsored Morning Watch (a time when students could come and have a daily personal prayer time) and Noonday and Vespers (noon and evening times for worship and brief preaching). Shirley was quite faithful at most of these events and so came to know Avery.

When Avery first started asking Shirley out, he would invite her to Wednesday evening prayer meeting. Shirley would decline, telling him that she worked with the Kickapoo Indian Church on Wednesday nights. She thought Avery might offer to come with her sometime, but he didn't pick up on that clue.

When it became clear to Avery that Wednesdays were not an option, he invited her out on a Tuesday. As it happened, there was a revival at the Kickapoo Church every night that week, including Tuesday. This time, Shirley countered by inviting Avery to go with her, and he accepted. Before the service began, one of the young boys she taught in Sunday School asked her about making a decision for Christ. Shirley stopped to talk with him about his decision. It made quite an impression on Avery.

Soon they were dating on a regular basis. Weekends were already committed to Avery's pastorate at Center Point, so time was spent studying together, going to church events, and Noondays, which Avery was leading. For Morning Watch, even if Avery was already there, Shirley remained in the seat she had routinely chosen. Rather than feeling ignored or rebuffed, Avery thought this independent quality might be useful in a wife.

First Love

Avery didn't let his romantic interests interfere with his commitment to Jesus. When their relationship deepened and became more serious, Avery startled Shirley one night, when he said, "Shirley, before we get married, you need to know that I loved someone else before you. That person captured my heart and will always be my first love. You will always be second."

"Who?" she asked quietly, with an edge of dismay in her voice.

"My Lord Jesus Christ."

After a brief pause, she pleased him with her answer, "In that case, I would rather be second!"[1]

Shirley referenced this conversation in the letter she wrote to Avery in his yearbook:

Dearest Avery,

I take my pen in hand to write you a little note—but that seems to be about as far as I can get because I don't know where to begin. How six weeks can pass by so fast or be so full, I'll never know! I only know that they've been six of the happiest weeks of my life. God has been really good to both of us in finally bringing us to know each other, hasn't He? When I think of all the good times we've had, and most of all, of all the things you've taught me in our many long talks together, my heart swells with gratitude to God and to you, and I know that words can never express what I find in my heart to say. Thanks especially for what you told me last night about your "first love", and please pray for me and help me to truly make Him my first love, too.

Avery, if you hadn't done anything else for me this year, the example which you have shown me of the kind of Christian I've always wanted to be would have been worth it all. But you've shown me much, much more—You've shown me a strong, consecrated Christian who is also a leader in many things, who has an excellent sense of humor, who is an extra easy conversationalist, and a very good speaker. I'm sure you didn't expect me to say all that and I hadn't intended to when I began, but somehow I had to try to put into words what you have meant to me, just as a friend; even if our friendship didn't go any deeper, you would still have been such a help to me, I would always remember you for it and thank God each time.

Your second love,
Shirley Morris
Senior 1955

Shirley Jean Morris, 1952

They began to discuss their mutual desire for overseas missions. Avery needed to have a seminary degree and some pastoral experience first, but he hoped to be overseas by age thirty. Shirley had taken extra classes and graduated in June of 1955, but Avery still had a year to complete his degree.

Shirley's plan was to go to Golden Gate Seminary in San Francisco, California, to further prepare for mission work. She was interested in ministering to Native Americans, having spent the previous summer teaching and leading Vacation Bible School at the Ft. Apache Indian Reservation in Arizona. The summer following her graduation, she worked among the Choctaw Indians in Mississippi. During that time, because of her relationship with Avery, she decided to return to Shawnee to work for a year, postponing her decision to enroll at Golden Gate Seminary.

Shirley kept the daily love letters Avery wrote her that summer, which reflect not only his heart but also some of his personality. He spent the beginning of the summer at sales school for Southwestern Company in Nashville, Tennessee. Avery had been very successful the previous summer selling Bibles, and he planned to do so again. His supervisor, Fred, suggested he recruit some of his OBU friends, and it fell to Avery to conduct the interviews.

Friday, June 4, 1955
Dear Shirley,

This morning I received your letter and was I ever glad to get it. I'm glad God keeps his telephone line open all night because I can't seem to pray with you at 10 p.m. Maybe I can for a moment tonight. [Avery and Shirley had agreed to both pray at ten each night so it would almost be like praying together.]

Last night was spent in Fred's office interviewing my salesmen again. Why did I get so many? Silly boy! Then this morning I did it. I skipped school half the morning (when I got your letter) and went shopping. When I get on a spree, watch out. There were some really good buys here so I phoned Dad and he let me draw a draft on him for $50. (I only asked for $35 but he insisted.) I must have faith in my selling for I'm buying like I had the money in the bank already. I've never done it before but it was fun. I bought two pair of pants, two shorts, a pair of shoes, belt, socks, etc. This, of course, will end my buying for a year or maybe two.

I decided to hitchhike to Huntsville to visit my high school friends before I headed home to Tulsa. [Omitted is a detailed account of a highly frustrating hitchhiking experience.] *We got to Huntsville at 9:15 p.m. I visited around until 12:30 a.m. I saw several people I wanted to see, and all the important ones.*

It was a truly beautiful southern night! The moon was full and the hills were beautiful. It was really perfect except the one thing that was missing! So it was like swimming in a lake without any water. They asked about my girlfriend and I told them about you and I showed them your picture. You sure got a lot of compliments. They all thought you were pretty. AMEN!

At noon, Bill and I will start hitchhiking toward Oklahoma. You can look for me when you see me coming. There's no telling how my plans will work out.

'Til then,
Avery

Infatuation

Avery returned to Tulsa and lived at home while selling Bibles. Unfortunately, the summer was less than profitable. Avery was so enraptured with Shirley that he could not keep his mind and motivation on his work and could do little else than think about her and write daily love letters.

Monday, June 27, 1955
My One and Only,

Honey, a Bible salesman just can't afford to be in love! No, I didn't work today, either! I got up this morning full of determination to work 50 hours this week. I ate and then went in to read your letter again. It surely looked good through my "roadmap" eyes. I lay there a while and moaned about having to go to work when I was so tired. Dad came in and said, "Why don't you just sleep till noon!" Now I've always been taught to obey my parents, no matter what, so I just lay there with my clothes on and thought of you. I fell asleep in this tranquil meditation and even dreamed briefly about you. I came back to civilization at 10:00 when your letter arrived. I read it a couple of times and finally got up about 11 when Bill Richardson called. He hadn't been to work, either. (We both noted it "sprinkled a little and was very overcast.")

On the way out to work, I stopped to get a check cashed to send to the company. Across the street from the post office, I passed a furniture store and there was Bill McBride selling furniture. I went in and talked to him about Bible selling. It was after 3:00 by then and I went to get a root beer. (I was surely hot!) I then got a map at a filling station to see where you were. By 4 pm, I was getting pretty good at rationalizing (understatement of the year)!

I went to get my flat tire fixed that blew last night and then came on home. I did read the Word awhile and then got down my Yahnseh [OBU yearbook] and looked up all the pictures of you I could find. Ain't it awful! (not the pictures but to be so much in love I can't—or won't—even work.)

The revival was good tonight. Angel Martinez preached a good message. He has gotten himself a new song leader that's really good! There were about 4500 people and there were over 20 saved and about 65 total decisions. It was out in the open in Skelly Stadium and the light on the emerald green grass and the stars overhead were like diamonds scattered over a piece of black velvet! The feeling that goes through a revival crowd just thrills my heart anyway! Honey, I really wished you were there. I wish the Lord would call me into that type of work even though it is such a hard life, for I love it. But that's His business and it doesn't look as if that is His will now!

Did I tell you the church got our air cooler in? I had to preach so loud I sweated something awful anyway—and I had a raw throat when I finished. The cooler and I are running competition another way, too—to see which of us can put the folks to sleep first!

So you were babysitting when you wrote to me last? Incidentally, I never asked you how many children you wanted when you get married?

I'm so proud that you are doing so well. I pray that the Lord is really using you, honey, for if He can use us, everything else will work out ok. You never can tell how much you have done with the kids but God knows and if we do all we can, He will take care of the rest.

Avery

Bill Richardson, Avery's OBU friend and Bible-selling recruit, recalled an event that summer. Bill was putting in time trying to sell Bibles but with limited success. One day Avery showed up and, rather than sell with him, suggested they go swimming. After a couple of days of doing anything but selling, they decided to go to a small town north of Tulsa. They were actually making sales until the police showed up. The policeman took them down to the station, saying they didn't have a permit to sell in that town. Avery explained that all he was doing was selling Bibles and pulled out the Bibles to show the officer. "Look at this comprehensive Bible," he said and started into his sales pitch. He was such an effective salesman that the policeman bought the Bible! Nevertheless, he told them they couldn't sell any more without a permit but did allow them to go back and deliver what they had already sold.

Engagement

Avery continued his impetuous, adventurous summer. The first week of July, Shirley was in Laurel, Mississippi, helping with Vacation Bible School in a Native American church. She was staying with an older couple in the sponsoring church. One evening, she and the wife drove into town to visit someone in the hospital, and on their way back, they got behind a blue '47 Chevy that Shirley said "looks just like my boyfriend's car, except he is from Tulsa."

While they made another stop, Avery drove to the house, parked across the street, and convinced the husband to let him in. Avery was waiting in Shirley's bedroom to surprise her. She wasn't permitted to "date" while serving as a missionary, but Avery convinced her it wasn't a date since she didn't know he was coming.

They drove to the gulf shore the next morning and sat in the car, talking. Avery asked again, "You never said how many children you want?" to which Shirley quipped, "You haven't even asked me to marry you yet!"

"Well, I was going to plan some fancy way to ask you, but will you?"

Shirley, of course, accepted. Her answer to the other question was four.

Tuesday, August 2, 1955

My darling, you don't know how happy you have made me by what you wrote after my depressing letter. My love really has grown as I read it. You make me a happy man by your spirit. I have always said I wanted a woman to pick me up when I'm down and you are already doing such a wonderful job. I am so thankful to the Lord that you satisfy all those worries that were once in my mind about a life's partner. Hon, you really fill the bill. With that kind of spirit and our kind of God, the devil and his hordes can't stop us in the work of the blessed Lord Jesus. Hallelujah! Isn't He beautiful! Won't it be wonderful to fight on the same side together for the enlarging of God's kingdom and the glorifying of our great King!

Hon, I think if a couple can't share everything, secrets and all, they won't be as happy as possible. Darling, I will be telling you my utmost because I want you to be a part of me and in a spiritual sense, you already are.

Your future hubby,
Avery

On her way back to Shawnee from Mississippi, Shirley stopped off in Oklahoma where Avery pastored. To her surprise, he introduced her from the pulpit as his fiancée.

Shirley worked as a receptionist/secretary for an architect in Shawnee. When she wasn't given time off for the wedding, she elected to work for a competing architect in town.

Avery and Shirley were married December 17, 1955, halfway through Avery's senior year at OBU. The wedding was held in Shirley's home church. Her family's pastor, A. A. Davis, officiated, and college friends were their attendants. It was not a fancy or expensive wedding. Shirley made her own wedding dress and all her bridesmaids' dresses. A florist in the church donated poinsettias. They honeymooned at one of the two motels in beautiful Branson, Missouri.

Avery and Shirley's wedding, December 1955

CHAPTER 4
Growing Churches, Growing Family

Yes, the church is the Bride of Christ, but we need
to see her more as the Wife of Christ.
We are not a bride in the sense of a wedding ceremony
but as a covenant relationship forever
—and as the bearer of His children into the kingdom of God.

—Avery

A fter their wedding, Avery and Shirley lived in a small one-bedroom apartment in Shawnee for Avery's final semester. Whenever they had visitors, they gave up their bed. Although it never happened to them, it seemed that every time a guest slept in their bed, one of the wooden slats would give way and slam to the floor during the night.

In the summer of 1956, after Avery graduated from OBU, Avery and Shirley moved to Ft. Worth, Texas, and enrolled full-time at Southwestern Baptist Seminary. Avery continued to pastor Center Point church, despite the 450-mile round-trip drive. At the time of the "annual call," when the church customarily chose a new ministerial student as pastor and pulpit supply, Avery chose to resign. *I knew that I could not do them or my school work justice if I continued.*

The Jar of Beans

That decision meant an end to steady income. Avery had sold some Bibles during the summer and preached several revivals for which he received "poundings," when members of the church would each bring a pound of food. Many of the church members were poor and on government commodities, so the food was often cornmeal, dried beans, and flour. Beans became a staple meal. Whenever money and food were tight, Avery would say, "Shirley, I guess you better get out the beans." Then another opportunity would arise to preach, and money would come in. When they packed to go to Indonesia, they kept one jar of beans as a reminder that God had always provided. Shirley still has that jar of beans.

Sunset Heights

During this time, the pastor of Connell Baptist Church, a good friend of A.T. Willis, asked Avery and Shirley if they would postpone taking a pastorate until January when his church would be undertaking a new mission work in the Arlington Heights area of Ft. Worth. At that time, there was a pastor/builder building in new subdivisions while simultaneously gathering a core group of people to start a church.

Avery became the first pastor of this church plant named Sunset Heights in January 1957. The mission church began with eleven people. He was paid $100 per month for the first couple of months; then he got a raise to $200 per month. That seemed like a fortune!

Shirley was pregnant with their first child. They had only been at Sunset Heights for two weeks when Randal Kean (Randy) was born. Labor began the night before Shirley's seminary finals. When her contractions were about five minutes apart, Avery and Shirley went to the hospital. Randy was born less than five hours later. The first thing Shirley heard Avery say was, "It's a boy, and he looks just like me!" Three weeks later, Shirley had to go back and take her finals. She took off the semester after Randy's birth; she later returned to seminary part-time for three more terms.

Between their inexpensive seminary insurance and the medical insurance from the new church, God provided payment for all of their medical bills surrounding the birth—with $5 to spare!

Church Growth

The church planting work was difficult but rewarding. According to his 1957 monthly reports, Avery visited, on average, forty-eight homes per month, and the church increased by nine new members each month. Baptisms occurred monthly. The monthly offerings more than doubled. Avery wrote, *We went through all that is involved in beginning a new church. God blessed and brought us through every problem. I had determined that if I could not grow a church in the U.S., then I could not go to the mission field.*

Young families taking jobs as engineers at Carswell Air Force Base were moving into the area, and church membership grew steadily. By May of 1959, Sunset Heights constituted as a church of 212 members. It was evident that God's hand was upon the young congregation. The first action of the newly organized church was an offering for world missions.[1]

That fall, the church bought a new house in the subdivision as a parsonage—only nine hundred square feet but with three bedrooms and air-conditioning!

Disciplemaker

While pastoring in Ft. Worth, Avery learned the importance of making disciples who make disciples. He wrote: *An internal conflict arose when someone asked me, "Where are all those people you led to Christ?" I could not find most of them. I realized the weakness of what I was doing. Something was wrong with my evangelism or my follow-up—or both!*[2]

He began to attend a Bible study in Dallas led by the Navigators. Eager to learn, he asked the leaders about their approach to intentional discipleship. When Skip Gray, one of the leaders, realized how intent Avery was to be discipled, he drove to Ft. Worth every week to spend an hour with him. Skip always brought someone along in the car to disciple during the two-hour drive, but met alone with Avery. Avery thought, *I would drive to Dallas to teach a crowd, but I doubt I would do it for one person.* Avery would later name Skip the second most influential person in his life.

A few months later, Avery heard a tape, *Born to Reproduce*,[3] by Dawson Trotman, founder of the Navigators. He learned the story of Les Spencer, a sailor who asked Dawson to teach him to use the Word of God to be an effective witness, as he had seen Dawson do. Les said,

"I would give my right arm to be able to do that." Dawson began to disciple Les, who kept his commitment to learn, became a disciple, and began to look for a man on his ship to disciple. When he found one, he brought him to Dawson and said, "Do with him what you did with me."

Dawson refused, saying, "If *you* can't do with him what I have done with you, I have failed."

Les began to disciple this friend and continued to make reproducing disciples so that by the time his ship was sunk at Pearl Harbor, 125 men had been led to Christ, and their influence had impacted fifty ships of the US fleet.

Joy and Pain

Sherrie Dennette was born in August of 1959. Near her due date, Shirley was not feeling well. So Avery asked one of the women from the church to stay with her while the men went to play in the recently formed church softball league. Sure enough, Shirley and her friend had to drive by the softball field to pick up Avery on the way to the hospital. He got them checked in and went home to change out of his sweaty softball clothes and cleats. By the time he returned to the hospital, Sherrie had arrived.

Joy turned to dismay the following month when Avery's father, AT, nearly died in an automobile accident. Returning home from preaching revival services, AT fell asleep at the wheel. His car went off the road and rolled several times, ejecting him from the car. He broke ten bones and his pelvis in three places. He was not expected to live.

Avery borrowed money from a friend to fly to the Memphis hospital where the family gathered to pray for healing and to grieve if healing did not come. Avery learned a great deal about surrender, the power of prayer, and ministry to the sick through the nine weeks of his father's hospitalization. He dropped out of seminary and did some part-time work selling records for the Word Record Company to help his dad, since AT had no income while he wasn't preaching.

Before AT was discharged, all five of his specialists gathered around his bed and told him, "We want you to know, you are not here because of us." Not one of them had thought he would survive.

Inglewood Baptist Church

Avery saw God grow Sunset Heights from the original eleven to approximately three hundred in three and a half years. He had planned to stay at Sunset Heights for a long time, but in the summer of 1960, he was recommended to be the pastor of another church plant, Inglewood Baptist in Grand Prairie, Texas, a small town west of Dallas.

We felt that God was leading us, although it was difficult to reason why. What caused us to accept the call to Inglewood was the great need they had and the tremendous "harvest field" around them. It was a new church, started at the same time as Sunset Heights, which had lost its pastor six months after it organized. They had been without a pastor for eight months. They had tried to expand beyond what they could afford and were now in debt. Attendance had fallen from 200 to 125.

Three months after we arrived there, it was back up to two hundred, but that was all the building could hold, and the church was too far in debt to build an expansion. Many came into the church by baptism and transfer of membership. A financial program put the church back on solid ground. But we began to learn the struggles connected with pastoring a suburban church.[4]

Inglewood Baptist Church, 1962

The new year emerged and, along with it, Avery and Shirley's third child, Wade Avery, who was born on January 1, 1961. Because it was Sunday when Shirley's contractions began, Avery took her to the hospital before the service and returned to preach. The doctor was a Christian, so he attended church first as well. Randy and Sherrie were put in the nursery, and someone was assigned to take them home. The doctor arrived after the church service, and Wade was born about four in the afternoon—too late to be a 1960 tax deduction or the first baby of 1961. There were now three children under the age of four.

Inglewood Baptist Church grew rapidly. The families were more established in finances and life-stage than the congregation at Sunset Heights. Since some of the people had prior church experience, they were more mature in the Lord. But for Avery, a new discipleship question had emerged: *How do you help those who have been spiritual babes for years begin growing as a disciple?*

Avery was still in seminary. Having completed his bachelor of divinity in 1961, he had begun work on his doctor of theology with a major in missions. When he first arrived, he had told the church of his plans to get his doctorate, but now that the church had begun to grow, some members felt he should devote his full attention to pastoring.

During the discussion of this topic at a church business meeting, a woman known for often saying the wrong thing, raised her hand and said, "I want to make a motion."

Inwardly cringing, Avery asked, "What is your motion?"

"I move that the pastor pray about it and do what he believes God tells him to do."

Avery did pray about it and chose to stay out of seminary for one year, while the church added an educational wing to the church building. Avery had produced a detailed book of demographics and information, which he took with him to the bank to borrow money. It helped cinch the deal. By the time the new 8,600-square-foot educational building had been completed in 1962, 440 people had been added to the church. By March of 1964, membership had grown to 541.[5]

Praying for Revival

In 1962, before the usual scheduled revival meetings, Avery told the church, *I am tired of scheduling "revivals" that are just "meetings." I have tried different programs and gimmicks to no avail, so I am finished planning programs for God to bless. Our job is to listen to His plan and do it. As I have studied revivals in history, it looks like the people prayed until revival came. When it does, we can invite someone in to preach.*

When the people agreed, he told them they were each a committee of one to pray actively and promote revival in any way God led them. They could have prayer meetings in their homes or anywhere. So the people began to pray.

That was in September. By January, I was getting desperate. I took several men to the state evangelism conference. We heard great preaching, but we weren't revived.

Out in the hallway, after the session, I visited with a former schoolmate. He told me of a revival in their church that had affected the whole city. The men from their church were talking to the men from our church. They got so excited that I began to listen to them instead of my preacher friend. One man with a speech impediment said, "We really had a revival last week. The preacher just sat in the audience and we men preached. Last Saturday night, I preached and five people were saved!"

I realized something dramatic had happened to cause him to speak so boldly with his speech impediment. When he heard we had been praying for revival, he said, "Say, buddy, I can tell you how to get yourself a revival. Just get down on your knees and pray until God sends you one. And if He don't, just call us collect and we'll come pray for you!"

That man got through to us. We returned home and begin to pray every night. God met us. We began to confess our sins. Some nights we prayed for several hours. The next week, we had two of our men preaching on Layman's Day. That night God sent revival. The altar was filled with people getting right with God and with each other.[6]

Revival had come. So when asked who should be called to preach the meetings, the men said, "We'll do it!"

"Who will do it?" Avery asked.

"I'll take Monday."

"I can do Tuesday."

One by one, the men spontaneously began to volunteer to preach for a night. Fifteen men preached in the next two weeks, and God sent a revival that set the church on fire. Through this, Avery learned to sense and follow the Holy Spirit's leading, which became particularly important later that year.

Test of Faith

Texas Baptists were planning a New Life Crusade in Japan. They were enlisting six hundred pastors, music leaders, and laypersons to serve as leaders during a three-week mission trip to Japan and Hong Kong. Avery really wanted to go but had not received an invitation.

One night, he couldn't sleep, and as he sat in his recliner at 3:00 a.m., he asked God why he had not been chosen. After all, he was the one who planned to be a missionary. Inwardly, he knew two things: he wasn't one of the two hundred well-known pastors being invited, and even if he were invited, he didn't have the $1,500 it would cost to go.

Still, he poured his passion and desire before God. Then he felt the Lord say, "You don't have the faith."

"Well, if faith is all that is needed, I will have the faith."

When an invitation arrived to go, Avery approached the church with his need for finances. The church began a special offering that quickly added up to $500 and then leveled off. (It turned out that some members were boycotting the offering because they thought their pastor should stay home and pastor the church.) The deadline arrived, and the mission trip sponsors called, requesting a commitment that day. Avery swallowed hard, and then said, "Yes, I am going. Count me in." Saying it out loud increased his faith, but didn't change the $1,000 deficit.

The next Sunday, Avery explained his situation to the congregation and invited them to give one last time. His sermon was about God telling the Israelites to go and take the Promised Land. The offering was taken at the end of the service, but before it could be counted, one of the ushers came to the front and said, "Brother Avery, you are on your way to Japan."

"How's that?" he asked.

"Several of the men have agreed to go to the bank and borrow the money to send you."

Avery thanked him but told the church he didn't believe that was how God wanted to answer his prayer. He believed the offering would be sufficient. After the service, the family went home. During lunch, the phone rang.

"Brother Avery, guess how much the offering was for your trip."

"$1,500!" he answered quickly.

"$1,503.43! The $3.43 must be coffee money!"[7]

New Life Crusade - Mission trip to Japan, 1963

Avery, Bud Wagoner, and Les Kennedy represented Inglewood Baptist Church for the three-week mission trip. Willis and Wagoner went to Fukui City. Meetings were conducted in the city hall auditorium and in the small Baptist mission, which had a membership of twenty-eight when the meetings began. Throughout the week of revival meetings, 234 people came to profess their faith in Christ for the first time. Kennedy went to the island of Kyushu, where 296 people came to faith in Christ. The three men went on to Hong Kong. The church there met in the fifth floor of an apartment house. That week, this small church experienced sixty-four professions of faith.[8]

Avery wrote in his journal notebook:

Never will I forget this—the greatest experience of my ministry. I still see people, people, people who are lost, who are receptive, who need Christ, and who will joyously serve Him. I don't know where we will serve Christ in the future but some of the ripening fields are our destination, I believe![9]

The impact of this mission trip on the church was life-changing. Over the next several years, eight families from the church went overseas as career missionaries, including the Willises and the pastor who succeeded them. The faith responses Avery learned in these settings set the stage to believe for greater needs when on the mission field.

SECTION 3
Church Planting in Indonesia

Spiritual Marker #5

God led the Willises as missionaries to Java, Indonesia.

Then I heard the voice of the Lord saying,
"Whom shall I send? And who will go for us?"
And I said, "Here am I. Send me!"
                                    —Isaiah 6:8 (NIV)

CHAPTER 5
Headed to the Mission Field

I want to win as many persons as I possibly can to faith
in Christ and to develop them in His image.

—Avery

In the summer of 1963, Avery and Shirley formally applied to become overseas missionaries with the Southern Baptist Foreign Mission Board. Avery's goal had always been to apply for mission service before he was thirty years old, after getting his basic theological education and some experience as a pastor. Though he had started work on his doctoral degree, he chose not to complete it for fear the board would place him in a seminary to teach. He felt his calling was to plant churches.

Rather prophetically, he wrote in his application:

The purpose of God's will is continually being revealed to me. I desire to have a witness to all men although in all probability I shall be limited to one area of the world. I want to win as many persons as I possibly can to faith in Christ and to develop them in His image. I shall continually seek new ways to reach more people for Christ. I will seek to establish growing indigenous churches with a great emphasis on the laity.

The significance of the church must not be overlooked in mission work. It is the spearhead of the gospel and nothing can replace it. The winning of peoples without a church to nurture them is doomed to be short-lived. It is my conviction that indigenous churches with little or no supplementary funds will be much more productive, although they may begin slowly. I feel it is my responsibility to encourage, to teach, to build up the nationals that they may do the work of ministry and the edifying of the body of Christ.

My larger purpose may someday lead me to teach in an institute or seminary, but I feel called to the task of field evangelism. I will cooperate with others, but I must be free to fulfill my ministry. It seems to me I can do this better if I am not burdened with the many processes of running the mission, or a school, or a hospital.

Destination: Indonesia

Shirley and Avery's FMB photo, 1964

When they met with Dr. Winston Crawley, Secretary to the Orient, to discuss where they might serve, Avery mentioned that he was interested in going to Asia. Shirley added she had been thinking about South America, and Brazil in particular. What they both agreed on, however, was that they wanted to be assigned to a new field where they could start churches. After hearing their hearts and looking at the options, Dr. Crawley said, "Well, from what you describe, Indonesia looks like it might be the best fit."

Thus, the move toward Indonesia began. After their appointment service on March 12, 1964, in Richmond, Virginia, they resigned the pastorate at the Inglewood church. During the interim period between the missionary appointment service and orientation, Avery spoke in churches or conventions from Tennessee to California every Sunday, every Wednesday, and other weeknights. He wanted five thousand prayer partners, so he began asking people to commit to pray for the family. At the Southern Baptist Convention, Avery stood in the hallways, passed out leaflets, and solicited people to be prayer partners, saying, *I am going to the mission field, and there is one thing I really need—for you to pray for me.*

Avery wrote an article, published in the December 23, 1964, issue of the Texas *Baptist Standard* paper, entitled "One Missionary Speaks for All":

My family and I sail to Indonesia on October 25th as your new missionaries. I must admit that I question you who send us. I do not question your motives or abilities, but I wonder if you will support us in prayer. Too often, your prayer support consists of the phrase, "Lord, bless the missionaries, especially those on the prayer calendar today." A stream of furloughing missionaries echoes the cry, "Prayer is our greatest need on the mission field." We do not face a difficult situation, but an impossible one! But God can do the impossible in response to the prayers of His believing people. Try to learn about your missionaries and the needs of their particular fields, and then pray, pray, pray for us and the lost millions we seek to reach for Christ.

Along with other missionary appointees, the Willises were presented to the Southern Baptist Convention in Atlantic City in May. Then there was a visit to the World's Fair in New York, family get-togethers, and finally back to Richmond, Virginia, for the week of orientation. During these three months, the Willises were saying goodbye to family and doing the required shopping and packing of items they would need in Indonesia. At that time, it was necessary to take everything from toilet paper and toothpaste to four years' worth of Christmas presents and a small washing machine and refrigerator.

Pulling Up Anchor

It wasn't easy for their families to let them go, but their parents' own commitment to Christ included the surrender of their children and grandchildren. Not long before their departure, Shirley's grandfather was in the hospital, near death. Shirley's father pulled her aside and said, "Don't let this change any of your plans." Her grandfather passed away not long after, and they were able to attend the funeral before they left. In a letter received on board ship to Indonesia, dated October 28, 1964, Beulah Morris, Shirley's mother, wrote:

> I have prayed to God to give me grace to accept what
> I knew was coming—separation from those we love
> for a long time. But I don't want to be, or say, any-

thing that might be a hindrance to what God wants both of you to do. He will provide.

On October 25, 1964, the Willis family boarded the SS *President Cleveland* ocean liner for a nineteen-day voyage across the Pacific, before flying on to Indonesia for their first four-year term. The family used the voyage on the ocean liner as a mission field in itself.

The Willises on board the S.S.
President Cleveland to Indonesia, 1964
Sherrie, Avery, Randy, Shirley, Wade (clockwise)

Avery began writing in a journal his second day at sea—a habit he would continue throughout the rest of his life.

SS *President Cleveland*, October 26, 1964
This journal is intended to be an account of my experiences as a missionary for Christ. It shall contain accounts, feelings, hopes, and failures. I have attempted to keep such a journal before but it never lasted more than three months. This time I feel the stewardship of my life and service demands it. It is primarily for personal use and evaluation. I trust

that anyone reading it will be kind enough to let it remain a personal accounting, letting it be a help to him personally if it can but not a conversation piece for gossip.

November 2, 1964

Yesterday I preached to nearly two hundred fellow passengers at the interdenominational service in the ship's chapel. My sermon was entitled "The Seeking Savior," taken from Luke 15. Several raised their hands for prayer but no one came forward. I have the names of some and plan to talk with them individually. I believe the gospel penetrated some of their pleasure-seeking hearts.

I have spent much of my time reading about Indonesia. It certainly looks like God has led us to a land that will tax all of our abilities. They are in a terrible position economically, politically, and spiritually. Only the gospel is adequate. I go in with great hopes, more in God than Indonesia. I know that God wants to save this world, especially those who have never heard. We will be so few. But if God is for us, who can be against us?

It was God's leading that set me in pursuit of 5,000 prayer partners. I argued its impossibility—yet He has led step by step at just the right time. I have over 2,000 definite commitments to whom I will send our monthly PRAY *newsletter.*

While on board the ship, the family joined in the nightly entertainment. On Halloween, the kids designed costumes and knocked on cabin doors, trick-or-treating. Avery and Shirley dressed as the ship's smokestacks, winning the prize for the best costume. Avery won the deck tennis championship, and Randy made it to the finals in shuffleboard. Sherrie sang "Jesus Loves Me" with the orchestra, and Avery performed two acts in the comedy show. Though this was all done for fun, the Lord used it to introduce the family to the fellow passengers and crew.

Avery performing on the ocean liner, 1964

November 8, 1964

Last night we had a talent show. I was the comedian and did the Bob Newhart driving instructor routine, as well as a parody of Camp Granada. I wrote my own words and changed the setting to the President Cleveland. I must say it was received as well as anything I have ever done like that. Several said that it was a sermon because it showed that a Christian could be happy and have fun. I know that the chapel service, what we did at Halloween, and the comedy routine have helped create friendships on the boat that I pray the Lord will use for future witness.

Learning about Revival

When the ship docked in Taiwan, the family was met and driven into the mountains to the Baptist Seminary where Dr. Charles Culpepper was president. Avery had heard and read about Dr. Culpepper over the years and looked forward to meeting this missionary whose life and testimony had impacted so many, not only on the mission field, but in the US.

Dr. Charlie, as he was affectionately called, would be retiring the following year, after spending forty-three years in China, Hong Kong, and Taiwan. He had experienced many victories and heartaches, having lost his daughter, Carolyn, to a fever in 1928, and having been imprisoned in the early 1940s for preaching the gospel.

Though he didn't talk a lot about those things, he loved to share accounts of the Shantung Revival of 1927– 1937 that began among the missionaries, and in turn resulted in a great harvesting of souls.[1] In 1927, missionaries from many denominations all over northern China had gathered for a time of spiritual renewal, even while the Japanese were threatening occupation. Marie Monsen, with the China Inland Mission, shared her experiences in the interior and the miraculous healings they were seeing. She then posed a question that would prove to be life-changing for many of the missionaries. "Have you been filled with the Spirit?" Dr. Culpepper, admitting that he had not given too much thought to it, later became convicted of "the sin of not being filled with the Holy Spirit."

Subsequently, in a prayer meeting that lasted four days and four nights, the Spirit of God fell in deep conviction. After times of confessing the sins of pride, broken relationships, prayerlessness, and other issues that had been hampering the work of God, the missionaries' hearts were renewed. During those days of revival, Dr. Charlie's wife, Ola, was miraculously healed of a serious eye disease, demonstrating the Spirit of God in their midst.

Over the years, the subject of revival became an increasingly important part of Avery's spiritual DNA. Though he didn't know it at the time, Avery would be similarly influential in introducing missionaries in Indonesia to revival through the work of the Holy Spirit. He would later become a moving force calling for revival in America, leading people in a call to prayer and repentance. His heart cry was for the church of America to experience an outpouring of the Holy Spirit that would shake her out of her lethargy.

Finally, after Avery preached a mini-revival in a Baptist church in Hong Kong, the Willises boarded their Garuda Airways flight to Jakarta.

November 17, 1964

Today is the day! Indonesia, here we come. You may never know we ever arrived, but by the grace of God, I trust that you will know Christ arrived on earth to deliver you from sin.

CHAPTER 6
Uncertain First Days

My days are in the hands of the Lord. I am
ready to go and I'm ready to stay.
I told God while I was in college that my life was for Him to use or take.
—Avery

Welcome ... ?

"Here is your house ... and here are the escape plans." It's hard to imagine a more ominous greeting as the Willises prepared to move into their new home in Bandung in 1964.

Prior to leaving the United States, Avery and Shirley had discussed their options of countries, with an eye toward the political climate. Upon deciding that God was leading them to Indonesia, Avery commented that "at least Indonesia has already had its revolution."

Indonesia, a republic of more than thirteen thousand islands, once known as the Dutch East Indies, was colonized by the Netherlands in the early 1600s. During World War II, when the Japanese occupied much of Southeast Asia, the Dutch retreated. Upon Japan's surrender at the end of the war, and before the Dutch could return, Indonesia proclaimed its independence on August 17, 1945. The forces of nationalism, communism, religion, and the army joined together against the Dutch with a zeal willing to fight against machine guns with nothing but sharpened bamboo poles and protective amulets.[1]

Years of political tumult were to follow the gain of independence, however. On August 17, 1964, three months to the day before the Willis family set foot on the island of Java, President Sukarno publicly denounced the United States in his Independence Day speech. Sukarno would subsequently lead a campaign against American interests, and in 1965, Indonesia would withdraw from the United Nations—the only nation ever to withdraw. The Communist Party of Sukarno's government would then call for "all workers and peasants" to arm themselves.

Home

The island of Java, the Willises' new home, was the world's thirteenth largest and most populous island—one of the most densely peopled places on earth. Approximately the size and shape of the state of Tennessee (population: 3.7 million people), Java was home to 105 million people.

The first Southern Baptists had arrived on Indonesian soil only thirteen years prior to the Willis family. Three men, leaving their wives at home, arrived on Christmas Day, 1951, to scout out the land for missionary work. In 1955, Dr. Kathleen Jones, the first Southern Baptist career missionary appointed to Indonesia, arrived with two nurses to open medical and church work in Kediri, East Java. Soon after, some of the missionaries who had been serving in China were transferred to Indonesia in response to Mao Tse-Tung's communist takeover.

Political turmoil only added to the initial culture shock the Willis family faced. Avery's journal entries give an overview of what their first year was like, spiritually and politically—a glimpse into the shaping God was doing in his personal life and ministry.

November 17, 1964

Indonesia at last! Almost one year from the day that we informed the Grand Prairie congregation that we were seeking appointment with the Foreign Mission Board, we arrived in Indonesia. We were accompanied by a beautiful sunset for several hundred miles. As we drew nearer, we saw twinkling lights in the darkness that turned out to be boats or buoys in the bay and the dim lights of Jakarta [the capital city of Indonesia]. *I thought of our missionaries here trying to eliminate the darkness with so few lights. I trust we can help.*

Missionary Leon Mitchell met the Willises at the airport to help them through the lengthy immigration process. As baggage and visas were checked, Randy, Sherrie, and Wade waited in a room to the side, listening to unfamiliar words and sweating in the humidity as they watched the *cicaks* (small tan geckos) running around the walls and ceiling.

We were met by a large crowd of people. Their brown faces with good-natured grins made us feel that this was our land. Jakarta was hot and sultry, dirty and old, crowded and noisy—and always needy. They think we may serve here. At present, I would rather go to a smaller place.

Though these were tense days, Avery and Shirley immediately got to work. The first items on their agenda were language study in Bandung and getting acclimated to a whole new way of life.

Cultural Adjustments

November 18–19, 1964
Bandung seems a paradise with its green foliage and high volcanic peaks. But looking at the people makes you realize it is a "paradise lost" as they carry heavy burdens on their backs, bathe in muddy streams and ditches, and drive water buffalo pulling old fashioned plows on their terraced rice fields.

There are people everywhere! People, people, people. People in need. In need of food, clothes, privacy, money—but mostly in need of Christ! Ninety percent of these 105 million people nonchalantly follow the teachings of Islam and its prophet, Mohammed. Some are dedicated, but most are as nominally Muslim as an American is a Christian.[2]

We have been received royally by the missionaries. We received our working expense of 200,000 rupiah. With the exchange rate, it is not really that much but it feels good to have 200,000 of anything! It is an inflation-depressed land and local goods and services are very cheap. Since we have already brought clothes, some food, etc., it is estimated that we can live on $75 a month.

Malaysia has placed an embargo on ships and planes that might be bringing arms into Indonesia. After January 1, they are invoking a complete embargo. I hope our freight arrives before then. There is a good bit of talk about the political situation but most people don't let it bother them. They say it is just propaganda.

I'm anxious to get started with language study so I can try mingling with the people and witnessing.

November 20, 1964

After registering with the city, I played golf with two of the missionaries on a beautiful course overlooking the city of Bandung. I decided I could afford to join the golf club when I discovered it cost $2.70 for the entrance fee and 3 months of dues!

I also decided that while we wait for language school to begin that I would sign up with the Famous Writers School to improve my style. Though I don't particularly like to write, I've never gotten away from what Martin Luther said, "If you want to change the world, pick up your pen and write."

Avery had difficulty seeing himself as a writer. He was almost through college, with a major in English, before he ever learned anything about his writing style, and when he did, it was not very encouraging. Avery will never forget what Mr. Espy, his English professor, wrote on one of his compositions: "Your style is atrocious, loose and awkward."

Avery recorded in his journal: *Since then I've tried to improve, but I'll never be a great writer. Some people seem to have a special gift, but nothing has ever come easy to me. It seems to usually be through perseverance and a lot of study with only a little above average intelligence.*

Little did Avery realize the important role in his life and ministry that writing would one day play.

November 25, 1964

One thing that has bothered me for several years is cropping up as I had expected, only worse: the wide difference between the economic standard of the missionary and the average national. We are rich here. Indonesians make $3–4 per month while we make one hundred times

74

that amount. Perhaps this is part of what they call culture shock. If so, my study lately in the gospel of Luke hasn't helped me. Luke 6:40 says, "The disciple is not above his master; but everyone that is perfect shall be as his master." Verse 24: "Woe to you who are rich." How can I be like Jesus? I know that we could live on a lot less but I doubt we could live long on their wages. Even if we cut down, we are still rich in their sight. I don't intend to just buy things because I can. For instance, I can't buy a candy bar that costs as much as I pay a woman to cook for us for three days. It just doesn't seem right.

We are experiencing many other adjustments. We don't have means of transportation or communication on our own yet. The four families in language school share two cars—one of which takes the kids to school and brings the language teachers. It takes two mechanics working several hours a day to keep them running. None of the cars are trustworthy to take out of town. The duty rate is so high that we can't get a new one. The telephone only works in spells. The hot water heater is broken. The gas is too low to heat water unless you leave it three to four hours. The stove will not bake and doesn't cook much. The water pressure is low and sometimes nil. The electricity is off and on. The trains and planes may or may not run. It seems that nothing mechanized is dependable.

The traffic here is different from other countries I have visited. You drive on the left—really you drive wherever no one else is at the moment. The streets are filled with tukangs [vendors], becaks [pedicabs], horse carriages, men pulling carts, bicycles, motorcycles, trucks, cars of all description and vintage, and people walking everywhere. How we keep from killing many of them and us is hard to understand outside the grace of God.

I suppose these are the little things they say are hard to adjust to. Thank goodness for Bandung's cool climate and fresh fruits and vegetables!

Crazy White Man Chases Dog!
(Told by Randy, Avery's Oldest Son)

One time, during my first year in Indonesia, when my parents were still in language school, Dad decided to take us swimming. Now, the way our house was laid out, our backyard was three or four feet lower than our neighbor's yard, with a barbed wire fence separating the properties. While Sherrie, Wade, and I were waiting for Dad to get ready, we saw a big black dog trying to climb over the fence to get into our yard. As he ducked under the barbed wire to jump down into our yard, his leg caught on the wire. He was suspended in air, with only the barbed wire in his leg keeping him off the ground. He was hanging there, yelping frantically, as he tried to shake loose.

Being a brave seven-year-old and wanting to help, I headed for the fence. As I drew near, the dog lunged at me, broke loose, bit me on the leg, and took off running. When I started screaming, Dad came running. He saw the bite and thought, "What if that dog has rabies?"

So he started off after the dog! In a moment of remarkable presence, he grabbed an umbrella, thinking, "If I catch that dog, I might need something to protect myself."

Now picture this. There goes my father, the new missionary in town, dressed only in his swim trunks, waving an umbrella, chasing a dog down the streets of Bandung—just so I wouldn't have to get rabies shots.

He somehow kept up with the dog, which eventually circled around to the house of its owner, with Dad still in pursuit. Dad talked to the lady of the house and was relieved to discover the dog had been vaccinated.

Dad often wondered aloud what the Indonesians might have concluded from this bizarre sight since black dogs are considered an Indonesian delicacy among the Batak people!

November 26, 1964

I'm trying to get to know the people by walking and talking in their kampungs [lower class neighborhoods]. *I'm beginning to feel the kindness of these people in spite of the political unrest and general anti-Americanism. It is among the lower class that the gospel is getting its best response. I'm told that there is very little response among the rich and intellectual who say they believe in God but won't recognize Jesus as being His Son. It seems that some people would rather work with the intellectuals even with little response than to work in the kampungs with good response among the illiterates whom they say lack leadership qualities.*

November 28, 1964

One thing I must keep in mind: there are many "Indonesias." One responsive group or area doesn't mean all are. I want to find the responsive fields. As far as I can discover, the Chinese are the most responsive ethnic group; the Javanese are next, and the Sundanese [of West Java] the most difficult.

We received the minutes of the Personnel and Planning Committee. They are temporarily assigning the Worten family to Bogor. Now I think that Bogor is where we would like to go. I have been praying to that end at least. I don't mind leaving it in God's hands but I'm not sure about the Personnel and Planning committee yet!

December 5, 1964

Language study is frustrating to me. By Wednesday, I almost despaired of ever learning a language. I have studied a lot, prayed, and everything else, but the language doesn't seem to be sticking for me like it is to Shirley. I suppose if I stop trying to compete with her I'll do better. Other language students say their wives surpassed them for about six months before they began to catch up. Of course Shirley is so adept that I don't know if I'll do as well.

Avery, however, was not about to let his frustration with the language stop him from using what he had learned to tell others about Jesus. He began to immediately use whatever language mastery he had as he took the four-hour express train to Jakarta. He sat on the hard plastic booth seats, his long legs squeezed in by passengers clutching their bags. Duck egg and fruit sellers pressed their goods against the window. Cigarette smoke filled the air.

77

December 21, 1964

The train pulled through the long valley that houses Bandung and began snaking its way between the mountains. The rice paddies stair-stepped up the sides of the mountain like patchwork quilts. Another train passed us with people sitting in the door, hanging onto the back, and perched on the engine. It probably had five to six times more people than seats.

I was seated with three Indonesians. Two were policemen. I began trying to use my three-week-old Indonesian on them. Soon the talk turned to Christ and I began my first personal witnessing in my new language. For three of the four hours I expounded the gospel. Can you imagine trying to explain the virgin birth, the new birth, the Trinity, the humanity-divinity of Jesus in a language you had only been studying for three weeks? The chief policeman, who showed a good bit of interest, also knew a little English, so when I couldn't come up with a word we would work on it together until we came up with what I wanted to say. Several times the third man would ask the policeman questions that he thought I could not answer but each time the policeman was satisfied. How I wish I could have pressed the claims of Christ better. He continued to ask questions each time I settled back to rest. I couldn't tell if he believed then or was only interested. I just praise God that I had the opportunity to share.

Sunday I preached the Christmas message in English at Calvary Church. There was no visible response from the 40-45 people present. In fact, I have yet to see a profession of faith in any service since we arrived in Indonesia. This is very disturbing to me and I think a growing concern in the Mission.

Not only was Avery aware of the spiritual destitution of the Indonesians, but he also sensed the spiritual needs of the missionaries. He wrote:

December 9, 1964

Last night, we had our regular prayer meeting for the "station" [missionaries living in Bandung]. Shirley and I gave our testimonies and they were well received. I believe we had the first real prayer meeting since I've been here. Gerald Pinkston prayed with a broken heart that our

Mission would experience revival and that our churches would really do something about winning the lost. John Smith was also weeping over the lost he had witnessed to. If we were all burdened about this, we could see a real revival here. It takes the same spiritual elements to bring revival on the mission field as anywhere else. Prayer for revival should top our prayer list. No spiritual victory is easily won.

One problem is our Adamic nature of selfishness. We have seen some of this with the language school students who have the attitude of being here first, or asking first. This attitude and lack of understanding, appreciation, and love cannot precede revival. I'm sure some would say, "We need revival? Who do you think we are? We gave up everything to give our lives on the mission field." Such an attitude should be evidence enough that we need revival. In devotions this morning, I studied the prayer of the Pharisee. Enough said.

In January, at the annual Bandung-Jakarta missionary prayer retreat, Avery was asked to preach in the evening session. He spoke on renewing a spirit of forgiveness, faith, and humility from Luke 17:1–10. Under the "spirit of humility," he pointed out that the Christian has given up the right of self-seeking, self-pity, and self-esteem. After supper, he led the group in a prayer period and introduced them to "conversational prayer."

During the conversational prayer, we began without many of the usual forms. Each person prayed in the first person; one after another prayed on the same subject before moving on to another topic—each adding their bit as they chose—just like in a conversation, rather than each person completing their list of prayer requests in turn. There was no set position, opening, or closing to the prayer.

Avery went on to write how frustrations and burdens were laid before the Lord and how people prayed for things they had not voiced aloud before—including forgiveness. He wondered if this might not be the beginning of a revival in the Mission. Many told him that it was the richest experience they had ever had in prayer.[3]

Political Unrest

Even while Avery and Shirley were progressing with language study, the political situation was becoming increasingly hostile to foreigners.

Thirteen days after the Willises arrived, the missionaries received word that all British personnel had left the country. How long they personally would be able to stay would be determined when, or *if*, a new US ambassador arrived, and *if* the US continued to send aid.

November 30, 1964

If we do leave, we'll only be allowed to take one suitcase per person. It would be hard to leave $10,000 worth of things we've accumulated, but as Dr. Cauthen [President of the Foreign Mission Board] *said: "Carry it in your hands; not in your heart." The thing I would most hate to leave are my files which could not be replaced.*

I heard on short-wave radio that twenty-eight missionaries, including three Americans, were massacred this week by rebels in the Congo. They said that some of the rebels were as young as twelve. I'm reminded that "He that loses his life for my sake shall find it." As long as one is going to die, why not be a martyr for Christ? Of course, I'm not going around looking for someone to martyr me, but I have given all for Christ—my goods and my life—so now I shall live in peace.

We've been told that demonstrations may start in Bandung. If protestors come to our homes, we'll hide the children and let them take our goods. They probably won't hurt us if we don't try to stop them.

January 3, 1965

The New Year is already providing surprises. We've been here less than two months and Indonesia has announced her withdrawal from the United Nations because Malaysia has been put on the Security Council. This now aligns Indonesia more with China. We don't know what effect this may have. Rumors have it that this is to be a month of surprises.

Avery and Shirley were in a restaurant one night when President Sukarno addressed the nation on TV. He explained why Indonesia had withdrawn from the United Nations and how they were now able to stand on their own. As he was saying that it was their crowning glory to be free from the UN, a waiter near them shouted, "Perang! Perang!" (War! War!). Sukarno went on to say that UNICEF and the World Health Organization were to "get out." He said, "To hell with your aid. Indonesia doesn't need your help. We will learn to do it ourselves." He said the longer Indonesia received help, the weaker it got. "Ever onward! Never retreat!" he cried. *This*, Avery thought, *is the end of all the UN work in Indonesia. I know our work could end as quickly. Whatever the final result, I feel that what is happening will stand out as a pivotal point in Indonesian history.*[4]

The problem of suddenly having to leave everything kept cropping up in Avery's mind. He decided to offer all his possessions as a sacrifice to the Lord like the Israelites used to do with sheep and bullocks. He wrote in his journal: *I would not just be watching them be destroyed by people, but would watch them ascend to God as a sweet smelling sacrifice.*[5]

Personal Growth

Another challenge for Avery was adjusting some of his mission philosophy to accommodate the Mission approaches and programs that had been in place for years. While waiting in the Jakarta offices to claim the newly arrived crates of belongings, Avery read *The Prisoner Leaps: A Diary of Missionary Life in Java* by David Bentley-Taylor. It was a story of an unusual working of the Spirit among the East Java churches in the late 1950s. Avery listed the practices that *describe so well my desires for missionary service* and contrasted them with what he saw happening in the Mission currently. He listed the following:

December 24, 1964

He [the missionary] *sought to work in the framework of the Indonesians and often under their leadership. He kept a close cordial relationship with the town officials. Whenever a problem came up, he let the nationals handle it.*

The missionary family used their own home as a meeting place for a women's group, a place of witness to children, and a weekly Bible class.

He ate and slept with the people. He gave out many tracts on evening strolls with his family, which gave him a contact, and let the people get used to him. They used Javanese more than Indonesian because it is spoken in the homes and marketplace. He did not support the work financially, except by his labor and his car. He refused to lend money.

The believers ordinarily met in people's homes. The meetings usually consisted of song, testimony, several sermons, and refreshments or supper. They spent much time in prayer together. Often, meetings lasted past midnight. They did not push decisions to get statistics, which let many curiosity seekers come and go. But they baptized almost immediately those who desired it. They used the new converts to witness. They were ever expanding into other villages.

In contrast, as far as I can tell,

We [our missionaries] immediately want to build a church building.

We want a full organization immediately, often modeled on Southern Baptist churches in the States.

We are so involved in keeping our machinery running that our time is all filled. It takes much of the missionaries' time to travel from one area to another for various mission committee meetings.

We attract many by our expenditures and their hope for gain. We let money, or its lack, stop us sometimes.

We lack a personal, day-by-day, night-by-night involvement in outreach and are failing to imprint our trainees with the evangelistic fervor that brought us here.

January 28, 1965

I have the impression that I need to ask Mr. Poei for the use of his cabin one day a month so I can spend a day in prayer and evaluation and projection of plans. I have begun a daily prayer list as well as my monthly one. The list is now over 2,000 people and includes all Indonesian missionaries and my prayer partners.

The practice of regularly setting aside a day or half day to spend alone in prayer and seeking the Lord's direction was one Avery would continue throughout his life. He took seriously the idea of prayer partners rather than prayer supporters, grouping them into days and praying for approximately fifty people per day so that he could pray for all of them. He also kept up correspondence, responding to anyone who wrote him, including Christmas cards.

Avery lived life on a learning curve, constantly striving to better himself, never satisfied with who he was and what he knew—always setting goals. He called 1965 a year of learning, writing out the following list of projects for the year:

1. *Learn Bahasa Indonesia well* [Bahasa Indonesia is the official language of Indonesia. Most Indonesians also speak at least one of the more than seven hundred indigenous languages.]
2. *Improve my golf and tennis, preferably with an instructor*
3. *Learn to play the guitar (and sing cowboy and folk tunes)*
4. *Continue to study the culture and history of Indonesia*
5. *Study how Islam has adapted to Indonesia*
6. *Learn patience*
7. *Practice intercessory prayer*
8. *Learn to do all kinds of repairs (electrical to plumbing)*
9. *Learn how a Mission functions*
10. *Become an effective writer*

Avery promptly beginning to work on his goals:

February 14, 1965
Last Wednesday I began taking guitar lessons.

March 28, 1965
I can so far pick out "Home on the Range," "Beautiful Brown Eyes," and "Goodnight Ladies." I believe this can be a real tool, especially working with young people.

Countdown

Due to the constant political tension and the daily reports of killings, martyrdom was never far from Avery's mind. He read *The Shadow of the Almighty*, the story of Jim Elliot, one of five missionaries martyred by the Auca Indians; and on February 17, 1965, he wrote in his journal:

Tonight I finished the biography of Jim Elliot. How he yearned to know Christ. Now he has His fullness. He willingly died that some who had never heard might live. His sacrificial giving was so like the Great Giver of Life he sought to imitate. This again tests my dedication. Here is a young man who lived a shorter life than I have already lived and God has used his martyrdom to call so many into missionary service. I haven't said much about it, but I told God while I was in college that my life was for Him to use or take. I felt that since we were all going to die anyway that I would be glad to give mine up anytime He would be glorified. I'm not seeking martyrdom and am planning to live at least my three score and ten. And since I have a family, I need to take precautions if danger threatens. Nevertheless, my days are in the hands of the Lord. I am ready to go and I'm ready to stay. God has protected my life thus far in an unusual way and delivered me from many dangers. Oh, Great Giver of Life, my Guide, my Strength. I want to live a redemptive life like Thee—or die a redemptive death.

Right now, I think it might be more difficult to live for Christ than to die for Him. This is a daily battle that Satan tries to win by temptation, over-activity, or by the inducing of spiritual slumber. Oh, Father of the Glorified, glorify Him in me.

Reading the life stories of others increased a sense of urgency on Avery's part to keep some kind of record of what was happening in his own life. He wrote: *I hope it isn't vanity to think that someday God might use the experiences I'm having, in one way or the other, though I doubt that anyone will ever care to write about me. Perhaps though, I can use the record I am keeping if I ever write a book.*[6]

On February 21, his thirty-first birthday and the thirteenth anniversary of the first time he preached "the wonderful gospel of Jesus Christ," Avery preached in English at First Baptist Church, Bandung, on "Jesus Christ, the Only Way."

I felt a great freedom and presence of the Holy Spirit. The people listened intently, but no one was saved. Oh Lord, how long? When shall I bear fruit in this land that will remain after I'm gone? My only fear is that we'll have to leave before spiritual sons and daughters are born.

The anti-American feeling is increasing. The protesters are shouting "Ganyang USA" [Crush the USA]. *The paper tonight said that there was a mass rally of 250,000 in Jakarta on Monday and that the American Embassy had been stormed to protest the assassination of Malcolm X. They sent a note to President Johnson demanding that all American institutions be shut down. All U.N. personnel are being ordered out now.*

Life in Indonesia was becoming a day-by-day gift. Decisions were made toward a future, but with an ear to the Lord and an eye to the surroundings—a daily walk of trust and making the most of the time.

CHAPTER 7
Preparing to Sow

Sharpen again Your sword in my hand, Your arrows in my quiver,
and Your battle plan in my heart.

—Avery

Avery's gift of evangelism caused him to desire indigenous missions from the start. He longed for the opportunity to implement his nontraditional convictions in an area largely untouched by the gospel. He felt that this could best be done in areas not yet influenced by other traditional church programs or expectations. He was convinced that outside finances and support stripped self-initiative and inhibited the spiritual growth process. However, missionaries were assigned to locations based on the Mission's felt needs.

Choosing the Plot of Land

Avery had a unique ability to negotiate because he knew in his heart who he was, what he wanted, and what he sensed God had called him to do. When the Mission's personnel committee met with Avery and Shirley to discuss their place of service after language school, Avery came prepared to outline his vision and explain his reasons. He presented his case and trusted the outcome to God.

He told how he had studied the field reports of Southern Baptist mission work over the past fifty to seventy-five years and how he had picked Indonesia because of its responsiveness to the gospel. During seminary, he had studied many books and methods on missions and was eager to begin an indigenous movement.

He outlined his plan. He felt it would be optimal to begin in smaller cities and towns. The discussion turned to beginning a work in Bogor, either by moving there or by commuting from Jakarta, fifty kilometers away. Having already anticipated and considered these options, Avery articulated his strong belief that it would be very difficult to be effective in Bogor while living in Jakarta.

Important questions remained.

March 13, 1965

They asked how we would feel about another new couple beginning with us. I said we loved people but I would think that it would be better if we had agreement in ideas and methods—at least to completely understand each other. They asked about us being alone in regards to children's schoolwork, etc. They brought up the problems of shifting responsibility to nationals, nationals going to seminary, and the influence of existing patterns. Finally, they wanted to know what we would do if the Mission as a whole felt that we should go to Jakarta and we didn't. I said that if God was in it and led them, He could surely lead me to the same conclusion. I did tell them that if, after considerable consideration, I could not feel God's leadership to go there, then I would have a problem. We left it at that.

Within six weeks, the planning toward Bogor took another twist. The national pastors of the West Java association of churches met to plot out every town in West Java with plans for future work. They elected to begin work first in Bogor with Peter C., one of the early graduates of the Indonesian seminary. Avery did not see this as competition, but he was uncertain about the attitudes and philosophy held by Peter. His work ethic had not left a favorable impression on the missionaries nor the Indonesian churches he served.

May 3, 1965

While in seminary, he led a student protest against the food, and in Bandung he demanded more money for salary. He was previously fired from our church in Bandung. He has lived in Bogor for two or three years and has done nothing to begin a work since he wasn't on salary.

I am not sure how indigenous a program I might develop if Peter is there. Some have told me that by the time I get to Bogor, Peter will have failed, but I doubt it in such short time. It's in the Lord's hands.

[Missionary] *Ray was quite upset about a similar mindset in Solo. The national pastors and six churches there are on subsidies and expect the Mission to pay for whatever they need (even for a flashlight for the preacher to use when visiting the villages). It is not the money that is so disturbing but the kind of welfare mentality it produces. It is difficult for indigenous work to get far enough away from the American influence to not be affected by it. The seminary seems to be one of the main problems. Boys who have never slept on anything but tikar [woven mats] now think they are too good for that. We graduate them to be frustrated preachers, unable to attain the missionaries' standard of living, and unwilling to live on theirs.*

Preparing to Cast the Seed—in Another Language

Avery strove to learn the language quickly so he could begin to preach. Fortunately, the Indonesian language is relatively easy to learn. Avery wrote his first sermon after only a few months.

March 14, 1965
Tonight I gave my first speech in Indonesian for a class on "Worship Through Prayer." The people were complimentary. After the service, Pastor Yo asked me to preach in Indonesian for him in both services on May 2 when he will be traveling with the seminary choir. He said that I didn't make a mistake in the class. He told me that I should preach my first sermon in Indonesian here, so no one would hear me. No one would hear me?!!! I think he meant that they would be sympathetic. I hope so!

If I agree to preach for him that will mean that I will be preaching in Indonesian less than four-and-a-half months after beginning language study. I told him I would preach one sermon and tell him whether I could preach a second one after a little while. I don't know if that isn't a little much for such a beginner but I'm a glutton for punishment and love a challenge. Time will tell.

Personal discipline was an increasing need and priority in Avery's life. In his morning devotions, Avery began reading a chapter per day from the gospel of Mark in Indonesian. His hope was to read the entire New Testament within the final six months of language study. He also tried to memorize a Scripture verse a day in Indonesian, mostly verses he had already memorized in English, but the task was challenging.

89

March 18, 1965

Fellowship in prayer refreshes my soul each morning. Since arriving here it has been easier to maintain a regular schedule. I usually study a chapter a day from the New Testament, make notes, and then pray for about a hundred people on my prayer list. All this takes about an hour, depending on the movement of the Spirit and the rush of other things. I have to lock my door, though, to keep from being disturbed.

I had the opportunity to witness to the cook at the club the other day after beating him in tennis, 8–6, 3–6, 6–1. What a thrill to be able to express the truth of the gospel without stumbling painfully. I'm still working on the best approach for witnessing to a Muslim.

Life Happens
(Bandung Journal Entry)

Then there were "those days" when little went right.

One day, Avery had gone to play golf with two other missionaries. Pelted with rain, they huddled under an umbrella for over an hour. But Avery was due at church where he was to lead the choir and sing a duet as part of the church's anniversary celebration. He called Shirley to bring some clothes and pick him up.

When she didn't show up in a reasonable time, the men went looking for her and found her down the hill. The car had run out of gas, and she had left it in neutral when she went to telephone. It had rolled into a wall! Fortunately, there was little damage. Since no one was available to bring her any gasoline, she was still waiting by the side of the road.

They found some gas and headed to church, but Avery was still in wet shorts. It was getting dark, so he tried to find an inconspicuous place to park and change clothes. In the first alley, he was met by a policeman who came running out with rifle pointed. Avery knew it would take too long to explain, so he just turned and walked the other way. He soon found another dark corner and changed. Avery and Shirley arrived at the church fifteen minutes late; the people were already praying. He sneaked in, sat down on the front row, and then stood just in time to lead the choir in the special music.

April 7, 1965

Today I finished writing my first sermon from Luke 15, "The Seeking Savior." Now I must learn it and try to pronounce the sounds like an Indonesian. It took me an entire week and all my language classes to finish it. I plan to start on the other sermon this week.

April 11, 1965

I've just finished typing the second sermon in Indonesian; "Hidup Kekal" [Everlasting Life]. Even though it is longer, it was easier to write because this is advancing my knowledge of the language rapidly. It feels strange to see an entire sermon I have written in a language I didn't know a word of several months ago. Sort of like a dream, though the effort to learn it hasn't been a dream.

Mr. The (pronounced Tee), Avery's Indonesian language teacher, told Avery that one sermon after five months of language study was enough and probably just one a month after that. Since he had already finished writing the second sermon, Avery was unwilling to wait when he already had an invitation to preach it in two weeks. He wrote:

I don't think he knows my bulldog tenacity, or stubbornness, as some would call it, once I have decided to do it. I have seen this perseverance rewarded hundreds of times in other ventures for Christ. Time is too short to waste.[1]

April 18, 1965 Easter Sunday

We attended the Easter Sunrise service this morning held in the parking lot of First Church. Over a hundred people were assembled in the fast fading darkness. The cloudy sky held the light of day captive until Daniel Tan was a third of the way through his sermon. Just as he told of the resurrection, the sun poked its head through the clouds as scores of birds began announcing its arrival. I thought of the clouds that are hiding the face of the Son here in Indonesia. How I long to see Him break through the clouds in all His glory and dazzle the unbelievers of this land.

Easter is essential to our witness here because Islam teaches that Jesus didn't really die, nor was He resurrected, but that He just ascended into heaven and Judas died in His place. How the craftiness of Satan has stolen the heart of the gospel and substituted a worthless life in its place. How I long to witness to the truth!

May 7, 1965

Only two more days until I preach my first two sermons in Indonesian! I think I have them fairly well in hand, though not quite memorized. I've been torn between memorizing them or just speaking extemporaneously; though to be candid, I don't have enough command of the language for that. That will be my goal, however—to speak with only an outline in the next few months.

May 14, 1965

Both messages last Sunday went better than I had expected. Of course, there were a few mistakes, but no serious ones. The problem now is that I will be on inspection and people may expect me to know more than I do. No one made a profession of faith but a young man seemed to be under conviction.

September 18, 1965

I have written a new sermon entitled "Repolusi Jesus" (The Jesus Revolution) *or "Kemerdekaan Allah"* (Freedom of God). *I have had really good responses to it from my teachers. Mr. Markonda says it's the best sermon he's ever heard and he is trying to get it put in the paper. He even wanted me to preach it at the party last night—and he is a devout Muslim!*

Escalating Political Tension

Encouraged that he was gaining ground with the language and the gospel, Avery was simultaneously aware that it could all be for naught if they weren't allowed to stay long.

March 28, 1965

Friday at 3:15 p.m. a huge bomb in an ammunition depot exploded. We could feel it miles away where we live. They estimate that hundreds are dead or wounded. A one-ton bomb is still alive and surrounded by fire. Six villages have been cleared in case it explodes. We have begun collecting clothes and money for survivors who have lost their homes.

We had to move the equipment out of the American school because AID [Agency for International Development] *leaves Monday and the government will take the building. The government has banned several newspapers and any periodical must have the backing of three parties to exist. The Postal Trade Union boycotted all American mail, telephone, and telegraph services for a day.*

April 7, 1965

The Ford Foundation will leave within two weeks. This leaves only the missionaries, two Peace Corps boys, and members of the Kentucky teaching team at the ex-patriate school. Mary Alice said that the deacons and pastor of Raya Barat church have asked that no more missionaries join the church. The church feels that they must "make friends in their new location." They are receiving much criticism from the neighborhood, which consists primarily of Muslims and Communists. If this attitude became a trend, it could spell the end of our effectiveness as missionaries.

May 7, 1965

We have been told to be extra cautious, especially from May 10–20 and on into August. The Communists are growing in strength and there may be fighting ahead. The newspaper has reported that plans are in the works to break off all relations with the U.S. If this happens, it will probably be of little use to stay. An American presence might hinder the work here more than help.

June 13, 1965

Three church members in Sukabumi took us to dinner. Just as we were seated in the restaurant, a Communist parade started. It took the entire street and lasted over an hour. It was led by a corps of drummers followed by marchers dressed in red, kids carrying hammer and sickles, men dressed in yellow, farmers straight from the fields, night watchmen on motorcycles, more marchers, floats carried by men, riders on horse-back, a band of children playing the anklung [bamboo instruments played like a bell choir]*, and hundreds of others. It had a real effect of* *strength and magnetic pull to be one of those on the bandwagon. It made my blood run cold.*

June 19, 1965 (excerpt from a letter home)
This week we are having air raid drills. We have to turn out all lights while they shoot off a lot of big guns. There will probably be a lot of news about Indonesia coming out of the Algiers Conference next week.

Spiritual Traction

In the midst of this, the Lord was moving in Avery's life and in the lives of those around him.

May 18, 1965
Station meeting met at our house tonight and I spoke on James 5:13–20. I suggested we pray with our eyes open as if speaking in the presence of Christ. I asked Bob to start and it was almost funny to see him start to bow his head and rest his head in his hands. He hesitated, pulled back his hands, smiled, tried again, and then said, "I can't pray and look at you, Avery." He suggested I begin the prayer. It was a good prayer time and about half participated with eyes open. It helped make us uncomfortable in our "rut." One person said he could imagine us in heaven someday face to face with Jesus, bowing our heads and closing our eyes while talking to Him!

June 4, 1965
This morning I'm at Mr. Poei's cabin on top of Bukit Dago, looking over the city of Bandung that is encircled by these hills. Gorgeous lavender and orange flowers surround my little prayer chamber under a cedar tree. The cool breeze reminds me of the refreshing of God's Holy Spirit. About fifty feet away a man is digging with a grubbing hoe in his tapioca field. God loves him as much as He loves me, although we are worlds apart in our educational, social, and religious backgrounds.

I need this time to get God's perspective on Indonesia and particularly His desire for my life and its part in this land. I must do this often in a prolonged exposure to His presence if I am to walk in His ways without branching off on my own. How often the flesh wants to become entangled in selfish pursuits!

Oh God, I long for You to do with me as You will. May You conquer the world, the flesh and the devil in this progressive, escalating conflict. Sometimes I go too long before opening my entire thought life to You, and some of the ideals You inspire lose their sharp, pricking power. Sharpen again Your sword in my hand, Your arrows in my quiver, and Your battle plan in my heart.

June 13, 1965

Last Thursday, I was asked to preach at the church in Sukabumi while the pastor was in a revival meeting. The whole family drove down. When we arrived, they asked me to teach Sunday School, which started in fifteen minutes—the pastor had said whoever came would. I had my hands full with the two sermons. The morning sermon went better than any so far. Five ladies came forward at the invitation. It really did me some good to see my first decisions in Indonesia when I preached.

Coming home tonight, Randy said he knew what I was going to preach on. I told him that it shouldn't be too difficult since I only have two sermons. He said, "At last that sermon did some good!" Then he said he would have made a decision himself if he hadn't been afraid. He had made his decision to follow Christ in the U.S. but knew he had sinned again. I talked with him about the daily need for believers to ask for forgiveness and he rededicated his life. Then he went to sleep on my shoulder the rest of the way home.

July 11, 1965

Much has happened since I last wrote here. Camp Miki [an annual week-long summer camp for missionary children] *started last Wednesday night. All my sermons had a space theme. By the end of the week, nine of the ten children present had made decisions, four to be missionaries, two for special service, and three rededications.*

I've received an invitation to preach the Sunday morning message at Mission Meeting [the annual meeting of all of the Southern Baptist missionary families], *which is a bit surprising since Shirley and I are still in language school. I wouldn't think they would listen to anything we had to say until after our first term. I am torn between preaching on an approach to mission work and the power to accomplish it. Perhaps I should be quiet on methods until I've had opportunity to do it and then have something to back up what I say. I'll just look to the Lord.*

Celebration

July 21, 1965

This is the night before our first Mission Meeting. It looks like it is going to be a full one for us even though it is our first. I'm going to preach Sunday morning from 2 Corinthians 10:1–6 on "God's Mighty Weapons." I really have a lot to say—I hope I can get it all in. Shirley and I will also be giving our testimonies, and I'm sure I'll have a part in the "Hootenanny" on Saturday. I will also be directing and playing the lead in the play I wrote on mistakes missionaries make in the language. And I thought I'd just be listening!

Today, the Executive Committee met and decided to recommend a new station—BOGOR! Bob said: "Unless you go home, I think you'll be going there." They started to link it with Jakarta but changed their minds. God is still working. But I had already received the victory about Bogor when I read Hebrews 11:1 in the Living Letters translation two weeks ago: "What is faith? It is the confident assurance that something we want is going to happen. It is the certainty that what we hope for is waiting for us even though we still cannot see it ahead of us." Whatever is ahead, I know God is leading. I am amazed at how good God is to me. I never will understand it.

July 26, 1965

As I was preaching the Sunday morning sermon, I was speaking but I felt like a spectator as the Holy Spirit moved. So many have come to share a blessing from the hour.

Then Sunday night I witnessed a direct answer to prayer (of our prayer partners and others). Bob led a prayer and testimony time. I was actually embarrassed as he mentioned my name several times as he told of the conversational prayer times I had led in the Bandung Prayer Retreat.

Another missionary followed, and again talked about my influence during the Bandung Prayer Retreat before leading all of us in conversational prayer and confession. Oh, how God moved as we prayed, confessed and worshiped. Then one missionary who had written a rather harsh letter to another missionary concerning a matter—and sent copies to all stations in the Mission—stood and publicly asked for forgiveness. It was reciprocated and God greatly moved in our midst. It was revival in the true sense.

The fire lit at Bandung is spreading. God is at work. Bob reported that something similar had recently taken place in a prayer meeting with national pastors. How different this meeting is turning out to be than the year before when some harsh, personal things were said in the public meetings.

I had trouble sleeping last night. I was trying to assimilate the blessings of the day and especially the repeated references to my ministry relating to prayer. I am amazed at the entrance God has given to me. I walked the street from 1:00 to 2:30 a.m., soul searching. I know how poorly I do God's work and want to be so sure I don't give any foothold to the devil. I also tried to process my being so accepted by the Mission as a first-term missionary. Then suddenly I knew what was making the difference: our prayer partners—the two thousand prayer partners who have been praying for Shirley and me!

During the Mission meeting, the board recommended that Avery and Shirley pioneer the new work in Bogor after they completed language school. This would be only the second time in the history of the Mission that a first-term missionary would be sent to begin a new work. There was no opposition.

July 30, 1965

Bogor! The Mission had felt for years that work should begin here and now we are the ones to do it. They "warned" us that Peter had begun work in Jakarta and that the church in Sukabumi had already voted to pay the expenses of their laymen and pastor to start work in a home in Bogor. But all of this sounds wonderful to me!

They assigned us a car, the Ford Econoline, effective now. So this morning, we drove over the Punjak Pass through the mountains into Bogor, Indonesia's second capital. It is a beautiful city in the foothills of the extinct volcano, Mt. Salak. The world famous botanical gardens, established in 1745, join the spacious palace lawn, where deer walk freely, with the palace gleaming in the center like a pearl. We met an American family who said about 200,000 people live here. They earn their living working with rubber, rice, tea, and fruits. Because of its various schools, it has been called the City of Science. There are already a Sundanese, Batak, and Gereja Kristen [Christian Protestant Church] and a large Catholic church and school. The people seem more accustomed to Americans and friendlier than in Bandung. The school board member welcomed us to put our children in the six-pupil remnant of an American school when we arrive. I also learned that Bogor has one of the best nine-hole golf courses in Indonesia!

Sowing the Seed

Avery's personal witness was beginning to bear fruit. He stepped out of the house one day to find Usubarnas, the husband of Juwarsi, one of the housekeepers, standing in the driveway, waiting for her to finish working. He smiled broadly beneath his black Muslim *peci* (the national hat), bowing in greeting, anticipating another one of the brief chats he and Avery usually shared upon meeting. He was born a Muslim and a Sundanese, a combination that almost precluded the possibility of his ever becoming a Christian.

To Avery's surprise, Usubarnas accepted the invitation to go to church with them and hear Avery speak. His whole family accompanied them that evening, and afterward, Usubarnas read aloud to his whole family from the children's Sunday school lesson his daughter had brought home. They came back for more the following Sunday, and as they listened to Avery preach, their intent faces gave indication to the Holy Spirit's work in their hearts. The next Sunday, they returned to accompany the Willises to a third church where Avery was speaking. Due to a misunderstanding, the pastor was there to preach the morning sermon, and Avery was asked to speak in the evening instead. In the crowd that evening were Usubarnas and Juwarsi, who had walked to the evening service. During the invitation, Usubarnas looked resolutely ahead, pushed past his wife, who was trying to block his way, and grasped Avery's hand, bowing his head and confessing his desire for Christ to be his Lord and Savior.

Not long afterward, Avery witnessed to a vegetable vendor named Enju. The man had set down the baskets and pole he carried on his shoulder and squatted down to smoke. He listened to the Bandung revival services through the window but remained outside of the church because he was too ashamed to go in, dressed as he was. As Avery spoke with him after the service, the vendor asked for some clothes so that he would be appropriately dressed to go to church.

Avery knelt by the vegetable stand and told him, "I would like for you to go to church and sit with me, for real Christians look at the heart, not the dress. But if I gave clothes to everyone who came, I would have thousands who came for the wrong reason. I don't know your heart, but God does. If you are seeking God, you will find Him, and He will help you get clothes." Afterward, Avery wondered if he had said and done the right thing—up until 6:45 a.m. on Sunday when Enju arrived with his brother, Oji, an hour early for church.[2]

September 19, 1965

Today I preached the new sermon to a full house, half of which we brought. All of our household servants, the two fruit vendors, Mr. The, and a missionary family came with us. The fruit vendor showed up this morning with good (albeit, too large) clothes on, and brought his brother with him. The Spirit blessed the service and Juwarsi and the two vendors came putting their faith in the Lord. I think I'll try to start a new Christians' class for all three of these.

The Folly of Fury

August 25, 1965

Word has just arrived from our Baptist Hospital in Kediri of a tragic chain of events. On August 14, a sign was placed over the entrance to the hospital by workers in celebration of Indonesia's Independence Day

[August 17]. *It included the word "NASAKOM," a combination of the words NASionalisme [Nationalism], Agama [Religion], and KOMunisme [Communism]—a major platform of President Sukarno. When he saw it, Dr. Bob Lambright proceeded to climb up the structure and rip off the portion with the KOM, march into the office and demand an explanation as to why the hospital would be supporting PKI (the Communist Party), and give a lecture as to why communism was evil. After hearing the workers' explanation, he put the sign back up but in the meantime, the workers had become very upset, feeling that this was an affront to the government. Someone outside the hospital had telephoned the authorities and so representatives from the police, military, and civil organizations came and interrogated Bob. The officials told him to write a letter of apology and state his reasoning—that this was an action of religion and not politics, but before he could do so, the PKI arrived. The final outcome was that Bob was given twenty-four hours to get out of town, and the hospital had to make a statement that they did not approve of his actions. The Lambrights left five hours after the notice and are in Jakarta now awaiting further instructions, an early furlough option, and exit-re-entry visas, should they be allowed to return to the country.*

It seems such a pity that one impulsive act should undo eight years of goodwill he had created with his medical practice and study center. He was said to be closer to and to better understand the Indonesians there in Kediri than did any of the other missionaries.

From this, I have learned:

1. *"He that controls his own spirit is better than he that defeats a city." (Proverbs 16:32)*
2. *Nothing should be said or done that could be construed as anti-government. (Romans 13:1–4)*
3. *We must not compromise the pure Gospel but not muddy it with our own political presuppositions.*
4. *We must use every opportunity for witness we have because we never know when we may have to leave. We are pilgrims on this earth and in this land.*

September 8, 1965

Tomorrow all foreign missionaries are to meet with officials from the Department of Religion. We don't know what to expect. We may be given a warning.

September 9, 1965

Sure enough, they asked us to sign a paper they had prepared that we would abide by the laws of Indonesia, not do or say anything against the government, and that we would help in nation and character building in our respective duties. After making a few word changes, we signed the paper for a release to the press, radio and the offices we deal with. We didn't like the way it was handled but basically we had already agreed to these things when we came as missionaries.

Internal Angst

It wasn't long before Avery recognized the incongruity of his philosophy and his actions.

August 5, 1965

It occurs to me that I have said the West Java Association of Indonesian Baptists couldn't do much since they don't have funds. To think that is to deny what I want to show: that the spread of the Kingdom is not dependent on foreign financing. I can see that I need to review my own presuppositions and methods.

As I face this new work, I am faced again with the question of how indigenous to be. When the money is available and the desire is to make an impression on this important city, it is tempting to go the way of most American missionaries. But I ask, "Would a building on an important corner impress them with the power of God or of the power of the American dollar? Would not several cell groups with devotion impress them more of a spiritual force at work?"

Right now I think I should train some Christians before trying any mass rallies; that is, if I can win enough before then. I may have to have a film rally to get an initial start. But if there are no mature Christians to help those reached, it could slow the work down in the long run.

And I must reach the Indonesians. In my conversations with Pastor An and Pastor Rembet of the Association, it became clear that a Chinese pastor can rarely reach both Chinese and Indonesians. In no time, the congregation becomes predominantly Chinese. It might be necessary to start several groups simultaneously, i.e. Sundanese, Chinese, English speakers, illiterates, intellectuals, poor, rich, etc.—whatever groups will automatically stick together to begin with.

Pastor An, head of the West Java association of churches, came to visit Avery, bringing a letter from the association concerning work in Bogor. The letter stated that the association had postponed their plans to begin work there. They requested, however, that Avery channel his efforts through their association and that property be purchased by the Mission but loaned to the association for the work of God. They felt this would protect the work so that it would appear to be at the invitation of the Indonesian association and not an American venture.

Avery realized the focus was on finding a public meeting site first, and as soon as thirty or more adults or young people began to come, they would want a church building. He immediately asked several clarifying questions. Would the "right to invite" also suggest the "right to dismiss" or the right to direct the work? Avery said he had already been invited/assigned by the Mission, so difficulties might arise if he had two bodies to which he was responsible. If the Mission owned the property, but it was "on loan to the association," who would be responsible for the bills and upkeep of the building? If they did send a national pastor to begin the work, who would pay his salary? Would their approach to evangelism and church planting be similar enough and as deliberate as Avery had intended? He shared with them his personal approach of gathering people in homes rather than focusing on a place to meet.

Unbeknown to them all, the intended cooperation in Bogor would be interrupted by an attempted overthrow of the government four days later.

Spiritual Marker #6

The Willis family survived an attempted coup
that brought spiritual renewal to Indonesia.

"Why do the nations rage and the peoples plot in vain?"
Now, Lord, consider their threats
and enable your servants to speak your word
with great boldness.
—Acts 4:25b and 29 (NIV)

CHAPTER 8
Revolution! The Indonesian Coup

My only fear is that we'll have to leave before
spiritual sons and daughters are born.

—Avery

Indonesia's first and only president, President Sukarno, was adored and almost deified by the Indonesian people. A skilled orator and charismatic leader, he had molded many islands of diverse peoples into a nation rich with natural resources. He gave the people a language of their own, raised the literacy rate from 6 percent to over 55 percent, and gave the people intense pride in being Indonesian.[1]

From the first national election in 1955, the PKI—the Indonesian Communist Party—was one of the four largest political parties in the nation; by 1957, it ranked first. By the time the Willises arrived, Indonesia had the third largest communist party in the world, behind only China and the Soviet Union.

Sukarno withdrew Indonesia from the United Nations on New Year's Day, 1965. A strong nationalistic and anti-American sentiment followed. Communism had infiltrated many areas of Indonesian life, and the government media increasingly followed a straight communist line. President Sukarno denied being a Communist himself but definitely held socialist views and backed the PKI as "the nation's most progressive party."[2]

In May 1965, the anniversary of the PKI's founding was widely and extravagantly celebrated, with financial aid from Peking—and with Sukarno's blessing.

By September 1965, Communist leaders believed everything was in place to seize control of the government. They had the support of the people and the implied, if not explicit, support of President Sukarno. Calling themselves the "30th of September movement" and master-minded by PKI leader D. N. Aidit, the plotters intended to complete the attempted Communist coup of 1948, which had been defeated on September 30 of that year. October 1 also coincided with Red China's celebration of its National Day, so it would serve as "a birthday gift to the People's Republic of China."[3]

Execution

Under the cover of early morning darkness on October 1, 1965, Lieutenant Colonel Untung, Commander of the President's Palace Guard, along with seven detachments of troops, left from the Halim Air Force Base on the outskirts of Jakarta with plans to seize power and communication centers, Radio Jakarta, and the National Bank.

Last to move out was an elite squad of men trained to torture and kill, assigned to kidnap eight generals—all senior members of the Army's top command. Three of the generals were killed in their homes. Another three generals were taken alive, but were soon tortured and killed, their bodies thrown in an abandoned well, called *Lubang Buaya* (Crocodile Hole).

At 7:15 a.m., Lieutenant Colonel Untung went on the airways falsely claiming that the "September 30 movement" had foiled a plot by the Council of Generals, that those generals had been arrested, and President Sukarno was "safely under protection." He later announced the establishment of a forty-five-man Revolutionary Council to take charge—President Sukarno's name strangely absent from that list.[4]

Two generals survived—one who was attacked and one who was not. General Nasution, Minister of Defense, escaped as troops stormed through his house, a young aide giving his life to stall them long enough for Nasution to flee, breaking his ankle as he jumped over a wall into a neighboring embassy. Major General Suharto, Commander of the Army Strategic Reserve, was at the hospital with his fever-stricken daughter and not home the night of the attack.

If General Suharto was thought to be "insignificant," it was a seri-ous miscalculation. General Suharto moved quickly and decisively to crush the insurrection, taking command of the Army and persuading naval and police commanders to join forces with him. Within twenty-four hours, they had wrested back control of the government in Jakarta, recaptured the radio stations, and claimed that President Sukarno and General Nasution were safe. Jakarta was declared a war zone, and the nation was put under martial law.

Truth or Lies?

Substantiated news was difficult to come by; rumors, however, were plentiful. The missionaries who lived through these events often knew less than the outside world. Avery's journals describe the confusion and rapidly changing winds of politics from the inside.

October 2, 1965

It is now twenty-four hours after the "re-coup" and this is a very unsettled, unsure situation. Speculation is rampant. The six kidnapped generals haven't been heard from. General Nasution, head of defense, is reported wounded along with his daughter. One report said his wife was dead. General Nasution and President Sukarno, who are now supposed to be in a safe place, have not been heard from.

The fight for power has evidently just begun. There is a good possibility that the fighting in Jakarta and Central Java could spread into a national struggle for power between the right-wing generals and the Communist Party.

Much hangs on whether the President is still alive and what is to be done to or with him and by whom. He is the one person who could weld the divergent opinions into a semblance of national unity. It will also depend on the power behind him. If he is dead, there is little doubt there will be a real struggle. Yet if the Army and Navy and Islamic groups would unite, they would probably win over the Communist forces.

The hardest thing is to tell the good guys from the bad guys. General Suharto himself is an unknown factor. No direct communication to the outside world is being made except by the government radio station. All communications have been seized.

As far as we know, all the missionaries are safe, but we have had little communication.

Evidence of the president's safety was a two-minute recording calling for calm while the rebels were being rounded up. President Sukarno said he was still head of state and that he had placed General Suharto and two other generals in charge of carrying out his orders. In a separate but equally brief broadcast, President Sukarno again asked for calm and ordered people to turn in their weapons.

October 7, 1965

Tonight the news blows from a different direction. President Sukarno announced no reprisals would be made against the murderers of the six generals. The PKI announced that they were behind the President and that they had no part in the September 30 movement. They called it an internal army affair. The President said that the movement was "normal in a country undergoing a revolution," and was to be expected. This announcement is a bitter pill for so many who have spoken out against the Communists.

To gain support against the Communists, grisly photos of the generals' mutilated bodies were shown to the public. Aborted plans for terrorist activities and atrocious murders were revealed. These scenes offended the gentle-natured Indonesians. People began to clamor for the banning of the PKI and punishment of all who took part in the attempted coup.

Violent Response

October 8, 1965

Five hundred thousand people in Jakarta demonstrated against the PKI. The PKI headquarters was burned and a demand was sent to the President that all PKI organizations be disbanded. Over two hundred Communist leaders were arrested for their involvement in the coup. Five were arrested for the murders of the generals and three have confessed. A request has been made that the Cabinet be purged of Communists.

The Armed Forces Day Parade, scheduled for October 5, was replaced by state funerals for the slain generals. The next day, the five-year-old daughter of General Nasution died from bullet wounds inflicted at point-blank range during his escape. It was at her funeral that the Navy chief admiral spat out one word to the anticommunist Muslim student leaders: "Sikat!" (Sweep!)[5]

The sweep was violent. The smoldering resentment, fear, and hatred of the Communists suddenly exploded in white-hot retaliation. Over the next six months, people suspected of being part of the PKI began to simply disappear, taken under cover of darkness and their throats slit. Official government estimates were eighty thousand lives lost, but more common figures ranged from three hundred thousand to five hundred thousand. Bodies filled rivers and mass graves as the anticommunist nationalists and Muslims waged war on the atheistic "infidels."

October 12, 1965

The army is stepping up its campaign to capture the rebels. Communists have taken to the hills. Demonstrations continue... curfews are imposed... ten communist newspapers have been banned and the PKI Ladies building burned. U.S. Embassy personnel are being evacuated as a precautionary measure.

October 13, 1965

The reaction to the heavy hand of the army, which has captured thousands of Communist leaders implicated in the coup, has begun with terrorist type killings and mutilations. The American Ambassador has requested permission from Washington to order all American dependents (women and children) to leave the country. If we have to leave we'll be given a motor escort to Jakarta from Bandung and flown out on commercial jet. Lead us aright, O Lord; our times are in your hands.

Although the political climate was treacherous, the Willises couldn't hunker down indefinitely to wait for a resolution to the conflict. So with underlying tension as a constant backdrop, they moved ahead with their plans.

October 20, 1965

We still hope to go to Bogor this weekend. The whole situation gives one a sense of "floating," just suspended until President Sukarno makes his direction clear. I am full of news, but like a dope addict, I still look for more on every broadcast. The transition from language school to permanent work is also on my mind. With all the tensions that have built up, I really think that what I need to do is to go to a quiet place and spend an entire day with the Lord.

Spared!

New information revealed that the missionaries' lives would have been at significant risk had the coup succeeded. It called to the forefront and tested the commitment of laying down one's life for the cause of Christ.

October 22, 1965
A Naval Attaché has reported that they have documented proof that the PKI intended to exterminate all white people, including Russians, if the coup had succeeded. They would have killed generals, the President, all religious leaders, and all foreigners.

October 26, 1965
We've heard that the PKI had a list of 30,000 Americans and their sympathizers that they were planning to eradicate. They had our names and addresses! We've been told not to open the doors at night for anyone—even if it is a man dressed in an army uniform because the PKI has stolen uniforms.

October 31, 1965
Last night I was awakened by gunfire at 1:30 a.m. In the morning, I found out that a Jeep of nine Communists refused to halt and were mowed down by police with Tommy guns. The American Embassy has asked all their employees' dependents to leave.

November 8, 1965
The head guards of our neighborhood and "hansip" [civil defense organization] have been arrested, along with several others in the community for implications in the 30th of September movement. They were

our local night-watchmen! Our very protectors were to help kill us. Surely our protection is from the Lord. We dare not trust in men.

A vacation trip to Bali brought new tales of atrocities being carried out against those who were considered Communists. On the small island of Bali, over thirty thousand people had been killed, as many as three thousand in one day. Members of the PKI were asked to turn in names of their leaders as proof of their loyalty to the new government. PKI prisoners were released to their own villages for execution. Approximately fifty thousand people had been killed in the area of Kediri in East Java. One of the rivers near there was called the Red River because the blood ran so freely in the water, and it was said one could walk across the river by stepping on bodies.

November 15, 1965

Demonstrations as large as one and a half million people continue against the PKI in Jakarta. In Central Java, homes of PKI members have been burned. Chinese schools have been closed. Terrorism is rampant. One man had the flesh ripped off his legs, then his eyes were plucked out. Even babies have been murdered.

The situation has become so tenuous that it has also had its ludicrous moments:

At the radio station in Surabaya, a loyalist officer arrived early in the morning, dressed as a rebel, and told the soldiers and drivers to go eat breakfast. While they were gone, the loyal troops walked in and regained control of the radio station.

A general tricked his would-be captors. When a soldier was sent to arrest him, his response was: "All right, all right. So now that I'm under arrest, go get me some tea." The soldier did and the general telephoned for fifty tanks!

A pickpocket was caught in Jakarta. People begin to cry, "PKI, PKI!" When the policeman arrived, the man shouted, "No, no, no, not PKI! Pickpocket, pickpocket, I'm only a pickpocket!"

November 19, 1965

Yesterday was the first anniversary of our arrival in Bandung. What an exciting year it has been! We are more sure than ever that the Lord has led us here. We will never forget the wonderful times here on the language school "hill."

I know I have learned a lot of things, including that I still have a temper to keep under control. Perhaps the most important lessons have come from the school of prayer. God has opened heaven's windows and poured out overflowing blessing. I have also learned a good bit of the language, how to play the guitar, customs and beliefs of the people, the nature and methods of communism, and that God still rules the affairs of nations as well as men.

In the midst of the trauma, moments of peace and optimism peeked through. God had protected and was still at work.

Christmas Joy

December 25, 1965

Merry Christmas! This morning we really had an enjoyable family time. The kids were excited about the gifts we had for them, and of course, there were presents from the grandparents. The joy of Christmas is watching the joy of the children. I gave Shirley an ornately carved seven by eight-foot teakwood screen. She had wanted it when it cost $250! Fortunately, it was one thing that didn't go up when the foreign currency exchange rate went up, and after several weeks of bargaining, I got it for $40! She likes it very much, as I do. [Over fifty years later, this screen has a prominent place in the Willis home.]

We invited any or all of the Bandung missionaries to share Christmas dinner and twenty-two people came to our house. It was the next best thing to getting together with real relatives.

Now, here it is Christmas night and I have so much to write about. What a wonderful, different, and exciting Christmas it has been. Maybe it could best be described by the parable of Jesus in which the rich man invited the poor and the maimed to a banquet. Jesus says for us to follow His example of giving to those who can't give back.

We began on Friday, the 17th when we had all the helpers on the "hill" and their families for a "pesta" [party]. We ate barbecued chicken and all the trimmings [seventy-five chickens and 175 big servings of rice]. They really ate!! Afterward, over one hundred people crowded into our house for the program. I told the Christmas story in Indonesian. I also played the guitar and Mel led the singing. Afterwards we broke up into groups and gave them all presents. The ladies got "kains" [sarongs], "kebajas" [blouses] and shoes. The men got dress pants and the children received toys and Bible-story books. It was a joy to be on the giving end.

On Saturday night we had a party at church with games, Christmas carols, and a big cake. I sang "What Child Is This?" with my guitar.

Sunday morning, I preached "The Shepherd's Story," a dramatic monologue I made up. Monday night was the annual station meeting party and Tuesday night was a party for all the language teachers.

Thursday evening, we had a showing of the Ben Hur movie. The crucifixion scene really touched my heart and I spent a good while processing it with the Lord. It was an experience I've needed for a while. I also had a burden for my own impure thoughts and the Lord gave me a way to deal with it. So far it has really helped.

I asked for whatever the Lord wanted me to have or do for Him. I especially opened myself up for any gifts He wanted me to have—even tongues—if He desired me to have them. It was hard to say that I was willing, but I did. No such experience was given.

Afterwards, God laid it on my heart to pray for Doc Oliver. He has found a tumor in his neck after having one removed twelve years ago. He is going to New Orleans next week for surgery. Although we had all been praying personally, we had not prayed as a group in faith. I called the group together and through tears told them about my experience and James 5:14–15. We all prayed and I felt led to lay hands on Oliver, though no one else did. Yet, I felt that the prayer was answered when Von prayed just before I did. I didn't feel that this necessarily precludes medical treatment, but I believe God will be glorified by this act of faith that God inspired in our hearts. I believe Doc is a good as healed!!

I don't understand some of the things I feel led to do like the laying on of hands. I do wish, however, that I had suggested we all do it and anoint Oliver with oil. Perhaps the oil is a symbol of the Holy Spirit. It was a very warm and heart lifting experience for all of us.

Inflation

December, 1965

The political situation gets increasingly serious. We aren't particularly afraid. If we were we would never have gone anywhere, including Indonesia.

I wonder how much of the Kingdom's progress is stymied by fear. W. A. Criswell said: "Take not counsel of your fears!" It may yet be the death of me but I'd rather die advancing the Kingdom than sitting on it.

The big news this month is that all the money has been reduced 1000%. One thousand rupiah is now one rupiah. Also, the government automatically deducts 10% from all bank accounts and all money exchanges. It caused a panic and people tried to spend all their money immediately. Merchants generally profited by raising prices exorbitantly when a soldier wasn't near.

January 14, 1966

The political situation seems to be improving but the economic situation worsens. The change of money has caused prices to skyrocket, speculators to get rich, and store owners to lose. For example, the price of public transportation was quadrupled and then quadrupled again. The previous price of a ticket from Surabaya to Jakarta was only a few thousand rupiahs. It was raised to Rp. 138,000 when we flew and the next day to Rp. 535,000 a person.

The Tide Begins to Turn

The struggle for power and control seesawed back and forth. President Sukarno retained his position as legitimate head of the government, but his actual power was unclear. He still refused to openly denounce the Communist Party. It was as if he was riding a large tidal wave on a surfboard, sometimes standing, but ever likely to slip and plunge into the depths of political suicide.

On February 21, 1966, President Sukarno announced his "political solution." He named a new cabinet, including members who were Communists, and relieved General Nasution of his position.

The people expected Generals Suharto and Nasution to respond and prevent President Sukarno from returning to power. In the indirect manner of the Javanese, however, General Suharto patiently waited to play his hand, attempting to avoid a civil war.

It was ultimately student demonstrations, from the university down to the elementary level, that turned the tide. In retaliation for the protests, Sukarno banned the student protests and prohibited meetings of five or more people. This only incited the students further. Fifty thousand demonstrators brought Jakarta to a standstill on February 26.

Sukarno called a cabinet meeting for March 11, 1966. As he sat in that meeting, he was informed that Army troops were marching on the capital. He quickly fled in his helicopter to his summer palace in Bogor and there was forced to sign an agreement turning control over to General Suharto.

General Suharto banned the Communist Party the following day. One week later, Prime Minister Subandrio and many other cabinet members were arrested. Only then did Suharto issue a command to cease the killing of the Communists.

Atheism Banned

In an effort to eradicate the possibility of a communist resurgence, the government returned to the *Pancasila*, a statement of the five principles upon which Indonesia was founded. The first principle was the belief in one God and his divine omnipotence, allowing for religious freedom, but not atheism. A decree was passed, requiring all citizens of Indonesia to believe in God and profess one of the sanctioned religions: Islam, Christianity, Catholicism, Hinduism, or Buddhism.

During the period of 1966–1967, millions of people became Christians, seeking the protection, peace, and stability of the church. Other religions similarly gained in numbers, but a disproportionate number chose to believe in Christ. This revival became the subject of Avery's doctoral thesis and his book, *Indonesian Revival: Why Two Million Came to Christ.* In his introduction, Avery wrote:

I believe the hand of God moves in all the activities of men to produce a responsiveness to the gospel throughout the world. I have been privileged to live through a bloody, abortive communist coup d'état that changed the direction of the fifth most populous nation in the world, to partici-pate in a revival of religion that resulted in unprecedented opportunities for evangelism in Indonesia, and to experience a spiritual renewal that influenced dramatic changes in mission methods.

Had they followed their heart and not their Lord—and been evac-uated with the other ex-patriates that left Indonesia in 1965—Avery and Shirley, and their fellow missionaries, would not have had the opportunity to witness and participate in this great outpouring of God.

Spiritual Marker #7

Avery opened new work,
attempting to plant an indigenous church.

Some of them, however, men from Cyprus and Cyrene,
went to Antioch and began to speak to Greeks also,
telling them the good news about the Lord Jesus.
The Lord's hand was with them,
and a great number of people believed
and turned to the Lord.
                                        —Acts 11:20–21 (NIV)

CHAPTER 9
Beginnings in Bogor

Prayer is our greatest need on the mission field.
We do not face a difficult situation, but an impossible one!
But God can do the impossible in response to
the prayers of His believing people.

—Avery

Life Must Go On

For weeks after the attempted coup, peace eluded Indonesia. The Willises' personal safety was juxtaposed against the need, the desire, and the recognition that their time may be short. In the midst of the political chaos and an uncertain future, Avery began laying the groundwork for a new church plant in Bogor. Avery and Shirley intended to move ahead, as long as the Lord would allow.

October 23, 1965

Pak [Mr.] Slamet, a retired forest ranger who is now a contractor, has located a house for us to look at in Bogor. It is a fabulous place with marble floors and many huge rooms, three of which are big enough to hold church services in. Maybe we could have simultaneous services going in three different languages!

It is the home of a deceased doctor; his widow, Mrs. Zahar, is willing to let us have a three-year lease with an option to extend. It is twice the house of the other one we looked at and is only one-third as expensive. In our conversation with her, we discovered that no one is presently occupying the wing of offices that were Dr. Zahar's clinic adjoining the house. There are four rooms which we could use as an office, receiving room, schoolroom for the children, and guestroom. We felt it was better to rent it ourselves than take any chances on an undesirable tenant. We'll hope that the size of the house is not a hindrance by being too "pretentious" and that we can make it livable.

The Chinese man who helped us look for a house earlier asked us not to call on him again. A military man had questioned him about our activities in Bogor and had made him very fearful.

November 8, 1965

We went back to Bogor this week and signed a three-year contract on the house. After the signing, which was attended by the Lurah Rohani [Spiritual Chairman], the Polisi Daerah [regional police chief], and the R.T. [neighborhood leader], we asked them to help our intentions in Bogor be known. Afterwards, Keith Parks and I visited the mayor's office and police department to clarify our presence. We want to head off any suspicion.

We have been told we can have the entire American school library from the Ford Foundation since their families have gone home. It contains several hundred volumes of school textbooks, fiction books, encyclopedias, etc., along with maps, blackboards, desks, and bookcases. The Lord is surely looking out for us.

We have also talked with the four servants of one of the American families who are leaving. They seem to be exceptional and the cook is supposed to be the best the Americans have hired. All four are Sundanese. We also have two American-trained teachers from which to choose.

Jan. 14, 1966

We stopped in Bogor to check the painting being done on the house on our way to vacation in the island of Bali. We stopped to visit Pak Slamet and were shocked to learn he had died of a heart attack. We had so hoped to win him to Christ and felt we had already begun a friendship. How quickly the opportunities for witness are lost. How long is eternity!

Our guide in Bali, Mr. Oka, was a man who had professed faith in Christ while going to school in Kediri six years ago. He had been a real witness. When he went back to Bali, he won his brother, who became a faithful Christian, but then succumbed to social pressure himself and became a secret disciple. He is hiding his light under a bushel. This shows how much we need to prepare our converts and how much we need a church for them when they go back home.

Bali is beautiful. White sand, large waves, and mosquito netting over the beds. We stayed at a lovely hotel on the beach and really enjoyed it. The second day, however, Randy stepped on a "bulubabi," some kind of urchin in the ocean, and got over fifty quills in his feet. He wasn't able to walk for two weeks. We carried him on our backs.

There wasn't much to do at night but listen to the waves so we read considerably. I read the autobiography of Benjamin Franklin and determined to try his thirteen-week plan of improvement. I changed his thirteen "virtues" to fit my needs. I ended up with thirteen areas and thirteen projects to be worked on each quarter—one attitude and one project each week: writing, prayer, Scripture, language review and learning more about such things as mission history, radio and TV, photography, the study of Islam, and approaches to witnessing.

I plan to keep a regular check on the virtues, concentrating on one a week while keeping score on the others. During that same week, I'll work on my project. I think this is going to help me discipline my life. I believe anyone who knows what he wants to accomplish can get there with a burning desire and discipline. I did not include things like daily devotions, writing in my journal, etc., because they are already in the realm of habit.

March 3, 1966

I have just returned from two prayer retreats. We had the West Java Prayer Retreat after finally getting government permission. I led the prayer sessions. We had times of personal prayer, prayer partners, prayer in small groups, and united prayer with an emphasis on conversational prayer. There was genuine confession of sin and some testimony but I think the note of victory over sin was generally missing. We should have had testimonies that claimed the victory of forgiveness through the blood and power over temptation. We particularly prayed for God to call out Indonesian laborers into the harvest. I also felt that we needed to seriously pray for our upcoming nationwide evangelistic revival in 1967.

Two days later, I left for the East Java prayer retreat. It was held in Kediri near the hospital so the missionary doctors and nurses could attend. The pressure of work when not in prayer sessions distracted and tired the Kediri personnel; even so, I believe it was more spiritual than the one in West Java. I preached on the broad themes of the Lord's Prayer. I also led the final prayer time using conversational prayer. It was the crowning session of the retreat with genuine confession of sin and joy of faith.

It is a real joy to get home again, ready to plunge into the new work. I have been uplifted and renewed by the prayer retreats. I had counted on them to prepare me for the work here because I had gotten in a rut and had missed the freshness of the Spirit. Now I'm rarin' to go.

Early Stages

February 9, 1966

BOGOR!! When I first mentioned the city of Bogor, I really never expected to be the one to open the work here, but by the grace of God, here we are. Our furniture arrived on two trucks and a trailer on February 1. After a little over a week we are about to get things halfway straightened up. The carpenters are still working on the house and that complicates matters somewhat. Hopefully, they will be finished before long. So far my "work" here has consisted of going to offices and going through all the "red tape" and trying to get organized. I had to go to Jakarta on Saturday to learn "how to be a station treasurer in one easy lesson."

February 14, 1966

On Friday, I got a good bit of information from the Department of Religion. 1,501,537 people live in the area surrounding Bogor. They gave me this breakdown of the number who claimed to be of each faith:

Islam	*1,472,242*
Buddhist	*11,991*
Hindu	*990*
Protestant	*6,410*
Catholic	*3,960*
Pagan	*2,209*

In the area, there are a total of 6,185 mosques and Muslim prayer rooms. In contrast, there are nine Catholic and nineteen Christian churches. Do I need any more incentive for witnessing here?

I've been passing out tracts, getting acquainted with those around us, including the night guards at the City Hall across the street, and getting ready to go on the offensive. Tonight before supper, Shirley and I rode our "bicycle built for two" to the shopping center. You've never heard the likes of the "Oohs" and "Aahs" and the yelling. We created a mild sensation riding this "modern invention." Maybe next time, we can pass out tracts and talk with them.

Seeing God at Work

Avery had to develop his mission strategy as he worked. His Baptist background and experience were more ingrained than he realized. Because he was in uncharted territory, many times it was Avery who was surprised at God's interventions.

March 4, 1966
Kang Shu Wi, a local pastor, came to see me. Now here is a man after my own heart (and I have been praying for some men after my own heart). He and I feel nearly the same in regards to mission methods. His church is going to send a busload of members to help us when the seminary choir comes in April. We are going to try to rent a theater. He will help me invite the people.

March 9, 1966
I am so anxious to reach people here that it's hard to sleep at night. I know the subconscious urge to "make a showing" threatens to overrun my principle of work and am praying for patience. According to my plan, I expect the introductory phase will last until August. Then we will begin to move more rapidly. I must wait for the leadership of the Holy Spirit. The first advertisement about our Bible correspondence course will be in the weekly Bogor paper this coming Sunday.

I've been trying to decide if my intention to wait before starting worship services is correct. I need to have a service to invite people to, but must also have a nucleus. I hope I can start by the time the seminary choir comes. We are planning to follow the Indonesian custom and invite our neighbors for a "selamatan" [housewarming reception] in the near future. We'll also have another one for "pembesars" [the VIPs].

March 21, 1966

This week I talked with one of the original pastors who started the Bethel Full Gospel church fifteen years ago. He claims they have seven hundred churches that are strictly indigenous, one of which has three thousand members. Most of them are "house churches" with a hundred members or so. Basically Bethel has had no missionaries or out-of-country funds. In the same length of time, Baptists have less than fifty churches and have poured millions of dollars into Indonesia.

While exploring the spiritual climate, Avery spoke with a Catholic priest who had taught school in the nearby town of Sukabumi for eleven years. The priest told him that in the beginning, they did not teach religion so as not to scare off the Sundanese people. After four or five years, they began holding voluntary classes of religion. In all that time, they had only reached one Sudanese family—who had a very difficult time. A few single people had been reached, but due to the strict social structure, they often reverted to Islam if they married. In Bogor, of all the people they had reached for Christ, two-thirds were Chinese and one-third were Javanese.

The Servant of God
(Avery's Journal – July 24, 1967)

Tonight I was enjoying TV after returning from a meeting when a grandmother and a young woman knocked at the door. The old lady asked to borrow some ice for a seven-month-old baby who had a high fever. She told of her desperation as Shirley got the ice and put it in a plastic bag. She said the child's mother had died December 29 in childbirth and, as the grandmother, she was trying to care for it. She said that the young Sundanese lady with her was trying to help. Of course, she was Islamic (and as I heard again today means she believes Christians are heathen) but she had told the old lady, "Let's go to the house of God's servant [hamba Tuhan] and ask him."

That is the greatest compliment and title I can ever receive! "And whosoever gives a cup of cold water [or a plastic bag of ice cubes] in my name shall in no wise lose his reward."

March 25, 1966

Response to our first week of advertising the correspondence course on the book of John has netted about twelve responses. Still no hope of invitations to homes for Bible study but everywhere we go we have chances to witness.

God has opened another unexpected door. Three different newspapers picked up and ran the ad for the Bible correspondence course which poses the question, "Who is Jesus Christ?" They are printing it free since the government is urging everyone to have a religion. We have received requests from people who answered the ad in each of the papers. The chaotic political situation should plow these fields so that the seed can be planted, but unless the dirt stops falling (i.e. some stability), people will not have their minds on such things.

I am increasingly convinced of the need to study the language. I have begun studying a bit every day plus reading the letters and newspapers I receive and reading books in Indonesian. I think I will get a lot of help from Nana, my new secretary. She has been a Kentucky team secretary for eight years. I am impressed with her first week of work and think she will be a real asset. There should be a good opportunity to win her to Jesus as she will be grading the Bible course lessons and writing the letters I dictate to answer their questions.

Some of the responses to the correspondence course have been encouraging. Several Muslims have responded. One person poured out his heart in a three-page letter of his conversion from a strict Islamic background. He said now he wants to be baptized by me and spread the gospel, even though his parents may disown him.

April 1, 1966

Plans are crystallizing. We are choosing Easter week for our three initiatives. The housewarming reception will be here at the house on the 10th, with neighbors, officials, and pastors invited. Then we will host a concert by the Baptist Seminary Choir from Semarang, led by Bill O'Brien. Since we are new to the city, we may only have two or three hundred people show up, but we'll use the city theater that seats eight hundred. I have invitations being printed, posters being made, and banners prepared to put up. Parkindo, the Indonesian Christian Party, is helping with getting permission. Pastor Kang comes Monday to work on visiting the "pantjatunggal" [government officials].

I think I'll try having a service the Sunday following the concert to see what response there might be. I really wanted to do the Bible studies first but there seems to be a need for a place of meeting now and no classes have yet been started.

April 3, 1966

"Commit thy way unto the Lord and He shall bring it to pass." Instead of having no help, I have several wanting to do the same job! I think Kang will be surprised tomorrow that all he intended to help us with has been or will be done by friends here who have volunteered. Foremost among these is Parkindo. Their secretary brought me other people I needed to know and who could do specific things to help. They will distribute the invitations through their six hundred-member youth group. They are getting a piano, which I had failed to find. Their number two man wants to take me to the surrounding areas to become acquainted with leaders. Mrs. Selamat has taken us to visit people she thinks we ought to know—like the chief of police, a relative of hers. Painting the street banners and posters are some talented Muslim youth. I really think one reason we never receive such help in other places is our isolationism and working only within our own groups.

This morning, we went to visit the Assembly of God church and the visiting preacher preached one of the best sermons on giving I've ever heard. He proved by his experience that the Indonesians can be used of God to do as well in this difficult economy as we saw Him do in the U.S. in response to our faith and obedience. They build their churches themselves and God blesses. I have not seen such spirit in any of our Baptist churches. I doubt that we will do so well with our missionaries because

a) *we live so "high" that it is hard for us to evoke sacrifice,*
b) *the people see no need to sacrifice when it is much easier to ask the Mission for things, and*
c) *we seem to lack the fire to expend our very souls for theirs. (For example, the Assembly church has had a ninety-minute prayer meeting every morning for the last two years.)*

No wonder many seek a place where they know the Spirit moves. I do not understand why we are so reticent to receive or use prayer in the healing of the body as well as the soul. In Acts, it was an essential part of spreading the gospel and seems to be needed today if we are to see great moving of peoples to God. I have seen a few brief flashes of God's power to heal but not many and not often. If He were to use such means today, I wonder if He could convince me of their validity and reality. Sometimes I wonder if I will spend my whole life sitting on the fringes of God's power waiting, "looking at the moving of the water," but never able to feel its fullness. I cannot get away from the conviction that God intends to do something with me and my life to reach great numbers of people, but again those sad words: "Not yet." In thy time, O Lord, make me ready in the day of Your power!

Rising Enthusiasm

April 7, 1966

How can I tell it all? These days have been crowded from morning until night. I've started getting up thirty minutes earlier (6:30 a.m.), but people still come before breakfast, or before it's eaten. Most visits relate to the housewarming or the concert in some facet but some have a spiritual problem.

Today I gave out many of the housewarming invitations and met most of the neighbors. If we listened to all the suggestions of our advisors, we'd have five hundred people present. We are inviting 180 and hope to have one hundred show up. (At least, that is how much food we are preparing.)

Preparations for the concert are really snowballing. Tonight we worked until the street banners were put up (9:30 p.m.). At the Jembatan Merah *[Red Bridge], I must have given out three-to-four hundred invitations and was mobbed for more. The crowd was pressing me up against the car, trying to get some, even to jerking and pulling my arms. I am taller than most Indonesians so I tried to pass them out individually as they jumped for them. I looked over to where I had seen a policeman a few moments before to get some help, but he wasn't there. Then I looked down, and there he was, along with soldiers and Air Force men, jumping and grasping for tickets with the rest of the crowd! I just threw the rest of the tickets up in the air and let them scramble for them! We may not have any left for Parkindo people to pass out. In fact, we may run out of the two thousand we have printed!*

April 14, 1966

The Housewarming on Sunday was a success. With the helpers, we fed one hundred people. The neighbors and some "big shots" came. We combined the suggestions of many and made it a Christian reception. I preached a sermonette on Freedom in God and told them about Baptists and our intentions.

Last night I went to the theater to see a show, to see how people reacted in theaters, and to see our advertisement slide. They showed it just before the film and held it quite a long time. Then, in the very climax of the film, when the hero and his army were cornered between a battalion and a sea monster, they stopped the film and showed our slide! (Of course, they knew I was there.) The people hollered at first but not against the slide. When everyone had had enough time to read it twice, they flashed it again, and then went back to the action. At least all eyes were focused on the screen!

People keep asking for invitations to the concert, so finally we decided to have the choir sing again at 8:00 the same night. I had eight hundred more invitations printed for that time. We added banners announcing the extra concert to the original ones, saying "by popular demand." Perhaps this is too optimistic.

Avery was speaking with Gus, his secretary's husband, commenting on the number of invitations he had passed out. Laughingly, he said, "It's a good thing they won't all come."

"What do you mean? How many invitations did you pass out?"

"About two thousand, I think. Hey, I've been a pastor in America for ten years. They won't all come."

"In Indonesia, they will!"

Stunned, Avery asked, "What will happen if they can't all fit in?"

"Nama Baptis akan bau sekali!" (The Baptist name is really going to stink!)

Chapter 10
Breakthrough

It is My strategy that causes these words: "awe,
wonder, amazement, surprise, astonishment."
—Avery's word from the Lord

Avery was astounded at God's faithfulness and handiwork. His fears were overwhelmed by the fragrance of God.

April 16, 1966

Great is the Lord and greatly to be praised! His abilities so outrun our faith. He is able to do exceeding abundantly more than we are able to ask, think, or imagine. In fact, the comprehension of how he has opened the door to Bogor has only begun to dawn on me. I awoke at 5:00 a.m. (as I have for several days) and have been fellowshipping with the Lord since then.

Last night, over 1,700 people heard the seminary choir in the two performances and had an opportunity to hear the gospel!!! A packed house listened enraptured to the first performance of the cantata, "Hallelujah, What a Savior!" which had been translated into Indonesian. The 6:00 p.m. performance filled the auditorium and included the mayor and other officials. (In fact, it was terribly hot because we had to shut all the doors since others wanted in.) They cheered zestfully when the mayor gave a welcoming speech to Baptists, when I explained our purpose here, and when the choir or Bill O'Brien sang Indonesian national songs.

I asked the ushers (members from the Sukabumi church who had chartered a bus at their own expense) to let the people in for the second performance. After fifteen minutes, less than fifty people sat scattered throughout the huge theater. I began to feel that I had been too optimistic in having a second performance. A look at the theater entrance changed that. Due to a misunderstanding, the doors were still locked, and a surge of people pressed against them, waving their invitations and clamoring to get in! When the doors were opened, they overflowed available seating and stood around the walls! At each performance, a seminary student gave a powerful testimony of the power of Christ to save. Behind him a forty-five-foot banner proclaimed: "Jesus said, I am the Way, the Truth, and the Life." During the concert, the president of Parkindo leaned over and said, "The door has been opened to the gospel now—before it has always been closed."

One reason I couldn't sleep this morning was that I was wondering what to do if we have more people tomorrow than we can get into the house for church. Many have said they will come, including Muslims. We could take care of one hundred, manage 150 in other rooms, but will be swamped if more come.

April 17, 1966

On this first day of services in Bogor, nearly fifty people attended and another sixty people stood outside the windows, listening. They were shy about entering because they were mostly Muslim children and young people. Most of those inside were adults and most of them ethnic Chinese. Several were from other churches. I led the singing, read the Bible, and preached "The Seeking Savior." Peter Cho and Elsie Tan came to present themselves as the first candidates for membership.

I had explained beforehand the elements of Baptist worship, including taking an offering. We received over 90,000 rupiahs. I think as soon as we have several candidates for membership, we'll have a new members class (which will become an evening worship) and then let them organize into a church. They can decide on how to use the money. It may take four or five months to become an official organization.

I am still quite concerned about breaking through to the Sundanese people here in West Java. They are prohibited from attending church and are called defectors if they do. They also have tremendous community and social pressure if they don't follow Islam. Home Bible groups may have to be constructed as a dialogue with Islam to get them to hear the gospel. I'd rather not use the indirect approach but it could be done simultaneously while the direct approach is being used with others.

The second week, about twenty adults attended with over eighty children, young people, and the occasional passerby looking in the windows. In the next few weeks, the number settled in between twenty-five and thirty adults, with the number of children diminishing as their curiosity was assuaged.

Each time Avery preached, a few more people made decisions to follow Christ, so he began to focus his energy on the new converts. An increasing number attended the Sunday evening "discussion groups" on comparative religions. He began to meet with several of the new converts individually to train them in leadership.

He considered starting a Sunday School class, and one of the men in the class felt they should start a prayer meeting. Shirley wondered how she could best start a Sunday School for the many children. She had no doubt the children would come, probably up to a hundred of them, if it was held in the front yard under the trees. But without other trained teachers to help, it didn't seem wise yet. Since Avery and Shirley would bear most of the burden until others could be prepared to help, the question became: *How much, how soon?*

April 28, 1966

I have just finished reading Glenn Bryant's biography of Billy Graham. How inspiring to see a man God can use like that. Undoubtedly he has had a great effect on me and my ministry throughout the years. His directness, humility, sincerity, and devotion to Christ contribute greatly to his effectiveness, but there is no explanation of him outside of God. I wonder how much his example figured in my college aspiration to be an evangelist. One thing that I'm certain of is God called me to be an evangelist! Perhaps not the itinerant kind, like Graham, but certainly to spread the gospel to as many as possible.

I often wonder about God's ultimate plan for my life. I feel a divine compulsion that in His own time God has a special work chosen for me in reaching many people for Christ. I think this is not worldly ambition for I'd like nothing better than this present type of work where I have plenty of time to withdraw to Him and plenty of opportunities to search out new ways to reach people. I hate to think there might come a day when I'd have to leave here. But, oh, isn't that presumptuous on my part?

Perhaps God has chosen me to do work that only He sees, and I'll not realize until I get to heaven. I have felt that each year has been another step in preparation although I've been used in His service. That is why I'm trying to do the thirteen projects I initiated in January—whatever He has in mind, I want to be ready.

Spiritual Attack

In the midst of increasing interest and a growing church nucleus, Avery was struck ill for about two weeks with influenza and bronchitis. But even more distressing than the physical weakness was an onslaught of spiritual attack in the form of temptation.

June 3, 1966

Satan seems to be pressing his attacks in spite of daily prayer, Bible study, and witness. How I have fought him in the battlefield of my heart these past weeks. Just when I think the battle is over, I find that my tactics have only caused a lull, and then Satan begins tempting afresh. I have used every weapon in the arsenal of God and then just had to resign and say, "Lord, it's in Your hands; it's bigger than I can handle. Teach me how to daily gain the victory."

The Lord has prevailed but too much of my time and thought has been occupied by my personal battles rather than those of the people I came to serve. I feel deeply the need for a new filling of the Holy Spirit.

July brought a respite and encouragement through the annual Mission meeting. Bill Tisdale, missionary from the Philippines, brought messages on the Holy Spirit, speaking directly to the need in Avery's life.

July 26, 1966

One of the helpful emphases is on how the "old man" (our natural sinful self) still fights to control even after we have the Holy Spirit and new life within us. Never can I remember messages coming home to me so much and that is because the devil has really been pushing the old man in me. This past month has been the worst yet! Bill said that God would allow almost anything to show us how sinful the old man is and to show us our utter helplessness without God's power. Certainly, he has shown me as never before the capabilities of the old man in me if given his way. I have fought him every step of the way, but most of the time it has been a slow retreat. I have used every means: Bible, prayer, work, etc. to help but with only temporary success. By God's grace, He has prevented me from falling into gross sin but that did not prevent the sins of the mind and desires.

I have made progress in the last two weeks but this week is going to be the victory, I believe. I am drawing much closer to the Holy Spirit whom I have grieved. His grieving has caused me grief and I have been miserable in the no-man's-land between the old and the new man. I have tried to assess the causes, such as challenges of a new area, boredom, and a hundred other things, but I know it all comes back to Self, and circumstances just give Self a chance.

I believe I will be able to be much more effective in my ministry to others because of this experience. Only the Holy Spirit can help me through a refilling.

July 28, 1966

I led the prayer times here at Mission Meeting with an emphasis from Norman Grubb's book, Continuous Revival. *We had real confession of sin. I presented myself afresh to the Holy Spirit. Bill taught that though it is hard to present our spirits, it is clear what Romans 12:1 means on presenting our bodies. It was not a dramatic infilling, but I believe the channels have been unplugged and the river of life in the Spirit is flowing again. I dread putting it to the test back home because experience has taught me the conflict that follows.*

Momentum!

In Bogor, people began enrolling for conversational English classes based on the Bible—either direct Scripture or simplified Sunday School materials. In two days, the Willises enrolled thirty people who answered the ad and interviewed them for skill level. Nearly half of these were Muslim and many were Sundanese. By July, the numbers swelled to over 140.

In the midst of this excitement, Shirley developed a light case of hepatitis and was required to be on six weeks of rest and a low-fat diet. By the time she received a doctor's permission to resume daily duties in late August, there were 175 enrollees, and more on a waiting list! This resulted in eight weekly classes of twenty students each, at vary-

The church in Bogor meeting in the Willis home

ing levels of ability in English. Avery taught three classes, and Shirley taught the rest. Some who attended the classes began attending the worship services, and others began to express interest in the gospel.

Since Bogor was a university town and young people seemed to be the most responsive group, the majority of the converts in the new Bogor church were between the ages of twenty and thirty-five. Throughout Indonesia, the university and high school student groups began calling themselves the '66 generation. They had been instrumental in overthrowing communism and in leading government reform. With an average life expectancy in Indonesia of only thirty-two years, these young people were ready for action.

They asked to organize and had already nominated leaders. This temporary group of young people would work to reach the lost, follow up on new converts, encourage the fellowship, and help in the general church work until the church formally organized. They also began choir practice and a monthly recreational event. They remained under the direction of the church, but forming their own organization allowed for leniency in who could lead. For example, they chose an Islamic Sundanese (Nana's brother) to lead the recreation and a former Assembly of God preacher to lead the prayer meetings. Twenty-six people came to the first midweek prayer service, and twelve attended the first choir practice.[1]

Avery wrote, *I had not planned to start with a youth organization, but at least this will be a good experiment in being indigenous. It will give vital experience, use new Christians, strengthen the saved, and contact the unsaved. Will they make mistakes? Certainly. But an honest mistake is better than a missed opportunity. There is hope for a young enthusiast trying to follow Christ, but there is little hope for the sleeping saint that takes counsel of his fears.*

August 26, 1966

This has been a week of beginnings: eight English Bible classes, a mid-week prayer service, choir practice, visitation, and planning for recreation day on Saturday. This gives us at least two classes or services every day except Monday, which we have purposely left free for family time. Although this quickened pace is going to be more tiring and confining, I believe it will be more joyful. We always live and feel better when we are busy, especially in the Lord's work.

On Sunday, I plan to talk to all the converts about baptism and church organization. I will propose that we organize the church the first week of December and on the same day baptize all the new converts so they will become charter members. Some seem anxious to be baptized, but I think it will be better to have a solid foundation to start the church on. After that, we will baptize people sooner.

Moves of the Spirit

August 6, 1966

I have been pleased with the presence of the Holy Spirit in my life since we returned from Mission Meeting. I have felt this nearness in everyday living more than in a long time. Also, I have remembered the word "Present your bodies" from Romans 12:1. It makes dedication more concrete and realistic. By presenting my body, I am led to "renew my mind" each time my body wants to stray. It helps me remember "that I am not my own." The ties of sin are not strong enough to hold a body presented to God.[2]

September 9, 1966

The Holy Spirit moved in a special way last Sunday morning. I preached on "Scattering Fire," the Holy Spirit-inspired spreading of the gospel. No response was made in the invitation time but when I called on Mr. Tambunan, principal of a Christian school and our language teacher, to lead the benediction, he said, "O Lord . . ." and could go no further. His large frame shook with emotion as he began to weep with a half-groan. After about sixty seconds, I led in prayer and then asked if others would like to pray. Over half a dozen prayed earnestly, and then Mr. Tambunan asked if he could say something. He said that he had been raised in a Christian home since a child but that he had never been touched like this before. He said that every word of the sermon from the first to the last pierced his heart and broke it. He confessed his unworthiness before the Holy God. He spoke for nearly fifteen minutes, thanking God and me profusely for "this message that has filled my heart." (Strangely enough, I had asked for his opinion of the sermon when I practiced it with him Friday and he said it was all right but "kurang menarik"—not very interesting. I told him later that the only real difference in the two was that when I preached, the Holy Spirit was working.)

All this time, we had been standing. We were seated and I asked for other testimonies. Many testified and we stayed over an hour more. It was the first such moving of the Spirit in our young work. I felt that they began to come of age in this service.[3]

People here come to me looking for spiritual help with every conceivable problem. On one Sunday I counseled with:

- *A young man who wanted to be saved*
- *A fugitive from the law (in Indonesia and several other countries) who was tired of running from God and the police*
- *A young man with marriage troubles*
- *A new convert facing stiff opposition at home from his ancestor-worshipping parents*
- *A teenage school dropout and new convert who had been left by his parents in the care of friends and was having problems*
- *Some people who wanted to enroll in the English Bible classes*
- *A man with mental problems who attempted suicide*

I sometimes feel like I am a mechanic dropped into a gigantic junkyard of wrecked cars and told to get them all running. I told Shirley the other day that I didn't know if everyone in Indonesia has problems or just the ones we know. Of course, I can't repair the wrecked lives—I just introduce them to the One who can!

And it can have a humorous side. I took the man who had attempted suicide to the mental health clinic in Jakarta. While I spoke to the psychiatrists about the patient, the man filled out the admittance forms. He registered me as a patient, too! I told the doctor, "He may be crazy, but he isn't dumb!"

October 12, 1966

On Sunday, October 2, we had our first Sundanese convert, Suardi! He was first enrolled in the correspondence course and had visited church several times. I personally didn't think my sermon was effective but God uses his Word as He wills.

I preached ten days of revival meetings at the Grogol church in Jakarta from October 5–16. God blessed the Saturday message on "How can we receive the baptism of the Holy Spirit?" About twenty-five knelt with me to receive the filling of the Spirit. God really broke many hearts. I felt from my recent study on "the filling" that I should lay hands on them as was done in the New Testament. I asked the pastor to help me and God blessed the service.

Several wanted to ask questions at the end so I stayed until 9:30. It was 10:00 p.m. before I got a bite to eat and started back to Bogor. I passed some soldiers near the traffic circle in Grogol. Because it was raining and dangerous, I didn't pick them up. Wham! They shot at me! I guess they weren't really trying to hit me. I felt around and didn't feel any wounds so I just took off! I got home safely and have since learned that Jakarta folks won't travel that road at night because of all the muggings, car thefts, etc.

I found it quite a strain to preach in Indonesian every day but the people have been very complimentary. I made one or two big mistakes with the words "mengandung" and "mengantung." Apparently I said I was "pregnant" instead of "hanging off a cliff" and then I said "ijazah" instead of "jenasa"—after the crucifixion, the disciples asked for Jesus' "diploma" instead of his "corpse"!

Sometimes, I still feel the frustration of cultural differences. I want to feel like one of the Indonesians and understand their daily life and thoughts. Using a daily illustration in my sermons was as natural as breathing in America, but I struggle to know how to make those kinds of connections here.

And yet God blessed. The attendance was the highest they have had in a revival. Seventy people made decisions during the revival, twenty-four of them professions of faith.

November 4–17 brought a much needed midterm vacation for the Willis family. They boarded an Italian ocean liner, named the *Victoria*, to Hong Kong via Singapore. Much of the time at sea was spent resting, and much of the time in port in Singapore and Hong Kong was spent shopping and eating! They returned to Jakarta on November 17, exactly two years from their original arrival date, with very different feelings—this time they were returning home!

A Dog's-Eye View of Missions

The Willises acquired a full-bred boxer during their time at Bogor. Because many of the Jeep vehicles in Indonesia bear the Willys brand, the boxer was named "Jeep" Willys, as were his successors—a play on words the Indonesians completely understood.

Avery created a column in his monthly newsletter called "A Dog's-Eye View of Missions," which became a favorite of readers. In fact, "How is Jeep?" was a familiar and often primary question when the Willises were on furlough.

The column allowed Avery to write more creatively and humorously and sometimes send a message in Jeep's voice, which might have seemed offensive if stated directly.

Samples of "A Dog's-Eye View of Missions" by Jeep Willys

August 1969

Now I don't know much about the new math but the old math is enough to upset me when it comes to missions. Every day 180,000 people are born, or sixty-five million a year. This means that Southern Baptists in America and all their mission-related churches around the world did not baptize a number equal to a year's increase of the population last year—even as the most missionary of denominations.

On the average, it takes 9,558 of you to put one missionary couple overseas. You gave $1.15 per member, on average, through the Cooperative Program, $1.29 through the Lottie Moon Christmas offering, and $.18 through other sources for a total of $2.62 per member last year. Excuse my sarcasm, but you are lying like a dog if you say you are mission-minded and don't do better than that. So for now when you talk about missions, I'll sing "Games People Play." When you quit playing and get down to business of sending more missionaries and supporting them, I'll change my tune.

June 1970

Have you ever noticed how dogs like to congregate? Have you ever wondered what we are doing? You should. We are having committee meetings! We try to decide on things like who is going to howl at what hour, whose turn it is to find the tomcat, who is going to pay for the midnight snack, and other important matters like that.

I have noticed that most churches and mission groups meet a lot to decide things almost as important as ours, but they take a lot longer. Missionaries spend half of their time going to meetings. Tuan [Master] Willis is on the Personnel and Planning Committee, the Evangelism and Church Development Committee, the Baptist Survey Committee, the Area Prayer Retreat Committee, and is a trustee of the seminary. When mission committees meet, it means that more time is spent traveling than meeting. Tuan usually has to spend the night en route because it is so far. Several of the meetings are in Jakarta which is six hundred miles away. If they keep on committeeing, they may commit themselves to the grave.

As a joke, some missionaries rewrote the words to "Home, Home on the Range" to poke fun at the endless discussions at Mission Meeting, per Robert's Rules of Order as they worked to rewrite their Constitution:

"Moved, moved to amend/Let's change what it was we just heard/ to say one more way/ what was said yesterday/And reword the reworded word.

Moved, moved to amend/We change it around and about/It's revised and rephrased/and then all are amazed/When we move to just strike it all out.

Moved, moved to adjourn/We really would love to meet more/ to keep dragging our feet/tiring out all our seats/but there's nobody minding the store!"

November 1970

I always did like a good dog fight, especially between friends. You know, like which one of us gets to go after the next cat. But the mission-aries have started an argument that I think is hilarious.

I suppose it started because most missionaries are sent out to do field evangelism and so are called "evangelists" anytime they are referred to as a group. I first noticed a protest among the doctors who let it be known that they were evangelists, too. Then the student work-ers began to call themselves "student evangelists." The field evange-lists countered by calling themselves "general evangelists." That has a nice sound to it when they say, "We are going to have a meeting of the generals."!!

My family has been in that group until Tuan Willis moved to the seminary a few weeks ago. A field evangelist retorted, "There goes another evangelist being gobbled up by an institution." Tuan didn't take too kindly to "being gobbled up" and the next time it was mentioned, he let it be known that in the three months since he "left evangelism," he had helped lead eighty-five people to Christ. I think it's crazy. Don't you wish all the members of your church were fighting to be evangelists?

February 1971

In Memoriam

Jeep Willys, famous missionary dog, made the supreme sacrifice— martyrdom—on January 3, 1971 at the age of four-and-a-half. When we returned from out of town, we could not find him. When the chil-dren knocked on neighbors' doors to see if anyone had seen him, they were told, "O, barangkali dimakan." (Oh, maybe he was eaten.) We had been told for years to guard him carefully, because Indonesians, partic-ularly Bataks, regard dog meat as a delicacy. (He is not the first Baptist martyr in Indonesia: Lymon and Munson, Baptist missionaries from America, were eaten by Bataks in 1878.)

For all his friendliness, love, and joy of life, Jeep exhibited the cynical, questioning side of his nature in his monthly column that exposed many of our foibles. We like to think that his close-to-the-ground view of missions helped some of us to be more realistic, and yes, even more dedicated. Jeep, we will miss you.

Sadly, Jeep was never found and would be replaced by other full-bred boxers over the years: Jeep II and Jeep III, who continued to write the column. They came with other names, but those didn't stick.

CHAPTER 11
Church Planting Expansion

Help me see Your hand at work and to know
when Your finger beckons me
to follow You into a situation or just admire You at work.

—Avery

Launch

The new church in Bogor was officially organized on December 10, 1966, with twenty members, thirteen of whom were baptized that morning. Twenty-seven other new believers would be readied for the next baptismal service. With the plan to be self-supporting from its inception, the church used its available money to provide a meal for two hundred guests who observed the baptisms. They gave their first mission offering toward the anticipated 1967 nationwide revivals.

Baptisms in the new Bogor church, 1967

By mid-February, Sunday morning Bible study began with eight classes and twelve teachers (only four of whom had prior experience teaching and most of whom had been Christians less than a year). At the same time, an evening service started. Within a month, there were forty-eight members in the church, and professions of faith were a near weekly occurrence. The Santosos, Christians for only four months, opened a Christian bookstore in their home. Mr. Santoso soon felt ill-equipped to answer all the questions he was being asked about Christianity, so he began to read all the books in his store!

Visiting speakers and musicians from the United States helped launch an outreach crusade in Bogor. In April, Dr. Leroy Fowler came from Houston, Texas, to preach nine services over a four-day evangelistic crusade. It was called GEHIBA—*Gerakan Hidup Baru*—the New Life Movement. Since the Embellishments, a singing trio from Texas, were also coming to Indonesia, Avery booked them for two concerts on the first night.

May 1, 1967

Inviting the Embellishments meant we would need to rent a theater. But I was worried about the other three days that Leroy was here. I felt it would not be evangelistically or psychologically right to come back to our home to preach the Word, so I contracted for four nights at the 800-seat theater. The theater wanted $1,800 but finally settled for a little over $200 even when prices were high. Then I had to get to work finding some way to fill the place—and to prepare our people if all the people came.

The program included Lie Yit Tong, a concert pianist whom I baptized on Easter, for Monday night. Tuesday night a young Ambonese men's choir from the Maluku island sang along with six men from Kalvari Church's men's choir, and on Wednesday, Leroy showed slides of three countries in which he had traveled.

Avery even served as part of the entertainment! Since many Indonesians enjoyed watching Westerns, their image of Americans, especially Texans, was that they were cowboys. So Avery donned his cowboy hat and boots and sang his Texan favorites with his guitar. He was a hit!

Willis draws cheers with cowboy attire and songs.

Discipling

It was time for the young church to prepare to receive and train a harvest of new believers. Avery had been training four men in earnest, meeting with them individually and each Thursday night as a group.

Avery playing guitar and sing western songs at the GEHIBA rally, 1966

I am teaching a "cadre" or "cell group" of four men on the fundamentals of the Christian life (i.e. how to pray, study the Bible, witness, follow-up, etc.) They will be my leaders and "lay preachers." They will also be responsible for teaching others everything I teach them. This gives me a solid base and four men that are faithful enough to depend on. They have been elected as chairmen of the respective committees for GEHIBA.

Having learned some lessons from the first crusade, we've decided to have tickets with numbered seats for each night so we won't have too many people come. If they want tickets, they must come to the church to pick them up and give us their names, ages, and addresses. Only those over the age of twelve can sign up for tickets and people may not get tickets for others.

Avery adapted follow-up materials from Billy Graham and the Navigators and taught a course on counseling and follow-up for six nights, two hours a night. Twenty-one people from the church were prepared to counsel during the crusade and in follow-up visits afterward. Each night, lost people came to the training, so there were "live" opportunities to train in witnessing. Several of them became Christians through this process.

This laboratory method could have had a negative effect, but it only seemed to implant the gospel in their hearts. Even one, Suharsono, who said that he now knew the Christians' secret of persuading people to become Christians and that "it looked like they were practicing a play," made a profession of faith the final night of GEHIBA.

Go Time!

Promotional street banners, circulars, posters, radio and newspaper advertisements, special invitations to VIPs, and a sound truck announced that free invitations to the rally were available at the church. The event became the talk of the town. In two days, the tickets were all claimed, so more were printed for a second service each night, beginning at 9:00 p.m., and a third service on Sunday. When those tickets were gone, all the church members could do was ask forgiveness. There simply were no more seats.

Help came from people outside the church as well. Between the theater's final movie showing at midnight on Saturday and the 10:00 a.m. service on Sunday morning, the theater was decorated by several Muslim youths, a piano was moved and tuned, counseling rooms were built of bamboo, lights were hung, and a sound system was set up.

Human Frailty

The response to the crusade was clearly a movement of God, but spiritual opposition and human shortcomings surrounded the event. The most obvious evidence of antagonism were the words scrawled by militant adversaries across Avery's car during the event: "The director of the concerts is a liar; God is a lie; and the Communist Party is God."[1]

The event was nearly hijacked before it began. In a period of rapid inflation, postal rates had increased seventeen times, making it impossible to keep proper denominations of stamps on hand—so the postal service simply did away with stamps! This led to fraud as postal workers simply stamped an amount on the letters, kept the money for postage, and disposed of the letters. Avery was writing Leroy regularly about plans for the crusade, but Leroy was not receiving any of the letters. Leroy tried to phone Avery thirteen nights in a row to see if the event was still on. He finally sent a cablegram—only half of which arrived—but it was enough for Avery to respond that the plan for Leroy's visit was still intact.

Tensions were escalating against Chinese Indonesians suspected of having connections or loyalties to communist China. The day before the crusade, students in Jakarta ran amok, burning Chinese stores and killing several people. Members of the church, many of whom were Chinese, questioned the wisdom of having the crusade in that climate.

Due to the riots, the Chinese (who owned most of the public transportation) would not allow their vehicles to go to Jakarta. As a result, the Embellishments were housed in Sukabumi, a four-hour round-trip for the band and those who transported them.

By 8:00 a.m. on Sunday, no one had come to unlock the utility box to provide access to electricity for the first crusade service.

The platform lights, loudspeaker, etc. could not be checked. So I took things in hand, went to the director's house, and with temper just under control forced them to wake him, only to be sent to another man's house who had the key. We went as far as possible on the scooter into the kampung [village] and then walked the rest of the way to his house. He said he would come as soon as he had his morning bath. But Ryanto had to threaten him before he would do anything even after he came!

By 10:00, the Embellishments, [missionary] George Trotter, and [interpreter] Daniel Tan had not arrived, but the audience had. They were a rather rowdy bunch because the mothers had brought all their children with them (and no extra seats were available). The first service was a bit rough on the edges but it did begin when the entertainment arrived about 10:15. Still, everyone seemed quite pleased with the services and we were a tired but happy crew when we got home after midnight that night. Over 2,200 people had heard the Word in one day—probably the most ever in Bogor!

Before the first service on Tuesday evening, the rain came in torrents, just when people would be arriving. As Avery drove to the theater, he prayed for the Lord to stop the rain if it was His will and told God that he would give Him the glory. He later journaled:

I am writing this to say the rain began to slack off five minutes later and was almost completely stopped by the time we started! The house was full. Rain began again during the service and didn't stop again all night, so the crowd for the second service was our smallest.

When it was time to begin the service, the choir had yet to appear. Avery returned home to check on them. They were at the house, dressing for the show. When Avery asked where the bus was, they said, "Outside." It wasn't. No one had told the driver he was to take the choir on to the theater. So Avery drove the first group to the theater, and Shirley shuttled the second group. Then, while the service was in progress, Avery had to find housing for everyone for the night since the bus driver refused to take them back to Jakarta late at night.

Wednesday evening, youths from a Muslim organization sought to disturb the invitation time by loudly laughing at and mocking those who came to profess their faith in Christ. Several times they physically restrained their friends from going to the altar, discouraging some; others pulled free from their grip and marched victoriously forward.

On the final night, armed soldiers intimidated the ushers into letting them enter the crusade. Scalpers were selling the free tickets for forty rupiah. Someone authorized tickets from the previous night, so that the auditorium filled and people began lining the walls. When Avery realized what was happening, he had to shut the doors, leaving two hundred people with legitimate tickets waiting outside the packed theater. He begged their forgiveness while offering them first entrance into the next service.

The overcrowding led to trouble, so that Avery had to tell some people who were creating a disturbance to leave (including a group of unattended children who had sneaked in). He also strategically stationed himself and a couple of the soldiers in the midst of the noisiest groups.

Victory in Jesus

None of these setbacks could undermine the triumph of the gospel. Despite the tensions and chaos, to the credit of the church members and their helpers, the general public witnessed only welcome entertainment and penetrating preaching. At the end of the four days, six thousand people had heard the gospel, and 114 had responded during the invitation—eighty-four of whom surrendered their lives to Christ.

One man came expecting to see an Elvis Presley movie but was allowed in on a ticket from a friend. Although he had never been to church before, he heard the gospel, and came weeping over his sins.

A soldier marched to the front, and his response to God was to stand at attention for the remainder of the invitation.

The three Air Force personnel who ran the loudspeaker system began the week very skeptical and uninterested. By the third day, they were asking questions and asking Avery to pray that they would be saved. They sang all the songs and, since they were in the counseling area, had read all of the follow-up material. They had not reached a final decision by the end of GEHIBA, although one man brought his wife the last night, and they all seemed to be sincerely considering following Christ, despite being Sundanese.

During the response time on the final evening, many came forward, weeping. Next came those who had helped in the preparations—including those who had made street banners, painted posters, helped decorate, and ushered. Even some theater employees, who had hindered more than helped earlier in the week, made a profession of their faith in Jesus.

As I told the audience during the disturbed invitation, "Christ died surrounded by a howling mob, but in the midst of it all, the condemned thief found peace when he cried out for mercy." And so did scores from Bogor when the Prince of Peace spoke to their hearts, and they decided to follow him regardless of the cost!

On Saturday, three people came to the house wanting to be saved. Two of them had not attended the meetings but had heard the news through their friend who had been saved. The following Sunday service we had our highest attendance in the church at the house, over eighty in the morning and forty-four in the evening, with two more people giving their lives to Christ. We have much follow-up work to do when our people can get rested up. We are all like the cow who had the new electric milker left on all day—proud but pooped!

Gospel Conversation
(Avery's Journal – January 29, 1968)

I have just finished talking to Dr. Saerun who came to talk about selling his house in Bogor. He said his house was second only to the summer palace of the President. He continued, "I have plenty of money and have been a success in life, but I have heart trouble and so I want to divide my inheritance between my children before I die so they won't have trouble later."

Then he tried to acquaint me with himself. I suppose he is between sixty-five and seventy years old. He wore a nice suit with matching tie. He showed me pictures of himself with General Darsono. Besides being a hero of the revolution, Dr. Saerun became a noted reporter, was very successful in the hotel business, and even now is president of the IKIP University in Bogor.

He pulled out his medals, which included some for helping in the revolution for independence and the Distinguished Award for Leadership from the Educational Center of Asia in Manila. To explain his medal on social service, he said, "Among the 23,000,000 of West Java, my name is at the top in social service. Every orphanage receives help from me and I am on the board of directors. During Lebaran [the Muslim holiday], *I gave all the old folks at the rest home a kain and kebaya* [skirt and blouse]. *He mentioned giving land, etc., for other social projects.*

I sought for a way to witness to him but didn't know how to open the conversation without offending him. I told him it was good that he was so socially minded but that no matter how good we were that it was not enough to get us to heaven. He looked at his watch as if he had to go.

I continued, "I think that it is good to get ready and prepare for your family, but we all need to prepare for the next world, and although it is meritorious to help others, all of us have sins which need to be forgiven."

"But," he said, "it's the good men that get to heaven."

I told him that was not necessarily so.

"Why not?" he asked.

"Because the sins we have committed can't be forgiven by doing many good deeds." Then I gave him the illustration that if a sick person came to his hotel, perhaps he would be allowed to stay on credit temporarily. But after he got well and wanted to stay permanently, the manager would ask him to pay. Suppose the man said that he would pay cash from now on. Sooner or later the manager would try to collect the thousands of rupiah the man still owed. "Suppose he said, 'Don't worry about that. I'm paying now.' You would not be satisfied because you would remember the debt. Even if you are perfect from now on, you still have sins, like all men, which haven't yet been forgiven."

He answered, "May I smoke? I want to hear more. No one has ever talked to me like this. I know all the religious leaders and pastors but perhaps they always thought I had too high of a position and was respected too much. None of them ever talked to me like this." He settled back in the carved rattan chair to listen, his chauffeur forgotten.

I began with the story of a rope that was broken. Man's efforts to contact God from his end were futile. Only when God lowered His end could man contact Him. This He did in Christ. He is the only way.

Dr. Saerun said that he never chose any particular religion or denomination, although he was a "statistical Moslem." I told him that I was not talking about various groups but God's only way for us to get to heaven: Jesus Christ. Then I told him of man's plight of living in darkness. The prophets were candles to help man see God but were insufficient. Then God sent the light, His Son, to really show us God and also to bear our sins on the cross.

I gave the illustration of a tukang [vendor] whose child was kidnapped and the ransom was a billion rupiah. The tukang could never pay that, but Dr. Saerun could.

"We are like the poor man and God pays to redeem us," he answered as he grasped the truth. Then he said that he understood why we needed a go-between. He wouldn't just rush into the head of the area or the governor's presence—he needed someone to usher him in. If his son, who graduated from Harvard, brought an American friend home, the friend would receive a ready welcome and an honored place in the home because his son brought him. He said he understood why God's Son could bring us to God.

Then I read John 14:1-7 and told him that even as Dr. Saerun was preparing for his children after his death, so Jesus was preparing a place for us. Dr. Saerun was thinking of earthly preparations while he also needed to think of heavenly preparations.

"Yes," he agreed, "we only stay for a short visit on earth—like stopping at Tjibonong for fruit on our way from Jakarta to Bogor."

Before he had to go for another appointment, he leaned forward and said, "They say that I am a good man when I give my employees a bonus of ten thousand rupiah, but really, I'm only looking out for myself. You are right when you say a so-called 'good man' is not necessarily good. In fact, I always count up what I'll receive from anything I do for someone else. I'm not a good man."

I told him he was close to salvation. He had admitted his sin (selfishness) and his need of a Savior. Now he needed to finish the third part: repent and believe in Christ. He agreed and thanked me for telling him for he was still in the dark and had no basis for faith.

Then he really did have to go but asked for an opportunity to come again. He also took several tracts to read. Who knows whether in the mercy of God this man will accept the Savior now at the end of his life or reject him like the rich young ruler?

How many of the respected are lost and no one has the courage to witness to them? I told him that I witnessed to him because I thought, "How sad for a man to get everything else ready and lose his soul. In Christ, I loved him and wanted him to know Christ."

Thrust

The New Life Crusade was a catalyst for continued growth in the Bogor church. Every Sunday following the GEHIBA crusade, more people came to Christ. One Sunday, a Javanese, Sundanese, Chinese, and Timorese person were all saved in the same service. By May, the Sunday Bible study enrollment had risen to seventy-five. There were 321 people enrolled in the Bible correspondence course, and two hundred enrolled in the English Bible classes. The space in the house was no longer adequate, so the church agreed to start two new missions in July if they could find spaces. Six laymen agreed to help with the preaching at the new sites. When Avery went to preach the Semarang revival in June, the men asked him not to bring in a guest speaker so they could practice their preaching.

In June, the Bison Chorale from Oklahoma Baptist University came to Bogor. They sang five concerts in two days to people from all levels of society at the rather run-down theater in town, allowing Avery to preach to three thousand people, resulting in ninety-six decisions, including seventy-three new professions of faith. The number of new converts in Bogor was now over two hundred.

This rapid response to the gospel in the aftermath of the Communist coup was being mirrored throughout Indonesia. The simultaneous GEHIBA rallies across Java in July 1967 recorded 2,681 new converts, with hundreds more occurring before and after the meetings. In North Sumatra, 1,900 people were baptized in one day. In Borneo, thirty new congregations had sprung up with five thousand members. In Central Java, the center of the Communist revolutionaries, sixty-five thousand people had been converted in the two years since the coup, according to the Indonesian Bible Society. Outer islands reported miraculous turnings to Christ as well.

This kind of response in a nation that claimed to be 90 percent Muslim could not long be ignored. Persecution and backlash from the Muslims arose. They advocated curtailing of visas for missionaries and protested help from foreign countries. Churches were destroyed in Celebes, a hand grenade blew up a Catholic church in Surabaya, and the Baptist student center in Jogjakarta was threatened.

Perhaps this persecution will be a means of strengthening the faith of the real Christians. Unless it is very grave, persecution usually spreads the faith instead of stopping it. As Paul says in 1 Corinthians 16:9(NIV), we say, "I will stay on . . . because a great door for effective work has been opened to me, and there are many who oppose me."

In August, one of the Bogor church members began a mission in their home, starting with twenty-five people. They soon had to knock out a wall and then began looking for another location. When Avery was showing a guest around Bogor, the man remarked, "*Gereja Baptis*—there's a Baptist church."

"Where?" Avery countered, "Oh . . . That's our new mission. I hadn't seen the new sign. They started services while I was out of town!"

In October, a 185-by-185-foot site (a huge plot in a city with 1,400 people per square mile) with a strong, four-thousand-square-foot masonry house was purchased for the church with funds from the Lottie Moon mission offerings (given by Baptist churches in the US to support the work of the Foreign Mission Board). The site was four blocks from the presidential summer palace and two blocks from the market where two main streets intersected. The members planned to remodel the building themselves and began giving sacrificially to do so. The remodel included an outdoor baptistery on the corner of a busy street so that each baptism was a distinctive witness. Although the church began meeting in the building, official permission to use the building was delayed for a year by Muslims, either for religious reasons or because they were awaiting a bribe.

At Christmas, the church's choir was invited to sing on the radio, and Avery brought a message to a potential audience of seventy-five million people.

Childbirth
(Told by Sherrie)

One of the difficulties international missionaries face is the choice they must make when the time comes to give birth. Do they use local facilities and doctors or relocate to cities with larger hospitals and/or missionary doctors?

The Willises had gone to Bandung for their annual checkups in May of 1967 and discovered that Shirley was pregnant, due in late November. They considered having the baby in Bogor by a German doctor who planned to move there. Ultimately they decided to return to Bandung because there was a surgeon there in language school and a Seventh-Day Adventist hospital. However, that meant taking Shirley to Bandung by November 6 in case the baby came early and allowing her to remain there at least ten days after the birth. That left Avery and the children in Bogor for three to six weeks without her. Thank goodness for house servants!

On the day that Shirley went into labor, a call was made to Bogor. However, in true Indonesian fashion, the call did not go through immediately, so the time needed to make the drive was shortened substantially. Avery burst into the children's schoolroom, saying, "We need to go—*now!*" Everyone threw some clothes into a bag and headed out the door within fifteen minutes. Sherrie remembers that her prayer life ratcheted up several notches that day as the car careened around the curves of the mountain at much greater speeds than usual. The drive that would normally take two-and-a-half hours was shortened by forty-five minutes! Avery was still thirty minutes late to the birth of Krista Dawn Willis, born November 22, the day before Thanksgiving.

A search committee began looking for an Indonesian pastor for the church. It was important now that the church be indigenous and self-sustaining, especially since the Willises would be going on a year-long furlough the next summer. (Twenty months passed from the time the pastor search process began until Pastor Sarkono from the seminary in Semarang accepted the call to pastor the Bogor church.)

In January of 1968, the Bogor church had doubled the number of Sunday morning classes and teachers; and in February, two members of the church, Mr. and Mrs. Djaja, moved to the island of Timor to serve as their first missionaries.

On the home front, the landlord wanted to raise the Willises' monthly rent by almost 1,700 percent, from $30 to $500 per month when the lease was renewed in November. Amazingly, when the Willis family left for furlough in June, they were able to sublease the remaining four months of the three-year contract at a price greater than their total rent payment for the three years!

In a surprising and rapid turn of events, the mission assigned the Trotter family to continue the work in Bogor and asked Avery to either begin a Bible Institute in East Java or begin evangelistic work in the city of Jember, 990 kilometers away, when they returned for their second term. It had been an incredible three years of seeing God at work and the birth of a new church. The future, though, was pregnant with new opportunities when they returned to Indonesia a year later.

CHAPTER 12
Furlough: Reporting, Reconnecting, Reenergizing, and Reproducing!

Furloughs (stateside assignments) are designed for rest and reconnection with families and prayer supporters and to provide opportunities to speak in churches about what God is doing overseas. Avery advanced beyond the expected "missionary slideshow" and created a film of Indonesia and the cry of the lost to show in the churches in which he spoke.

Hidden Talent: Moviemaker

With a long-held interest in photography, Avery liked to try his hand at special effects, even in home movies. He had purchased equipment while on vacation in Hong Kong: a Super 8 mm movie camera of the latest style, a projector, film editor, voice synchronizer, and splicer.

The Willises had taken vacations to exotic Bali and to north and west Sumatra, and Avery had visited the jungles of Borneo. He took time to shoot film in each location. Initially, Avery combined his footage and his hobby to create a tourism movie about Indonesia for a national competition. His film won third place! The film was entitled *Columbus' Dream Come True*. Avery's script told the story of an Indonesian foreign exchange student to America who attempts to convince his host family to visit Indonesia. Besides scenes from the islands, the film included clips of President Sukarno and of an interpretative dance of the story of Mary Magdalene, created by Mr. Bagong, New York World's Fair director of Indonesian dances, who had recently become a Christian.

More importantly, Avery took the opportunity to simultaneously create another film entitled *Edge of the Light* to use in speaking engagements while on furlough. This movie documented the sweeping religious revival of over four hundred thousand baptisms to Christianity following the aborted Communist coup.

Avery said:

I just felt that this story must be told, so I plunged into movie-making before I fully realized how much was involved.

Faith is a strange thing—it causes us to do things that we would not do if we knew all the facts. It seems God has always led me into deeper waters by faith than I might have gone had I known what was awaiting me. Then He enjoys taking me through the deep waters to show His power and glory.

The latest case in point is the 16 mm color/sound movie I am making. Through a series of events, God led me to plunge into this project. I thought I could do it for minimal cost. Imagine my surprise a few minutes ago when I sat down by the public relations director for the U.S. Embassy in the Jakarta airport and he informed me that it costs them $60,000 to make a twenty-minute color movie with sound! Like I said, God leads me into things I wouldn't do if I knew the facts. Yet, I am not worried because He always supports His projects and I'm sure it can be done for a fraction of the Embassy's cost.[1]

Since Avery was on a low budget (his personal cost totaled $2,250), his movie crafting was essentially homemade—before the days of digital photography, editing software, or computer graphics. He was recklessly confident in his willingness to do whatever it took. Truett Meyers of the Southern Baptist Radio and Television Commission later told Avery, "I am surprised that you could make such a movie. Your greatest advantage was in not knowing what couldn't be done, just going ahead and doing it."

It wasn't all safe. To create the dancing flames on the title page, Avery created and filmed a massive bonfire in his backyard. For one scene, he wanted to film a preacher and needed to zoom in closer and then back out. Since he didn't have a dolly, he moved chairs to widen the aisle and then filmed from the inside of a *becak* (pedicab) while the man holding the camera lights sat on the bicycle portion and pedaled him forward and backward.

Another time, Avery got a hundred yards behind a jet taking off to get some footage, and described it as being inside a "blast furnace turned tornado." Then he had the audacity to ask a pilot of a flight he was booked on to taxi his plane down the runway while he filmed it, and then stop and open the door again so he could get on. They did!

Avery's hair was prematurely gray, so in an attempt to look younger for the movie, he borrowed some hair dye from an American woman in Bogor. It turned his hair orange! After a good laugh, he went to wash it out, but then it turned green! Since he was due to go to Bandung for a meeting, he tried hair darkener that looked more like black shoe polish. He finally went to a hair salon for some permanent brown-black dye. It worked for the movie, but then came the painful process of growing his hair back out to its natural shade of gray. He massaged it every day hoping to speed the process before he left for America in two months.

Edge of the Light

The *Edge of the Light* film begins with Sudiono, an Indonesian student in critical condition, being wheeled into the operating room of an American hospital. His pastor (Avery) rushes in, realizes his condition, and begins to pray as he thinks through the student's brief experience in the United States. The screen goes black, and a lantern approaches out of the dark, and then the title *Edge of the Light* burns across the screen. A flashback shows the student's arrival in the United States, boarding in the home of the pastor and his family, and his subsequent conversion to Christianity. He tells of his experience in Indonesia where he often stood outside of Christian services at the edge of the light and listened. Now he is concerned for his family and friends who are still at the edge of spiritual light. He wonders why more Americans, including his pastor, do not go to tell them the way to God. Using a series of descriptive flash-forwards showing the family enjoying their time on the islands of Bali, Java, Borneo, and Sumatra, he begs the pastor's family to consider going.

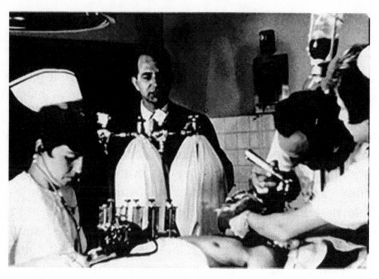

Opening scene from Edge of the Light movie, 1968

Standing at the young man's deathbed, Avery resolves to take his place in spreading the light of the gospel in Indonesia. As the screen darkens, Avery picks up the overturned lantern and carries it into the darkness. While the student's voice pleads, "How will they know unless they hear? And how will they hear unless someone tells them?" (Romans 10:13–14), others pick up lanterns and form a procession, expanding the edge of the light.

God used the movie to impact people with the spiritual need of the world and called them to respond. Johnny and Diana Norwood tell of the movie's effect in their life:

As young missionary candidates still in seminary, we were seeking the Lord's direction to some particular country. Knowing we were called to be "pioneer missionaries" to a place where people had not heard of Jesus, we were constantly praying over the mission map.

> One Sunday evening, a furloughing missionary couple came to our church to show a film they had made about Indonesia. It was a re-enacted drama depicting the urgent need to take the gospel to the villages of Indonesia—Central Java, in particular. Avery and

Shirley Willis had a passion for Christ and for the lost. It was contagious. Diana and I spent some time with them after they spoke that evening. They prayed with us, and we knew this was the Lord's answer to our question, "Where, Lord?" After four more years of preparation, we arrived on the island of Java—specifically Central Java. After a year of language school, we moved to the tiny village of Gombong to become pioneer church planters among hundreds of nearby villages where the gospel had yet to be introduced. During our time in Gombong, we often fellowshipped with the Willis family in meetings and personal visits. Now as colleagues, they continued to be our mentors.[2]

Stateside

Adjustment to America was its own kind of culture shock, especially for the children. Sherrie, age nine, asked, "Want to know which I like more: America or Indonesia? It must be Indonesia because when I am in America, I miss Indonesia, but when we were in Indonesia, I didn't miss America." (Of course, she didn't have much memory of America since the family had left when she was barely five years old.)

Avery wrote:

A friend was telling me he recently asked a missionary's two sons if they liked their dad being a missionary. They replied, "It's the most fun thing in the world, unless maybe he was an ice cream man." The next day, while we were driving home from church, I told our kids the story, and they all responded, "We would rather you be a missionary because we want to go back to Indonesia." This was really something for them after not having much ice cream for four years! My heart was singing as I turned the car into the Dairy Queen.

Then came another surprise:

The Foreign Mission Board has one policy we feel a need to break! They require all missionaries to have an annual physical exam. Last year, we went to Bandung for the physicals and the doctor broke the news that

Shirley was expecting. Our annual check-up this year was in Fort Worth, and again the doctor revealed that Shirley was pregnant. That does it! We're not having physicals next year! This number five is due in April.[3]

Rest was certainly not at the top of Avery's priority list. He began work on his doctorate and completed his oral exams. Nearly every Sunday, Avery preached in churches around the country, and Shirley had multiple opportunities to speak more locally during the week. December was an especially busy time because it was the emphasis time for the Lottie Moon Christmas Offering for Foreign Missions, which funded a majority of the Baptist mission work around the world.

Five Thousand Enlisted

A major milestone was realized during this stateside year when the monthly *PRAY* newsletter was printed and mailed to over five thousand homes, meeting Avery's prayer partner goal.

After we were appointed as missionaries, I contacted everyone I could to become prayer partners. I personally challenged friends to do one thing for us: pray. By the time we got to Indonesia, two thousand people had covenanted to pray for us, and that number has continued to grow until now over five thousand are translating their prayer time into missionary service. Many told us they did not miss praying for us one day in five years. We have only had a small part in what has happened in Indonesia, but I do believe that God spared that country from communism and opened it to the gospel in answer to the prayers of His people. Over 400,000 people received Christian baptism in the first three years following the attempted Communist coup. During this time Baptists almost tripled their membership and number of churches. To God be the glory![4]

Looking Ahead

After a sizeable Christmas, including time with extended family and enough gifts to make up for four years of absence, shopping began in preparation to return. Over the next few months, Shirley would take advantage of sales to buy nonperishable food items and paper products, fabric to sew homemade clothes, and a generator for use during power outages. Packing and crating these items was an arduous task, all completed while Shirley was in her final trimester of pregnancy.

Avery, Shirley, Randy, Sherrie, Wade, Krista, Brett Willis, 1969

Brett Lane Willis was born in Ft. Worth, Texas, on April 12, 1969. He lived two and a half months in America before the family returned to Indonesia. As they prepared to leave the country, Avery summarized the year:

Furlough is....
Traveling 63,000 miles... visiting the Holy Land and Europe... participating in the Baptist Youth World Conference in Switzerland... and coming home to family reunions.

It is... speaking four or five times per week... studying ten to twelve hours a day... getting ready for a new baby... talking with prospective missionary candidates... visiting with old friends until past midnight... hearing your children ask why you always have to go to some other church instead of going with them... making thousands of new acquaintances... showing our movies... adding prayer partners until we have five thousand who receive our monthly newsletter.

It is... seeing the first men go to the moon... skipping a Philosophy seminar to watch the last game of the World Series... taking in a college football game... too brief visits with relatives... Christmas with our parents... buying and selling a car in a year... shopping for the next four years.

It is... drinking water without boiling it... eating ice cream whenever we want... eating out... long distance direct dialing instead of placing a call and waiting for hours... having a choice of more than one TV channel... dashing to the airport to catch another plane... saying goodbyes... and looking forward to getting back to the work that matters for eternity.[5]

The Eagle Has Landed—a Prophetic Word
(From PRAY, September 1969)

"The Eagle has landed!" crackled over my shortwave radio in Surabaya, Indonesia and I breathed a sigh of relief along with millions of others around the world. In the days that followed, many Indonesians went out of their way to congratulate us on America being the first nation to put a man on the moon. Two days after the astronauts splashed down in the Pacific Ocean, President Nixon was welcomed to Jakarta.

I, too, joined in this euphoria until a word from the Lord shattered my pride. Obadiah 1:4 states, "Though thou exalt thyself as the eagle, and though thou set thy nest among the stars, thence I will bring you down, saith the Lord." Though the original prophecy predicted the fall and destruction of the Edomites, it can also apply to America whose "pride of their heart has deceived them" to reject God. God had couched his words in terms that speak to us in the space age.

My recent furlough in the United States only confirmed what the prophets had said about God's people having a "form of godliness but denying the power thereof": the deterioration of the home, sexual indulgence, rebelliousness, a lack of concern for the unfortunate, and a love for the things of this world. I know it is not popular to predict the downfall of a nation at the height of its power, but the prophets made a habit of it and now speak a word to us. Amos' call, "Prepare to meet thy God, O Israel" (4:12) was not an exhortation to repent as we usually think; but a declaration that judgment had begun and must be faced without recourse. Has America reached this place of no return, or is there still time to repent?

CHAPTER 13
Jember: Church Planting amid Opposition

The Willis family arrived in Jakarta on July 4, 1969, in time to celebrate Independence Day with a picnic and fireworks at the American club and enjoy a reunion with Indonesian missionaries. The following day they went to Bogor, arriving in time for church. Though the church had a pastor now, it had not grown much numerically during the past year. Nevertheless, Avery and Shirley were pleased to see that almost everyone to whom they had preached the gospel during their first term had remained faithful and were still part of the church. Avery was able to speak to the group for thirty to forty minutes and only needed to grasp for a few words.

Relocation

The Willises were assigned to East Java as evangelists to Jember, a city of 350,000 in an area of ten million people with no missionaries of any Christian denomination. More than half of the people in Jember were from the island of Madura, deeply Muslim and traditionally hostile to the gospel. Evangelistic work in this city would begin with the more receptive Javanese.

Fellow missionary John Ingouf had begun driving to Jember from Surabaya to conduct services, so there was a nucleus of five faithful attendees meeting in a Red Cross building, having been ejected from their prior meeting place due to Muslim protests.

July 17, 1969 – Letter

The Muslims are strong there, but the government is standing its ground on the Panjasila, which guarantees religious freedom. We have not found a house yet in Jember. I plan to go back this weekend to look for one and conduct services for the first time. We are in a temporary house in Surabaya. It is really hot here and there are millions of mosquitos. I am sure glad we will not be living in Surabaya permanently. For now, I will make the 115-mile trip there every weekend.

August 13, 1969 – Letter

I think we are nearing the end of the all the red tape after fifty-six visits to the government offices! We will have to repeat the process when we move to Jember. We have a possibility of a house to buy. The family is going with me this weekend to see it. It will need a lot of remodeling.

October 6, 1969 – Letter

We will remodel the house after we move in because we don't want to wait several months for them to get finished, and at the same time we can supervise it more closely. It will be messy for a while, but we will at least be in our own house and will be able to work better there. We are going to put in an American-style kitchen (meaning inside the house), add a couple of baths, move a couple of walls to make the bedrooms larger, and paint it inside and out. In Indonesia, that will take a long time to get done. We discovered that much of our furniture stored in Bogor during furlough was eaten by termites. We burned some of the infested furniture, and we are having some repaired. We are reminded of the transitory nature of this world and the permanence of Heaven where "moth and rust does not corrupt and where thieves do not break in and steal."

Because he was out meeting people and establishing connections, Avery was home only two full days during the month of October.[1] Through the newsletter, Shirley requested prayer as she began home-schooling for the first time. School started late since the books had to arrive in the delivered freight and Shirley needed a few days' head start to prepare to teach.

Encouraging Signs

October 22, 1969 – Letter

Jember is surrounded by about 250 plantations of various kinds: sugar, tea, coffee, cocoa, tobacco, rubber, and of course, rice. Last week I got an invitation to go to the Wonowiri plantation about eighteen miles from here to talk about having services. We were received royally and they are excited about our coming there, perhaps every week. They have about two thousand people on the plantation—six hundred are adults and about 150 have a Christian preference. We will start with evangelistic services and later see if we can begin a church.

Now that we are here, the church here in Jember should begin to pick up. The church has between five and fifteen adults coming, and this week I have already had several visitors come to the house. A sixty-five-year-old man was the first to make a decision to follow Christ since we arrived here. But increased pressure exerted by Muslim leaders now means that we are no longer allowed to use the Red Cross building. We are rotating the services in the homes of the members each week. It is a problem because new people who want to come don't know where we are meeting each week. But at least we are being more like the New Testament church.[2]

December 1969 – PRAY newsletter

Our invitation to the plantation was more than we planned for. Joining our family in the car were four church members who formed our evangelistic team and the local minister of religion. To our surprise, the manager of this government plantation (who is not a Christian) had sent trucks to three neighboring plantations to pick up people who wanted to attend. By the time the trucks had disgorged their passengers and the people from this plantation had assembled, we had five hundred people present, not counting the scores of people leaning over the rail around the meeting hall. At least half of them were not Christians and many more were prominent Muslims.

This area saw tens of thousands of Communists killed in 1965, and many of those remaining are asking for spiritual direction. After several speeches, all of which emphasized the freedom of religion, I preached on

"The Seeking Savior" and then showed a film on the prodigal son. The minister of religion and the chief military leader have taken a personal interest in our work, so God may be providing the necessary backing as we face religious opposition.

Much like they had done in Bogor, the Willises held a traditional housewarming meal in their home, serving nearly one hundred city officials and neighbors. Because it was held during the week of Christmas, they were able to offer an invitation to a special Christmas service. Over a hundred people attended the service, in spite of rain, to see a film in Indonesian about the birth of Christ. Two people accepted Christ as their Savior. After the service, the film was shown again for approximately a hundred more people who had gathered outside, requesting to see it.

On March 20, missionary Bill O'Brien brought American and Indonesian singing ensembles to Jember and conducted the first concert ever held in this city. Police prohibited passing out circulars, using a sound truck, or hanging street banners as had been done in Bogor, but they could not stop the Indonesian "grapevine." Not many came for the free tickets on the first day, but by the third day, people had to be turned away! Twelve hundred people attended! If the auditorium had been large enough, hundreds more would have claimed tickets.

Besides the goodwill created in the community by the concert, two responses indicated God's activity. The man who had created the most problems with the local government concerning the church's meeting place thoroughly enjoyed the music and warmed up to the church considerably. Furthermore, early the following morning, a sixty-seven-year-old man who had never been to church came to the Willis home seeking the way to Christ. He surrendered to the Lord that day and continued to be faithful.[3]

The Seed of the Church

The first nine members of the Jember church were baptized on Easter Sunday, March 29, 1970, in the Bedadung River. We had planned to have the baptism in the local swimming pool, but the evening before, the motel director withdrew his permission under pressure from the Muslims. We notified the members that we would have the sunrise Easter service and baptisms regardless. The people began arriving at our home at 4:15 a.m. and before daybreak, we walked the four blocks down to the river. As the sun rose, people lined the bridge over the river, watching the nine adults be immersed. That did more to tell the Easter story than my brief sermon![3]

Easter morning baptisms in Jember, 1970

Though response to the gospel was much slower in this region, the small church began to reproduce. The new fellowship began witnessing to their friends and bringing them to worship services. Visitors often responded to Christ after a few visits. The principal of the local elementary school began spreading the gospel through a Bible study booklet *The Heart of the Faith*. Other teachers began taking the booklet to their schools and teaching it in the extracurricular religion classes. Another member began teaching it in his role as Boy Scout leader. Several of those baptized on Easter soon led others to the Lord.

Expanding the Stakes

In May, the small church began to extend ministry in all four directions from Jember. The Inspector of Community Education from Bondowoso, the county seat twenty miles *north* of Jember, came to the house asking if services could be started in the home of the county midwife. *They have asked for a service every Saturday night. Although the work will be slower among this Madurese community, it might grow stronger under opposition.*

Avery took five men from the church to the village of Curahnongko, twenty miles *south* of Jember. The highest official of this village had asked them to come pray for his sick wife and to give spiritual instruction to the twenty thousand people under his jurisdiction. The attendance at the second visit doubled the first. The majority of the four to five hundred people were non-Christians. The thatched-roof meeting hall could not hold them all, and many were beyond the light of the kerosene lantern. It was as if Avery's *Edge of the Light* film had come to life!

Two new Christians from Jember gave thrilling testimonies before Avery preached on New Birth. After the service, the group distributed tracts and booklets of the gospel of John and showed a film about Jesus. Then the village head stood up and told them that they should all believe in God.

A seminary student sent the name of a Baptist man who had moved to Jatirejo, a village sixty miles *east* of Jember, in the midst of two million Javanese. Plans were made to start services in his home that month.

The pastor of the Javanese Protestant Church introduced Avery to a man from Tanggul, twenty miles *west* of Jember, whose grandson had offered his home for services in the village of Pondok Jeruk.

The church attempted there by Pentecostals was closed down after Muslim demonstrations. We plan to begin quietly with a home worship service and let it grow into a church. I pray that each of these preach-

*ing points will become launching pads into the smaller desas [villages]
that surround each of these cities. I pray that Psalm 107:2–3 be fulfilled:
"Let the redeemed of the Lord say so . . . whom He has gathered from the
lands, from east and west, from north and south."*[4]

Implosion

Surprisingly, the Willises were to remain in Jember less than a
year. An April Fools' incident revealed how a very difficult eight months
had tested Shirley to her limit.

The crash started with what Avery thought would be a harmless
prank. On April 1, as the family was sitting around the dinner table, Avery
began with, "Oh, Shirley, I got a letter from the Filipino mission today
[where he was about to go and lead their camp for missionary children].
They have invited you to come with me." As she began to eagerly ask
questions and start to problem-solve about where the children would
stay, Avery realized she was far too excited and blurted out, "April Fools'!"

Staring at him in dismay, Shirley suddenly burst into tears and
fled from the room. Surprised, he looked around at the children who
were sitting in stunned silence, and then followed her to the bedroom.
Hours of conversation would follow as Avery began to realize the magnitude of the load on Shirley's shoulders. While he was spending much
of his time out at the plantations, she was homeschooling three children for the first time (all subject areas for grades 3, 5, and 7) with a
two-year-old and newborn baby, and was directing (sometimes redoing) the remodeling of the house. Adding to the stress, Randy, and possibly Krista, had hepatitis, which required rest and a special diet.

Crisis of Belief

This created a crisis of faith for Avery. His wife and family held priority, but his heart cry was evangelism. He began to earnestly seek the
Lord anew for direction. En route to Hong Kong and the Philippines on
May 18, Avery wrote a letter to his parents, who were scheduled for a
three-week visit to Indonesia at the beginning of August.

There is a good possibility that we will be moving from Jember to Semarang in Central Java for me to become a professor in the seminary there and direct the 125 students in evangelistic outreach. If this is a surprise to you, it is also to me. The new president of the seminary has talked to me several times about coming there to teach and told me if I ever wanted to, to let him know. I have always turned him down to date (although I thought I might eventually accept after a few terms) because I wanted to open new work.

Several things have happened recently to move up my time schedule. The need at the seminary has really been on my heart since the revival there, but I have pushed it aside. I can help fill the vacancies left by Keith Parks who is leaving to become the Area Secretary, by Ebbie Smith who will open the mobile Bible school in Kediri, and by Clarence Griffin, the evangelistic director who is leaving for furlough.

The other thing that has precipitated this is that Shirley is unhappy in Jember. The school situation and living with the carpenters for several months hasn't helped. I feel that for her good we ought to be closer to other people where she will not be so isolated. All of these things have come to a head in the last couple of weeks.

I will hate to leave Jember just as we are really getting started in the city and surrounding villages. But God knows best and a new missionary will be ready to move to Banyuwangi in July, and he could take our place. Don't let this alter your plans. Just pray for us that God's will be done.

While in the Philippines, Avery recorded his back-and-forth struggle and his ultimate surrender.

May 19–June 1– Journals, taped

I have to look at all angles for the will of God, especially in regard to past direction, past guidance from God and past preparation. As far as I can tell, it looks like the circumstances point toward the move to the seminary. As far as Shirley is concerned, it gives the last push that is necessary. The bobsled is going down the hill.

There are some disadvantages in going to the seminary. We will be busier and have less freedom to do what we want. Two weeks ago, when

I was there, I almost shuddered thinking about these students and their expectations for subsidies.

And yet, more and more, I begin to feel there are advantages to working with these young people. The seminary seems to be quite the center of our work. Most of the conferences are held there at the campus and I think we can have a real testimony in the work with these students. Maybe I could teach them the biblical basis of the laity and how they must develop, teach, and use laymen to reach the people, particularly in the villages. I will be glad to be close to the radio and TV center there in Semarang. Perhaps I could use a little of my creativity. With the drama classes at the seminary, maybe we could make a film. Maybe some creativity could be used in the way of outreach in the evangelistic program there.

I sure hate to leave just when things are getting started, but I can also see the hand of God in our going. I am glad to have things started so that maybe the next missionary can come and carry on the work here. The work is still new, but we have the base and we have the four new area services starting up. I also asked the cooperative committee of nationals and missionaries to consider sending an Indonesian pastor to the area.

Last night, at the MK camp, the youth and I each made a collage by tearing from magazines pictures and words that described aspects of our lives and collecting them on a poster. Then we were given about ten minutes to try to write a poem or folk song or something to express it. It really helped me see where I was. I think I was able to put into words the decision I have been struggling with. Here is what I wrote as I was seeking the will of God for my own life:

God, tie it together.
I wander down a dusky path
To the unknown that God hath
He has a plan
A plan for His man –
But I only see it when the lightning flashes.
The rain falls
And the dam breaks.
The surge of circumstances beats against my will.

I'll make that hill, I will. I will!
But I won't...
Because the flood takes me,
Carries me,
And then lifts me to higher ground
Where He is waiting.
I'll fight no more till I am breaking.
I will ride the crest of His will
I'll make the quest Through the dark.
God, help me stand the test.
You know what is best.
There I'll let it rest.

Which is a way of saying that I will no longer resist what I interpret to be the will of God as going to the seminary—though I have resisted a long time, and though it has taken many, many things to help me get there. Maybe there was no other way for me to get there. Maybe I was not willing to go under any other circumstances and maybe it had to take something like this. So unless there is a change, I see this is as what God wants us to do. In fact, I believe this is what God wants us to do. I will just stand on it. At this point, I think we will move after the revival services in June.

Goodbye to Jember

The Semarang station voted immediately to request, and the executive committee unanimously approved, for the Willises to move to Semarang. Four seminary students from Semarang were assigned to help in Jember in the short term.

Avery returned to Jember for the June revival, which had been planned in conjunction with Kabaria '70 (simultaneous revivals throughout the country). He was very pleased with the results and the number of decisions, especially the salvation of Mr. Sujiwo, the husband of a woman saved at Christmas. Sujiwo had opposed his wife's baptism and refused to accompany her to church until the final night of the revival, when he declared himself for Christ. Eight new believers now joined the fellowship, bringing the next Sunday's total in the church to thirty adults.[5]

Avery chose not to tell the members of the church that his family was moving until the final day of the revival meetings, lest it distract the church from its greater purpose. He did share with the seminary students who would be taking over in the interim, and most painfully with Faisal, the new convert that Avery had spent months discipling.

Living Discipleship—Faisal's Story
(From Avery's Taped Diary, June 1970, and Retold in PRAY, August 1970)

When the Willises moved to Jember, people from the church helped them unload. Among them was a man named Faisal who had begun attending the gatherings. When they finished, Avery took the crew out for an iced drink, laughingly quoting the Scripture "those that work, eat." Faisal blanched because he was not currently employed.

In 1957, Faisal had moved to East Java from the Minangkebau area of Sumatra (where no one had become a Christian in the past eighty years). He had married and served as a schoolteacher. The man he boarded with at the time of the 1965 coup was a Communist and Faisal was arrested along with him. Faisal was interrogated over a period of three months, but because there was no evidence against him, was exonerated. By that time, however, his teaching position had been terminated and his possessions sold. Then his wife died. Depression set in. He was unable to get another job and had to be supported by his family in Minangkabau. Ultimately, he met a Javanese woman in Jember, married her, built a small home, and did odd jobs around town.

As the Willises began home Bible studies, Faisal attended, curious about Christianity. After firing their gardener/handyman for stealing, Avery offered the position to Faisal, even though it was "below his station." Faisal agreed, primarily to study with Avery and to secretly observe the Willis family to see if they lived out what they taught. He was particularly attracted by how Avery "treated everyone the same, including him, regardless of their position." Sometimes after working all day, Faisal would go home to bathe and then return to visit in the evening as a friend.

Faisal carefully considered his decision to follow Jesus. He had seen others commit and slip back. He also knew that his family in Minangkabau would likely cut off support if he made this decision. Avery had told him clearly that Jesus required a full commitment.

The evening Avery returned from the Philippines, Faisal came to speak with him. Faisal could not sleep that night as he wrestled with his decision. He returned to the Willises before 5:00 a.m. the next morning. He was so eager to make his commitment to Christ that he had forgotten to bathe himself [unthinkable for an Indonesian] and didn't even want to wait till Avery dressed and shaved. Immediately after professing his new faith in Christ, Faisal went out with the seminary interns to pass out invitations to the upcoming revival.

When he went home that night and shared his commitment with his family, there was much resistance. His father-in-law, who lived next door to him and on whose land Faisal's home was built, was a strong Muslim and vehemently opposed Faisal's new faith.

The next Sunday morning, Faisal made public his profession of faith and gave his testimony to the church. He feasted on the revival meetings all week and planned to be baptized with the group the following Sunday. Each night, when he went home, he faced such opposition that he began to believe he would need to sell his house and move. But he told his father-in-law, "I have spit on the ground, I will not lick it up."

On Saturday, the night before the baptisms, Avery felt that he must not wait to tell Faisal that he and his family would be leaving Jember, lest Faisal feel that he had been duped or betrayed when the announcement was made at the end of the revival. This news was another blow and challenge to Faisal's new faith. Nevertheless, afraid that he might miss the baptism since he did not have an alarm clock, Faisal barely slept that night and arrived around 3:00 a.m. at the river where the baptism would take place and waited for the others to arrive.

When they left Jember, the Willises offered Faisal continued employment if he wanted to move to Semarang with them. Faisal agreed, sold his house, and moved his family. His wife was soon saved as well. He wanted to "become a strong Christian this year so that I might attend the seminary, and become a pastor to my own people in Sumatra."

It was a tearful goodbye to the church and a busy final week. Avery went to each of the four locations outside of Jember for a final service. Some of the work in these locations and in the English classes would need to be altered or postponed.

A Pastor's Heart

Before leaving Jember, Avery was forced to deal with a difficult situation that threatened to leave the tender, young church in disarray. Some Muslim neighbors protested the use of films during the revival, claiming they had been used to draw children to convert them to Christianity. When the church secretary, Sujoko, was called before the county official to respond to the complaint, he denied even knowing about the revivals.

Sujoko went home and wrote up a resolution that he sent to Pak Salam, head of the Religion Department, requesting that future church services be canceled, that no missionaries be sent to replace Mr. Willis, and that all control of the Baptist work be turned over to him and those whose names were on the letter. Sujoko criticized Avery specifically, falsely accusing that: (1) he had gone out to the villages without informing Pak Salam; (2) his dogmatic teaching (that Christ was the only way to salvation) would split the nation; (3) Avery was financially irresponsible with funds designated for sharing the gospel.

Pak Salam informed Avery of the letter. Avery had already planned to meet with Sujoko and the treasurer to discuss some discrepancies in the church bank account. Avery confronted Sujoko about the accusations he had been spreading about him, about the church finances, and an unpaid debt. Sujoko confessed his resentment toward Avery and that he had fallen away from the Lord. Still, he and the treasurer remained unrepentant and evasive about the missing money.

It sickened Avery that when opportunities were opening to the church and new converts were being realized that sin and opposition should come from within.

The conflict was resolved by the church's election of a new secretary and treasurer. A seminary student was asked to serve as interim pastor and members were assigned to help him. Pak Salam assured Avery that permission was granted to continue services and that he would take personal responsibility if further up line permission was needed.

Avery felt he had addressed each wrong and each accusation with the truth and remedied as much as possible. It was time to look forward.

SECTION 4
Serving as Seminary President

Spiritual Marker #8

Avery found new focus in teaching
and equipping at the seminary.

And the things you have heard me say
in the presence of many witnesses
entrust to reliable men
who will also be qualified to teach others.
　　　　　　　—2 Timothy 2:2 (NIV)

CHAPTER 14
Semarang

It takes the same spiritual elements to bring
revival on the mission field as anywhere.
Prayer for revival should top our prayer list.
No spiritual victory is easily won.

—Avery

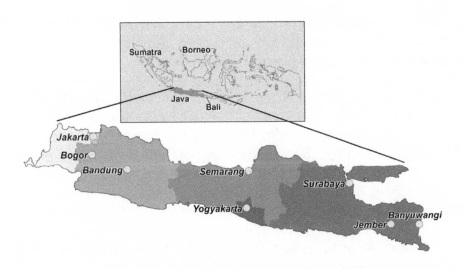

The Willis served in Bandung and Bogor of West Java,
Jember in East Java, and Semarang in Central Java.

Adjustment to Semarang came quickly. Packing and moving
was made easier because most of the items brought back from
furlough had remained in a warehouse while the Jember house
was under construction. Although the house in Semarang needed
painting and other work, it was a large home with an even larger

yard full of trees. It sat on a hill overlooking a valley. The children roamed over the hills, exploring, riding bikes, and playing with both Indonesian and American children. For the first time in five years, they not only had other missionary kids (MKs) to play with, but there were neighboring American children from other mission and business groups.

School took place in a one-room schoolhouse, a former chapel on the seminary campus. The American families in town joined together, and each mother taught one subject area to all grades. Each grade had at least two students, so the students remained in their grade-level cubicles, while the teachers rotated. Shirley was in charge of teaching language arts, a subject in which she excelled.

Seminary

Avery's responsibilities at the Indonesian Baptist Theological Seminary (STBI) included teaching classes on philosophy of religion, advanced preaching, and personal evangelism.

When we returned from putting Mom and Dad on the plane in Jakarta [Grace and AT had spent three-and-a-half weeks visiting Indonesia], *I really had to dig in. We drove back on Sunday and classes started the following Wednesday. Classes have been going for two weeks now, and I may have them fooled about how much I know. I am only a day or two ahead of them. But I am enjoying it. It is a real satisfaction to be able to teach these young people who want to learn.*

He was given oversight responsibility for twenty churches and chapels in the Semarang area.

A.T. preaching and Avery, Jr. translating in Indonesia, 1970

August 1970 –Taped Diary

As Dad (AT) preached and I translated in the different churches while he was here, I noticed again how much Dad counts it a personal ministry and feels like it is his job to help everybody be better in witnessing and that every church ought to grow. He sits down with them, gives them advice, and prays with them. It taught me how I need to a better minister to these pastors—not to just expect them to know how to help their churches—but to pray with them, visit with them, and try to encourage them. This was a good lesson for me, coming into the seminary with all the assignments I have with the churches.

Some of the area pastors have come to me and asked for all sorts of things from ceiling tiles to lanterns to songbooks. I am trying to teach them the necessity of standing on their own two feet—that it is their responsibility. So I have declined their requests—but it is not as easy for me to "cut the water off" as it has been for others to turn it on all these years. I have tried to make it a spiritual ministry in all these cases. When

183

anyone comes, I have made up my mind always to pray with them before they leave.

Furthermore, Avery led the "dropping" program at the seminary, originated by Keith Parks, in which the students went out in teams to evangelize. He was in his element as he found new ways to disciple, equip, and mobilize students, and as he directed the results of the new evangelism efforts back to the local churches.

We started the "dropping" program last week—a term taken from the war in New Guinea to describe the parachuting of troops behind enemy lines—only we drop from pickup trucks instead of airplanes. I have made up my mind that any time I am in town I will go out with the students. I need to, not only to teach them, but for the souls who are lost. I need it for my own spiritual life. I also want to keep contact with the people. I feel more cut off here than in any place we have lived because we are up on Candi hill, where we are not surrounded by people. The seminary campus is enclosed as well, so we do not always have people in and out of our house like we did in Bogor.

A downside to the dropping program is that the gatherings of people who have been converted by this program have formed churches almost as satellites of the seminary. I met with all the pastors of the Semarang churches and gave them a vision for each of these new pockets of converts to be connected to a local church, as a mission of that church, rather than to the seminary.

I asked the students to turn in reports on how they were spending their time. It was revealing to some of them as to how little personal witness they have done. Some of them were not too happy that they had to turn it in because they were afraid of the accountability. I feel, though, that it will help them and us know what they are doing so we can train them better.

Joy in the Work

It was not long at all before Avery felt completely at home in this new position and fully immersed in the ministry, unlike what he experienced in Jember.

Every Sunday I am preaching somewhere and have had several invitations to preach revivals. I may take some but I will have to decline others. I cannot be gone that often. But I am having plenty of opportunity to preach and serve and witness.

I am really happy to be here. I have a sense that this is where God wants me right now—a sense that I had a hard time finding in Jember. I worked at it and maybe by the end of our time was deciding that it was a good place to be after all, but I never had the sense that everything was clicking like it ought to. Nothing clicked there. I have the same sense here that I had in Bogor of being right in the center of the will of God.

Avery and Shirley were members of Puspawarno
Baptist Church in Semarang, 1972

Texas 42 Championship
(Taped Diary)

"Texas 42," or just "42" as it is known to most missionaries, is a domino game with a strategy similar to the Spades card game. Winning or losing a "hand" (one deal of the dominos) is based on whether the bidder and his/her partner make their bid. A game is comprised of winning seven "hands," and usually a night of play involves one or two games.

Avery and Shirley had been playing 42 regularly with their close missionary friends, Bill and Dellanna O'Brien, during the eight-month period the Willises lived in Semarang. In order to keep frustration of "bad plays" from marring marriages, they teamed up with each other's spouses so that Bill and Shirley regularly took on Avery and Dellanna. Unlike most players, however, in addition to their weekly games, they kept a running total of the number of hands won and lost. Amazingly, the score had remained quite close throughout all their games. Avery tells the rest:

About a month ago, we were five hands behind, then eight hands behind. The next night we thought we would play it off so we played fifty-two hands in one night and we won an equal number of hands, meaning we were still eight hands behind. Then, on Friday night, we played and caught up to within one hand, but the longer we played, the more we lost, until by the time we quit playing, we were thirteen hands behind. Bill said we had "really cooked our goose."

The next Wednesday would be the final time we could play for three years because the O'Briens were returning to the U.S. for a longer stay, and by the time they returned, we would be on furlough. So we dubbed this the "42 Olympics."

That night, we won five of seven games, closing the gap on the number of hands we were behind. By midnight, Shirley and Bill were ready to quit, but Dellanna and I would not agree. We offered to play till we could break even. By then, it was nearly 1:00 a.m., so we all decided the next hand would be our final hand, regardless of the outcome. We were still down three hands. We realized the only way to stay in the fight was if one of us bid two marks [worth two hands but not a single trick or domino can be lost] *and the other bid three marks.*

Although I did not have a very good hand, I bid two marks. Shirley almost raised it to three marks but didn't want to gamble when they were ahead. So Dellanna raised the bid to three marks. Any other time, Bill would have bid four marks just for the competition, but realized that if he did and lost the hand, they would lose. He said, "You are going to risk it all and end up more hands behind."

I retorted, "You know it, buddy! But when you are behind and it gets down to the last ten seconds, you have to throw the long pass!"

Dellanna had a good hand to start with, and I saved the right domino for the last trick, and we won! That meant after all these months, we came out exactly even, which was perfect, better than if either team had won. I laughed, and laughed, and laughed till they all thought I was possessed. It was just such fun! I could hardly sleep that night for the excitement of it.

Released to New Vision

Avery was a man of vision. He had arrived in Semarang in August, and by his journal entries in September, it was obvious that he had already begun to dream and plan how to maximize spiritual impact by discipling and equipping the seminary students, and training them to disciple others.

September 1970 – Diary

I am enjoying teaching the Preaching class and I am going to add some time in the schedule to allow the students more practice.

We are going to train some weekend revival teams which could go out to the churches here in Semarang, and later further out. In addition, we are training other teams who could teach on The Deeper Life, on Soul-winning, on Stewardship, or on Teacher Training. My plan would be to take what I have taught on these and use the Navigators approach (or my modification of it) and give these students some actual experience. For instance, when I went to the Pekalogan church to teach the stewardship seminar, I took all the first and second year students with me so they could learn how to teach the presentation. Perhaps they could present to the churches being led by the third- and fourth-year students.

I have also worked out a witness system with the Benar Benar Merdeka [True Freedom]—*a modern translation of the gospel of John that includes illustrations of present day Indonesians and verses already underlined. The students can use it as a tool for evangelism and then leave the book with the person. In the first few weeks, we have given away 149 books and had seventy-three professions of faith. The students have been very surprised at how quickly people have been willing to say yes to Jesus when the gospel is presented in this simple, positive approach.*

We also hope to work on a home witness plan, where you go visit a family and you only give the testimony to entire families. If the whole family will gather, you study with them for four weeks and then you bring them to a commitment to Christ.

I had a discussion with Ebbie Smith when he was here and he has some important thoughts on theological education by extension. He wondered if the mobile Bible school he has started in East Java should be a branch of the seminary and even offer degrees for the students. If that was appealing, perhaps we could continue to produce materials for those who want to learn in other cities and villages, and they could be trained without leaving their homes to come to the seminary.

We have also discussed making a film documentary of the seminary on the pastoral call and training. But honestly, I don't know when we could do it. I have far more responsibilities now than I am able to manage.

In September, Avery chaired a committee to organize the national churches into a cooperative union of churches. The committee voted to send an Indonesian missionary to Banyuwangi, near Jember, funded exclusively by the churches. Avery was excited for this first indigenous missionary. He said, *I believe it is a significant step.*

By February, Avery's film idea had become a reality. He worked with the Indonesian Radio-TV Commission, using Super 8 film and a magnetic soundtrack, to create a movie called *Angkatla MataMu (Lift Up Your Eyes)*, which demonstrated the internal struggle of a young man who feels God's call to the ministry. The lens became the eyes of the man, and viewers heard his thoughts as he faced the commands of Scripture, the crying needs around him, and his own personal desires. The film was made to be shown in the Indonesian churches as an attempt to mobilize people toward outreach and missions.

We worked hard and were able to complete all the filming in two weeks. We filmed at the leprosarium, the literacy class, and the commissioning of the first Indonesian missionaries, Pastor Sarbini and his wife.

A Visit to a Leprosarium
(Quoted from PRAY, June 1971)

We visited a leprosarium during the shooting of the film "Lift Up Your Eyes" to get some shots of human need. The lepers were thrilled that anyone would pay any attention to them, even if it was to photograph their plight. After the shooting, I suggested that Bill O'Brien sing a song or two for them. One of the men spoke up and said, "I can sing a Christian song." With that he began to sing, in English:

Come, every soul by sin oppressed,
There's mercy with the Lord,
And He will surely give you rest
By trusting in His word...

While we were getting our emotions under control, he
broke into another song, even more apropos:
The great Physician now is near,
The sympathizing Jesus
He speaks the drooping heart to cheer,
Oh, hear the voice of Jesus.
Sweetest note in seraph song,
Sweetest name on mortal tongue
Sweetest carol ever sung,
Jesus, blessed Jesus.

> *He sang slowly, with deep feeling, and as we looked at those disfigured faces, stubs of fingers, and missing feet, we got a new appreciation of God's love.*
>
> *I made arrangements to come back and hold a service for them later. I took ten seminary students with me. They led the service and then we talked with each patient privately. Eight of these oppressed souls trusted the Great Physician.*

Always on the newest edge of technology, Avery had begun using cassettes to record his diaries and send letters home to the US. Now he envisioned and began a "cassette recorder ministry" in conjunction with the Radio-TV Commission to place cassette recorders in areas without a Christian witness, using the language of the area.

Besides all of this, Avery felt a strong sense from the Lord during several times of prayer that he needed to work in earnest on his doctoral thesis on the religious revival in Indonesia following the Communist coup. Although he still had his normal responsibilities, he declined preaching any revivals for the summer to set aside time to do his research and simultaneously gather information that might enable him to write a popular book on the same topic.[1]

He was also considering writing a book on revival, especially outlining his own experiences with the filling of the Spirit and including revival experiences he had witnessed during his time in Indonesia.

God at Work: The Way of Revival

It seemed that revival often broke out when Avery preached. In each case, Avery anticipated the Holy Spirit's desire to change hearts and thus created an environment for prayer, confession of sin, commitment, and fresh visitations of the Holy Spirit. He believed no real heart change could occur without these.

He recorded the following occurrences in his monthly *PRAY* newsletters over the years:

Youth Conference at the Seminary in Semarang - September 1967

I brought a series of messages on the Holy Spirit over the five-day conference. On the fourth night, we invited them to come and kneel at the altar and be filled with the Spirit. Moving prayers signified the penetrating presence of the Spirit as broken-hearted confession of sin emptied hearts for the forthcoming filling. Many were the evidences of a renewed faith and power in the lives of these youth, 90% of them attending their first youth conference. By the final night, over a third of the attendees declared their willingness to serve Christ as pastors and full-time workers so that all Indonesia might hear the Gospel. They returned home with spirits ablaze heralding, "Let's win Indonesia in our generation!"

Surabaya Rally - January 1970

Recently, I preached in Surabaya at a city-wide rally in preparation for the 1970 Asian Evangelistic Campaign. After preaching from Jeremiah 8 when God called his people to repentance, revival broke out. People streamed down the aisles, broken-heartedly confessing their sins. After about sixty had made soul-wrenching decisions, I asked if they would like to share with us the sins they confessed and for which they had received forgiveness. One after another, they stood with tears streaming down their cheeks to tell of their sins and ask their fellow Christians to forgive them, too. This is difficult for anyone, but it is especially difficult for Indonesians who do not want to "lose face."

One man confessed hating another who was present (calling him by name). Afterwards, I saw them embracing.

Perhaps the most moving moment came when the treasurer of the host church confessed to stealing from the church because he was out of work. He promised to pay back every rupiah. A member of a sister church stood to say that God had blessed him for tithing and he would repay the debt of the first man.

The service lasted three hours and I finally had to stop. But revival had begun.

Seminary Revival - April 1970

A feeling of anticipation filled the air as 125 Baptist seminary students stood to sing the revival theme song. For months, they had planned for revival and for the past four weeks had met every morning at 5:00 a.m. for an hour of prayer.

I preached morning and night for the five days on the theme, "The Servant that Pleases God." I led the morning prayer meetings in conversational prayer. God visited us in these times of fellowship with Him.

The invitation given the last night and the following morning became a Pentecost for us. Five seminary professors received those coming to make decisions. One of the professors suddenly made his way to the platform to tell me, "I didn't come to receive others. I came to confess my sin. Pray for me."

At the close of the service, the entire front of the auditorium was filled with students, many of them freshmen. They stood one by one to confess to their fellow students the sins they had already confessed to God. They confessed loss of faith, hating other students, desires to give up the ministry, etc.

The next morning, we all knelt for prayer and I prayed for them to be filled with the Spirit. Never have I seen more broken-heartedness for sin. They took up the prayer and wept their way to the throne of grace. Although they were crying and praying at the same time, there was no sense of disorderliness; rather, we sensed the Holy Spirit's leading to a deeper walk with God. After nearly thirty minutes of prayer, they asked for time to confess their sins. This time it was the junior and senior students who led the way. The song leader confessed he had planned to leave seminary the next week if he hadn't experienced a personal revival. Other pastors told of blaming their churches when they were at fault themselves. Another told of hating a professor, others of lying, and on and on. It was two hours after the message before we were able to bring the service to a close.

One sign of true revival was evident when I asked many of them to consider going back to the desas [rural villages], *which was considered a step down for an educated graduate.*

Many responded, saying they felt the burden to go to these poor areas where 80% of the Javanese people live. We shout with Zechariah, "Not by might, nor by power, but by my Spirit, says the Lord of Hosts" (4:6).

Semarang Revival - August 1970

The Faith Baptist Church in Semarang has demonstrated again that revivals come through prayer. They began praying and preparing for the Kabaria '70 evangelism campaign two years ago, along with the other churches in Indonesia. Six months ago, they organized fourteen neighborhood prayer groups, which met weekly in the homes of members. They invited their lost friends, and many made decisions before the revival meetings began.

The week preceding the revival they gathered at the church at 5:00 a.m. daily to pray for an hour. The twenty-four-hour prayer chains brought everything to a climax. The chairman of the prayer committee took her vacation time to be able to pray and visit each day. As a result, people were saved every day of the revival meetings. During the week, 142 people made decisions, forty-five of them—mostly adults—to follow Christ. The prayer groups are continuing to meet weekly and are becoming "follow-up" fellowships where the new converts can grow in an atmosphere of love and prayer.

Minahasa Revival - August 1972

Minahasa is the far northern tip of the Sulawesi island of Indonesia. Over 95% of its six hundred thousand residents claim to be Christians. I was invited to preach at the triennial convention of the seven thousand-member KGPI denomination. Many of their leaders had graduated from our seminary and have pastored Baptist churches in Java.

One of the reasons I accepted the invitation was that I felt that the people of Minahasa could be ideal missionaries to all of Indonesia. They are easily accepted by all ethnic groups, and their unusual wealth could support a large indigenous missionary force. They raise thousands of tons of cloves a year and give liberally. Another reason was the many people who profess Christianity without possessing Christ.

During the first week I preached in several churches in the mountains; some had not had a white man in the area for seventeen years. The second week I taught the Bible and preached to their convention an average of four hours a day. One of the things that made this revival unique was the opportunity to lay a theological base for God's plan of world redemption through the spiritual ministry of all His people. Every morning at 5:00 a.m. we had a prayer meeting attended by over a hundred delegates. The first morning some of them were two-and-a-half hours early to the prayer meeting. They woke us up at 4:00 a.m. singing. I introduced conversational prayer and God used it to spark revival as He has in every other place I have introduced it in the past ten years.

The second night the president of the convention and many others stood and confessed their sins. Preachers who had hated one another for years confessed openly and were reconciled. Confession continued the next morning at the prayer time as we prayed in twenty small groups.

The third day I taught for four-and-a-half hours about the Holy Spirit's ministry, His gifts to equip His people, and His power to work through them. It was climaxed by a sermon on how to be filled with the Holy Spirit. After explaining the absolute demands of the Spirit on our lives, I asked those who wanted to be filled to kneel. I expected a few to do so. To my surprise almost everyone kneeled. Great soul-wrenching prayers went up to God as confessions were made; then praise rose up to Him as the refreshing showers fell. It was certain that the Spirit had filled the place and the hearts of His servants as they prayed for over an hour.

The Lord intervened in the plane schedule so we could stay for the final Sunday service—truly, the climax of the week. At this final service I called for a dedication of this denomination to missionary service. From the beginning of the invitation I was flooded with people who wanted to surrender themselves as missionaries, who wanted to use their means to support missions, who wanted to rededicate their lives, etc. The president called on those preachers who had already made decisions to help receive those who were coming. We were still overrun, so he said, "This week we have learned that we are all ministers. There are not enough preachers to help, so you all should minister to one another."

It was glorious! I have never seen God turn the leadership of a denomination so thoroughly upside down—or, more accurately, right side up. They established a department of missions and made plans to send missionaries to Borneo, Sumatra, and Sanggir Taluud. The president said to me, "God has dropped an atomic bomb on us. We will have to rebuild along His lines. We will be calling on you for more help and advice! We pray that this revival will spread to the other churches of Minahasa and the other islands of Indonesia."

Sequel to the Minahasa Revival - January 1975

Avery returned to northern Sulawesi in January 1975 at the request of the leadership of this now ten thousand-member denomination. During the 1972 revival, the president of their convention had said, "You have dropped a bomb on us." When Avery reminded him that it was God who had dropped the bomb, he replied, "You, at least, pushed the button."

Now Avery had been invited to speak on missions at the pastors' conference.

Alex Tairus, the president, greeted him with the question, "Well, do you want to see how that bomb is still exploding? We have become a missionary church."

In two short years, they had sent missionaries to the Indonesian islands of North Sumatra, Borneo, Halmahera, and Central Sulawesi. "But we are having problems paying our missionaries. We had voted a four-million-rupiah convention budget, including their expenses, but as soon as a new missionary would be appointed, some individual would say, 'I want to be responsible for paying their salary.' So after sending four missionaries, we still have all that money. Therefore, we are planning to appoint five more this year. God has blessed us financially since we became a missionary church. We have already spent six million rupiah this year and have another five million in the bank. We have more money than missionaries right now. That's why we wanted you to come preach on missions to our pastors and their wives."

In the week that followed, Avery taught mission methods to nearly a hundred conferees and preached to approximately four hundred each night. Twenty-five people, mostly pastors and their wives, surrendered to go as missionaries to other parts of Indonesia.

He was also invited to speak to the convention on theological education by extension. They had already voted to close their seminary and moved three professors out to various areas of Sulawesi to begin the programs. They expected to enroll up to 150 people, including many of the pastors who had not had the opportunity for seminary education. "We anticipate that, by this method, we can equip our missionaries, and at the same time provide new leadership for the churches they will leave," claimed Rev. Tairus. "I have already told the deacons of the churches that if God sends *all* the pastors out as missionaries, they should be ready to take over and lead!"

Healing in Vietnam
(Told by Sam James, Steve Brown, and Avery's Taped Diary)

Steve Brown, new journeyman missionary to Vietnam, took one look at Avery Willis, wearing his white pants, maroon shirt, and white sports coat (a "'70s outfit" purchased on furlough and worn for the cool mountain temperatures) and thought, "Oh, no. They sent us an evangelist!"

It was November 1974, and the situation in Vietnam was precarious. The American military had withdrawn the year before, and it was evident everywhere that the Communist forces were gaining momentum. Baptist missionaries in Vietnam were seeing good response to the gospel, but times were increasingly tense. The Mission decided to have its annual spiritual retreat in the central highlands city of Dalat, known as the City of Eternal Spring. These retreats usually afforded a good balance of spiritual enrichment and encouragement mixed with times of fun and fellowship. Ernie Bengs, who had been one of the "inner circle" of the Spirit-filled prayer meetings at OBU, was Mission chairman and had invited Avery to come from Indonesia to lead the spiritual retreat.

As Avery began to speak on the need for confession of sin, forgiveness, and reconciliation, Steve felt the Lord convict his heart. During the ministry time, Steve invited John, another journeyman, to go outside with him. They sat on the steps, and Steve confessed his dislike, anger, and jealousy toward John and asked for his forgiveness. It turned out the feeling was mutual. The two talked more about their differing personalities but asked for and received forgiveness for their attitudes toward each other's ministry.

When they walked back in to the room, others were sharing. Steve asked Avery to come off the stage and be seated with the others. He asked Avery's forgiveness for judging him and then shared the experience he and John had just had.

After the program finished, Avery suggested that anyone who would like to stay was invited to join him for a time of spontaneous prayer and sharing. A few gathered in a small room, lit a fire in the fireplace, sat on the floor, and allowed the Holy Spirit to lead. From time to time someone would share a Scripture verse or begin singing a song or just utter a spontaneous prayer of praise, confession, or supplication. Each night the group grew until the room was almost at capacity.

One of the missionaries, Prissy Tunnell, had been suffering from advanced inflammation and fungus in her ear. Rachel James, nurse practitioner and medical consultant for the Mission, had gone with her to every ENT specialist in Vietnam, but there was no improvement. It was decided that she was going to have to go to Hong Kong for special treatment as the pain had become unbearable and there was concern that she could lose hearing in that ear.

On the final evening, missionaries continued to open up, share, and ask one another for forgiveness. Relationships were renewed and made whole, sins confessed, and needs met through prayer, affirmation, and laying on of hands. That night Prissy came to the prayer time. Sam James recalled, "As the evening progressed, the presence of the Lord among the group was especially intense. It was as though the Spirit of God was at work in everyone as they prayed and sang. At one point in the evening the room became quiet. The atmosphere was unusually spiritually charged, as though we could actually touch the presence of God."

Slowly, Prissy moved to the center of the room on her knees and spoke. She said that her ear was aching so badly she could hardly stand it. The noise in her ear was deafening. For a long time, she had not been able to sing anything because the noise in her ears was so great that she could not find the notes. She begged, "Please pray that the Lord will take away the ache and the deafening sound in my ear." The missionaries gathered around, laid hands on her, and prayed for healing.

She returned to where she was sitting. Again all was quiet for a long period. Suddenly, she moved forward. "It's gone! It's gone!

The aching is gone! The noise in my ear is no longer there!" she announced.

Someone said, "Sing, Prissy, sing." She then began singing a version of the Lord's Prayer so beautiful and Spirit-filled that everyone was in tears.

The next morning Rachel went to Prissy's room with otoscope in hand to examine her ears. Her ear was completely clear. No fungus could be found anywhere. A divine healing had occurred.

Six months later, South Vietnam fell to the Communists, and the missionaries were forced to evacuate. Steve was given options for reassignment, and he ended up choosing to work at the student center in Semarang, where Avery and Shirley lived. As hot as it was in Semarang, Avery donned the white sports coat to meet Steve at the airport.

Little did either of them know that Steve would one day be Avery's son-in-law. One Christmas after Steve and Sherrie were married, Steve opened a gift from Avery. Inside was the white coat.

Revival

Revival through the work of the Holy Spirit was central to Avery's life message—one he would preach repeatedly. However, he had little hint as to what would be in store for him when God sent revival into Avery's own sphere of influence. Even while he was teaching at the seminary, a confluence of events was setting the stage for dramatic changes that would ripple not only through Avery's leadership in the seminary, but through the entire Indonesian Mission and national churches—and even to other parts of the world!

CHAPTER 15
Collision Course

Two swelling tsunami waves, one divine and the other human, were headed toward each other, destined for a collision! The Spirit of God was hovering over the souls of men, calling them to find refreshment and power through Him. At the same time, a groundswell of unrest, coupled with an unwillingness to yield power, was brewing a storm of conflict.

The Wave of the Spirit

Spiritual revival and renewal began, as it often does, in the lives of individuals.

January 26, 1971

The Lord has really been doing something with Bill O. It began with the shortage of funds in the station accounts. No one has been able to figure out what happened to the money. But Bill added it up and decided that the shortage was nearly equivalent to the back tithe he had not yet have given to the Lord on his U.S. account, so he offered to make up the difference. This act of obedience jumpstarted his spiritual pilgrimage. Now he comes in almost every day with some exciting thing that has happened to him or another witness he has been able to make: helping a starving boy, testifying to his Dutch teacher, etc.

From various quarters, we are seeing a movement of the Spirit among us. Ruth V. had a unique experience. She had served two terms in Indonesia as an accomplished anesthetist before taking a leave of absence and returning to the United States in 1969, a spiritually defeated missionary. Through an unusual working of the Holy Spirit, she came to

God in confession of sin that culminated in what she described as her initial conversion. The following day she was filled with the Holy Spirit. During the next few months, God miraculously opened the way so she could return to Indonesia. In the few months since her return we have all agreed with the Indonesian who said, "That's a new Ms. Vandy."

Bill S. has been reading the journals of John Wesley and the daily miracles he experienced. I noticed Von was reading The Holy Spirit: Who He is and What He Does.

Roger, a missionary friend in Mexico, reports weekly and monthly of miracles, people being saved by the scores, people healed, and even reported one raising from the dead as if it were a common daily occurrence.

I am thrilled to see more emphasis on the daily movement and immediacy of the Spirit, but some of these things I don't know how to take. It is easy to believe whatever you want if you accept it all with a non-critical mind. Or are these things really happening and because of my scientific orientation, I hesitate to accept some of the real miracle-working power of God? One thing difficult to deny is that there is a great change of life among most of the people I have seen who encounter the Spirit.

My concern for my own life is that I don't bypass anything the Spirit has for me or any way He wants to use me. I am convinced of the filling of the Spirit in my own life, and yet I realize there could be an even fuller experience of the Spirit—perhaps related to a deeper prayer life, because my prayer life has slipped this past year from what it used to be. I realize a need for more prayer. I keep hoping and praying that the Lord will give me more openness to Him and that I will be a better channel for His work.

God had been working in the lives of many individuals in the months preceding the annual prayer retreat such that many came expecting God to work. Many prayer partners and churches around the world had been asked to pray for this retreat, including over five thousand families that received the Willises' monthly *PRAY* newsletter. Prayer retreats in other areas had been more spiritual than usual, but it was at the Central Java prayer retreat in February 1971, where the Spirit moved mightily.

The program for the retreat was a Bible study, led by Marvin Leech, on the "Fullness of Joy" and messages on the "Fullness of the Spirit" by Ed Sanders. Avery led the prayer times that followed each session.

On Friday night, I explained briefly how to pray conversationally and how to create a loving group that could receive anyone's confession of sin. One by one, missionaries began to pour out their hearts asking to be filled with the Holy Spirit. The barrenness of heart, the powerlessness in service, and the emptiness of living by human power instead of in the Spirit were confessed for two or more hours.

Everyone assembled the next morning with a new expectancy and desire to pray. Early in the morning, prayer partners went up into the hills and found a quiet place to pray. Later, men and women prayed in separate groups. In the men's group, one missionary said that before he could pray he had to confess negative feelings he'd had about another person in the group. He asked for forgiveness and received it on the spot. Another man, who had experienced a particularly difficult past two years, poured out his heart to God, requesting forgiveness and help. Someone suggested that we lay hands on him as was done in the New Testament. Never have I seen such love poured out on a person as was poured out on him through his brothers in the Spirit.

On Saturday evening, the prayer time began with confession to God and prayers for forgiveness. The Spirit began to probe deeper and deeper into our lives, motives, and relationships. Hypocrisy, bitterness, lust, hate, grumblings, skepticism, selfishness, covetousness, and sins of the flesh were laid before the forgiving Lord. Lives were presented to Christ to be filled and be baptized in the Spirit. Who knows what time we went to bed that night?

One missionary requested prayer for a serious illness which five doctors had been unable to help cure, even with an operation. As we prayed for him and laid hands on him, an unusual river of the Spirit flowed over us. Some sobbed uncontrollably. Some fell on their faces unable to do anything else. Someone began to sing the Lord's Prayer and others joined in. It was as if a Great Conductor led in the most beautiful rendition of the song any of us had ever heard. The man is going out of the country tomorrow and will be examined. We are confident that God has worked a miracle in him.

On Sunday night, I opened the final session as an unstructured testimony and prayer time and then tried to stay out of the way so the Spirit could move. Testimonies of praise moved into prayers of intercession and then into songs as described in Ephesians 5:18–20. No one wanted to stop the worship. We had begun at 7:30 p.m. and reluctantly stopped at 2 a.m. The usual games of cards or dominoes were replaced by spontaneous prayer.[1]

One missionary reported:

I personally didn't really know what revival meant. But at that time, I experienced what love was—what God's love was for me. I found out how other people loved me and how I could love other people. It was just as though God Himself walked into that meeting and descended on us all in the form of love. Because of that, I am a different person. I am not a better person. In fact, I realize now more than ever my shortcomings and faults—my sins. But I have a new capacity to love God, love others, and love myself.

Dr. Catherine Walker described it this way:

I think what was most characteristic of the retreat was the total honesty and openness and freedom from play-acting. The first night when we began to pray, there was such an openness to tell God, even in front of other people, all that we were not experiencing but wanted to experience, all of our heart hunger. The prayers seemed to be such a deep crying out to the Lord with great agony of soul. I was astonished at the thoughts expressed, because looking at people outwardly, I would not have known they had such doubts, unbelief, and emptiness. If I was so deeply touched by those prayers, how must the Lord feel? I was confident that He would bring refreshment and comfort and joy.

I think we felt that this was not a passing event but something that would go on, because we knew that Christ had taken hold of us. I know Christ will begin to pour out on the seminary and I know this is going to spill over to our national brethren and our families at home—in the life of anyone who will let Christ come in and be in charge.[2]

The revival spread to missionaries in other parts of Indonesia and into the churches. The Sunday following the retreat, Avery preached in Solo, and people streamed to the altar during the invitation. The wife of the local missionary told the congregation about the prayer retreat and asked their forgiveness for her bitter feelings against some of them, her laziness, her obstructing a revival there the previous June, and more. Church leaders led the way as people came to confess sin and repent.

In the two months Avery preached after the prayer retreat, over four hundred people made decisions, including 130 for salvation and seventy for special service.[3]

The revival spread to the Seminary. Indonesian professors brought messages in chapel about the Spirit. The students shared what God was doing in their lives.

One student told of receiving the Spirit and he was now seeing conversions in his church.

Another told of feeling so empty that he tried to get other people to preach for him. He thought perhaps he would leave the church. But as he began to pray, he saw all the troubles in the lives of the members of his congregation. As a result of his prayers, he began to see those issues turn around.

Several students who were about to drop out of seminary, and maybe the ministry, have been revived. One student who was to be sent to a psychiatric hospital discovered that his problem was spiritual. When he dealt with it spiritually, he no longer needed treatment. Dramatic reconciliations between students have brought a new fellowship in the Spirit. There is a fresh wave of faith that God is doing something great![4]

The Wave of Human Conflict

During 1970, the Indonesian Council of Churches had begun an in-depth study of Indonesian churches, culture, politics, religion, and economics. Avery was the chairman for the Baptist contribution to the study. He was pleased to review the surveys as this study dovetailed nicely with his own doctoral research. He compiled the results and summarized the data in a seventy-five-page document for the Baptist leadership to study. The dialogue with the national pastors about these results was so successful that the survey was extended to all Indonesian Baptist work.

In June 1971, Avery met with the committee known as the BKS— *Badan Kerja Sama* (Body Working Together)—whose task was to formulate a structure to organize the Indonesian churches. They were to make their recommendations at the Musjawarah in August. A *musjawarah* is an Indonesian concept where all parties come together, give input, and mutually negotiate a solution. The growing pains of an evolving organism became obvious as the discussion deepened.

This was one of the most fruitful meetings I have been in with our Indonesian brethren. We came to look at ourselves: our history, attitudes, statistics, goals, hopes, and our working relationships. We quickly learned where the key problems lie: how we work together—and the part that money plays in that.

We compared our relationship to that of a father and adolescent son. The national churches are not quite mature enough to create their own organizational structure yet. They are trying to develop so they can take equal roles with the missionaries. But they are becoming frustrated in the process.

The Mission as a whole is making an effort to allow the nationals increasing control, but have an established structure we don't really want to set aside. The missionaries have continued to plan and make decisions about allocation of personnel and finances as they have been accustomed to doing.

This has exasperated the national pastors. They are significantly impacted by the Mission's decisions, yet they have no voice into the proceedings. They feel "completely in the dark about what the Mission does and wants to do, that they are not trusted to make or be involved in any major decisions, and their plans can be overridden by the Mission."

In fact, a group of national pastors has already met in Sukabumi because they felt that dealing with the Mission was "like going up against a wall." It had its own structure and rules, and there was no way to change it. They had given up trying to do so and wanted to form their own union of churches and work on their own—without missionary input or oversight.

I was sure this was a mistake. Working as separate units would be like a man standing with one foot each in two boats—sure to result in trouble.

Avery knew relations had reached a tipping point.

This is really a critical time for Baptist work in Indonesia for the next 10-20 years. If our Mission will work with the nationals as brothers on the same level, I think we will head off trouble. But if we are hard-headed, there will be a rupture in the fellowship and they will go off on their own.

So we have to ask ourselves this question, "What would happen if missionaries and nationals worked together to decide how to use capital funds or determine personnel assignments? This would certainly be a radical departure from how we have been functioning because we have not involved the nationals in our decisions.[5]

Too often, mission strategy is a conglomerate mess of individual opinions, historical precedents, half-formed hypotheses, and emergency actions. More often than not, our decisions are based not on disciplined research, but personal preferences often acquired long before we ever arrived on the mission field. It is no wonder that nationals want to know where we are going.

Strategy is not a one-way street. Effective strategy must involve both nationals and missionaries with all the knowledge and abilities at their disposal. Usually we shrug it off by saying that we are waiting for the nationals to take the initiative. Of course, they must determine the direction of Baptist life in their own country, but instead of our encouraging them to take the initiative, we often put them off with our happenstance strategy until they rebel and take over.[6]

Eddie W., a national pastor and leader, adamantly promoted the option of establishing a *Gabungan*—a self-directed national union of churches—but letting the Mission continue to be responsible for everything else (hospitals, publishing, Radio-TV, etc.) until the Union had grown to sufficient strength to take on further responsibilities.

By the time the BKS meetings ended, further self-discovery and self-determination was the assignment. Before the Musjawarah meeting in two months, all sides would decide what they could and were willing to do. The Mission would discuss what they would be able to surrender over to the Union. The "Sukabumi group" would discuss how they envisioned the Union working. The BKS committee would get feedback from pastors.

Simultaneously, the Mission was hearing from their own sources. They reviewed the report of a survey that missionary Ebbie Smith had administered on attitudes of church members, pastors, and missionaries. In addition, two US seminary professors of missions, Dr. Cal Guy and Dr. Bryant Hicks, came to Indonesia and traveled throughout Java, listening to missionaries and pastors to formulate recommendations for improvement. Their findings shook the Mission to its core, calling into question the effectiveness of years of mission strategy.

June 1971– Taped Diary

Dr. Cal Guy and Dr. Bryant Hicks have arrived and have conducted their survey work in Semarang. The results were similar to what they have found in other places. Almost uniformly, they said the pastors were denouncing missionaries, and church members were denouncing preachers. The unhappiness of the pastors toward the missionaries stems from experiencing a lack of love and trust and not feeling on the same level with them. They are also generally unhappy because they want more money for buildings and salaries. Church members feel the pastors are not working hard enough and are acting as dictators.

Dr. Guy and Dr. Hicks were keenly disappointed at finding so much friction tied to money and property ownership. They were so upset by the product our seminary was putting out that they thought the seminary might ought to be closed entirely. They even thought we might need to "write off" a whole generation of students and buildings and start over out in the villages. These positions were quite radical, but they felt if we didn't make some drastic changes, they couldn't return to the U.S. to advocate for our mission work here.

On Monday, I met with Pastor Sudarso. Now I am beginning to understand how they feel if they have met pastor after pastor who feel like Sudarso. He said that the big problem was that the missionaries came to Indonesia to spread the gospel, but in practice, it was really the Indonesians doing it. It was alright if he were used as a tool to do so, but that the tool should be well taken care of and well paid. He said he would work better if he had more money. After eight years, he was an unhappy pastor with a building and thirty-five to forty members who were not doing much in evangelism. I could understand why Drs. Guy and Hicks questioned the value of the seminary if this was the type of pastor it produced.

I have been trying to sort out my feelings about the results of this survey. Dr. Guy and Dr. Hicks are committed to the idea of winning the most people in the shortest amount of time and believe the way to do that is through the laymen, without subsidy. It will be interesting to see what happens at Mission Meeting.

Avery anticipated that adjustments would be made based on these recommendations, but he could not have imagined the magnitude of change God had in mind!

Spiritual Marker #9

Spiritual revival among the Indonesian missionaries
brought sweeping and dramatic changes
in how the Mission operated.

*They stood where they were and read from the Book of the Law of the
Lord their God for a quarter of the day and spent another quarter
in confession and in worshiping the Lord their God . . .
[and after understanding God's word]
. . . In view of all this, we are making a binding agreement,
putting it in writing, and our leaders, our Levites
and our priests are affixing their seals to it.*
—Nehemiah 9:3 and 36 (NIV)

CHAPTER 16
Spiritual Breakthrough

One thing difficult to deny is that there is a
great change of life among most of the people
I have seen who encounter the Spirit.

—Avery

"Spiritual revival swept among the missionaries at the annual Mission Meeting held in Tretes, Java, in July 1971. Its impact revolutionized the Indonesian Baptist Mission, producing new directions and unprecedented changes in their personal lives and work." So begins the recording "Spiritual Breakthrough in Indonesia." What follows in this chapter are excerpts from the live recording of that event, written and narrated by Avery.[1]

The Mission Meeting of the prior year had been a low spiritual point for many missionaries. Important decisions were needed in light of a shrinking budget, but redundant discussion and pettiness limited the time to make them. After they dispersed, discouragement caused people to seek God anew, and He began renewing individual hearts in response to their prayers.

Dellanna O'Brien spoke for many when she told of beginning a search for a new relationship with her Lord:

> About eight or nine months ago, I woke up one day to what I had really become. I was so unhappy during Mission Meeting last year because there was so much strife and disagreement. I was very critical of my fellow missionaries and of their work. I kept

blaming everyone else. Then I realized it was not so much the Mission as it was me!

Not long after, I was teaching about the Spirit of the Lord descending on Jesus in the form of a dove and that He was baptized in the Spirit as well as water. One of the ladies in the class wanted to know how this related to our lives. What did the baptism of the Spirit mean to us?

Although I tried to give an answer, it certainly didn't satisfy me, and I felt sure it didn't satisfy her, either. At that time, I didn't know what it meant—but I couldn't admit that I didn't know. Here I was, a missionary and a long-time Christian, and I couldn't even tell her what baptism in the Spirit meant. It continued to nag me until I became even more dissatisfied. One day, I came to the point of saying, "I can't stand this type of life anymore. There's got to be something else." At that time, I was willing to let go, and let the Spirit enter my life in a new and meaningful way. I began to realize real joy in turning myself over to the Spirit.

Shot to the Heart

This year, with the fresh wind of the Spirit beginning to give new hope, the missionaries came together to discuss the opportunities facing them and the obstacles hindering them in the work they had come around the world to do. The report of Dr. Cal Guy and Dr. Bryant Hicks shattered their complacency like a bombshell on the second day of the meeting.

Dr. Hicks, himself a former missionary to the Philippines, told of his own spiritual pilgrimage related to the survey:

I came here with the knowledge that God had communicated to me internally in a way I cannot define, nor am I accustomed to, that I wasn't coming out to participate in a survey but to participate in a most amazing growing kind of experience in the Holy Spirit that Southern Baptists had ever known—not a revival where you get worked up for six weeks but the kind that has residual and growing impact in the lives of people—on the order of Pentecost.

This spiritual experience that God has foretold may be as quiet as a gentle breeze or may be a whirlwind. I don't know—and I don't care—but I believe it is going to happen. It has already started. I have seen God bring you to the place where you are saying, "Oh, God, *anything* but what it is now."

Our responsibility is to bring up areas of general concern, some of which are so touchy that they have not received the needed ventilation or been laid out in the open where we believe they belong for the good health of the whole Mission. And secondly, we are to bring concrete recommendations to be discussed and decided by *all* of the Mission. It is time to look at the total work to reach millions of lost souls in Indonesia. If after hearing this, you make decisions to protect your own feelings or situations, rather than the harvest of souls, it will be an incredible failure.

Dr. Guy joined in:

The first necessity is to be vessels, willing to be filled with the Holy Spirit and coming to the end of ourselves. I think many of you have joined many of us in America who have acted as field generals, and in quiet despair, want Him to take control again. We don't think this will be an occasion for embarrassment, except where it is necessary to go down in order to go up. Whatever God calls for, we will do. This is a great day and I am scared to death.

In a twenty-page report, Drs. Guy and Hicks reported the strengths of having churches and missionaries in all of the most populous areas of Java and Sumatra and a record of growth that was one of the best in Southern Baptist Convention mission history. But they also pointed out failures in the work. It was clear a Western style of church life had been imported and imposed on indigenous cultural patterns. The missionaries realized they had often acted unilaterally and paternally toward the maturing Indonesian leadership, causing tensions to mount.

The men reported:

We found almost absolute dependence on Western funds for any consideration of further development. This is a crippling preoccupation. Such dependence is disastrous if it continues. Dependence on Western methods, buildings, and programs has effectively blocked communication and become a non-reproducible system.

We must radically redirect the work. We recommend switching to a pattern of producing congregations that can be infinitely multiplied by local leadership and economy. This means a New Testament pattern of "the church in your house"—which requires no money—and a lay leader who requires no salary. Each missionary should plan for and conduct the most extensive program of training to develop local lay pastors and other volunteer leaders.

An Organic Move of the Spirit

In the presence of the Holy Spirit and one another, the missionaries reflected on themselves, their reasons for coming to Indonesia, and the work they had done. As they did so, they began to confess their shortcomings and deep hunger for the work of God.

Again and again, the set order of service was set aside as one or more of the missionaries led in spontaneous prayer, testimony, confession, and praise. One missionary confessed, "In fifteen years on the mission field, I have not led one soul to Christ. I have taught the Bible and tried to do personal witnessing, and I have helped some people come to the Lord. But I have yet to experience someone actually giving his life to Christ as a direct, immediate result of my testimony."

Another stated, "Few, if any of you, have ever seen me angry. But there is one in our fellowship who has repeatedly felt the venom of my wrath." He sobbed out the rest, "And that's my wife."

A new missionary relayed, "I was recently treated at the hospital for blood poisoning. But the poison in my body was nothing compared to the poison in my soul—the critical, unforgiving attitude I have had toward some of you older missionaries. Praise the Lord, both poisons have been drained!"

One man told of his experience of pouring out his sin after a motor scooter accident several months prior:

> While my wife was in school those mornings, I lay in that bed and I just looked at myself. I said, "Lord, I am going to name them all to you." And I poured all my sins that I had been holding in my life since a child. I tried to name them one by one because though Jesus has forgiven me of my sins, the devil through the years has come back time and time again and accused me—and I couldn't forgive myself. I couldn't be convinced that God really loved me. In the last four months, I have discovered that God loves me! He loves me!

On the fourth day, Dr. Guy led the Bible study from 1 John 4: "Beloved, let us love one another, for love comes from God. Since God so loved us, we ought also to love one another. If you say, 'I love God', whom you have not seen, but do not love your brother whom you have seen, how can you say you know love?" Dr. Guy then invited the missionaries to express their love to one another.

The sound of revival and a flood of love inundated the room as individuals went to one another and shared the depth of their love and appreciation. Sometimes, they needed to first confess their sins to each other and make right their relationships.

For some, it was the highest peak of their spiritual lives. But they weren't going to wait long before there was another work of the Spirit—this time among the teenage children of the missionaries. The adults were back in session when suddenly twenty excited teenagers burst in, saying, "We know what you've got, and we've got it too!" Tony, a nineteen-year-old student worker from Georgia, explained what had happened:

> We were about to have a debate, when one of the teenagers said that a missionary had come and asked his forgiveness for harboring hard feelings against him because of his shoulder-length hair. The teenager said, "The adults have something we don't have." So we began to pray, and study the Bible, and confess our sins, and praise the Lord. We, too, have felt the outpouring of God's Spirit.

After embracing their parents and missionary "aunts and uncles" and confessing, through sobs, their genuine love and regret for past misdeeds, the young people picked up guitars and led the adults in worship.

This love extended to lost people living near the meeting site. The young people fanned out over the mountain, passing out five thousand tracts, and witnessing in Indonesian, Javanese, and English, singing, and holding brief services—one of them in a nearby open field, when a man's home proved too small to hold the crowd. They returned, rejoicing that an elderly woman had turned to Christ.

Dr. Guy summed up the awakening hopes of joining God in His work:

> I want to share with you my amazement that a group of missionaries would be willing to move as boldly as you have moved. It is a new thing on this earth. In so many ways, God is putting together a number of factors that have us standing on the threshold of

something exciting beyond description. Somewhere our conversation has changed from praying for 70,000 to 80,000 or even a half million new baptisms by 1981 and now we are talking about a million. We believe this is God. We think in your hands is the opportunity to galvanize Southern Baptists for a new day in foreign missions. Your mature, eyes-open response to the offer God is making to you may take us beyond talking about the difference between 10,000 or 20,000 or even between 80,000 and a million, but may have worldwide implications.

The Rubber Hits the Road

In the midst of these uplifting spiritual hours, however, missionaries were brought back to reality by the frightening proposals hammered out in the wee hours of the morning. Among the more startling ramifications of changing the mission strategy were the gradual ending of mission subsidies for Baptist churches and pastors, the discontinuation of the current seminary education program into a new design of field evangelism, fuller cooperation with Indonesian Baptists, and considerable change in the lifestyle of mission families.

Coincidentally, or providentially, Dr. David Stewart, a psychiatrist who worked with the Foreign Mission Board, was present at the Mission Meeting that year. He shared his insights:

> A scientist must be prepared to re-evaluate a thesis he has worked on for twenty years if his hypothesis does not bear out. If, by his own hand, he proves it false, he must pick up the pieces and go again in a different direction.
>
> It takes real courage to make a basic change on an individual or collective basis. It takes courage to pile up all of your life's winnings to this point and risk it all on one turn of the wheel. But there are points in life when we, as Christians, can do no less. If we

believe what we say we believe, and God is directing, then of course, it's not even a gamble. But it can be frightening because we are human. It can be painful because we are uncertain, and it may feel like groping in the dark. There are no guideposts for the way you are headed.

The report of how evangelism would be carried out became the foundation of the entire New Pattern of Work. It began with a confession and then outlined the proposed changes:

We, the missionaries of the Indonesian Baptist Mission, confess and sincerely regret our failure in spiritual life and many aspects of our method of work. We have not properly functioned as the Body of Christ in that we have become too involved in organization and materialism to the neglect of spiritual ministry. We feel that we have limited the Indonesian Baptist churches from evangelizing the masses of Indonesia by imposing upon them a Western pattern of Christian life, which is not in keeping with the national culture, economy, and aspirations.

Therefore, having been led by the Holy Spirit to recognize the limitations of our past approach to win the masses of Indonesia to Christ, we feel compelled by the Holy Spirit to follow what we interpret to be a better way.

First, missionary energies should be directed immediately toward the priority of the evangelization of the masses of Indonesia through the establishment of thousands of house churches. These house churches shall consist of several neighbors, gathering daily if possible, in homes, to be led by their natural lay leader in unstructured worship, centered around the reading of the Bible. In light of the definition that a church is "a body of baptized believers in Jesus Christ as Lord and Savior, covenanted together for worship, fellowship, study, ministry, and witness," these house churches should choose their own spiritual leader and observe the ordinances, as they feel led by the Spirit. Each believer is a priest before God with the freedom and responsibility to spread the gospel and lead his family and others in worship, centered around the Bible. We will depend upon the Holy Spirit to lead these people in ever-widening circles to begin new house churches.

Development beyond the house church stage will be entirely in the hands of these Christians. No subsidy shall be given to any leader or group for salary, house, equipment, transportation, or meeting places. This includes mission funds, gifts, tithes, or special gifts. The missionaries' tithes and offerings shall be given carefully so that no church is dependent upon them.

The role of the missionary is to:

- minister in the Spirit, building up Christians so they can minister to others;
- itinerate in new areas, seeking responsive people, who will begin additional house churches; and
- serve as a teacher for Christian leadership training.

Dr. Keith Parks, Area Secretary, expressed the difficulty of implementing this pattern in an emotion-filled speech:

> There will be a reaction [to the removal of subsidies]. Unless we are convicted that we can win more people and see the vision of ultimately impacting this nation, we will not be able to stand the coming pressure.
>
> Love wants God's best for all of His people. In these cases, love is not reacting to pressure nor being guided by emotion. When you sit down to talk to these pastors and students whom you love, who were called to preach while you were preaching, and say to them, "we are changing" when they won't have this background of revival . . . well, they won't understand. They will hate us, some of them, and they will accuse us of not having any compassion or any love. This is the thing we fear the most. When they accuse us of not loving them because we will not help them, we may prove that we love ourselves more than we

love them by doing something to please them so they will think well of us. We must not be so tempted. The level we now need to move in is deep, spiritual conviction. We'll not go through this otherwise. But if we truly believe this is the best way to win Indonesia, the Lord will show us the way to solve these practical problems.

The recommendation that brought about the greatest negative reaction from the missionaries, the nationals, and even the Mission Board was:

In light of the above, the present program of seminary training will be discontinued at the end of the next semester. Missionary personnel there will be re-deployed to develop leadership training programs.

Among those standing to concur with this decision were Frank Lewis, acting president of the seminary; Dr. Catherine Walker, one of the original faculty members; and three other seminary teachers[2]— including Avery.

The Difficult Choice

The missionaries concluded that, ultimately, it was preferable to provide training for hundreds of laymen to lead house churches than to provide a seminary degree for dozens. As it was, the seminary was establishing expectations of a pastorate of a Western-style church complete with a building, salary, transportation, and a full program of church life—something few Indonesian churches could realistically provide. The students became accustomed to such nice accommodations at the seminary they did not want to return to poorer rural areas where the need was greatest. Forty seminary students were to graduate the next year, and many of them had no place to serve. In addition, the imported theological curriculum did not adequately deal with the practical issues faced by the students. It needed to be revised.

While the mature leaders could not leave their work or their family to come to the seminary in Semarang, the seminary was training young people who were not yet considered leaders in the Indonesian culture. A pilot project, the East Java Bible Institute, had already effectively reached these mature leaders as the teacher went to the students' villages.

Dr. Marvin Leech, who had just completed language school and moved to Semarang to teach in the seminary, told of his reaction to this decision:

> I knew basically what the strategy of indigenous missions meant. I was not exactly prepared for the philosophy to be applied in such a specific and direct way to the seminary which means so much to people in Indonesia. [With 125 students, the Indonesian seminary was the largest one in Southeast Asia.] Of course, since it had direct consequences to me, I did have an emotional response of loss and maybe arriving at a dead-end street. But I think I have come to terms with it. I feel the Lord has revealed a new day for us. I feel that I am part of something of permanent significance that will be able to continually reproduce.

After proposing sweeping changes to the seminary, the missionaries addressed the touchy topic of their own standard of living. Many missionaries lived in older Dutch colonial homes, built for the tropics, with their high ceilings and large rooms. Though not large or luxurious by American standards, they were palatial in comparison to Indonesian standards. The recommendation was made to restrict house size to a maximum of 1,600 square feet, closer to the standard of middle-class Indonesians.

Dr. Catherine Walker, professor of counseling at the seminary, led a session to help the missionaries recognize the cost these radical changes would bring. She said:

221

I started grieving yesterday. Since I have been here, I have wept tears of repentance and tears of joy, but now I am weeping tears of grief. I want to tell you that we need to weep. We need a funeral, because we are cutting off or cutting deeply into things we are tied to—things that are precious to us. I know none of us are talking about poverty, but if I move into something less than I have now, that means something has to go. And anything I have now, I have because I like it! I like my space—I don't part with it easily. And I don't part with privacy easily. I don't want to give up my guest room. I like company. I like pretty things.

It's not about being willing to sacrifice. Everyone here is willing to sacrifice. But it hurts. It costs. And we might as well say it does. Under God, I am confident what we are doing is right. But it is going to hurt at some point. So I suggest we face what it will really mean for us—and pray for each other.

Another proposal was the simplification of the entire mission structure and a gradual release of leadership to the Union of Indonesian churches. This was to prepare the way for revival among the nationals. Underlying all the discussion was an awareness that many Indonesian Baptists would not agree with the new directives. Regardless, the Mission felt it must make these decisions about future missionary roles before surrendering the direction of corporate Baptist life to the national leadership.

Though other matters still needed discussion, the final business session was preempted for a worship service. The twenty missionary representatives who were designated to share these ideas with the nationals were asked to kneel, and for forty-five minutes, the other missionaries came to lay hands on them and pray for them.

Ever-Widening Circles

At the close of the Tretes Mission Meeting, a letter was drafted to the other Baptist missions of Southeast Asia to relay the experience of the Indonesian Mission and ask for prayer.

> We have been led by the Holy Spirit to a point of utter despair concerning our failure of nerve and our failure of love in mission work in Indonesia. We have spent these ten days of Mission Meeting, examining our personal lives and our total mission philosophy and practice. We have surrendered ourselves to a new direction and a new lifestyle as a Mission family.
>
> Now we must face the consequences. We desperately need your prayers during the crucial months to follow. Our greatest need is forcefulness in communicating our new directives and genuine love in carrying them out. We beg you to covenant to pray, individually and corporately, that the work God has done in our hearts here will be implemented by His Holy Spirit, in total singleness of service and mission with our fellow Indonesian Baptists. During the next few months, we will be making the necessary transitions that will potentially transform Baptist church life in Indonesia.

What occurred in Indonesia served as a catalyst to other mission fields to seek the Holy Spirit for their own lives and work. In all the Baptist Mission Meetings of Southeast Asia that summer, great outpourings of God's Spirit were felt. In Thailand, the revival involved the conversion of one of the missionaries. In Vietnam, the revival took much of the same spiritual tone as the one in Indonesia. In the Malaysian Mission Meeting, the annual message was only five minutes long, but the invitation lasted for two hours.

Avery summarized his perspective:

At this stage, no one can predict the final outcome of this spiritual break-through, but we believe God has a great plan for Indonesia's evangelization and eventually, the evangelization of Asia and the world. Our spiritual breakthrough at Tretes has shown us a vision of revival in people movements.

One by one, and as a group, the members of the Indonesian Mission went through a judgment, a death, and a resurrection. The holy light of the Spirit exposed our sins and weaknesses. His fire burned away the works of hay, wood, and stubble. We died, along with the work we had painstakingly built up over the years. Of course, some of it stood the test, and shone through the smoke as gold, silver, and precious stones. Yet much of it was no more than human effort, based on human popularity and an open pocketbook.

But from the ashes of that death, the Holy Spirit resurrected us to walk in His power and at His bidding. He has given us a vision of a new pattern, a pattern of Indonesian Christians dressed in their batiks, singing an indigenous song, worshipping in an Indonesian way, and sharing the gospel with their friends and neighbors in their Indonesian homes.

The trajectory has been charted. The goal is in the sights. The power is available. We have been launched. From here, we go by faith.

First House Church Beginnings
(Told by Missionary John Smith of Jogjakarta)

Actually, I had gone to Mission Meeting, thinking it would be my last—that I probably would not be back. If we stayed this year, it would probably end my missionary career. After Tretes, I went back to Jogja as excited as I had ever been since arriving in Indonesia. It was a renewal of spirit. I just knew I had to get back to Jogja and share.

On the first Sunday morning at the English service, a seventh-year medical student attended for the first time, invited by a friend who had been attending for some time. He made a confession of faith that morning, and after the service, he asked, "Mr. Smith, when can we get the Bible and sit down and let me learn more about this?"

"How about tomorrow night? I will plan to be at home at six p.m."

From 6:00–9:00 p.m., we went through the gospel of John, and the student was deeply moved by the teachings of Jesus on the doctrine of salvation and new life.

At the end of the time, we prayed, and then he said, "Mr. Smith, my parents must know. When can we go to my village and share this with them?"

"Well, how about tomorrow afternoon?"

The student picked me up on his Honda motorcycle, and we went ten kilometers down through the rice paddies to his village. There we met his ninety-seven-year-old father, stately and reserved, and fluent in Indonesian, though his wife only spoke Javanese. The student read to him from the Bible in Javanese, and his father would stop him every little bit and ask for an explanation. I would explain in Indonesian what had just been read in Javanese, and then the old man would explain to his younger wife in Javanese what he had just learned. Both chose to follow the Lord that day.

They live in a large house in the village, and this man is likely the village leader. I am sure that this will be our first house church to spread the word of the Lord to that village.

CHAPTER 17
Backlash and Turmoil

If you're going to be a leader, expect to get some arrows in your back.
                                                                    —Avery

The seminary closure became a focal point of challenge and strife. What missionaries called the "new thrust" and offered as an opportunity for national pastors to mature and gain independence was received more as a "new threat." It was seen as yet another unilateral decision by the Mission, who held the power to now take away the supports Indonesian Baptists had come to depend on.

The first missionaries to share the plan with their national partners were those who lived in Kediri, where the hospital was located. The demeanor of the missionaries was immediately noticed and the new direction embraced. As the missionaries went individually to the pastors, others would stop whatever they were doing and pray for understanding and unity. One pastor was sure it had come from the Holy Spirit because it was "so radical that all of the missionaries wouldn't have been in agreement unless it was the Spirit." Another listened and then said, "I have felt for some time that Indonesia was ready for this but that we were not—missionaries or pastors."[1]

For the missionaries in Semarang, the home of the seminary, the response was radically different. The students and prominent Baptist leaders characterized the Mission action as "drastic" and "fatal." Some of the students threatened to demonstrate or go to the government or, as a last resort, to burn down the buildings if the seminary was closed. The two Indonesian professors urged patience. The seminary board of trustees, comprised of both missionaries and nationals, met but time and again failed to reach a solution. Dr. Frank Lewis, acting president, expressed the frustrations everyone felt.

"We met for two full days and didn't reach one conclusion. I was afraid for our Baptist work. We had just demonstrated that the two factions of seminary leadership couldn't come together. How could we possibly find unity from all over Indonesia?"

Sobering Reality

Catherine Walker sent a letter to the missionaries expressing the pain she was hearing and the reality of its impact:

August 7, 1971

After three days of seminary board meetings and two days of reflecting, I have seen myself and our Mission with a floodlight of truth turned on us.

In spite of endeavoring to gradually share and cooperate, to have an Indonesian voice on our boards, and to work for a future convention, at this high spiritual moment, our stance as a Mission was that the Baptist institutions were under our sole authority. Our unconscious view of the seminary was that it was ours. We did not even go through the formality of recommending to the board to close it. We felt the right to do whatever we felt guided to do. Whatever our minds or lips say about cooperation, we did not feel that Indonesians and missionaries were jointly responsible for managing Baptist work.

I personally feel that our seminary board meeting was the last time they will plead and argue their rights with us. Almost all missionaries have warm personal relationships with Indonesian Christians, but none of us practice true shared responsibility in organizational or administrative matters. Our best friends, therefore, can love us, but they do not want to work under us any longer. If we can see ourselves as we really have been, without continual self-justification, we may be able to not unduly wound each other in the severance process and not sully the name of Jesus by any unChristlike response in the situation we now find ourselves.[2]

Avery recorded his own thoughts: *Without a miracle, it will be impossible for us to come together. God must work in everybody's heart as we face each other and listen to what the Holy Spirit says to us. I am expecting a miracle from God.*

One in the Spirit

The Musjawarah was the triennial meeting of the Indonesian national pastors. This year they were gathering to determine the viability of creating their own union of churches and the leadership structure necessary to bring it about—essentially their "constitutional convention." There was a palpable tension in the air. Very few meetings in Indonesia had been covered—before and during—with so much prayer.

Some influential pastors sensed a need for spiritual unity above all else. The program was altered to allow more time for prayer. On the second day, one of the leading pastors changed his sermon and preached on unity in Christ. He then called on everyone to lay aside the program and pray.

When the missionaries shared the spiritual breakthrough that occurred at Tretes and how the Lord worked even among the youth, some of the seminary students began to weep. One missionary described, "I felt like the sweet breath of God had blown across me and the Indonesian brother next to me." The entire congregation joined in the song "We Are One in the Spirit, We Are One in the Lord." The missionaries explained the *Corak Baru*, the New Pattern of Work, and answered over fifty searching questions. They concluded by saying, "God has led us. We must do His will. We can do no other."

National leaders began to work behind the scenes to calm the explosive situation. Time and again, pastors led by the Spirit rose to lead the representatives not to make a wrong decision. The selected officers were not the ones vying for the position but warmhearted, coolheaded men. The seven men installed during the final session knelt for an hour as missionaries and nationals laid hands on them.

It seemed the spiritual change that occurred at Tretes set the climate in which the Indonesian churches could actually form their new coalition of churches. Ed Sanders described it as

> somewhat like birth pangs. It allowed for a healthy start. When we first came here, we were talking about the Holy Spirit, Holy Spirit, Holy Spirit until some of these guys were sick of it. They felt like we were using this as a tool to manipulate them: If the Holy Spirit did it, then it couldn't be wrong. Then I noticed by the end of the week, the nationals were talking Holy Spirit, Holy Spirit, Holy Spirit until we are *all* convinced this was a work of the Holy Spirit.

On the final day, a formal statement was issued by the representatives of the newly formed *Gabungan* (Union of Indonesian Baptist Churches) on the missionaries' New Pattern of Work, agreeing with the concept of house churches and lay training, but insisting on a resident seminary in Semarang.[3]

August 1971

I have been reading a lengthy book by Ralph Winter on theological education by extension. The Presbyterian seminary in Guatemala began doing what we are talking about back in 1962. Since then there has been a groundswell and over fifty institutions have gone through extension training. They did not do away with the resident seminary as we are trying to do.

October 4, 1971

The first week of seminary was a very tense time. The students had very pointed and emotional questions. They asked why we didn't think of them, and what did we think of them, if we could go ahead and make such plans, leaving them out completely. Truly, we could not have designed something that would have shattered them more. First, we took away their subsidy, then we took away their free buildings, and then we took away the seminary that produced them. But we felt responsible for what we had done in the past and felt we had to correct our mistakes.

Unexpected Opposition

Protest came next from an unexpected source. Keith Parks's reports concerning what had occurred during the Mission Meeting, addressed to the Foreign Mission Board in Richmond and to the furloughing missionaries—including three of the seminary faculty, had been lost in the mail. Consequently, when these missionaries convened for Missions Week at the Glorieta Baptist Assembly, rumors were rumbling of the seminary closing, but no one understood the reasons behind it. Immediate reaction from the Foreign Mission Board was that the seminary must *not* be closed completely, and that no action should be taken until the matter could be reviewed at their October meeting.

September 16, 1971

My first response was: if we are also getting opposition from our Foreign Mission Board, we may have to lose the battle after all. My second reaction was that they are not God, and the Lord can do whatever He wants, even if the board of trustees does not agree. Keith plans to present our position. He is wondering how the board will respond if the Indonesian Mission holds firmly to their position.

Compromise

Meanwhile, the faculty of the seminary sat down to discuss the plan for the extension seminary. Indonesian professor Chris Marantika felt that if the brand-new Gabungan was immediately required to open a replacement seminary of their own, the burden would be so great and the resentment so deep that working relationships might be damaged beyond repair. The opposition might even block the plan for extending the seminary out to the villages.

The seminary board considered the option of continuing the seminary until the current student body could graduate. A compromise was reached to remain open for three semesters and graduate all current students in an accelerated program. In response, the nationals agreed not to open their own seminary for five or six years, giving time for the extension seminary to be implemented and gain ground.

Pressed on All Sides

Despite the negotiated compromise, peace proved elusive. Because of his key leadership position in multiple facets of the changes, Avery was forced to stand between two opposing forces and determine when to bend and when to stand firm.

October 15, 1971

It appears that all of our negotiations may have fallen through. The education committee of the Union is demanding the continuation of a "high level of education on the campus." But since the nationals have neither the funds nor the teachers to provide that, it would mean continuing the seminary much as it is.

They want to ensure a highly trained, selective clergy, while our goal is to train as many of the people of God for ministry over the widest area to reach the most people in the shortest period of time. What they are advocating is essentially reproducing what we have been doing for the past seventeen years—to our regret!

This morning, we had an unusual experience. Two students—Youtie L and Yeti—asked to speak with Marvin and me. I was impressed with Youtie when he came to work with us in Jember.

Youtie told us his story. His father is a wealthy man. He himself planned to be an economist and give large sums of money to the church. But his preacher told him that as a preacher he could win ten economists to the Lord. He was one of the five who stayed up till 3:00 a.m. when they first heard the news of the seminary closing to write protest letters and then focused on forming the new Gabungan.

After the revival on the second night of the Musjawarah, Youtie came to ask forgiveness for his attitude. Now he was encouraging the close of the seminary because many of the students he had polled were happy to graduate by December anyway.

Youtie and Yeti said, "If this is the will of the Lord, and the Holy Spirit is leading you to do this, do not back off because of some students, because if you do, we may miss what God wants to do. We want to see a million souls won by 1980. We can see how we (the Indonesian churches) can send missionaries out to Kalimantan and Sulawesi and Sumatra.

One missionary could go there to teach and we could multiply ourselves by many people. Then we could reach a million people—more, even."

October 31, 1971

We got a letter from Keith Parks about his report to the Board and their recommendation. I admit this letter sent me into a deep cloud of despondency and disappointment because their recommendation is that we maintain a central seminary.

A summary of Keith's letter was that the Foreign Mission Board maintained its right as an overseeing agency to "review any major decision by a mission and to confirm, modify, or veto those decisions" since they were responsible for the past, present, and future work in Indonesia. Therefore, they went on record, indicating the "necessity" of keeping a central seminary for those seeking the highest level of education. They also felt a central seminary would serve as a "touchstone to give guidance to the whole program."

The board was "highly supportive and generally enthusiastic about the extension program and the strength it will give to the total outreach. They were enthusiastic and deeply grateful for the spiritual breakthroughs occurring in Indonesia and in other countries. Most of them were able to accept the house church concept warmly, although some were confused and needed considerable clarification."

In the face of confusion and criticism for the "rapid change of events without consulting the board, furloughing missionaries, or the Indonesian convention," Keith explained that he felt that he had no alternative but to compromise at the point of the seminary in order to keep support for the whole program. He pleaded for understanding and continued prayer rather than frustration from the missionaries.

Keith added, "I believe there is flexibility enough that we can have a happy blending of the approach you desire and which they can support . . . I believe that this difference at the point of the resident seminary is not something that will appreciably diminish the thrust that the Mission is seeking."[4]

October 31, 1971 (continued)

I think I understand Keith's situation. He <u>didn't</u> have a choice. I don't resent or feel bad at all for what he has done, but I feel very strongly about the action the Board has taken. It seems to me they have misunderstood, either purposely or unintentionally, that the seminary training we are proposing in the extension program is equal to what students are receiving now.

Operating a resident seminary "for any who seek the highest level of training," an additional program of study beyond what we are currently offering, would sap much of our time, effort and personnel away from creating the area seminaries. I have not felt right in their decision. I recognize that this decision is almost exactly what the Indonesian Baptists have asked for. I think it disturbed me to see where we really stand—that the Board has the ultimate control. Maybe this is the same feeling the seminary professors felt when we wanted to close the seminary.

Soul-Searching

I have prayed a good deal about this this week. I need to wait and try to see all the alternatives. The decision will be made at Tretes II. Although when I pray and read my Bible, I can get peace, and when I teach, I feel the presence and blessing of the Lord, it is as if I am carrying a cloud around with me. It is a burden. It's a grief, I suppose, much like when you lose a loved one. It is hard to think about anything else, really. We went swimming yesterday, and I couldn't really enjoy that. I'm not sure whether this is a grief of the Holy Spirit or whether it is grief related to self-pity because I have stuck my neck out and got it chopped off both ways.

I came home and spent a lot of time praying. I have been working on a message on the Holy Spirit, and I have read many books preparing the course on the Holy Spirit. I studied the chapter in Roy Hesson's book on the Spirit-filled life. The verse "be ye filled with the Spirit" is to be a continual thing. And the evidence is that we will sing spiritual songs in our hearts to the Lord and that we submit ourselves to one another. I must admit, that if I am filled with the Spirit, those evidences are not much in my life right now. I could not sing many spiritual songs or really thank God, nor willingly submit to this decision.

I came to a time of prayer and confession of my own concerns and of my self-pity, trying to understand myself, and wanting to repent of all my sins, and the sin of unbelief in particular, in relation to this deal. The Lord blessed me with some passages from chapters three and four of the book of 1ˢᵗ Peter. I then read a book by David Wilkerson called Have I Got Problems! *It was made to order for me. It emphasized how to ask the Lord to help us in times of afflictions and that the Lord delivers us out of them all. Wilkerson said: "To be a man of God, we have to drink the cup of pain, go through the night of confusion, and experience the hour of isolation. But through it all, we must rest." He also spoke of the "prayerful act of violence," quoting the verse, "the kingdom of God is advancing and violent men take it by force." This is interesting to me because I have been asking the question, "Were we too rash, too forceful in the decisions we made at Tretes?"*

What does this mean for me? It could mean that I would have to resist what the Board has said to the point that I could not work any longer in the seminary. Maybe I could work in extension; maybe I could go back to evangelism. It could come to the point that I couldn't work with the Foreign Mission Board. It will take the whole Mission to decide how to respond, but at this time, I'm prepared to do what I feel is the will of God, no matter what the cost may be—even if it means I do not continue to work here.

I am most frustrated with the proposal of the nationals. They want us to take students with only a high school degree, give them the three years of extension work, and then provide a Masters' degree at the campus in three more years. That means six years and another whole seminary, just a notch higher, which is still education for a few of the "in" group that will bypass the multitudes who are waiting right now for the gospel—and they can't wait ten years—or five years!! We must get to them now!

I don't know how I can get to them if I don't work within the structure of the Mission, because I know how little one person can do. But I have this confidence now, that I must believe God and not accept anything as final—to trust God that He is going to bring His own purposes out of this. I pray His wisdom will overcome any faults in our understanding and that He will show us as a Mission and as individuals what to do.

Voice of a Prayer Partner
(By Marvin Leech)

I was Avery's prayer partner during the period following the Tretes decisions—after the formation of the Union of Indonesian Baptist Churches [GGBI] and throughout the period of time that the new Union had declared a moratorium on working relationships with the Indonesian Baptist Mission. Avery had three primary concerns that we spent much time praying about: family needs, establishing healthy working relationships with the Indonesian leaders of the new Union, and the implementation of the New Pattern of Work.

Avery was very, very troubled about the extreme opposition that the nationals demonstrated toward the New Pattern of Work. His pleas to the Lord reminded me of David's pleas for God's intervention to preserve and enhance all that was good and right and to remove all that was destructive and self-serving. He never doubted God's intention to establish and multiply new believers, emerging leaders, and new house churches all across Indonesia.

We seldom met for prayer in our homes or offices on the seminary campus. Our prayer times usually were held away from the seminary in places to which we traveled together to consult personally with Indonesian pastors and missionaries in their churches or homes. Other times we would go to designated "prayer sites" in beautiful natural settings. We carried enough food for a meal and spent half a day in prayer.

On occasion, we were asked by our Mission leadership to intervene on behalf of missionary personnel in our area who were going through very difficult and even tragic challenges in their family life. Our prayer time together proved to be a very stabilizing factor that empowered and equipped us to deal with those situations and see the Lord work—sometimes bringing reconciliation and sometimes bringing divine discipline.

I enjoyed praying with Avery on family concerns for which we sought concrete answers, whether in his family or mine. He was extremely open and honest with God in my presence, as I learned to be with him. The depth of our trust and respect for each other intensified as time went by. We often prayed heartfelt pastoral prayers for one another because of the depth of feeling we shared with respect to our wives and children—and the variety of situations they faced that needed God's intervention.

Avery loved to keep up with his past prayer requests and seek to ascertain when and how God answered those prayers. He usually identified prayer promises in Scripture that for him served as a more objective basis for his requests. He helped me to learn to ask, seek, and knock with greater faith and confidence in God's grace and His desire to answer our requests "above anything we could ask or think, according to His great power that is at work in us."

Tretes II

The seminary dilemma was the subject of three more months of consultation and conflict, but the broad outlines of a new theological program were worked out and agreed upon at a specially called November Mission Meeting, dubbed Tretes II.

The new program emphasized the beginning of branch seminaries in the major cities. The emphasis was expansion of theological education to more people and improving the quality of theological education by linking it with practical experience in natural settings. All the branches would meet in church buildings and use programmed instruction to standardize and guarantee the quality of instruction, and to allow the professors to teach in multiple centers in outlying areas.

The Semarang seminary facilities would serve as the administrative center of the entire system and as a resident seminary for those who wanted to complete their education in three years. The new class of students would study the same programmed textbooks as the extension centers and have traditional teaching methods for courses not yet programmed. A one-year course of study would be available for qualified graduates of any of the centers who sought to become seminary professors.[5]

I think the students were very much in prayer for this Mission Meeting. As I was teaching the class on the Holy Spirit, there were serious ques-

tions asked about the leadership of the Spirit in these matters. "How could God lead like this, to lead you one way, and then turn around and lead a different way? Won't it be a sin if you go back?" One student asked, "I believe the seminary ought to close, but if you leave it open, I see the benefit of it and I would continue to attend. Would that be a sin?"

At the Mission Meeting, Keith laid out his recommendation that at minimum, we take one more group of students after this one, beginning with the 1973–1974 school year. During this time, we could begin the extension seminary and be able to show the impact and value of it. We discussed the house church, the ramifications and the problems. Several missionaries had testimonies of how they had begun small groups and turned leadership over but none as we had originally planned—where it initiated from a natural leader, evolving out of the situation, and our supporting him. So our greatest need right now is for actual evidence that this is a working model.[6]

CHAPTER 18
Seminary Development

The Reformation was never completed. The leaders proclaimed that the priesthood of the believers means that as priests we have access to God though our High Priest, Jesus Christ. But they failed to implement the corollary truth that, as priests, all believers are to minister to mankind as Christ's representatives. They allowed the clergy-laity structure to rob the whole people of God of their right and privilege to be ministers. They failed to understand that the Holy Spirit gives spiritual gifts to all his children so they will have a ministry. This doesn't do away with the "ministry"—it does away with the "laity!"[1]

—Avery

In December 1971, word came that Dr. Schweer's return to Indonesia had been postponed indefinitely, vacating his position as president of the Baptist Seminary in Semarang. This left only Dr. Catherine Walker and Avery to maintain the resident seminary and begin the extension seminary concept.

This leadership vacuum created a tension Avery had to wrestle with—it was important to fill the presidency with the right qualifications and the right spirit of leadership.

Seminary Presidency

December 10, 1971– Taped Diary

No one is currently serving as a leader, and we haven't really done all we were supposed to have done by now. We really need a leader to minister to us, to encourage us, to direct us, to interpret and reach out in the New Pattern of Work.

I spent a whole day driving to Jakarta yesterday—about eight or nine hours of pleasant fellowship with the Lord. I dedicated that time to Him. One thing I did was reflect on myself. I traced back as far as I could my image of myself as an evangelist, as a pastor, as a teacher, as a person of authority in the Mission, and even the secular part of me from my childhood that wants more of the fine things in life.

I was looking at these images of myself in context of the role of seminary president. I never wanted or sought the job, but it was suggested that I might be the one recommended. From my time with the Lord, I have arrived at an image I am satisfied with: the image of a <u>servant</u> and a <u>minister</u>. God has given me gifts in evangelism, in preaching, in pastoring when I was in that role, and in teaching (although that gift has not been exercised as well as some of the others).

Dr. Ebbie Smith is the one who wants the role and who is really more qualified because he has taught two terms, already has his doctoral degree, and has two more years left in this term. He should be the permanent president. If I had to do it, I would only want to be an acting president for a year. I could do it as a servant but I would not have plans beyond that. In fact, I don't even have plans to do it at all unless the Lord especially leads and the Mission insists.

I have not wanted to stand out as one who is trying to push himself forward. But if I can honestly take the image of a servant, I think I can live with myself better and I will be more helpful, because whatever I do, I can direct my help to this Body of Christ in Indonesia. I could help, not in leading the New Pattern, but in serving in the New Pattern, giving theology to it, helping direct it, and giving inspiration.

In March, the seminary board asked Avery to be the acting president of the seminary until Dr. Schweer would return. Avery wrote to his parents:

This will involve getting the whole new seminary system started and being president (Rector) of the campus one. I really didn't want it because I'd rather spend my time in evangelism and more direct teaching in the new seminary branches. But the committee thought I was the logical one since I had worked out the first proposal for the expanded seminary. I asked the Central Java missionaries to pray that God would give me a gift of administration. They laid hands on me and the Lord really ministered to me.[2]

The new position also meant the Willises would move again—this time to the president's home on the seminary campus. The home sat perched atop the hill, overlooking the river dam and *pasar* (market) outside the gates, the schoolhouse for the children, and a tennis court. Behind the house were the seminary dormitories. A sidewalk ran alongside the house toward the circular drive in front of the offices and classroom buildings.

Shirley would have preferred not to move, but their other house was to be sold as part of downsizing missionary houses. This would be the fifth consecutive June the Willises would relocate, and the upcoming furlough the following summer would result in packing up a sixth time! But at least the president's house did not require much remodeling. The real remodeling work was to be done in the new seminary.

Racing a Train
(PRAY, August 1972)

Shirley's parents, Clarence and Beulah Morris, spent a month visiting them in Indonesia. One day, while waiting at a railroad crossing, a man reached through the open car window, snatched Clarence's glasses and hat, and took off running.

When Avery saw the hand come in, he immediately realized that the glasses were the target. Knowing how desperately Clarence needed glasses in order to see, Avery jammed the car into park, jumped out, and gave chase. The thief hopped on a freight train going by, with Avery in hot pursuit. The man was shocked to see Avery sprinting alongside the track, demanding that he return the glasses. Realizing Avery intended to keep running until he got the glasses, the thief pitched them to Avery and rode away. It was a rare moment of effective heroism, and Clarence was able to see the remainder of Indonesia!

Seminary Curriculum

New materials were being developed by missionaries and national writers under the name *Pemuridan* (discipleship) and were designed to teach not only the Bible but also how to put the commands of Jesus into practice.

June 24, 1972 – Letter home
We are making real progress on the new seminary program, but the amount of work involved in setting up a new school like this is staggering! I can see that writing this programmed instruction will be more difficult than we imagined. It will take up to five years to complete all the writing. We will need to average writing and printing a new textbook a month while still teaching the resident program here in Semarang.

July and August, 1972 – Taped Diaries
As we are getting units back from our writers, there are many changes that need to be made. We may not be able to start in January or February as planned but I would rather hold off and have the materials be correct from the start.

I have had so much responsibility correcting and ordering the units being written by others that I have had little time to write myself. I know I need to try to write because that is the only way to really be able to critique or instruct others.

I have almost finished a little booklet on the filling of the Spirit and on spiritual gifts. I am writing it in Indonesian and I hope it will be used. I have also been teaching on the laity and think I finally impressed on the students the idea of "the whole people of God, filled, given gifts, witnessing, serving, and ministering, and those few, specially appointed workers (apostles, prophets, evangelists, and pastor-teachers) serving to equip the saints." Not all have accepted this completely, but we are making progress.

School began the first of August and I have been able to line up enough people to teach the various classes. The students are in good spirits and things are going well.

Challenge at the Line
(Told by Von Worten)

One afternoon, needing a break from their meeting, Von and Avery took on Ebbie and Marvin in tennis on the seminary court. Avery was playing at the net and smashed a return. Ebbie immediately called the ball out. Avery quickly insisted that the ball was on the line and therefore good.

The two men proceeded to challenge each other's ruling for several minutes, and then Avery headed over to the line to point out where the ball had hit. As he reached out with his racket to tap the spot, both men were startled and then embarrassed to see the ball wedged into the V opening in the handle of Avery's racket. Speechless, they returned to their places on the court. Von is still laughing.

Seminary Extension

The expansion seminary began to get underway at the beginning of 1972. The site near Semarang enrolled over forty people from seventeen nearby villages; the Purwokerto extension branch began training in three new places; and the East Java Bible school continued its eighteen training locations. The seventy-five resident seminary students were to each start a home Bible study group during the semester.[3]

The house church model was gaining momentum. One of the seminary extension centers produced testimonies of significant life change:

A man named Mr. Samusi visited his relatives in a village near Semarang over the holidays. He discovered that several of them had become Christians and had started a church in their home. He asked many questions, then returned home and invited his siblings to join him in becoming Christians.

When they agreed, he visited the newly established seminary training center and asked the Baptist pastor to hold services in his village ten miles away. Mr. Samusi then invited five of his closest friends to receive and listen to his guests. All chose to believe in Christ.

A seminary student visited Mr. Samusi's village every weekend. Services and follow-up questions would last till midnight. By the end of January, an initial group was ready for baptism. Thirteen men were baptized in the river, and two weeks later, thirteen women and children followed. After the second baptism, the people got a loud speaker and sang and testified for hours to their whole village and to visitors from several surrounding villages.

Mr. Samusi was invited to begin services in a second village. "Pak Willis and Pak Chris went with me, but we all agreed it would be best if I led the services. Eight men and fifteen children attended the first service. Perhaps many will become Christians. I went several kilometers in another direction to begin teaching a family who want to become Christians but are surrounded by Muslims. I also got a letter from Skopek, a three-hour walk over the mountains, to begin services there. We know of two more villages that have shown interest, and we hope to go soon."[4]

Mr. Dahlan, a lay pastor for several years, shared, "I visited a village ten kilometers from my village, where we had once thought about starting a church but decided it was too far. Now I am ready to go myself! Last week I met with four families there who want me to come teach them about Christ. I told them the first thing they were to do was to get their neighbors to attend. Two of the men have offered their home for a house church."

Mr. Hardi, a layman, said, "I gave a man a lift on my bicycle last week on the way home from seminary. I began to witness to him with the verses we had learned. He said he wanted to become a Christian, so we stopped the bicycle beside the road and he trusted Christ. I gave him the packet of verses and so I need another one."[5]

Bill Bright of Campus Crusade for Christ came to Indonesia to lead a conference in witnessing using the Four Spiritual Laws tract. Part of the training was going out to witness for two afternoons. As he participated, Avery engaged a pedicab driver in conversation. Others gathered around, and he continued for an hour and a half to speak and witness to those who came by. Many heard the gospel, and seven responded in faith to Christ. The next afternoon, Avery was invited into a *warung* (roadside eating stand), and six others made a commitment to Christ. Avery says, *I am convinced that this pattern can be repeated every day in most parts of Indonesia and the results can be conserved in house churches.*[6]

Seminary Graduation

In April 1972, the Indonesian Baptist Seminary graduated thirty-eight students, the largest class in its eighteen-year history. Most of them were weekend pastors of small churches that could not provide them a living salary. This created a crisis of faith for the students, because the Mission subsidy was being reduced each quarter until it would be discontinued completely within two years. Yet many testified that God was already meeting their needs, and all committed to serve even if they had to take multiple congregations or multiple jobs for a season.

The Spirit moved deeply during a special service to ordain them. At the close, they all joined hands and sang "Blessed Be the Tie that Binds." Then they turned to face outward, rejoined hands, and repeated the song, indicating that they were still united, even while moving out to serve in scattered places.

Remaining at the seminary were twenty-five who graduated in December and twenty more who graduated the following April, after which the established program of educational training was phased out and the new one inaugurated.[7]

State of the Disunion

Although the new plans for evangelization and seminary extension were being put into place, tension was still mounting between the Indonesian pastors and the missionaries. Both wanted to move forward, but in different directions.

August 9, 1972 – Letter home

We received a letter from the Indonesian Union of Churches stating that they intended to open a theological academy, beginning next January. They have asked Eddie W., our remaining Indonesian professor, to be the director of the academy. They also said they would not appoint members to our seminary board and would withdraw representatives from all boards but the board which approved loans.

I do not see that we should try to talk them out of their school in any way. They want to be indigenous in origin, in design, and in planning. I see this as them standing on their own feet. But if Eddie goes to direct the academy, that only leaves Dr. Catherine Walker and me to teach, write, and oversee the regional centers. And I worry about how we will be able to work with the nationals in the future, if they see themselves at cross-purposes.

Despite the Mission's efforts to establish an organic, indigenous house church model, the Indonesian Baptist pastors wanted more traditional, centralized organizational control. Their *keluarga besar* (big family) concept referred less to spiritual fellowship, and more to a presbyterian form of government, in which "the parents make the decision for the family." Among other things, the Union leaders insisted that

1. the ordination of pastors and pastoral changes must be approved by a central committee;
2. only ordained pastors could administer the ordinances and perform weddings and funerals;
3. new churches could only be started by a church in that area;
4. new areas of work could only be initiated by the Union;
5. missionaries should no longer begin churches on their own or in new areas;
6. each church should give 10 percent of its income to the Union; and
7. theological education must be done by the Union.[8]

Meetings and consultations to work out differences only increased national versus missionary friction. Proposals from each side were met with suspicion and counterproposals so that possible solutions were mired in deadlock.

In December 1972, Avery sent a passionate message to Keith Parks, Area Secretary, requesting that he come back to the field to serve as a mediator for the next "consultation" of the nationals and the missionaries. In it, he described his perspective on the issues. He also began to share some of the issues with his prayer partners through the *PRAY* newsletters.

The Heart of the Matter

I think we are in a serious situation. Both sides have continued to polarize. There is a basic mistrust on each side about what the other one says. Motives are suspected and words are played with. Every time we take the next step with the Gabungan [Union of Indonesian Baptist Churches], *they come back with a harder line.*

In essence, the nationals are demanding complete control of all Baptist churches and institutions <u>and</u> the determination of the missionary's place of service and methods of work.[9]

Initially, the Union set their own house in order. They affirmed that they are both Baptist and Indonesian and that they are responsible for their own nation and program of work.[10] *The relationship of the missionaries or groups who want to work with the Union was defined as that of helpers or assistants. They did not specify what the relationship would be to the present mission institutions such as the seminary, publishing house, hospitals, mass media, and student centers. At least they did not limit or attempt to control the Mission's work.*

At its base, much of what the nationals are doing is positive:

1. *They feel that Indonesians must win Indonesia to Christ.*
2. *They feel they must establish indigenous churches with indigenous patterns. They are not satisfied with the old pattern either.*
3. *They want the missionary profile to be lower, which we have also said we wanted.*
4. *If they administrate more things, it would free up the missionaries to have a more spiritual ministry.*

But at the consultation that followed, the leadership demanded that the Union be the policy-maker and the missionaries be their assistants and partners. They would not agree to even discuss cooperative efforts until we agreed to that point. The ambiguity between "assistants" and "partners" was clarified by their explanation that although they would discuss their plans with us, they would make all decisions. Missionaries would no longer take the initiative or plan programs, but would work only within the Union's programs.[11]

247

They say this is the Indonesian pattern, and I think they believe in what they are doing enough to try to get it at any cost. They have not come to the place where they will kick us out of the country, but we have experienced some veiled threats. It might give them just cause for further action if we instigate another pattern of work which they could not control or they feel is in competition with their proposals.

We have several factors against us:

The broad base of discontent revealed through the surveys is dry tinder to kindle the flames of nationalism. Due to the Indonesians' history of resistance against Dutch colonialism, emotions of nationalism may rise stronger than Christian values of love, respect, and equality. Three and a half centuries of domination have resulted in a chronic cultural "inferiority complex," but the fight for independence instilled the belief that all obstacles can be overcome through revolution. The idea lies deeply within them that during revolution, it is acceptable, even necessary, that some must die or be sacrificed in order to accomplish the aims.

We encountered the essence of the problem when we discussed the role of the evangelistic missionary. They claim missionaries should not open work in the villages because it gives the wrong image. If the missionary comes in with their car and prestige, and then the Indonesian comes peddling in on a bicycle later, the people will look to the missionary as the leader. Instead, the Indonesian must be the leader. The whole image must be national. For instance, in Purwokerto where Von has opened a number of small churches—none of which are organized and therefore not under the jurisdiction of the Union—they feel they would probably need to remove the missionary from that region because the "image" and plan of work is "American." They would put a national there instead.

The best it can mean for the missionaries is that when they make a request of us, e.g. to go to a specific location or do a certain project, we would have veto power. We would have no initiative but we could refuse to do what they asked. Missionaries are still needed as teachers in their academy, but would not be allowed to influence the students against the policies of the Union.

In a sense, their desire for control is rooted in fear that the missionary, given freedom, has the ability, the means, and the prestige, to once again influence their followers more than they can.

Secondly, there is a strong resolve for power and a subconscious desire to do to the Mission as they have been done unto. Eddie W. [Seminary professor and leader of the Union] *said, "It is only natural. Formerly, the missionaries were on top and made the policies. Then we tried to work together, and that didn't work, so now it is only natural that we be on top and you be on the bottom."*

Finally, a feeling of resentment exists among the nationals, especially related to economic inequality. Thus far, there has not been a strong move in our Mission to bring our economic standard of living into line—even bringing our houses down to the established limit.

What does this mean for us?

The Indonesian leadership claimed missionaries should not direct work in a city where there are already churches. They could open work in new areas, such as on the outer islands, along with other Indonesians. Again, the Indonesians would carry the national image and would decide the place and the policy. The missionaries would be their helpers or friends. When asked about work on Java, they said all evangelists would be put under the authority of Mulus Budianto, who has plans to have mass crusades. The missionaries could help and would be allowed to witness personally there.

They rejected the extension seminary outright. They are not against programmed literature except that it teaches our plan of evangelism. Since the regional/extension seminaries are the vehicle the missionaries want to use for evangelism, the nationals cannot support it.

The real key for us is our freedom. I don't suppose any of us want to give up control and power. Because of our desire for freedom and independence as Americans, we don't want to be controlled—in spiritual, economic, or other matters. We feel we must be free to evangelize, free to start churches, and free to train people (which sounds like the Great Commission to me!). We want the basic rights to evangelize under God.

The primary goal of missions is to win people, form them into New Testament churches, and train them to lead their own people to develop self-determining, self-supporting, self-propagating, and self-expressing churches.

As he continued his letter, Avery expressed the essence of the dilemma:

Are we going to be the servant and surrender or really stand up for our right to evangelize? So we face these paradoxes:

- *We have the desire to be free of administration but an unwillingness to relinquish the power.*
- *We have the desire to be servants but an unwillingness to surrender to the will of another, which is the definition of a servant.*
- *We have a desire for them to take the initiative but we want them to take it along our prescribed lines instead of theirs.*
- *We have a desire to fit into the culture but an unwillingness to do it economically or sociologically.*

There remain only three ways we can go:

- *We break this deadlock and work as cooperating but independent bodies.*
- *We be willing to be under them, no matter what they say.*
- *We split.*

Unfortunately, we feel a bit like a couple headed toward a divorce. We have ceased to communicate; we question each other's integrity and react based on sensitive feelings; we are seeking a third party; and we may even be headed toward legal issues. We must stop the deterioration and then work back toward trust. That is why we need you to come, Keith. They trust you as an outside voice.

We want to find the will of God. We have a real burden for Indonesia and seeing the greatest number of people come to know Christ as Savior. We can't win Indonesia as missionaries and they cannot win Indonesia as pastors. Yet they refuse the very method by which God could use all His people as witnesses to reach this land.[12]

Resolution

Ultimately, discussions and meetings continued over the next two years until the Union of Indonesian Baptists and the Indonesian

Baptist Mission reached an agreement on a cooperative plan for theological education in Indonesia, stating that both groups wanted to work together in one endeavor.

For the immediate future, the Mission would have prime responsibility for the seven regional seminaries under the name STBI—*Seminari Theologia Baptis Indonesia* (Indonesian Baptist Theological Seminary). The seminary would be designed for men and women to live at home while they studied and continue to serve a church or support their family while doing so.

The Union would have prime responsibility for the resident theological school, the ATBI—*Academi Theologia Baptis Indonesia* (Indonesian Baptist Theological Academy). The academy would serve people who could live at a resident seminary and go to school full-time. It would be housed on a portion of the seminary grounds in Semarang.

Initially, joint boards with Indonesian and missionary representation would be responsible for running both schools. Missionaries and Indonesians would teach in both programs.

Avery was elected to serve as the permanent president of the seminary (following his stateside year), and Eddie Wiriadinata was selected to preside over the academy. The goal was that eventually both schools would be under a common board and under an Indonesian president, after the regional seminary concept had been proven effective, and the Indonesians were able and ready to assume full responsibility.[13]

While the Willises went on furlough, Dr. Ebbie Smith was asked to serve as the acting president. However, the tragic death of his son, Roger, in a motorcycle accident in July meant that Ebbie never served in that role. Ross Fryer became the acting president.

CHAPTER 19
Stirring the Nest

"How Odd of God..."

T he first stop out of Jakarta on the way home for furlough in 1973 was Bangkok, Thailand, after which the Willises intended to tour Spain and Italy. Avery left the hotel to go out jogging early in the morning, but when he didn't return on schedule, Shirley began to worry. When it was nearly flight time, she decided something was dreadfully wrong and called the Thailand mission office, who called the police.

It helped that Avery had worn a gold OBU jersey with "Willis" imprinted on the back. He was found wandering around another downtown hotel, asking for the hotel manager, and was taken to a hospital. He had bruising on his left side and a total loss of short-term memory. The conclusion (a guess, really) was that he had been sideswiped by a car or motorcycle and perhaps hit his head on the pavement when he fell.

When the family arrived at the hospital, his repeated questions: "Where am I? How did I get here? What day is it? Where is the hotel manager?" were interchanged with chuckling about the clever lines running through his head: "How odd of God to choose the Jews!" and "It's funny to be disoriented in the Orient!" After hundreds of repetitions of the above, he began to read the faces of his family members and added another question: "Have I said that before?" only to repeat the complete loop again.

Avery's memory became more operative over the next couple of days, but the accident hijacked the Spain portion of the trip, and he was tentative throughout the visit to Italy. The concussion served as an excuse for any memory lapses for several months!

Upon their return stateside, the Willises were invited to live in a missionary house in Cleburne, Texas, a suburb of Ft. Worth and a thirty-five-minute drive from Southwestern Baptist Seminary. The Eric Gustafsons had purchased the home and remodeled it, and members of First Baptist Church of Cleburne had furnished it with everything from beds to a potato peeler.

ThD

Avery's primary goal for the year, beyond speaking in churches on a weekly basis, was to finish writing his dissertation on the revival in Indonesia—why two million people joined the Christian churches from 1965–1971 following the attempted coup. He had hoped to remain mostly nondescript while at the seminary so that he could get as much work done as possible. However, that hope was gone after he preached at one of the first chapel services on September 12.

Challenging the Status Quo

In his sermon, Avery recounted the revival in Indonesia among the missionaries and how God was at work. He remarked, "Before going over, one of our missionary leaders commented that 'we are establishing Southern Baptist churches overseas just like they are here in America.' My response then was, 'Lord, deliver us!'" At that, the students broke into applause. Avery went on to say that when he got to Indonesia, he discovered that, in fact, missionaries *had* transported an American church to Indonesia, "stamped MADE IN USA." He continued, "You know, Southern Baptist churches are not necessarily synonymous with the New Testament church." The students clapped again. Avery went on to explain the changes that had occurred in Indonesia: the move to house churches, how all the people of God must be equipped to minister, and even some of the miracles that had occurred.

After the invitation, Dr. Naylor, president of Southwestern Seminary, came up to the platform and gave a rebuttal. He said, "I heard your reference to Southern Baptist churches not necessarily being New Testament churches. A chill went up my spine when these students clapped for that. These are God's churches. I was saved in a Baptist church and called to preach in a Baptist church."

Avery told it this way:

He took several minutes to refute what I had said. I was standing down front where we had been receiving people making decisions. I questioned in my own heart, "Should I go back up there and respond to what he is saying?" I recognized that there could be misunderstanding of what I had said or what I really meant. But I didn't want to take the edge off what I had said. So, I listened to the Holy Spirit, and felt like I should go back up on the stage. I went up and stood behind him waiting until he finished his remarks. It was quite obvious I intended to speak.

When he finished, he turned and asked, "Now, uh, Avery, did you want to say something?"

I said, "Well, yes, I do." I slipped my arm around his shoulders and thanked him for the opportunity to get things straight, lest there be misunderstanding. "I, too, am a Baptist, and a man of the Book. What I am trying to say is: Don't take the forms and structures of church that have come out of America and the needs in America and try to export them to another country where they don't fit. But I would also say: Don't get so bound up in religious forms in this country that you continue to be bound by them, if they are no longer meeting the need for which they were designed!"

Evidently, this sermon became the topic for nearly all of the seminary classes following the chapel service. Several professors, and especially Dr. Guy, were angry at the president's response but realized that the event had underscored the most important idea of the message, so that no one could miss it. And since my response had been loving and full of the Spirit, it had taken the sting out of the moment and refocused my intended message.

However, it has now become almost impossible for me to get any studying done. The message struck such a responsive chord that everywhere I go on campus, students have been stopping me to talk, and even coming by my study carrel to ask me questions. They are interested in so many big ideas the Lord has gotten me involved in: the filling of the Spirit, the miracles, theological education by extension... If we start talking about the lay movement, the time disappears.

Little did I think I would be thrown into this kind of situation, here in the U.S., this soon. Although I have often remarked that if the same things being said in Indonesia had been said here in the U.S., there would be a similar reaction from many of the hierarchical leaders and many of the pastors. Several have approached me to apologize for the felt "attack," but after the last few years in Indonesia, this didn't faze me. In fact, I sort of enjoyed getting back in the fight. It had been nearly a month!

God has revealed to me the beauty of being His son and not needing to be threatened by anyone. Just last week, I couldn't sleep, so I went in to pray, and said, "Oh, God, I want to be your man. There are so many forces trying to shape me here, both within and without, that I am tempted to fit the mold. I want to say what they want me to say. But what I really want is to be yours, totally and completely, and listen to the voice of your Spirit—and not just do things automatically." There was a real peace in my heart—no vindictiveness at all.

I went back to talk to Dr. Naylor in his office. I went to share with him about the seminary and what had occurred. Where we really disagreed, more than on any other subject, was the idea of the laity as ministers versus the "called clergy" and he could not be dissuaded.[1]

On Eagles' Wings

Avery's chief message in churches that year was taken from Deuteronomy 32, entitled "On Eagles' Wings." He spoke of how the Lord had led Israel as a mother eagle does her baby eaglets: at first providing comfort, protection, and nurture, but then stirring the nest to cause the eaglets to rise up and learn to soar. He used the metaphor to explain how God had been at work in Indonesia and how God was stirring the nest in America. This teaching would become a repeated theme for Avery for years and become the structure of his book, *Learning to Soar*, published in 2009.

God's Provision

In June, as they were preparing to return to Indonesia, the Willises began to sell what they had bought for use during the furlough year:

their TV and two used cars. In all three instances, only one person ever responded to the ad, and that person purchased the item for only $50 less than the Willises paid for it. As Avery was walking back into the house after the final sale, praising God for how He provided in the little things, he said, "Lord, You are so wonderful! You just take care of everything. There is only one other thing I thought You might do that You haven't done yet. That is, to provide us with another boxer puppy to replace Jeep [Jeep II, who had died in Indonesia of an infection during the year]. But I won't go back on my agreement with You, although I could afford to buy one."

As Avery laid down to rest, the phone rang. It was a man in Dallas who said, "This is a little unusual, but my mother-in-law wants to give you her six-month-old registered boxer puppy to take back to Indonesia." Mrs. Orr, recently widowed, had prayed for the Willis family since 1965 and had heard there was an "opening for a missionary dog." So the Duke of Lancastershire became Jeep III and would endure a seventy-five-hour sojourn of airports and plane compartments from Ft. Worth to Semarang.

Avery receiving his Doctorate of Theology at
Southwestern Baptist Seminary, July 1974

The Willises were granted a three-week extension so that Avery could be present at the actual diploma ceremony for his ThD (doctor of theology) at 10:00 a.m. on July 19, 1974. They left for Indonesia at 3:20 that afternoon so that they would not miss any more days of the annual Mission Meeting, being held in Semarang on the seminary grounds.

CHAPTER 20
Decentralized Theological Education Works!

Returning from the US, the Willises were met at the airport in Semarang by some of their close missionary friends with the sign, "Welcome to our new Chairman: Dr. Willis!" The annual Mission Meeting had already begun, and Avery had been elected as the Mission chairman for the coming year, in addition to his responsibilities as seminary president.

Though Avery had not even considered this possibility, the Mission felt he would be best suited to lead during this transitional and difficult juncture of the Mission's life. This responsibility would engulf 50 percent of his time leading meetings, consulting with the Indonesian Union of Churches, ensuring that mission decisions were carried out, working with others to evaluate mission strategy, and coordinating long-range planning. He still had the responsibilities of coordinating the seven regional branches of the seminary and overseeing the production of the programmed theological textbooks. In addition, he was teaching at the seminary, preaching in churches, and writing textbooks himself.

He made a request to his now seven thousand prayer partners to *"pray with us that the work will be done under the initiation and control of God and be accomplished by the power of the Spirit so that it will be obvious that only God could have done it."*

Theological Education by Extension

This third term on the mission field would be full of challenges in three areas: establishing Theological Education by Extension (TEE), writing effective curriculum, and long-term planning.

The Indonesian Baptist Theological Seminary (STBI) opened its seven regional seminaries in January 1974 with forty-six teaching centers. Seminary professors were placed as directors of all of the teaching centers in their geographical area. The TEE concept enabled students to attend seminary classes without leaving their homes, jobs, or church. Instead, the teachers went to the students. It enabled the training of lay leaders, not just those who desired to be full-time pastors. The key to its effectiveness was contextualization. The students could immediately put what they were learning into practice in their local church.

Unique to the Indonesian experience of TEE was that the textbooks were written in Indonesian for the Indonesian culture, not translated from other sources. The classes were open to anyone who could read and write. The students learned simultaneously from the self-study programmed textbooks, weekly class sessions, in-service ministries, and quarterly weekend retreats for in-depth study.

And it worked! By 1975, of the 450 students, only 4 percent were full-time pastors. The immersion of students across society was evident: 19 percent were farmers, 17 percent government workers, 16 percent white-collar businessmen, 13 percent schoolteachers, 5 percent merchants, and the rest peddlers, soldiers, university students, and other professionals.

By the time Avery returned from furlough, he was convinced that their model for writing the programmed literature was flawed. The materials were too content-laden and insufficiently practical or applicable to life and culture, lacking models as to how to work out the teachings. The initial registration for the first two quarters of TEE had been overwhelmingly positive with over 440 registered, but there had been a tremendous dropout rate. The stringent requirements for getting into the school had not been enforced, so the students were unprepared to study five hours a week. Also, the books had been so difficult that many students attended only once or twice and did not return.

Avery immediately set about to correct these weaknesses. The books were changed from 90 percent informational content to how to apply the information learned. The branch seminaries also reregistered students to attract those for whom the program was designed. Attendance through the following year stabilized with about 355 enrollees.

As they became available, the discipleship materials were field-tested in churches and then taught at the seminaries in six successive semesters. Eventually, most of the missionaries serving in Indonesia and the Indonesian Baptist pastors and leaders completed the training.

Seeing the Future

A year later, the results were dramatic. A retreat was held for the TEE students on the seminary campus. Attendance was intentionally made difficult. Only students who had successfully completed three quarters of study and who could pay their own way were invited. Nevertheless, 228 people attended, with a majority aged thirty or older. The students attended six classes per day (one beginning at 6:00 a.m. before breakfast) in addition to two worship services, two prayer groups, and a choice between choir practice and a class on creating spiritual adaptations of cultural art forms. They approached these events with a seriousness not often seen among the resident students. The spirit of God moved among them.

1975 Seminary Retreat

Avery said:

The revival I had been hoping would break out in Indonesia since the 1971 revival among the missionaries seems to have begun during this retreat. This spiritual event solidified and strengthened the students and boosted the reputation of the regional seminary concept.

Pastor Raharjo wrote: "STBI has opened the way for Baptists in Indonesia to step forward and become effective leaders. It is my hope that through this form of learning, the Lord Jesus will train these students to plant at least 250 new churches in the next five years. I believe it. I experienced revival myself and all of Baptists in Indonesia will experience it."

One said, "Since our pastor moved, our church has been led directly by the members. Ten of the members are studying in the seminary, and we take turns preaching each Sunday."

Another claimed, "Since I have been going to seminary, I understand how to help my pastor. Seven of the thirty members of our church study in the seminary. Because of the witness of these, the thirty has now become ninety in attendance."

Full Circle
Making Disciples Who Make Disciples
(PRAY, October 1975)

One of the first persons to become a Christian after the Willises moved to Jember in 1969 was Mr. Mulyono. Pak Mul, as he was called, testified before his baptism, "I came to Jember because my doctor said I needed a change of climate for my narcolepsy. I heard Pastor Willis telling how he had prayed for a sick man. When I made my way to the front to profess my faith in Christ, I also believed God would heal me. He healed me instantly!"

After that, Pak Mul made a habit of going with Avery to the villages around Jember to spread the gospel. Even after the Willises moved to Semarang, Pak Mul faithfully served one of the village congregations a hundred kilometers from Jember for two years. He felt that the Lord wanted him to go to other areas to spread the gospel. He moved to a strong Muslim area and began to witness while commuting to a regional seminary in Surabaya seventy-five kilometers away.

At the national seminary retreat in April 1975, he felt led by God to go to one of the outer islands as a missionary. Some seminary graduates from North Sulawesi also in attendance invited him to come work with the Javanese who had transmigrated to their area. He replied, "I believe this is God's will for me, and I will come as soon as I finish the course I am studying on the Holy Spirit." A few weeks later, he came to seek prayer from Avery before leaving by boat to Sulawesi.

He later wrote to Avery:

I arrived at the transmigration project on July 15 and received a happy welcome from the Javanese people. All around me is jungle. We are seventy-five kilometers from the nearest town. I often eat wild boar meat because there are many wild boars in the jungle.

There are already 350 families, plus another 150 due to come later from Java. Many of these people are former criminals, beggars, prostitutes, etc. Before I arrived, there had already been a murder and several thefts.

I ask for your prayers, Pak Willis, because this is not an easy job. I have no power to serve the Lord. I am convinced that in this project, many people are open to Christ, but I must be faithful and patient. With His power, I am sure things will go fine.

After receiving the letter, Avery mused, *We cannot know the extent of our influence in spiritual generations when we serve as disciple-makers. Only in heaven will we see the impact of the ripples and how far-reaching they can be from one changed life.*

Nonetheless, Avery sought to improve the quality of the textbook writing. Ted Ward, the top educator of "nonformal" education in the world and the only American to receive the Dag Hammarskjöld award for his contribution to Third World education, came to work with the seminary textbook writers in a three-day workshop.

In a letter to his parents on March 28, 1976, Avery wrote:

We were really surprised and encouraged that he thought that STBI was doing the best job in the <u>world</u>! He has worked in thirty-three countries and had connections with extension seminaries since their beginning, so what he said wasn't just off the top of his head. He asked me to co-author a chapter in a book on <u>Theological Education of the Future</u> compiled by experts. He asked us to include our philosophy almost verbatim. We worked until 1:30 a.m. last Saturday night to finish it. He believes it will have an impact on seminaries in the U.S.A.

In November 1976, Avery wrote:

This last week we had a writers' workshop for new Indonesian writers. Most of it was planned and taught by our Indonesian staff. I was thrilled to see our work with the staff bearing fruit. It gave real hope that they could administrate the entire program in the future.

The Indonesian government has begun revising its educational system and they have requested the seminary's model of "The Taxonomy of Educational Objectives" and distributed it to two hundred high school teachers in central Java.

Ione Gray, writer for *Commission* magazine, was invited to Indonesia to write articles on theological education by extension and house churches. The interview with Avery was recorded and produced in full. Such publicity was a boon for the seminary.

The new seminary concept in Indonesia was seen as pioneering. Avery wrote an article on the "Contextualization of Theological Education in Indonesia" for the Asia Theological Association[1], which received circulation in other countries and was reprinted in *Theological Education*, receiving worldwide circulation. He was invited to speak to the leaders of seminaries throughout Asia. Requests for copies of the materials came then from other countries, so Shirley began translating some of the textbooks into English to be retranslated into the languages and cultures of those countries.

Projection to the Twenty-First Century

The Foreign Mission Board tasked Avery, as Mission chairman, and the planning committee with projecting the next twenty-five years of mission strategy—to have a "bold advance and challenge for the remainder of the century." They were asked to outline strategy with the question: "What could you do if you had unlimited personnel and unlimited funds for the next twenty-five years?" Linked to this was the board's question of how to better use short-term lay missionaries.

The paradox was that the missionaries were being asked to design these strategies and make recommendations when they had just turned over the role of "policy maker" to the Indonesian Union of Churches. To bring the nationals into the planning with the idea of unlimited resources was to set up hopes and expectations that could not be met. And while it was a positive step for the board to build a larger base of short-term mission volunteers, it conflicted with the new strategy of creating indigenous, self-sustaining churches.

After months of prayer and meetings, the committee's strategy report was submitted to the other missionaries at the 1975 Mission Meeting. It consisted of three emphases: partnering with established work, evangelizing new areas, and turning the power and leadership of the institutions over to the nationals in a more concrete way. Although the report was approved with few changes, it raised expectations and caused dissension, even among the missionaries, on how funds could best be spent. This would have been exacerbated had the nationals been included in the discussions. The irony was that, in the context of discussion of unlimited resources, the Mission had to cut its budget!

June 1975 marked a significant step in the devolution process when Tertius Sudiono was appointed as the dean of education and student affairs at the seminary. It marked a new level of Indonesian leadership. He became a central figure to help link the seminary to the local churches. He also helped the staff work together with a national spirit.

As positive as all this was, the "cold war" with the national leadership continued, especially concerning the seminary. In October of 1975, the Executive Committee of the Union voted to freeze all cooperation with the Mission. They rescinded two mutually agreed-upon declarations—one that established joint national-missionary boards for both the extension seminary and the academy, and secondly, a declaration that "where the Union could not take direct responsibility in evangelism, missionaries could serve as helpers."

Nevertheless, Avery was invited to speak at the Indonesian pastors' conference in November. It was the first time in four years that a missionary had been invited to speak to the Indonesians. It was obvious the missionary-national pastor roles had reversed when they not only paid for Avery's flights, but, after he finished speaking, they gave him fabric for a new suit!

In 1976, the academy opened in a church in Semarang with five students. At the request of the Indonesian Union president, the Mission recommended reopening the seminary campus in Semarang in addition to continuing with the TEE centers. Missionaries and nationals alike hoped for reconciliation at the upcoming congress in November 1977. Avery and Shirley were asked to stay through this meeting.

However, their youngest son, Brett, now in first grade, was having significant trouble learning letters. He had been tested and found to have a reading disability. Avery and Shirley began to plan for an early six-month furlough beginning in August 1977, following Sherrie's high school graduation, until January 1978, so that Brett could receive special education services.

SECTION 5
Equipping the American Church

Spiritual Marker #10

God led Avery to equip and disciple the American Church.

It is He who called some to be prophets, some to be evangelists,
and some to be pastors and teachers, to prepare
God's people for works of service,
so that the body of Christ may be built up
until we all reach unity in the faith
and in the knowledge of the Son of God and become mature,
attaining to the whole measure of the fullness of Christ.
—Ephesians 4:11–13 (NIV)

CHAPTER 21
About-Face: Call to America

The Willis family planned to spend six months on furlough in Tulsa, Oklahoma, before returning to Indonesia in February 1978. Living in Tulsa kept them close to Avery's parents and sister, Shirley's parents, and Oklahoma Baptist University where Randy attended and Sherrie would begin her freshman year. They planned to get advice and treatment for Brett's learning disability.

Burnout

They also desperately needed to re-engage with family and prayer partners, rest, and reenergize. The years-long conflict surrounding the seminary issues had taken its toll. Shirley wrote:

I came home from Indonesia in August both emotionally and spiritually drained. Avery and I had discussed it in Indonesia many times and doing so seemed to relieve the pressure, but after a few weeks it was always back to the same pattern. I knew I had had about all of the Indonesian Union/Mission feud I could take. I also knew that somehow I had to find my place of ministry, but I didn't have the spiritual resources to do it. We had even talked about my getting professional help when we got back to the U.S. because Avery felt my problems were deeper than he could handle. In the rush of getting settled, though, nothing more was said or done about it.[1]

Avery wanted to join Eastwood Baptist Church in Tulsa. He had preached there during the previous furlough and was impressed with the church's growth and its pastor, Tom Elliff. Shirley would have preferred a church smaller and closer to home, but allowed Avery to make the decision. She later testified:

Although I didn't feel it at the time, I now know that this was definitely the Lord's will for us. Although the worship services were helpful at times; for several months, I definitely was not getting much from the church fellowship (my fault, not theirs). After a couple of months of being in the U.S., the problems in Indonesia seemed to be growing smaller—distance and time have a way of causing that—and I thought maybe I would be able to get things under control.

Then, in October, during a time when Avery was out of town for three weeks, we got a letter giving all of the details and reactions to the consultations between the Mission and the Indonesian Union. Nothing was really new; just the same old hassle but I realized then I was not nearly ready to go back in three months; maybe no nearer than when I got home.

Since Avery was gone and I was desperate to talk with someone, I caught our pastor before supper on Wednesday evening and asked when I could speak with him. My main question was, "How can you know the will of God? Avery feels he should be in Indonesia. As a wife I am to support him, yet I continually have all these doubts." Of course, I had to tell him about the letter and the problems in Indonesia, some of which he already knew.

Before leaving Indonesia, Avery and I had registered to attend a Marriage Enrichment Retreat and it happened to be at the end of this three-week trip. I sent all the accumulated mail, including the letter from Indonesia, to Avery so that he would process it ahead of time. The retreat was helpful, but I don't think we were able to get the full benefit of it because, at the time, neither of us fully realized how far apart we had grown—especially spiritually. It was a habit we had slipped into over the years that three days couldn't erase.

During the weekend, I discovered that Avery was to talk with Pastor Tom almost immediately after our arrival at home, so I had to tell him I had talked with Tom after getting the letter. He didn't say a lot then and it was only later that I realized how much it "shook the troops," because I am not normally one to talk about my feelings or problems—especially to someone who is almost a stranger, even if he is my pastor.

We got back home and things rocked along; I picked up a few things to take back to Indonesia with us. But that seemed to be all I could make myself do. Then it got to be December and if we were going back the first of February, things needed to be done. If we weren't, we needed to make <u>that</u> decision.

It was obvious I was not ready, and I'm not sure anyone except Wade was ready because to that point we really hadn't had a furlough; Avery had so many speaking engagements, it had been one of the busiest and most separated few months we had ever spent. So we decided to extend our leave for a couple of months with the expressed intent of getting me some professional help—so I could get ready to go back. Since Pastor Tom already knew some of our history, he was willing to help.

Shirley was initially hesitant to accept Tom's help because he and the leadership of Eastwood Baptist Church has asked Avery to help them develop material for their small groups similar to what he had written for the extension seminary in Indonesia. Tom and Avery convinced Shirley it would not interfere with their working relationship, so in January, she began counseling weekly with Tom. Through these sessions, Shirley was able to identify family problems and see the resentments she was holding—especially in her relationship with Avery—as well as spiritual problems and personality issues from childhood.

The Lord showed me some very deep, long-term resentments I had toward Avery, especially for his lack of helping me grow spiritually (which was probably mostly my fault in the first place), and even resentment toward God because he didn't make me into the spiritual person Avery wanted me to be. It had gotten so bad that I had been resenting the changes Avery had been making to improve this situation!

In the days to follow, I began to learn much about submissiveness— mostly that it was an attitude, not an action. I was better at the actions than the attitude, and not even very good at that. I had problems with submission and delegation because I didn't feel that Avery had really ever delegated anything—that I had just inherited what he didn't want to do. And I resented it.

The counseling revealed a destructive habit Avery and Shirley had developed of criticizing one another. Shirley said, "I'm sure I do sometimes try to bring him down to my level that way, but goodness knows, I don't need him to bring me down any!" They also began to realize the children were fighting more and obeying less probably due to Avery's frequent absences and the resulting lack of leadership in the home. Those problems cleared up almost as quickly as Avery became aware of them and began to address them.

Interim Consulting

During the furlough, Avery was sought out by a variety of Southern Baptist organizations. Soon after he returned to the US, he consulted on goals and objectives for the training and orientation of new missionaries, as well as on evangelism training programs with the Home Mission Board, and training with the Mission Service Corps (a team of 1,400 self-funded missionary evangelists who serve for two years or more). Avery was also conferring with the leadership of the Church Training department of the Baptist Sunday School Board and with others who were considering a discipleship program combined with the house church concept, as it was being explored in Indonesia.

Avery began to sense that there was a *great movement among Southern Baptists to get on with the business of missions and evangelism in the U.S. and the world.* It seemed that the various agencies were moving toward a common goal in a way they hadn't done in years. He feared that without adequate training, these movements might dissipate—resulting in disillusionment and apathy in, or flight from, existing churches. He felt that he was being allowed to have a seminal part in a move of God.

God has opened a door wider than I ever imagined possible for me, the Indonesian seminary, and innovative education—too wide for me to ignore. I am talking with people that are shaping training for Southern Baptists for lay renewal, mass and church evangelism, church training, missionary education, and the new Mission Service Corps.

Envisioning

Avery soon began envisioning and writing action plans. He requested the materials he had created for the Indonesian seminary, began organizing and improving his presentation, and planning for a delayed return. He was trying to pull together all that he had learned about discipleship, house churches, and leadership training. He described his concept:

November 30, 1977

Southern Baptists need to develop a church model that is the equivalent of a New Testament church in the modern world. This can best be done in returning to the house church concept as the locus and focus of church development. These house churches should be led by local Christians who minister as "priests" without clergy-laity distinctions. These ministers must be developed as disciples, servant-leaders, and disciple-makers. Equippers must become enablers that equip the leaders and aid them in their ministries in the house churches.

We need a catalyst to design and test such a program in a local church setting.

In December, Tom Elliff proposed that Eastwood's Local Bible Fellowships (LBFs) could serve as a model for churches and that Avery come on staff at Eastwood to develop the training materials. He envisioned an integrated discipleship program, designed from the local church perspective, so pastors would not have to piece together their own program from various curriculum sources. Tom believed Eastwood could become a test case for both the house church concept and the discipleship materials, which would expand to other churches and have worldwide ramifications.

But Avery struggled with the notion of leaving the mission field to accomplish this.

My commitment to world missions takes priority over anything I do. The seminary program and the establishment of the New Testament church life in Indonesia may be subverted if we delay too long. My commitment to the seminary is to establish it in such a way that it will continue along the basic lines we set. At best, it will be difficult and long even with me on the job. We may need three to four more years and then the Indonesians should be able to run it.

Nevertheless, by January, Avery wrote in his journal that he felt at complete peace with what was developing, including going off salary and delaying the return for several months. Tom Elliff offered salary and housing for Avery to become a full-time, temporary staff member as his associate to develop the Local Bible Fellowships. Avery agreed as long as he was still free to continue speaking engagements and consultations with other ministries. He had already been invited to Atlanta to work with the Home Mission Board on improving TELL (a witnessing program) and their How to Build an Evangelistic Church seminar. The Church Training department of the Baptist Sunday School Board in Nashville had also requested his help.

Reconsidering

After accepting his new temporary position, he received a cassette tape and several letters urging his return to Indonesia to mediate a situation developing at the seminary.

January 27–28, 1978

The letters painted a pretty dreary picture of what <u>isn't</u> going on in the seminary extension. They intimated that the concepts I was promoting here in the U.S. weren't as "proven" in Indonesia as I might make it sound and that if I didn't return soon the new seminary structure might be swallowed up by the old pattern on campus. The letters came at an appropriate time since I was thinking that we would return in about four months when the school year ends and when the first round of Eastwood's LBF elder training would be completed. That would mean my involvement with the Home Mission Board would be limited to advice.

I'm not sure yet what I ought to do. The situation in Indonesia is improving, but it appears I do need to get back. The current Rector is not showing strong leadership but who else will be selected is unclear.

I think that subconsciously I've been trying to step down from the Rector's job for several years, partly because of my feelings about devolution and partly due to my lack of desire for that type of position, particularly with a campus program. But I'm not willing to step down if what we've done is not continued. So unless there is a negative event in that regard, I guess I'll still be required to be that servant the Lord asked me to be. I still look at it as a phase and not a lifetime commitment. My nature is to get something started, make sure it is working, and then move on to another challenge.

At any rate, this has solidified my commitment to missions, my desire to be directly involved, and my vision for reproducing disciples and house churches. It has redirected my attention to Shirley and caused me to re-examine my motives and contributions to the Kingdom. I need to make these next months as productive as possible.

In February, the Willises received letters from Indonesia saying that the nationals were definitely leaning toward an Indonesian rector of the seminary. That had been the long-term goal, and Shirley noted:

Something inside of me—whether it was woman's intuition or the Lord—said, "You're not going back to Indonesia." I never said anything about it to anyone but it did not encourage me to shop or learn more about learning disabilities or anything else that had to do with getting ready to go back.

In the same month, I finally got a Bible promise about staying in the U.S.: Acts 1:4 told me to "Tarry in Jerusalem until I was endued with power."—and Acts 1:8 said, "After you are endued with power, you will be witnesses for me."! These were the two things I most desired. Until then, I was feeling rather guilty because I had been the main person to keep us from going back.

Avery wrote in his journal on February 19, 1978:

As I read the most recent letters from Indonesia, my reaction was less than noble. I read the minutes of their meetings, and everything is now in national hands. This could be the effective death of the New Pattern or a rebirth. Today God showed me Jeremiah 33. I believe His intentions are the same and His covenant is unbreakable. He will do His work in Indonesia. My question is whether I will be part of it. My depression over this is that it may be another circumstance saying we won't return now. Shirley isn't ready yet and my work here is incomplete.

By early March, both the Home Mission Board (HMB) and Church Training department approached Avery about working with them full-time, but he gave them no encouragement since he still hoped to get back to Indonesia as quickly as possible.

Guy Leonard [of HMB] wondered if I would take the place of one of their men who had resigned. He said I was really the only person he knew "who had his whole act together to plan an overall strategy with all the agencies and then make it available to those who need it via modern technology to those here and overseas." It was affirming but I believe promotion comes from the Lord. I don't plan to carve out any kingdoms. I still plan to go back to Indonesia unless the Lord reveals differently. I just want to be free from my inhibitions and be blown by the Spirit.[2]

The Willises extended their leave until June while working on their marriage and seeking the Lord's will for their future. They still expected to return to Indonesia when the school year ended and before their current visa expired. They were newly learning how to understand the Lord's will through "Bible promises" in their LBF small group—allowing the Holy Spirit to provide direction for the day or longer-term concerns through their regular daily Scripture reading. But neither really knew how to get a Bible promise that would apply to ordinary problems and decisions.

Offers and Options

In the end, Avery looked to the Lord to decide between the multiple offers that he received.

Tom Elliff and the elders at Eastwood wanted him to lead a Bible Institute and be the director of the LBFs. Tom had received a Bible promise that God was going to give Eastwood a ministry in every nation.

Bill Hogue talked with Avery about becoming director of the Personal Witnessing department of the Home Mission Board—to lead in evangelism training and spiritual awakening. Though the witnessing and spiritual awakening appealed to Avery's gifts, he felt that the department was not set up for success because *if the men really meant business, the department would not be buried in bureaucracy, hamstrung for funds, with only two men available for its implementation.*

The Church Training department of the Baptist Sunday School Board (BSSB) asked Avery to write curriculum for them. Dr. Roy Edgemon phrased it as "writing curriculum for a lay seminary."

When Avery and Roy first met in 1977, Roy was moving into the position as the director of the Church Training department. Avery questioned Roy then about what he was planning to do in the area of discipleship. Roy responded that Dr. Grady Cothen, BSSB president, had already asked him to develop a plan; and because discipleship was the priority of his own heart, Roy had accepted the invitation to move to Nashville.

Avery asked Roy how he defined discipleship. Roy suggested they each write their definition on one side of a flip chalkboard. When they compared what they had written, the men were amazed because there was only one word of difference—a word Shirley had coined and suggested to Avery. The word was "pass-on-able," meaning everything a disciple learns should be reproducible for others they disciple.

Soon after Dr. Edgemon settled into his new position, he invited several prominent leaders on discipleship from across the country to come to Nashville to talk with his staff on the subject. Each leader was given opportunity to present their approach to discipleship. Roy saved Avery till last. They had stayed in touch since their initial meeting in Atlanta, and Roy knew that Avery was developing a discipleship plan for the local church, beginning with Eastwood Baptist Church.

Avery and Tom Elliff spent an hour presenting their plan for training church leaders in discipleship with Roy and Dr. Cothen. As they were leaving, Dr. Cothen asked Roy in private. "Is this the man you are suggesting to be the director of our adult section, and is this the new material you would like to use?"

Roy answered, "I haven't asked him yet, but with your approval, I would like to work with him. I would first ask him to write a book on the biblical basis of missions." The book would outline Avery's philosophy of discipleship and what Roy, Tom, and Avery believed was the New Testament model for church growth.

Decision

While Avery was preaching on missions at the seminary in Fort Worth, Texas, Roy called him to see whether they could meet to talk about the book. Avery agreed, but told Roy that Shirley was with him and that he would like her to be included in the meeting. To Roy, this was of God since his primary purpose for the meeting was to ask Avery to come and work with him at the Baptist Sunday School Board.

"At that point," recalls Roy, "I felt it was important that my wife, Anna Marie, join me. We picked Avery and Shirley up at the seminary and drove down to our hotel for lunch. After we had discussed the book, I told Avery that I had another agenda. I told him I had actually come to see if he would pray about working with me as the section director for our adult work to develop three curriculum lines: regular training, spiritual growth, and equipping centers—and that a part of the work would be to incorporate the material he had written on training leaders in discipleship."

Avery and Shirley asked many questions about the job and about living in Nashville. Roy told Avery that he could return to Indonesia and touch one country, but through this position, he would touch the world. Roy outlined how the discipleship and training materials would be used worldwide and translated into most of the major languages.

Roy was empathetic to Avery's situation because he had gone through a similar struggle when he left his own missionary position in Japan. He ended by saying that even if Avery didn't take the job, they would like to use the discipleship materials. Roy divulged, "I believe that this offer was a shock to Avery. I knew he really intended to spend his life in Indonesia, a place he loved, among the people he loved, but now, he was faced with a choice he had not anticipated."

Though the offer was enticing, Avery told Roy he still intended to head back to Indonesia in June and he would not have enough time to redo the materials, even with the additional writers Roy had offered.

It was sleeting and extremely cold when they got in the car and drove back to the seminary. As they stopped in front of the main building and Avery was reaching for the door handle, Anna Marie spoke up. "I'm deeply troubled, Avery, that you have made your decision without praying about it, and that we have accepted your decision without praying about it."

"Her statement shocked us," remembers Roy. "We had to admit what she said was true, so with the heater running, we just stayed in the car. After we had prayed for at least an hour, Avery said that he and Shirley needed more time before making a final decision. We decided that we would set aside the next three weeks to pray and then get back in touch."[3]

March 24, 1978

For the first time since Roy talked to me, I've looked more favorably on the job. The fact that they would put all three curricula under me sounds like I'd have enough freedom and the resources to accomplish something. But I don't really understand the job and feel I need to go talk to them to fully understand it. I've been trying to think toward Indonesia but have had some difficulty putting myself back in that position since they are choosing an Indonesian rector. I don't know what role I'd have or freedom and resources I'd be given. I feel very strongly about the need to help Church Training set up their concepts and discipleship before returning to Indonesia. But if we stay longer than July 23, our visa will expire and that may mean a permanent change or at least a long stay since visas are so hard to get now.

Finding Answers in Scripture

April 3, 1978

After my vision time on Good Friday, from 2:00 to 5:00 a.m., I feel I need to go to Nashville. I have outlined the vision the Lord has given me.

My goal is to present to the Southern Baptist agency leaders the vision of reproducing disciples and house churches as God's vehicle for renewal of the churches and Bold Mission Thrust throughout the world. The convention is in need of a new means to reach the lost. Shaking the tree doesn't produce more fruit if the roots are diseased.

I don't know why I feel that somehow all these things must come together to keep me from returning to Indonesia, but I do. I don't want to leave out any part of missions, discipleship, house churches, renewal, evangelism, and training of the laity and equipping of the clergy. It is too much for any man so I still need to hear God's voice and He needs to prepare the way and make the offer He wants.

In April, the Lord gave Shirley several scriptural promises in as many days. Philippians 1:9–10 was a promise concerning Avery and her "that your love will keep on growing more and more together so that you will be able to choose what is best."

I knew then that we were on the way, and probably soon would be ready to know what our decision was to be. Matthew 13:52 said to me that we would become homeowners and take things out of storage, i.e., stay here in America. Avery wasn't so sure. So then I had to talk with Tom about finding Bible promises together. What if we didn't both interpret them the same way?

Three Men at the Gate

April 14 was a turning point. Both Bill Hogue and Tom had told Avery they thought the first decision to make was whether or not to return to Indonesia; other decisions could be made if and when they resolved to stay in the States.

About ten that morning, Avery left his proofreading at the office and went home. He and Shirley prayed, talked, and read the Bible till it was time to pick up the kids from school. During that time, they read Acts 10 about the vision the apostle Peter received from the Lord to "kill and eat" the unclean animals. In the passage, though he was first appalled, Peter submitted to the Lord on the third command. Then the Lord told him that three men would come to his door and he was to go with them without hesitation, "for I have sent them." At that moment, three men arrived, sent by Cornelius, a Roman centurion, asking Peter to come and preach to his family. That led to the preaching of the gospel and the pouring out of the Holy Spirit on the Gentiles.

Avery wrote:

I can relate to Peter. The American church is already dead—I certainly wouldn't want to eat it! I see three men are at my gate but I don't yet know where they are taking me. Do I go with them to find out? Is the Lord pointing me back to the USA to help decontaminate and equip a large missionary force for effective work?

Avery and Shirley read Isaiah 43, a passage Avery felt the Lord had spoken to him earlier in the year, promising God would give him men and nations for his life. God gave them a definite promise in Isaiah 43:5–6, 18–19 that they would come back from the east... and they were to look and see what God was making happen! He promised to refresh them, form them, and pour out His Spirit that they should grow. And He was telling them beforehand as a testimony that He was God.

I walked the floor and prayed and committed ourselves to His will and said aloud, "We will not return to Indonesia." I really wept as I prayed that. I told God that it was too hard—that I couldn't do it without His help. Amidst sobs, I said I wasn't sure I could even do it then. But I gave myself to Him for His use and will.
There was no elation at having made the decision. Just grief. And a little relief at having made some decision.

Step 1 had been determined.

But, every time over the next two days, when Shirley mentioned not returning, I cringed.

Mutual Confirmation

Eastwood Baptist Church had a spring Bible conference ten days later. On Sunday evening, Avery and Shirley were in the prayer chapel. Avery shared a list of all the questions he hoped to get answered during the conference. The first verses Shirley read immediately after that were Exodus 19:10–11 and 16; and she knew it was a promise that if they would prepare themselves, God would reveal Himself by the coming Wednesday. So they fasted through the remainder of the conference. Avery was to go to Atlanta on Wednesday to meet with men from the Home Mission Board. Was the answer to come from there?

Shirley wrote:

I woke up very early Monday morning and couldn't sleep. As I got up and prayed, I realized that there were still problems we had not resolved and maybe that was the reason the Lord was still waiting. If we went anywhere right then, we would fall right back into the same old habits. My biggest problem was still the issue of submission: when to say anything or when to keep quiet. How many times can I bring something up before it becomes nagging?

On Tuesday, Avery and I talked again with Tom. I was rather apprehensive, but we had a good talk and were able to get through most of the remaining problems. We also told him about our promise in Isaiah, which helped to confirm the decision in our own minds. I told Tom about my promise in Exodus and he almost came unglued; he was so excited!

On Wednesday I woke up with the Pepsi commercial going over and over in my mind, "You're on the verge of something great ... This day is made to celebrate." Maybe not particularly religious but it expressed my feelings. That night during the service, the Lord spoke to me clearly— just as He had promised, but not at all like I had expected. Both speakers' messages came through loud and clear that God is sovereign and that His plan is best for us, no matter what it is. Several verses in Isaiah 45 and 46 showed me that God had big things in store for us which He will swoop down and accomplish. And even though we are stubborn and think victory is far away, it is really very near.

God really convicted me that I had been standing in His way and Avery's way for years because I thought it was my job to keep Avery's feet on the ground. Whenever Avery came out with his high dreams of God's calling, I either said nothing or quickly brought him back to earth. Of course, I had to ask the Lord to forgive me and ask Avery to forgive me as well when he got home. I wrote Tom a note and handed it to him after the service. He told me later that when he read it in the airport, he literally shouted! I wrote in my journal that night, "It is not going to be easy for me to change and allow Avery the freedom to do all he can and will—all that the Lord wants him to do. It's going to demand more submission on my part, both to God and to Avery. But I believe I'm willing to try for the first time. It should be a freeing process for both of us."

I still hadn't heard from Avery to see if he had received an answer on his end while in Atlanta, but I fully expected him to do so. I knew someone had tried to call him long distance about 5:00 p.m. When Avery got home, I learned it had been Roy Edgemon, calling from Nashville. Avery thought the Lord had missed his three days by a few hours; he didn't know Roy had tried the night before.

Dr. Roy Edgemon's call was good news! Dr. Grady Cothen had approved the writing of forty equipping centers over three years and budgeted two million dollars (the biggest outlay in the history of the board). Dr. Cothen wanted to meet with Avery and Tom on May 15 about making the discipleship curriculum Avery had adapted for Eastwood's Local Bible Fellowships part of the regular curriculum for Church Training. They felt Avery had both the theological and educational training to pull it off. They were excited about developing a discipleship training program and a launch point for the whole church growth movement.

April 30, 1978

Tonight, as Ron and Pat Owens sang in the service, I felt that God was asking me to be available and be the "face of God" to those who don't know Him. I really felt scared. He is asking me to do more than I have the ability to do, so He'll have to do it. I've got to come back to the point I began when I read Moody's book, "The world has yet to see what God can do with one man fully dedicated to God." I need to spend much more time in prayer so I can be His prophet.

Isaiah 49:6 promised that this ministry God was preparing would eventually have worldwide ramifications, but it was accompanied by a warning in Isaiah 5:19 to wait—God would carry out His plans if they would just be patient.

As Avery thought and prayed about how to answer Dr. Cothen, he felt the Lord speak to him from Nehemiah 2 and 1 Samuel 9–10. Avery felt the Lord wanted him to propose an American version of what was being practiced at the Indonesian seminary—that Church Training should become a "lay seminary."

Avery and Tom returned from Nashville like they were walking on air. The Lord had done more than either of them had dared hope. There were no objections to their proposal! Cothen and Edgemon had accepted the plan to enhance the ongoing curriculum with a discipleship institute with selected enrollment, self-instructional materials, accountability, and local recognition. Cothen said there was much to work out, but that the board wanted "to hitch our wagon to your star."

Avery had told the men that, due to a Bible promise, he would not give a final answer for seven days, so they waited. On the day that Avery and Roy had agreed to reconnect, Roy was in a meeting at the Nashville airport when he received a call from Avery. Avery first asked what Roy was hearing from the Lord. Roy responded that he believed it was the will of God and how soon could Avery come? Avery agreed. He too felt this was God's plan. So he and Shirley began making plans to move to Nashville.

Besides confirmation for the big move, Shirley was looking for a promise about whether to accompany Avery on a farewell return trip to Indonesia. They had already decided that Avery should go back for the Theological Education Consultation retreat and pastors' conference, even at their own expense. Tom convinced Avery that Shirley should go too. Shirley resisted:

That was the last thing I wanted to do! I knew how hard it would be emotionally—and spiritually—to say goodbye to everyone—both missionaries and nationals. I even said, "I think the Lord would have to give me a Bible verse that says, 'Shirley Willis, go to Indonesia' before I would be willing to go!"

Then on the day before Avery was to give his answer to Nashville, I got the promise. In my regular reading, I had gotten to Luke 8, the story of the healing of the Gadarene demoniac. Guess what Jesus told him to do when he had healed him: "Go back home and tell what the Lord has done for you!" (TEV) It didn't have my name in it, but I knew it was for me, and I just bawled—partly because I was so excited and partly because I still didn't want to go. But after a few minutes, I was okay, and then became very excited about sharing my story.

On that same day, Deuteronomy 3:23–25 was a confirmation that what we were getting ready to do was the right thing. This was followed by several verses in Deuteronomy 6 which warned us to never get back in the old rut we had been in together, but to continue with this "new life together" that God had given us. The next day, the day Avery gave his answer, I read Deuteronomy 9:1ff "You are about to cross the Jordan to go in . . ." with the promises that followed.

Knowing God's Will

While making the life-changing decision to leave the mission field to provide discipleship training in the USA, Avery listed the guidelines he used to determine God's will:

- Spirit – The Spirit must bear witness in my heart that this is right.
- Uniqueness – I should do only what I can do—if someone else can do it, I should let them.
- Significance – I should invest my life where it will do the most long-term good.
- Gifts – I should be in the place that is best suited to my gifts and abilities for maximum effectiveness.
- Receptivity – I should be where God is moving—a place of receptivity.
- Need – I should put my life against the greatest need. If other factors are equal in two options, then need is the basic criteria.
- Freedom of the Word – I should be in a place that allows complete adherence to the Word and use it as the testing standard.
- Family – I should serve in a place that does not violate my family responsibilities.
- Faithfulness – I should not renege on current commitments without obvious leadership of the Spirit.

Summary:

1. Situation: need, receptivity, and freedom
2. Me: uniqueness, significance, gifts, family, faithfulness
3. God: Spirit, Word, and timing

Guidelines for Movement from the Word of God:

1. God's promises to give the people new husbandmen and shepherds and that I should set up waymarks. Jeremiah 31–33

2. Move only when the glory of God goes before you as with His tabernacle. Exodus. 40:36–38

3. God's hand is not shortened, and He will take care of the how. Numbers 10–12

4. Move on God's timetable—not ahead like Asa, who relied on Egypt in 2 Chronicles 16, or behind like Israel after Kadesh—too late and in their own power in Numbers 14. I must follow His command when He gives it, not before or after lest God punish me.

5. I must not trust a means as Moses did with his rod or put myself in God's place. Numbers 20

6. I must not waver after God shows me His will though honorable men offer great rewards and fame—not even to go look at the possibilities with them as Balaam did. Numbers 22

7. God will give me a burden for the country He wants me to serve in as He did with Moses, even to being blotted out. Exodus 32:32

CHAPTER 22
Discipleship in America—and Beyond

What happened to discipleship?
People started making excuses instead of making disciples!
—Avery

In 1975, the Southern Baptist convention established an initiative to take the gospel to every person in the world by the year 2000 called Bold Mission Thrust. Although Avery fully believed in and embraced Jesus Christ's Great Commission to "go into all the world and make disciples of every nation, baptizing them in the name of the Father, Son, and Holy Spirit, teaching them to obey whatever I have commanded you" (Matthew 28:18–20), he was equally certain that the people advocating the movement didn't fully comprehend the enormity of the task or that reproducible discipleship was God's one and only strategy to accomplish it. This excerpt is from one of multiple settings in which he addressed the issue.

Discipleship: Man's Plan, God's Plan

In response, let me affirm the faith expressed by [the proponents of Bold Mission Thrust] *but I want to remind us that "starting five million new churches and reaching one billion souls" is not an easy goal to achieve. We need to realize that we are asking for a God-sized goal and one that won't happen simply because someone predicts or sets goals for it to happen.*

Do you even know how many a billion is? If a person had been baptized every minute since Christ walked out of the tomb, we would just reach a billion by the year 2000. And we think we can do it ten years?

You might say, "We could do it faster—baptize more than one person at a time!"

Ok. What if we baptized three thousand people a day like at Pentecost? It would still take almost a thousand years to get to <u>one</u> billion and 5,479 years to get to all five billion lost people in the world today [1975]. It would take you more than seven years to just <u>glance</u> at the faces of five billion people at the rate of <u>five faces per second</u>.[1] If you were to take the time to just say "Jesus loves you" to each one, it would take thirty-five years to speak to one billion people and 175 <u>years</u> to address all five billion lost people alive today.

And world population is outstripping our comprehension. In spite of these statistics, Baptists are saying they will share the gospel with everyone on earth by the year 2000. That means we have to witness to approximately 300 million people each year and that doesn't count the people who are born and die each year. All the modern means known to man cannot effectively present the message to that number of people each year, scattered as they are through the remote regions of the world!

AND YET! This was Jesus' specific command! He had a plan and we must recover it. He painstakingly discipled twelve men over three years and taught them by example to disciple others. Stated simply, God's plan is multiplication: One person is to disciple one or more until the one being discipled can disciple someone else. Then the two should disciple two others, and so forth. If each disciple could help another person to become a disciple every six months, it would take only sixteen and one-half years to total more than eight and one-half billion people.

But a critical point remains: To reproduce a disciple, one must BE a disciple. If the second disciple in our example above fails to reproduce himself, our final figure is cut in half. Or suppose that disciple is only half-hearted in learning and practices only one-half of what he has been taught. Then his disciple will pick up his half-hearted attitude and cut in half again the standard of the original disciple. If that pattern continues, the impact of future disciples becomes inconsequential.[2]

"Jesus did not call people to be Christians but to be disciples. He did not tell them how easy it would be but how difficult. He did not invite them to walk an aisle but to follow him in daily obedience. He did not tell them to forget about the cost but to count it. Jesus did not require anyone to have certain talents, to be educated, or to be a member of a certain

social class. He only demanded obedience. He took people wherever they were and led them to be more like Him.

If we are to do the will of God on earth, we must recapture the life of discipleship as the norm in our churches. A disciple is one who makes Jesus Christ Lord of his life. He may fail in the application of his commitment at times, but there is no wavering in his allegiance to Christ as the Lord of his life."[3]

Writing the Message

Reproducible discipleship was the heart of Avery's message that he would bring to the Baptist Sunday School Board in Nashville, Tennessee. Upon his arrival, Avery's first assignment was to get Ralph Neighbor's innovative, cartoon-illustrated approach to discipleship, the *Survival Kit for New Christians*, ready for printing. It was published in December 1978.

Avery's first book, entitled *The Biblical Basis of Missions*, followed in 1979. His interest in writing the book was sparked years earlier when a professor of missions remarked that a more current doctrinal book was needed on the biblical foundation for mission work. Avery wrote in the preface:

I was startled because I thought that everything on the biblical basis of missions had been written already. When I later wrote an outline and did research for the contents of this book, I realized I had not understood nor experienced all that I discovered in the Bible about missions. I had served one term of missionary service, but I returned to Indonesia to put into practice what God had revealed to me in his Word.

Through fourteen years of missionary experiences in Indonesia, God forced me to study his Word over and over for a deeper understanding of the biblical basis of missions and ministry and its implications for us today. He has given me a fresh perspective of His purpose and plan for the world and the ways He intends to bring people of all nations to Himself. I hope that this attempt to share these insights with you will result in your understanding the biblical basis of missions; but even more, I hope that it will result in your making world missions the overriding purpose of your life.

Avery and Shirley's 25th wedding anniversary celebration
Nashville, Tennessee, December, 1980

MasterLife

Avery was simultaneously writing his own discipleship training for leaders, adapting the coursework he had written in the Indonesian seminary and for Eastwood's Local Bible Fellowships, recontextualizing it for the American culture. Jimmy Crowe, Avery's associate and publishing expert, played an important role in making the materials, called *MasterLife*, into the powerful leadership training tool it later became worldwide.

Roy Edgemon introduced *MasterLife* in 1980 as "an in-depth training experience for discipleship leaders. Participants will have the opportunity to learn how to abide in Christ and live in the Word. It addresses prayer and faith, fellowship of believers, witnessing in the world and ministering to others. Participants will study how to discover their potentialities and spiritual gifts for ministry. They will

292

receive guidance on how to discipline their lives and enlist the help of others in reaching their goals for Christ."[4]

MasterLife was introduced with a new marketing strategy that publishing experts insisted would not work—called "pull-through" marketing. The plan mandated that only trained leaders could buy the material. Churches could not order the materials until they had a leader who had been trained by a *MasterLife* trainer. In doing so, the plan placed a value on training and reproducibility and separated out those who were not serious.[5]

Roy was convinced *The Survival Kit for New Christians* and *MasterLife* would prove to be revolutionary, both in their quality and interactive methodology. He arranged that the new *LifeWay* imprint first appear on these works. Subsequent decades have proven him correct. Both resources continue to have an overwhelming impact.

And What Do You Do?
(Told by Shirley Willis)

Since Avery was a frequent flyer on the airlines, he was often offered an upgrade to business class if extra seats were available. One particular day, on a return trip to Nashville, he settled into his upgraded seat and, after fastening his seat belt, turned to introduce himself to the man sitting next to him.

"Hello, my name is Avery Willis."

"Hi, I'm Ricky Skaggs."

"And what do you do for a living?"

"I'm a country singer," smiled Ricky, who had recently been named Country Music Artist of the Year. "What do you do?"

"I write materials to help people know how to master their life."

Interested, Ricky asked to hear more. Then he suddenly jumped up and got his *Survival Kit* from his briefcase in the overhead bin. The conversation continued through the flight, and when Avery disembarked, his traveling companions declared enviously, "I can't believe you got to talk to Ricky Skaggs! Did you get his autograph?"

"No," Avery replied. Then he added with an impish smile, "But he got my Disciple's Cross!"

Through the years, testimonies to *MasterLife*'s impact have demonstrated how God has used its powerful influence to change lives and churches.

Maryland: Great Commission Baptist Church, a dying church in a transitional community, turned around when the pastor first used *MasterLife* with his own family, then with his five leaders. The church later taught the *LIFE* (Lay Institute for Equipping) courses to meet the needs of their community. In 8½ years, the church grew from 32 to nearly 1,500 members and began ministering in multiple countries, with a primary focus in Guyana because immigrants from Guyana were part of the congregation.

Texas: Fellowship Church put *MasterLife* graduates on each of their sports teams, enlisted unbelieving players for the teams, and assigned the *MasterLife* graduates to witness to and disciple the team members.

Oklahoma: First Baptist Church, Moore, Oklahoma, began *MasterLife* in 1982. "In 1989–1990, we had 150 people in *MasterLife*. In 1991, we graduated over 300 people, and plan for 500 this fall. All 33 Sunday School department directors have finished the course and all officers are currently studying. We have grown from 1500 to 2500 in attendance in the past two years. We now have two worship services and three rounds of Sunday School. We plan to teach *MasterLife* in one round of Sunday School each year—and on Sunday and Wednesday evenings—while some leaders will teach it in home groups."

Texas: Don Dennis, a former convict, began using *MasterLife* in Texas prisons. Men's lives were being radically transformed, and they learned to share their faith and make disciples of others. *MasterLife* graduates were placed in inner city church staff positions when they were released from prison.

Florida: When Panamanian dictator, General Manuel Noriega, was captured, arrested, and extradited to the US, Dr. Clift Brannon Sr. sent him a Soulwinner's New Testament with the words "God loves you and so do I" in the flyleaf. When he received it, Noriega sent word through his lawyer that he wanted to know this God who loved him—now! With special permission from President Clinton, Clift and his interpreter, Rudy Hernandez, were given permission to enter General

Manuel Noriega's cell in Miami, Florida, and witness to him. This led to his placing his faith in Christ and the conversion of some of his family members.

Clift then turned the responsibility of discipling General Noriega over to Dr. Anthony "Tony" Ponceti. Tony had been trained in *MasterLife* with Avery, had been involved with the Texas Baptist Men's prison ministry, and had just moved to Miami, Florida. Tony met with Noriega for approximately ten hours a week for nearly nine years. When they finished *MasterLife*, they studied *Experiencing God* together. Tony said, "I discipled him for the first three years and he discipled me the next six years."[6] (For the full story, refer to the appendix "Reaching Manuel Noriega.")

Even after Avery's death, *MasterLife* has continued to impact lives and churches. In December 2015, Elizabeth Baptist Church of Atlanta, Georgia, held a graduation ceremony for 1,245 who had just completed the course.[7]

A key ingredient of the *MasterLife* discipleship process was the daily time each participant spent with the Lord. Participants were taught a simple tool of reading Scripture, writing down what the Lord revealed to them through the Scripture, whether it be an instruction, a reproof, a correction, or a training in right living (2 Tim. 3:16). Then they would speak back to God what He had said and what they would do in response to that word. The result was that their relationship with Jesus became dynamic. Learning how to listen to the Lord's guidance and obey created marked changes in their life. The extended time to complete the course (eighteen or thirty-six weeks) established that time and process as a powerful habit.

Avery reported:

What we are seeing in MasterLife is that people are getting in touch with the Word of God again and letting the Lord work in their hearts. MasterLife is essentially helping people understand what it means to abide in Christ. And they are bearing fruit as a result. We're seeing revival and renewal in the lives of people over a span of time to really change lifestyles and direction.

The keys are the modeling by those who lead the group and putting the learning immediately into practice. The only hindrance to the effectiveness of MasterLife would be exchanging the discipling process for a product and/or viewing MasterLife as an academic teaching tool.

Avery listed his hopes for the growth of *MasterLife* not in terms of sales or numbers but in the end product: *I'll tell you what I'm looking for. I'm looking for an army of 200,000 to 300,000 people who are ready to go anywhere, any time, and do anything the Lord says do—whether they're lay people or clergy—people who are disciples.*[8]

Expanding Beyond the Churches

By 1983, Avery was involved in the Sunday School Board's publishing of forty equipping center modules and a study course on the doctrine of the Holy Spirit, even as training people in *MasterLife* continued throughout the United States. Two of the Baptist seminaries soon added it to their curriculum.

In September that same year, *Commission* magazine reported that "already used in thousands of Southern Baptist churches in the United States, *MasterLife* is now being spread throughout the world by missionaries and national leaders in their individual countries." The article included reports from Holland, England, Israel, Austria, Venezuela, South Africa, and Japan. *MasterLife* had been added to the curriculum of Nigerian, Argentinian, and Malaysian seminaries.[9]

The next year, the Foreign Mission Board trained 1,500 missionaries in *MasterLife*. By then, it had already been translated into twenty languages and had been taught in more than a hundred countries. The *Survival Kit for New Christians* had been translated into more than fifty languages and was being used all over the world. Furthermore, by May 1985, discipleship training was being produced on video in addition to the live training events.[10]

By 1990, *MasterLife* was in fifty different languages, and approximately two hundred thousand people had grown as disciples and ministers by studying it. Avery was particularly excited about the work Don Dennis was doing with *MasterLife* in prisons, beginning in Texas, but expanding through the nation. Avery mobilized members of the Mission Service Corps to help with administration and work in the prisons.

Avery presenting at a MasterLife training, 1980s

Expanding Training

Avery completed *MasterBuilder*, a sequel to *MasterLife*, in 1984. Whereas *MasterLife* was designed to help a person become a growing disciple of Jesus and minister to others as they discovered gifts and areas of service, *MasterBuilder* was designed to take the *MasterLife* graduate into skill development as a leader. The tremendous response to both these courses and demand for training led to the creation of a new section within the Baptist Sunday School Board called Leadership Development. Avery was asked to head up this new section with Jimmy Crowe and Larry Roberts.

In 1987, Avery's Leadership Development section launched the *Lay Institute for Equipping* (LIFE), which consisted of intensive, experiential courses lasting approximately thirteen weeks. This planned educational system enabled leaders and potential leaders to grow at their own pace according to their life goals and spiritual gifts. Much like the students of Indonesia's TEE (Theological Education by Extension), participants spent an average of thirty to sixty minutes daily in a "personalized class" in their own homes, or place of their choice, using self-paced, interactive, individual textbooks. They were involved in on-the-job training for most courses. In addition, there were weekly one- to two-hour seminars with a leader who guided the participants in learning, reflecting, evaluating, problem-solving, and planning.

MasterLife in Europe

In April 1990, five months after the fall of the Berlin Wall, Avery traveled with a team to West Germany, East Germany, and Poland to visit the churches. Their escorts were Jim Smith and Bill Wagner, who had translated and taught *MasterLife* in almost every one of the European nations. It was a critical time to help the East German churches step out and take advantage of their new freedom from communism to make disciples. The church members wanted to be witnesses for Christ, but found it difficult to do so after being prevented from witnessing openly for so many years. West Germany had 2,000–3,000 people involved in *MasterLife*, and those pastors taught East German pastors.[11]

MasterLife in China

Avery was invited to China, Korea, and Hong Kong in 1991 to introduce *MasterLife*. Tom Elliff had accompanied Katherine Pih to China the year before, and on his recommendation of *MasterLife* as the "best leadership training they could have," the Chinese Christian Council (CCC) invited Avery and provided diplomatic passports for the team.

Christians in China numbered about seven hundred thousand when the Communists took over in 1949. During the "cultural revolution," all churches were closed, Christians were persecuted, and the church went underground. Forty years later, when the churches were reopened, the number of Christians had grown to five million in registered churches plus millions more remaining in the underground church. Most pastors were now seventy to eighty years of age, so the greatest need was for Christian leaders. Most of the work was currently carried by laymen or bivocational pastors.

God said to Avery regarding the Scripture in Matthew 10:16 to "be as shrewd as snakes and innocent as doves":

Many Chinese Christians understand these commands better than you do. They had no choice but to be sheep and doves and to be beaten, imprisoned, flogged, and killed. They have experienced much persecution that you can't understand. You need to go humbly and as a brother not as a benefactor or giver of material things. Be as shrewd as snakes because you are dealing with the Serpent's territory. He's held it for thousands of years and has wreaked his slaughter on the people, especially during communism. Be on guard against men. Although you go meekly and with friendliness, do not be gullible. You must be alert and not give Satan any corner in your thoughts and mind. He knows the importance of this mission both in Korea and the disciples they send out to the nations and in China with untrained leaders for the house churches. They are much like the Indonesians of 1965–1968 during the revival there—they are experiencing freedom in a political turmoil. You can't imagine what I am and will be doing there in the future. What you do has a significance beyond what you do on this trip.

Avery summarized parts of his journal:[12]

So much has happened to communism worldwide since we received the invitation to China that the government was putting pressure on Christian leaders. Newspapers assured the people what happened in Russia (the fall of communism) would never happen in China. Everything was very tight. It seemed that the government had decided to give us the VIP treatment and keep us so busy seeing the growth of churches that we would not have time to present MasterLife.

Never have we been treated so royally. In every city, we were entertained at huge banquets by Christian and government leaders. The

Chinese are the best cooks in the world, but they eat everything! We were served such things as squid, prawns, crab, eel, sea cucumbers, octopus, shark fin soup, fried fish gills, chicken feet, quail, snake, frog, toad saliva soup, and a few things I have tried to forget. Most were delicious. At the banquets, they gave welcoming speeches and told us how wonderfully the church had grown under communism. When I spoke in response, I relied on the Holy Spirit to direct my words so some of the government officials had the opportunity to hear the gospel.

In one town, people shot off fireworks as they led us up the street to the church where a brass band lined both sides of the entrance. Our interpreter said, "Even George Bush didn't get this type of reception!"

Nevertheless, it looked like we were not going to be allowed to do what we had come to do. But God led Katherine Pih to find ways for us to present in four seminaries, in churches in all the major cities, and to the Council. Their eyes lit up when we gave the MasterLife presentations of the Disciple's Cross, the Disciple's Personality, God's Word in Heart and Hand, and gave them Power Bands along with our personal testimonies.

We were warned to be very careful not to put the Christians in a situation that would make it worse for them. Our interpreter, a professor at the Nanjing seminary, told us that the committee had evaluated MasterLife and decided they would not recommend its use to the Council because it was too systematic and difficult for the average Chinese. Our presentation time had been reduced to two hours. He said, "If you really want to teach this, then you need to teach me so that in the future, I will be able to promote it." That crystallized our thinking that one of the main jobs we had on this trip was to disciple our interpreter.

As I walked the streets of Shanghai early one morning, I was just overwhelmed by the multitudes of people. I thought "God surely must love the Chinese. He made so many of them!" I found it difficult to grasp what it meant to love more than a billion Chinese. The Lord shared with me His compassion and tears continually came to my eyes as I walked, realizing that every one of these people would be in heaven or in hell. In the two weeks we were in China, a half million Chinese were born and almost that many died, many without knowing the Lord Jesus Christ. God is doing a great work in China, and we wanted to do all we could to help.

We gathered in our room to pray and poured out our hearts. We hoped the room was not bugged. As we prayed, Joe Barnes said, "It is already accomplished. God has already set His purpose, and He will accomplish it." Before I went to sleep that night, the Lord reminded me of 2 Chronicles 20, that "the battle is not yours, but God's." I once again claimed this Scripture which has been so pivotal in big events in my life. I believed God was going to give the victory but I did not know how.

We first met with the Nanjing Provincial Christian Council. They described the situation the church faced with so many becoming Christians and so few leaders being available. They were trying to do short term training but had few resources. Then they asked me to respond.

I compared their situation to Indonesia when two million came to Christ in five years. That gave me an opportunity to share about MasterLife and how it had developed. I also had the chance to share how the seminary program spread out to regional seminaries and teaching centers for people on different levels of education. They began to see that MasterLife held promise for their situation.

The meeting with the Chinese Christian Council was completely different. Instead of all the introductions and explanations, the leader began by saying that the committee would give their report. The members were very uncomfortable because it meant they had to criticize something we offered even before exchanging pleasantries. The leader, seeing their discomfort, asked how we should proceed. I told him it was up to him. He asked me to explain MasterLife in approximately thirty minutes. He asked if we had books for everyone. We quickly pulled out our Chinese and Basic English MasterLife materials. God guided our conversation and they expressed intense interest in using the materials.

I wanted to "close the deal" but God said, "No, Avery, this is your Isaac (my child of promise through whom God had promised to bless the nations). You must lay it on the altar and let me determine what happens next." I swallowed hard and quietly left it on the altar. That accomplished more than I realized at the time. It allowed the Council to not have to reject it as they had been told. They didn't have to make any decision. They will be free to do as God leads them. In fact, the committee never voiced a single criticism or even hint at rejecting it.

The key thing is that we felt we did everything God wanted us to do in the circumstances. Now we must walk in faith and watch for His next step.

In Korea, the team was privileged to introduce the *Disciple's Prayer Life* at the World Prayer Center on Prayer Mountain. Over the previous two decades, Korean Baptists had increased from seventy thousand to four hundred thousand, and now they were asking for help as they focused on discipleship over the next decade.

MasterLife in Russia

In 1994, Roy and Anna Marie Edgemon were Bible teachers for the Baptist missionaries from all the countries that had once made up the Soviet Union. The first night, the leader from St. Petersburg spoke of the small window of time in which they would have religious freedom. He claimed they did not have time to enlist and train leaders in seminaries. He publicly asked for one hundred teachers of *MasterLife* to come and train pastors for the future churches in Russia. Dr. Edgemon said, "We sent forty, but it was not enough."[13]

MasterLife across the Cultures
(Told by Randy Willis)

The organic nature of *MasterLife* discipleship was vividly illustrated in Paris in 2011.

Personal discipleship met opportunity on a short-term mission trip to Paris, France in the spring of 2011. That winter, I began discipling a handful of people in my home church in Oklahoma through *MasterLife*. We were halfway through *Book 1* when I was asked to lead a mission trip to help and encourage a Chinese church in Paris. A young couple in the *MasterLife* group, Chris and Aimee, signed up to go with me.

At the end of *Book 1*, each disciple is asked to give a presentation of what they've learned of the basic tenets of discipleship. Chris's presentation was such that I asked if he'd be willing to make the same presentation to the Parisian Chinese church in a few weeks. He was surprised, and nervous, but agreed.

That Sunday in Paris, Chris did so well before a full room of forty people that I decided he could repeat it the following night at a second church. He went with a translator while I stayed with the team. The next morning, we met up.

"How did it go last night?" I asked.

"Okay. But they were already aware of the Disciple's Cross."

I was surprised. "What do you mean . . . they already knew it?"

"It seemed like they already knew everything I talked about! They had some questions, but I told them to save all their questions until tonight, because the son of the man that wrote the material would be here to answer everything!"

Terrific. But I was not as concerned about unanswerable questions as I was wondering how these Chinese men in Paris might be familiar with *MasterLife*.

That evening, full of curiosity, I took the train to their neighborhood and climbed the long hill to the apartment complex. Before the church service started, I had opportunity to quiz the men in question. What does it mean to be a disciple of Jesus? What are the habits of a disciple? What are the characteristics of a disciple? I leaned in, listening to their answers through a translator. They had certainly been discipled by someone! I pressed on, asking what they had studied. One of the men disappeared to an adjoining room and returned with four books written in Mandarin—the four-volume set of *MasterLife* books!

I discovered that their discipler was a Chinese taxi driver in Paris—who had himself been discipled in Hong Kong using *MasterLife*. Across three continents and three languages, there had been one purpose—making disciples of Christ.

New Approach

In 1996, Avery and Kay Moore coauthored a revision of the *MasterLife* material into four six-week books. They had received feedback that the eighteen-week program of the original *MasterLife I* and *MasterLife II* was often so intensive and prolonged that it was difficult to complete. By creating a series of six-week studies that could be completed with breaks between each one, the material was accessible to more people with a variety of schedules and commitments.

Kay and Avery were outlining the revision of what was to become *MasterLife Book 3, The Disciples' Victory*. She recounts:

> After only a few sentences into his vision for the project, Avery scooted back in his chair as we sat at the table and looked at me squarely and soberly. "You know, Kay, you are going to experience spiritual warfare once you take on this topic," he warned.
>
> Inwardly I scoffed and mentally rolled my eyes. "Oh, Avery, been there, done that. I know how to deal with temptation."
>
> Still dead-on serious, he shook his head. "You've never known warfare like you will when you tackle this," he continued. "Just be on your guard and stay prayed up."
>
> I promised I would. And how right he was! Satan certainly didn't want *Book 3* to see the light of day. I experienced extraordinary troubles the entire time Avery and I worked on its revision. Of the four *MasterLife* volumes in the new format, it still is my personal favorite, *Book 3*, the book of my heart.

In 1998, Avery's daughter, Sherrie, coauthored a trade book version titled *MasterLife: Developing a Rich Personal Relationship with the Master*. It contained the same topics but was written for general readership, with discussion and application questions at the end of each chapter, rather than the interactive approach.

Clyde Meador, colleague of Avery in Indonesia and subsequently executive vice president of the International Mission Board, remarked, "Some folks who did not know Avery might think he was bragging when he talked about all that the Lord was doing, the way God was using him. But that was not what he was doing because he was a man in whom there was no guile. He was simply reporting what God was doing."

CHAPTER 23
Aligning the Leaders

Strategy is not made in the board room but
discerned in the prayer room.

—Avery

C laude King, design editor for *Lay Institute for Equipping* (*LIFE*) at the Baptist Sunday School Board, described Avery as a "door opener for many leaders. He was constantly on the lookout for people who had a life message needed by the body of Christ. He was committed to building relationships and networking for Kingdom purposes. He was not as concerned about denominational 'turf' as he was about seeing God's people strengthened and equipped."

Dr. Henry Blackaby

In the fall of 1986, Avery and Claude attended a conference to introduce lay renewal leaders from across the country to *LIFE*. Dr. Henry Blackaby, Director of Missions for the Capilano Baptist Association in Vancouver, British Columbia, was the keynote Bible teacher. He spoke on "knowing and doing God's will" during the afternoon free time. Nearly every attendee showed up. At the conclusion, Avery leaned over and asked Claude if he thought Henry would have enough material to write a *LIFE* course for them.

Avery was convinced it was an important and timely message for the church at large and was committed to creating an avenue to broadcast it. When they talked to Henry, he relayed that he had sensed for some time that God wanted him to write the message.

Over the next year, Avery recorded many of his and Henry's many lengthy phone conversations. He invited Henry to speak to groups at the Glorieta Baptist Assembly and to the employees of the Baptist Sunday School Board. Claude King took the transcripts and videos from those presentations, compiled them into a first-person narrative, and added learning activities to help Henry develop what would become *Experiencing God: Knowing and Doing the Will of God*, one of the pre-eminent Christian works for the next twenty-five years. Through this process, Avery, Henry, and Claude developed a deep lifetime friendship and partnership in the move of God to lead America into spiritual renewal.

In 1988, Dr. Larry Lewis, then president of the Home Mission Board, confided in Avery that he was looking for the right person to become the director for the Office of Prayer and Spiritual Awakening. He asked Avery for a recommendation. After spending time to pray, Avery recommended Henry Blackaby.

Larry asked who Henry was. Avery responded, "Your evangelism guys know him. Why don't you talk to them?"

The next day, Henry called Avery to tell him that Dr. Lewis had asked him to consider the position. That summer, Henry and Marilynn Blackaby moved to Atlanta, Georgia. Over the next two years, while Claude and Henry were developing the course, Henry traveled around the country teaching about knowing and doing the will of God. By the time *Experiencing God* was released in October of 1990, tens of thousands of people were eagerly awaiting it.

Dr. T. W. Hunt

Avery believed the world needed spiritual renewal in the Christian church—and that such a renewal would only take place with extensive prayer. He was thrilled to observe that an increased number of churches and agencies had begun emphasizing prayer, revival, and the need for spiritual awakening. Pastors were preaching on prayer and starting intercessory prayer ministries in their churches.

Avery and his team had been learning from Henry Blackaby the value of identifying where God was at work in order to join Him in what He was doing. Recognizing that God was calling His people to prayer, Avery, Claude, and the rest of the Discipleship Division began to pray about what part God would have them play.

At a planning session of the Leadership Development department in February 1987, one of the topics was promoting the new *Disciple's Prayer Life* by Dr. T. W. Hunt and Dr. Catherine Walker to be released the following January. Whenever Avery led a planning session, prayer was always a central component. Avery made it clear that he didn't want "our best plans," he wanted "God's best plans." As they prayed, Avery sensed they were to ask TW to join the team and lead a prayer emphasis, calling and equipping Southern Baptists to pray.

"Avery and I got on a plane and flew to New Mexico," recalls Roy Edgemon. "We arrived at Glorieta to find Dr. Hunt teaching an extra class for those who wanted to learn about the doctrine of prayer. We learned that he had actually skipped lunch to take on this class."

When Dr. Hunt was finished, they took him to a Mexican restaurant in the little town of Pecos and there asked him if he would be willing to leave Southwestern Baptist Seminary and become the prayer leader for Southern Baptists. In his humble way, TW told them that if they felt he should do this, they all needed to seek God's will in prayer. Dr. Hunt had been a professor at the seminary for twenty-four years. Leaving his post at this point would have a negative impact on his retirement plan. He also thought that his wife, LaVerne, would not want to leave their only daughter and grandchildren. But when he told her of the offer, she responded, "I think you should do it." Through prayer, God convinced them all this was His plan.

Shortly afterward, Claude and Avery spent a week with LeRoy Ford at his retirement home in Montrose, Colorado. LeRoy, who had been a professor of Avery's at Southwestern seminary, had developed the "interactive approach" to learning through written materials. He had traveled to Indonesia to train writers of the TEE materials and, at Roy Edgemon's request, had trained writers at the BSSB, who assisted Avery as he wrote the *Survival Kit* and *MasterLife*.

As they were driving through the Rockies, Avery began to pray. Claude described it as "a strange new experience for me, but I quickly picked up on what he was doing and joined in. We prayed for an extended time as we rode together. That wasn't the only time I got to prayer drive with Avery, and it marked me. It has become so natural to me that I catch people off guard sometimes, just like Avery did me."

Helping the Hurting

Avery realized that if spiritual awakening came, churches would be flooded with people with all kinds of significant spiritual, emotional, and social needs. Many churches were not equipped to help them experience the life transformation of the gospel. Avery had met with Robert McGee, author of *The Search for Significance*, in January. Robert had encouraged Avery to use *LIFE* (*Lay Institute for Equipping*) resources to equip laity to develop Christian support groups in churches.

Avery knew pastors were struggling with many of the same spiritual and emotional needs as well. Bondage-breaking needed to start with leadership, but presenting that idea would require delicacy.

July 1, 1991

God said to me: You are entering a time of intense spiritual warfare and jeopardy. When you try to help as I release pastors from bondage, Satan will not give up his stronghold easily. 80% of pastors are co-dependent and feeding off the sheep instead of caring for them. They must be freed and healed so they can allow me to heal the people. I am the answer but 12-step support groups may help people identify the bonds, apply Scripture to their needs, and seek Me. Seek my wisdom and the counsel of leaders in how to approach this whole situation.

Around that time, Carole Lewis asked if the BSSB would consider serving as publisher of *First Place: A Christ-Centered Health Program*—a ministry of First Baptist Church in Houston, Texas. Avery and Claude sensed God's urging to address such issues, but didn't see any human way they could do that within the current policy structures at the board. At that time, they were not allowed to use outside writers or pay royalties to entities like churches.

That summer, Avery and Claude King spent half a day in prayer. They hiked up a mountain overlooking the Glorieta Conference Center in New Mexico and began to pray about this opportunity. As they prayed, they sensed God was "inviting them to join Him in what He wanted to do, but they would need to make the major adjustments required."[1] They asked the Lord to reveal His intentions and concluded their prayer time believing God wanted them to return to the BSSB and ask for everything they needed.

Avery called Dr. Jimmy Draper, who had just been elected president of the BSSB, explained what they had in mind, and asked if they should even give time to create a proposal. Dr. Draper recommended that Avery and Claude prepare a business plan and present it to him. Avery immediately pulled together a whole team of people to help put together a plan.

In the proposal, they asked for everything they believed would be needed to develop what would become the *LIFE Support* curriculum. They requested permission to use and pay royalties to non-Baptist writers of other curriculum resources. They asked for a new unit of personnel and the top technical equipment to help produce the resources. They included a request to sidestep standard protocols in order to produce the resources on a fast track to get the help out to the churches. They asked to create LifeWay Press as a new imprint and market beyond the existing Southern Baptist base of customers. To top it off, they attached a marketing budget far beyond any prior request.

The requested changes were not accepted easily. Time and multiple meetings were given to negotiations concerning royalties, who held primary license, and what the BSSB would have to have from multiple organizations for it to work.

Other department heads questioned and attacked the men for trying to change how the board had operated for many years. Dr. Roy Edgemon described it as one of the most difficult experiences of his life. He said, "We put a lot on the line because we believed our churches needed this ministry!"

January 11, 1992

What a week this has been with meetings every day! And not just meetings—but confrontations that challenged the 100-year old traditions of the BSSB and how it operates. But we have rested in the shadow of the Almighty and He has been our refuge and fortress. He has been our Commander and our Rear Guard. He has walked with us/led us through the fire and we have emerged unscathed, praising Him.

January 13, 1992

From 2 Kings 13:10–20, God said to me, "What you are doing, Avery, is My work. I've put your hand on the bow and arrows to shoot My enemy. I am like Elisha, putting my hands over yours to guide your aim, give you power, and determine the timing of the shot. I'm telling you to take the arrows and strike the ground until complete victory is assured. Do not stop short. Go for it—be persistent—in how you use each and all the arrows I'm placing in your hand. As you believe and persist so shall the victory be.

The bow is prayer. You can only shoot as far as prayer will take you.

January 16, 1992

Today is the day. God gave me several promises through Proverbs. I have claimed the promises in Isaiah 61, including verse 4, "They will REBUILD the ancient ruins, RESTORE the places long devastated, and RENEW the ruined cities."

Lord, I believe You have gone before us and will open the door wide and give us the mandate and resources to implement LIFE Support Ministries. The battle will be fierce. But all this is in preparation for the attack on Satan's strongholds in the lives of people.

Until the morning of the presentation to the Senior Executive Team, only one person supported the plan. The other leaders and vice president resisted. The men broke for lunch, and for the first time in his life, Roy actually passed out (he believes from the tension) and was brought back in a wheelchair.

But God intervened during that lunch. When the meeting reconvened, everything had changed. Several leaders weren't there, and the attitude was different. When it was evident that an openness existed, Roy called in Avery and Claude.

Avery began with prayer, and then said: "Before we look at the business plan, let me tell you how we got to this place." He shared the spiritual markers of what God was doing around their work. He described the needs for churches to be prepared to provide help to many people struggling with addictions should God send awakening. Avery described the offers of curriculum from outside sources to equip laity through support groups. He summarized by describing the spiritual need in churches and his desire to help meet that need through the *LIFE Support* curriculum.

Avery then opened his black folder to begin the presentation when one of the vice presidents interrupted him. "I don't need to read this report. My people have kept me informed. I don't have any questions. I just came to celebrate."

Another said, "Avery, we'll have no problems with the board of trustees. I believe that if we tell the trustees we see this need in churches and want to work on a fast track to meet the need, we're liable to see a revival break out. I'm all for it."

The vice president of finance said, "My guys have been working on the numbers. They tell me it's a go." Even when warned of a potential first year deficit of as much as $278,000, he just flipped his hand and said, "We've lost more than that on ventures not nearly so worthy. Plus, the long-range potential is so positive."

Avery journaled:

For the next 30 or more minutes, the others did the talking and were just praising God. They even said this could be a model of how the BSSB ought to operate—find out what God is doing and search out how to make what we are doing cooperate with that. God, You are so good! You once again showed Yourself strong!

Every vice president at the table unanimously approved the project before any of the presentation was even made! That decision changed the future of LifeWay Christian Resources. LifeWay began moving beyond the realm of the Southern Baptists and incorporating the work of other Christian writers to provide resources for the Christian community throughout the world.

CHAPTER 24
Call for Solemn Assembly and Spiritual Awakening

If I were asked to give a speech to a convention, and at the last minute was told that my time would be limited to one sentence, I would say: "Most of the world is going to hell and most Christians don't give a damn!"

That statement was the final entry in Avery's journal as he prepared for furlough after his first term in Indonesia. He returned to the US to find a lethargy in the American Church, which deeply troubled him. He so desired to see revival and spiritual awakening rouse the nation's churches out of their "slumber" and arise to the task of taking the gospel to the world. Now it seemed God had brought him to the time and place to speak to the issue. He knew it would not happen outside of prayer and repentance, two ingredients Avery had experienced as foundational to revival over the years.

Beginning with the Intercessors

Avery, T. W. Hunt, Henry Blackaby, and Claude King began training prayer leaders to mobilize and equip an army of intercessors who would pray fervently and specifically, in unity of spirit and according to biblical principles, about the common purposes of the churches and the kingdom of God. They began training leaders of the National Prayer Corps.

Initial revival broke out during a training at Ridgecrest Conference Center on Tuesday, July 18, 1989. Leaders became convicted of their lack of urgency in sharing the gospel. God convicted others of specific sins. The sense of God's holiness had many on their knees and a few prostrate on the floor, weeping over their sin. That stirring continued all week.

The following Monday, Henry was leading a session on prayer and spiritual awakening in Nashville, Tennessee, when T. W. Hunt pointed out that widespread biblical revivals were always led by leadership, usually by a combination of prophets, priests, and kings. Three days later, Henry shared a summary of TW's findings on biblical revival with a group in Colorado.

Richard Owen Roberts, a historian of revival, spoke on God's remedy for corporate sin through the "solemn assembly." Roberts's message profoundly impacted Henry; he sensed God had spoken. In a meeting with Avery and the other prayer leaders, they all agreed God was calling Southern Baptists to solemn assembly.[1]

Call for Solemn Assembly

In the chapter on "Solemn Assembly" in his *Spiritual Renewal Manual*, P. Douglas Small describes the solemn assembly as a time for the corporate church to come together expressly for the purpose of repentance and confession, not simply for individual sin, but for corporate sin. Repentance must first start with the people of God—within the church. After its own purification, the church can act in its priestly role toward the world by confessing sin for the cities and the nations, sins against God that could invite His wrath and judgment. As the church stands in the gap for its cities, God sends revival and visits the unrighteous on behalf of the righteous. "Fasting is required. Contrition of heart is expected. Genuine humility before God is essential."

Solemn assemblies do not happen spontaneously. In the Old Testament, they were called during times of spiritual crisis, usually a crisis precipitated by the righteous judgment of God upon the sins of the people. It was an emergency action—a desperate plea to prevent further judgment. The words of the prophet Joel demonstrate this kind of urgency: "Consecrate a fast, proclaim a solemn assembly; gather the elders and all the inhabitants of the land to the house of the Lord your God and cry out to the Lord... Blow a trumpet in Zion and sound an alarm on my holy mountain! Let all the inhabitants of the land tremble" (Joel 1:14, 2:1a). God's call to corporate repentance through the solemn assembly is found in 2 Chronicles 7:14: "If my people, who are called by my name, shall humble themselves and pray, and seek my face, and turn from their wicked ways, then will I hear from heaven, and will forgive their sin and heal their land."

Throughout history, God has used the solemn assembly as a means to bring revival. Of the twelve periods of renewal recorded in the Old Testament, each one was preceded by the calling of a solemn assembly. Solemn assemblies are called when godly leaders sense the need to return to God. They, in submission to God's call and conviction on their lives, call the corporate body for which they are responsible to repentance and to a return to biblical order. In America, historical documents verify that before every major national revival, emphasis was placed upon fast days and solemn assemblies.[2]

The prayer leaders began to pray about how to share their message with other leadership. Within a two-week period, one or a combination of them had the opportunity to speak to all Southern Baptist presidents and agency heads, executive committee members, and top national and state Baptist leaders. Avery and the prayer leaders realized that no human could have arranged platform time with all the key leaders of the denomination in such a short period of time.

Though their message was warmly received, none of the other leadership sensed it was God's assignment for them to call for the solemn assembly. So after much prayer, the prayer leaders decided they were the ones that needed to issue the call. The prayer leaders of the National Prayer Corps issued the "Call to Prayer and Solemn Assembly" in a live national teleconference on September 17, 1989.

Call to Prayer and Solemn Assembly
Issued by the SBC Prayer Leaders on September 17, 1989

God has revealed (in His Word and to many of His people) that He is judging His church and the nation of the United States of America. This judgment is because:

1. His Lordship has been discounted by his peoples' selfish desires and self-serving practices.
2. His commandments and Word are not being used to determine right and wrong.
3. His Holiness is being ignored and impugned by impure living.
4. His Bride, the Church, is not preparing herself for the Wedding Feast at his Second Coming but has prostituted herself with worldly values, methods, and priorities/activities.
5. His people are disoriented to Him and apathetic to His voice and activity.
6. His warnings through the Word and His prophets have been largely ignored.
7. His house is not known as a House of Prayer for all Nations.
8. He is displeased with much religious worship and activity.
9. His leaders have not led His people to repentance corporately and individually, for many remain in sin and disobedience themselves.

Therefore, great calamity is hanging over America and the Church. His judgments will intensify in number and magnitude until we repent or are crushed.

God's remedy for corporate sin is "solemn assembly" called by the leaders:

- To humble ourselves
- To fast and pray and seek His face
- To confess corporate and individual sin and repent of it
- To uphold and practice His commandments
- To sacrifice and worship Him with our hearts

- To make a covenant with Him to follow His ways and do His will
- To serve mankind and proclaim His gospel to all people
- To become like Him and follow His leadership in our world

God promises to bless us if we do as He says and to curse us if we ignore Him. We are His people and carry His name before our world. He cannot and will not overlook our condition and response.

What shall we do?

1. If you are a leader at any level, call your people together for a solemn assembly: from a parent—to a church—to an association or denomination of churches—to political leaders.
2. Set regular times to pray for God's mercy and movement on us—1 to 2 hours weekly and a half to full day monthly prayer until God turns His wrath away from us and restores us to a place of usefulness and blessing to others.

Avery preaching

Preaching as a Prophet

Avery preached, "*God has convinced me of two truths. First, He has been judging America since at least 1963.*" He relayed data from the book *America: To Pray or Not to Pray* about the rapid increase in broken families, promiscuity, and crime since that time. Avery went on to describe the seven stages in the judgment of God upon a nation in which He

1. convicts of sin (John 16:7–11);
2. sends warnings by the Word and His prophets (Is. 5:8, 11, 18, 20, 22);
3. brings remedial judgment and allows the nation to experience the consequences of its sins (Is. 5:25–30, Gal. 6:7–8);
4. withdraws His presence (Jer. 7:12–16);
5. removes the hedge of protection and allows the enemy to ravage the nation (Is. 5:1–7);
6. gives the people over to their sin and its destructiveness (Rom. 1:24–32);
7. destroys them (Is. 5:13, 25–30).

Secondly, I believe God is in the process of bringing revival. God showed me ten years ago that He was going to send spiritual awakening in America. It was the reason I believe He called me back to help Baptists disciple people so we would be ready to reap the harvest.

When God pronounced a judgment against Israel, Moses interceded. God reduced his final judgment to wrath upon the few and remedial judgment on the rest. God is still punishing and will continue to do so in an intensifying crescendo until we repent or pay for our sins. There is a race on to see which will come first—destruction or repentance. The purposes and plans God has for us are to fully discipline us and then to restore us. We can't expect the second until there is true repentance. But He promises to rebuild and to plant as thoroughly as He destroyed. (Jeremiah 31:27–28)[3]

God is calling us back to what it means to be a Christian nation. If we refuse to be used, then He will leave us and go to someone else. If the church will become purified and get right with God, multitudes of non-Christians will begin to seek Christ." But he predicted *"disaster if Christians do not repent and if they turn away from God's call to Solemn Assembly."*[4]

God is letting us experience the consequences for our sins and our choices to leave Him out of our lives and our nation. We had our chance as a nation to be God's instrument for kingdom change in the earth. We would not send missionaries by the thousands, and so we have sent our soldiers into war by the millions and have lost hundreds of thousands in battle. Think how that many missionaries and that much money could have changed this world if we had done it God's way![5]

State conventions and associations began to invite the prayer leaders to help with solemn assemblies for their groups. Many sensed the building momentum toward revival and believed this might lead to another spiritual awakening.

Avery had long operated in the spiritual gifts of pastor, teacher, and evangelist and even apostle as he planted churches in Indonesia, but the prophetic role was a new one for him. Yet he believed God had given him a message he must preach.

He began experiencing criticism for speaking what his critics called gloom and doom. Critics claimed such things as: "I agree with all my being with Avery's theology on judgment, but he talks like a prophet, and I don't believe he is one. We don't have them today." "I think Avery has taken off on another agenda than discipleship training, and we shouldn't fund it." "I thought someone would have stopped him by now!"

In all these times they came back to commend my gifts as a communicator and preacher. But not my message! I would rather it be vice versa. The heart of the matter is this: Is the message from God to America today or is it my own concoction? Have I made applications on my own that God has not led me to make? Am I to defend God, the message, or myself by answering?

319

God does not need my defense. The message is sound and Biblical. The prophet's only credential was "thus saith the Lord" and whether it proved to be true.

Lord, cut out my tongue and still my voice before I say You said something when You didn't. Protect me from myself and my negative sense of Your people not following You when it is not true. Protect me from falsely reading the signs of the times. Show me the real ones. Speak to me with clarity or shut my mouth. Help me not to prophecy from man's projections but from Your revelations.

If You want me to qualify the seven stages of judgment or abandon that understanding, I am willing to do so, if You reveal it is Your will. I am Your servant and before You I stand or fall. If I am wrong, O Spirit of God, show me and I will apologize. If I am right, give me the boldness to say what You say and do what You do. I do not want to fear men. I do fear You. I'd rather die than besmirch Your Name, preach a lie, or make myself the issue.

After much prayer, honest inquiry before the Lord, and talking with the prayer team, my conclusion is that I must speak exactly what God says—nothing more or less. I need to clarify what is God's Word and what I believe/discern/think are the current applications of that Word and maybe state those as a question. Henry and T.W. have faced similar criticism. It is not personal but a resistance to anyone having a word from God and speaking as oracles of God. We must be ready for more and stronger attacks. We must maintain our integrity before God.[6]

Avery heard this from the Lord:

You are right to speak what I tell you. Just be sure it is Me, not you, speaking. You did not seek to be a prophet, but I have chosen you and will speak through you. Even among a rebellious people you are to bring My true word as I give it. Many will not like what I say and try to attack you. You'll just have to take it for My sake. Do not let it blunt you from being a "sharp threshing instrument." I've been sharing with you how Jesus dealt with opposition because I've shown you this day was coming. Go back and read what I've taught you. Listen to what those attacking you are saying. Separate what you suffer for Me and any wrongdoing for which you are responsible.

Within the same conversation, the Holy Spirit convicted Avery of using a borrowed software. Avery responded, *"Lord, I want You to cut away any part of me that does not match the pattern of Jesus. You have convicted me about using that program. I don't know how You can be so merciful to use me as I've used it to write these past couple of years. I repent and confess to You and am willing to confess to others. I'll pay for it. I will call* [the person he borrowed it from] *today.*

Fruit of Prayer

The Lord encouraged Avery and the prayer leaders to write down an accurate account of His movement, whether they understood it at the time or not—much as Luke heard and recorded the life of Jesus. They began documenting the acts of God in the 1990s as "Stories of God's Work in Today's World" in an *Experiencing God* magazine.

In his journal, Avery reported on the solemn assemblies for which he was praying.

The Foreign Mission Board had an "extraordinary time" at their solemn assembly this month. The solemn assembly for the Baptist Sunday School Board is scheduled for March 5–9 and the Home Mission Board will meet May 5. Seminary students are meeting to plan prayer strategies. Southwestern seminary has 11 such groups.[7]

God moved in a marvelous way at the National Spiritual Awakening conference in April. God freed people of past guilt, childhood sexual abuse, and much more. The Florida Solemn Assembly was very solemn but impressive. Before each session, a trumpet was blown and Scriptures were read. Each message was followed by corporate prayer and personal confession. In between, people wrote sins of the nation, of SBC, of pastors/staff, and themselves and attached them to a wooden cross covered with nails. My assessment is that God worked mightily in this. It is a good model for the pastors to use in their churches.

In November 1990, the prayer leaders of different Christian denominations met to share what God had been doing in their churches in the realm of prayer. Person after person told of God calling out prayer warriors in unprecedented numbers who were praying more frequently and for longer periods and how churches with strong prayer ministries were growing exponentially.

Al Taylor, of the Church of God, said, "You can look at the churches statistically and tell which ones are praying." David Bryant, head of Concerts of Prayer International, claimed the current prayer movement was unparalleled in three ways: the numbers of people praying worldwide, the diversity of those gathering to pray across racial and generational lines, and the focus of prayer as the lever to bring about global evangelization. He said, "God's plan for a city can only be completed when *all* God's churches, all His body—including the parachurch organizations—are united in prayer."

The same is true for a nation.

CHAPTER 25
Conviction of Pride

*Most people think the test comes in the hard times
when you are criticized or maligned,
but the real test is what you do when inundated with praise.*

—Avery

A repeated struggle for Avery was denying the pride that would creep up in his heart. One July night in 1989, during the season of seeking God for spiritual awakening, Avery woke up at 2:58 a.m. and heard the Lord say, "I have the time, do you?"

Avery sensed it meant this: "I have eternity, how long do you have? I am ready for revival, are you? I am available, are you? I am bringing judgment, will you take time to listen to Me and repent?" He wrote those phrases down to make it part of the next day's call to prayer, and then he lay back down.

God spoke to him, "I am asking *you* the question *now*."

Avery answered, "Yes, speak, Lord, I am Your servant."

God said, "You need a cleansing. Look at My holiness."

I began to look through my life. At first, I began to try to make myself feel guilty but then I sensed I was going about that my own way—actually Satan's way. I prayed, "O Lord, You be my accuser, not Satan." There is a difference in the conviction of the Holy Spirit and the blaming of the Accuser. Satan makes me feel guilty for the wrong things. He tells me that I am no good, that I have failed, that I can never measure up.

Then I saw my sin in light of God's holiness rather than some standard Satan would give me—like another person. So the Holy Spirit spoke to me through John 16. God said,

"Avery, you have not believed in Me first for every need. You first look to the agency who pays your salary and to the means at your disposal at work. You have been learning again to look to Me for everything but have a lot of learning to do if you are going to do greater works as I promised. *[I couldn't bring myself to write "greater works than I," which the Holy Spirit said "shows that you are not believing in me"! Ouch!]* Any confidence in the flesh—yours or someone else's—is lack of belief in Me. Do you really believe I can bring the US or the SBC to its knees—by Myself?"

Yes, Lord, I do, but I do not know how You will do it. One thing I sense is You're telling me these last four weeks that I need to bear witness to Your work, even when I am not the immediate instrument You use to initiate revival. It's been humbling to see You use T.W., Henry, and Claude while I was leading other conferences. I have been a little jealous of the fact I wasn't in on it all. So I need to confess it to be as real as if I had been the immediate instrument because it was never me anyway—I was just open for You to use.

"Avery, you are too distracted. You take your mind off Me to look at a passing interest, a person or a ball game, or a task to be done at work or for work. You move too quickly to the practical and don't stay long enough for the Holy Spirit to reveal all My righteousness and your unrighteousness. It is good that you ran out of time to speak on holiness and revival last week. You are not holy.

"You are used to speaking of what I have taught you personally so I have had to teach you more about believing Me and My Word.

- I taught you more about believing Me and My word for all occasions and claiming My promises through Tom Eliff.
- I taught you more about My person and nature through T. W. Hunt.
- I taught you to see Me at work in everything and to listen to My voice and respond to it through Henry Blackaby.

"Avery, get ready. Let me show you your sin now before I have to expose it to the world."

Yes, Lord, do so now. Show me the deceitfulness of my own heart that I don't know and all that I know but do not admit. I know it may take several encounters over the next days to see what You see. Help me see it and repent of everything that is not pleasing to You—lust, selfishness, pride, insensitivity to others, not taking time to share the "wonderful works of God" with them, lack of godly love, etc.

On another occasion, Avery journaled what he was hearing from the Lord.

March 11, 1990

God said to me, "You need to consider the ways you are still proud. Pride is a matter of the heart, not the outward expression that others may see.

1. *You have pride in what I have revealed to you and the ways I have used you. You accept the fact that I taught you MasterLife but you still feel you must let others know how widely it is used or how it has helped Me change peoples' lives so you can get some credit for being used.*
2. *You want to tell your relationship to what I am doing through prayer and spiritual awakening—that you were present when I did something. You want recognition that you were on the prayer leaders' team. Even if you don't say it, you think in your heart that you pushed the team to give information and then you wrote the first draft.*
3. *You have some pride in the gifts I have given you in that you will compare them to gifts I have given to the other prayer leaders, i.e. the ones they don't have.*
4. *You are envious—wanting Me to use you like I do others.*
5. *You have always wanted to know something that others don't know.*
6. *You notice when others do not notice "who you are." For example, when the college student prophesied this weekend that you are going to be used more, you thought "he doesn't know how I am already being used."*

7. *You are proud that your children have not rebelled and that they are faithful to Me.*
8. *You are proud that you were a missionary and a seminary president and that you were in the Indonesian revival.*
9. *You are proud that you get calls to go overseas each year.*

Now, because of your pride, humble yourself before Me by:

1. *Agreeing with Me that when you have done all that I told you to do, you are still my unprofitable servant. Luke 17:17*
2. *Agree with Me that only I can cause people to come to Me, to recognize truth, and to follow and serve Me.*
3. *Recognize that Jesus continually emptied Himself and gave credit to the Father for everything He did and said.*
4. *Give credit to the thousands of people, who have taught you, helped you, supported you, prayed for you, told others about you, promoted you, and loved you—beginning first with Shirley, your parents, and your children. Add to that your prayer partners and all of the people you have and do work with.*
5. *Give credit to Me for creating you and choosing you—protecting, calling, equipping, filling, sustaining, and loving you."*

I said, Lord it is as You said. I am nothing. Now I want to empty that nothing. I want to completely throw down the stronghold of pride and selfishness by Your strength and for Your glory.

By the end of his life, Avery would preach "God will not share His glory with anyone. So all great reports must be about Him and not me." Then he would follow up with a story of Corrie ten Boom. She was once asked, "Miss Boom, you have received so many accolades for all you have done, had books written about you, and have been on television shows. Do you ever sometimes feel proud?"

Corrie leaned forward and looked the interviewer squarely in the face. "Young man, the donkey that took Jesus into Jerusalem on Palm Sunday never once thought the crowd was clapping for him!"

Avery would end the story with, *I just want to be His donkey.*

For years, Avery carried a tract in his Bible called <u>Others May, You Cannot</u> that summed up his commitment to humility regardless of his position, preferring to be approved by the Spirit rather than men. He passed it to Sherrie during one of their discipling sessions. She still carries it today.

Others May, You Cannot[1]
(G. D. Watson 1845–1924)

If God has called you to be really like Jesus he will draw you into a life of crucifixion and humility, and put upon you such demands of obedience that you will not be able to follow other people, or measure yourself by other Christians, and in many ways he will seem to let other people do things that he will not let you do.

Other Christians and ministers who seem very religious and useful, may push themselves, pull wires and work schemes to carry out their plans, but you cannot do it, and if you attempt it, you will meet with such failure and rebuke from the Lord as to make you sorely penitent.

Others may boast of themselves, of their work, of their successes, of their writings, but the Holy Spirit will not allow you to do any such thing, and if you begin it, he will lead you into some deep mortification that will make you despise yourself and all your good works.

Others may be allowed to succeed in making money, or may have a legacy left to them, but it is likely God will keep you poor because he wants you to have something far better than gold, namely a helpless dependence upon him, that he may have the privilege of supplying your needs day by day out of an unseen treasury.

The Lord may let others be honored and put forward, and keep you hidden in obscurity, because he wants to produce some choice fragrant fruit for his coming glory, which can only be produced in the shade. He may let others be great, but keep you small. He may let others do a work for him and get the credit for it, but he will make you work and toil on without knowing how much you are doing; and then to make your work still more precious he may let others get credit for the work which you have done, and thus make **your reward ten times greater when Jesus comes**.

The Holy Spirit will put a strict watch over you, with a jealous love, and will rebuke you for little words or wasting your time, which other Christians never feel distressed over. So make up your mind that God is an infinite Sovereign, and has the right to do as he pleases with his own. He may not explain to you a thousand things which puzzle your reason in his dealings with you, but if you absolutely sell yourself to be his love slave, he will wrap you up in a jealous love, and bestow upon you many blessings which come only to those who are in the inner circle.

Settle it forever, then, that you are to **deal directly with the Holy Spirit**, and that he has the privilege of tying your tongue, or chaining your hand, or closing your eyes in ways that he does not seem to use with others. Now, when you are so possessed with the living God that you are, in your secret heart pleased and delighted over this **peculiar, personal, private, jealous guardianship and management of the Holy Spirit over your life**, you will have found the vestibule of Heaven.

CHAPTER 26
Seeking God's Next Assignment

*When God reveals a truth to you, He is trying to tell you what He is
doing because He wants to use you. He may have a lot more shaping
to do before He can do His work in you. Allow Him to do it through
spending time with Him in the Word and watching His activity.*
—Henry Blackaby

I n January 1990, in order "to have a greater impact on all adult training," Roy Edgemon proposed a departmental merger of personnel,
budget, and office space of the Adult and Leadership Departments and
asked Avery to manage it. Avery was promised the freedom to "ideate,
be out on the field, conceptualize, and manage how to make disciples
and equip ministers of all eleven million adult Southern Baptists."

However, it would greatly increase the amount of work and
responsibility for Avery at the office in Nashville just when he was feeling the need for more freedom to follow God in spiritual awakening
and world missions. Leadership at this level would mean managing
through associates and what Avery feared would be "management by
walking around." It would take a year to complete the reorganization,
two to three years to reshape the curriculum, and five years for the
changes to impact the churches.

*I told Roy I did not see curriculum development as my primary gift and
that I had done adult work only until we could start MasterLife—but
that I would pray about it. My question is "What is God doing?"* [1]

*The only important fact is God's will—not if it will be difficult, more
work, more conflict, etc.* [2]

Hearing from God

As was his practice, Avery set aside days for a personal prayer retreat to seek the Lord's purpose and plans, and his place in them, before he gave Roy a final answer. Avery wanted to hear from the Lord about upcoming events and the next stages for the prayer movement and spiritual awakening. He wanted to lay the plans for reorganization before the Lord to see what adjustments needed to be made to match what God was doing.

He listed his steps to hearing from God:

1. *Review Scriptures through which God has directed me clearly in the past. Check the spiritual markers. Open myself up to hear through other Scriptures.*
2. *Review what God has done, especially over the last nine months, in light of Scripture.*
3. *Consult with other leaders on what I am seeing.*
4. *Consider whether God is continuing a pattern He has been developing in me or taking me in a new direction. Compare that with what is being proposed in the reorganization.*
5. *Spell out where I think God is moving in my life and adjustments I need to make personally and adjustments that may need to be made in the department.*
6. *Inquire of God whether any of these moves would block my obedience or availability for future assignments He has for me.*
7. *Ask God to reveal specific Bible promises that will direct me now and in the future.*

By the end of his retreat, he summarized:

God, I see You calling Your people to repentance, to holiness, to prayer as intercessors, and ministry to the needy. You are calling leaders to respond to a call to prayer. You are stirring the people and calling them to discipleship and world evangelism. You are demonstrating Your great power in the tearing down of systems and nations of Eastern Europe. You are tearing down every religious ritual, program, and institution that relies on itself, seeks its own benefit, or gives glory to anything or anyone instead of You.

I sense God wants to change Discipleship Training, its curriculum and organization from the inside so that it will be a catalyst for the SBC to become a holy people before the Lord again. God is preparing his church to go to the world as His redemptive agent. He is putting me in a position with personnel and budget to accomplish the training function and preparation of people who are or will be on the front lines.

Our adult curriculum is currently a form that has outlived its function. It seems irrelevant to the current generation and to the inner city culture. God is moving us to deal with the poor, needy, oppressed, and imprisoned as Jesus did. We need curriculum for them and support groups. We have curriculum now for leaders and committed Christians but we need to focus on what is helpful to new converts from difficult backgrounds.

Even as Avery was envisioning Southern Baptists becoming a holy people, united and equipped to minister to those in this nation and to spread the gospel to the world, other events were indicative of the damaging toxin of disunity permeating the denomination.

A purposeful takeover of leadership through the strategic placements of presidents, trustees, and heads of agencies, seminaries, and state conventions had been orchestrated by conservative leaders of the Southern Baptist Convention (SBC) over the past decade. The inerrancy of Scripture was their primary platform and measuring rod. Although he aligned with the conservatives on most doctrines, Avery had intentionally chosen to remain uninvolved in the political workings. Nevertheless, he feared the repercussions of disunity throughout the convention, especially in light of the revival God was initiating. He wanted to preach reconciliation—not be courted or threatened by either group.

Lord, it's beginning to frighten me to see the conflict in the SBC and my more prominent position as a prophet. I'm aware that the stakes are getting higher, that my role is becoming more visible, that I'm going to be asked to take sides—not so much in any one action but in daily decisions that escalate to a turning point. I may have to make choices related to my work, location, direction, etc. because of what is happening in SBC and/or what You are doing in revival. I'm not sure what You have in mind for me but I've sensed for years You would choose me to be a leader for Your cause and mission. Help me to be true blue to You and to no man, group, or organization. Teach me step by step and word by word to only do and say what You say.[3]

Call for Reconciliation and Revival

Avery met with Morris Chapman, SBC president, to plan the theme for the executive committee meeting and the upcoming convention. Avery's desire was that a solemn assembly be called at both. He wanted to provide opportunity for reconciliation and revival. Morris responded by endorsing the prayer leaders' call to spiritual awakening and asking state leaders to encourage prayer-oriented times at all levels. The solemn assembly itself was scheduled for the 1991 Southern Baptist Convention in Atlanta, Georgia.

Who could have dreamed it possible?! Several times in recent years, people have said T.W., Henry, and I should speak to the SBC to seek for reconciliation and revival. I said, "Yeah, but they haven't asked." And if I thought they would, it would only have been to speak, not to call for repentance and give time for it!!![4]

Avery Willis and Henry Blackaby set to work on the solemn assembly for the SBC Convention. As they were planning the program, they wanted to list in the evening's bulletin the sins from which people might need to repent. They opted to list the major categories of sin and allow the Holy Spirit to direct individuals toward specific sins they needed to confess. They listed the first category as "Neglecting to love God with all our heart, soul, mind, and strength" and the second as "Neglecting to love our neighbor as we love ourselves." They had listed the third as "Loving the world more than the lost of the world," but when they attempted to list the Scriptural basis for each, they could not find Scriptures to validate the third. The Holy Spirit revealed to them that God had not called His people to "pray for the lost" but to pray for "laborers to go into the harvest."

Avery's evangelistic spirit was challenged when he and Henry began to understand that evangelism and people streaming toward Christ was a by-product rather than the essence of revival in the church. In a sermon, Avery shared, "When Christians repent and begin living holy lives before God, unbelievers marvel and turn to Christ. If God's people really return to Him, the world will turn to Him." So the title of the third section was changed to "Neglecting to live holy lives before God and the world God loves."

The time of corporate confession was held on Wednesday night of the SBC Convention. During a session usually attended by fewer than a thousand attendees, nearly twenty-five thousand gathered and prayed like they had never done before. It was a powerful evening with a strong emphasis in repentant prayer asking God to break through the divisive feud within the convention.

Avery wrote in his journal on June 10, 1991:

I am still basking in the glory of God manifested at the SBC—although I am completely given out. It was clear that people are interested in encountering God—from both conservatives and moderates. God is orchestrating a spiritual awakening. The presence of the Lord was obvious. I was thrilled by the confession and repentance that took place, the decisions made in the after-service time, and the responses of people since that time. People have asked for copies of the program so they can hold solemn assemblies in their own churches.

Isaiah 58 is the spiritual awakening we must have. God does not just intend for us to have a "big experience" even of solemn assembly. We must not see awakening as an event to be perpetuated but as a relationship with God to be deepened. He intends to turn our hearts toward Him again. Then He'll lead us to become a people who live out Isaiah 58 with personal righteousness and honor God instead of pleasing ourselves. What kind of radical adjustments do we need to make so He can use us? We have to find people ready to make those adjustments and be so Christ-centered they'll know what to do when judgment and/or revival comes.

Still, the political maneuvers continued. Throughout the early 1990s, professors and presidents of the various seminaries were fired and replaced with more conservative leaders. Hopes for resolution dimmed such that moderates no longer offered an alternative candidate for presidency of the SBC. Six thousand moderate Baptists met in Atlanta and formally organized the Cooperative Baptist Fellowship (CBF) of churches and their own missions body. In January 1991, Avery was dismayed when his boss, Dr. Lloyd Elder, president of the Baptist Sunday School Board, was asked to resign.

Nomination for BSSB Presidency

In March, Tom Elliff called Avery to ask for his resume so that he could recommend him as a candidate for the Baptist Sunday School Board presidency in the vacancy left by the removal of Dr. Elder. Tom had already spoken to the committee chairman who guaranteed Avery would be considered. When Avery responded with hesitation, Tom said he should at least ask God if it was His will or not.

March 29, 1991

The more I've thought about it since then, the more it has disturbed me. I've said before that anyone who wanted that job didn't understand the situation. Financially, we are not profitable as an organization, even after cutting costs for six years. Loyalty among churches and society is decreasing for institutions and programs. The move to computers and desktop publishing will eliminate the need for some of our publishing. The current controversy may mean fewer buy from the BSSB; they will print their own.

Is it even possible I would be chosen considering all the more qualified persons available? I am way down in the ranks. It would be like making a sergeant into a 5-star-general overnight. I am not one of the "political insiders" although I am theologically conservative. Many of them would question me and my loyalty to them, and rightly so.

Most of all, Lord, would this prevent me from being free to do Your will in revival and spiritual awakening? Or ... since we've been saying revival must come from the top, could this be the platform for leading revival? I've recently commented that the BSSB presidency is the most influential position in the convention because its programs affect each church. It, along with the mission emphasis, has been one of the cohesive factors to make the SBC churches similar—for good or bad. Would it be a position from which to fulfill the mission You have given me: to awaken, disciple, and equip the people of God for ministry and mission to the world?

Or would the daily responsibilities crowd that out?

This does not seem to go in the direction that I have desired/sensed. My heart and my hope has been to someday lead out in <u>*missions*</u>*.*

March 30, 1991

Here's where I am. I'm sending the resume' to Tom. I'm leaving it in God's hands. I don't think I should discuss it with anyone. If it progresses past this, then I'll need counsel of the brethren—who will really seek the mind of the Lord and not just tell me what they think I want to hear.

If it happens, I would see it as God's lifting the platform for such things as the Word being the center of all programming, the church as the focus of ministry in the marketplace and the world, evangelism and witness being the overflow and fruit-bearing result. It would involve bringing agency heads together for united prayer, cooperation, and contribution to other denominations to bring the gospel of the Kingdom to the nations. It could be the development of new wineskins for the new wine God gives us in spiritual awakening and a catalyst for God's agenda to lead us into the twenty-first century.

I do want to consider what God's purpose is in my even being recommended. It could just be to lift my vision and let me be a helper to the new president or prepare me to consider something else.

I don't know how to relate this to the fact that I've always thought there was the possibility that God would use me to lead the SBC in missions in some way. Keith Parks, being a compatriot, pretty much ruled out my becoming the FMB president when he assumed that position. My age of fifty-seven is about five to ten years beyond the beginning age for a normal head of an agency. In two to three more years, those positions will be out altogether. I am healthy and I have the sense that I can serve the Lord until at least age eighty—half of that could still be as the head of something—if God did it.

March 31, 1991

Two hours in prayer only confirmed that I am his servant. Only when He calls can I obey. Until then I'll be obedient in all He has already asked me to do.

Within a couple of months, it became clear that the board of directors were looking at other candidates; and in June 1991, Dr. Jimmy Draper was elected as the new president of the Baptist Sunday School Board. But God had used that time to put Avery on alert. In prayer, he sensed that God was directing him to a new platform.

May 5, 1991

I sense You are preparing me for a change as You have at other times in my life. I don't know what it will be but I need this time to just know You and experience Your Presence more. I sense You are assigning me several things that I am to do while waiting for Your next "significant assignment."

SECTION 6
Expanding World Missions

Spiritual Marker #11

God granted Avery a ten-year window
to design and implement new mission strategies
for church planting movements throughout the world.

Therefore go and make disciples of all nations,
baptizing them in the name of the Father,
of the Son, and of the Holy Spirit,
teaching them to obey everything I have commanded you.
And surely, I am with you always, to the end of the age.
—Matthew 28:19–20 (NIV)

Chapter 27
Back to Missions

Lord, keep me in mind in Your plan to reach the nations.

—Avery

I n the midst of all God had called Avery to do, his heart cry was still to return to missions. His desire would slip into his journals from time to time. The nearer he came to retirement, the more he feared the possibility might slip away due to his age.

November 24, 1990

Lord, I see You doing so much overseas that once more I ask You to let me be significantly involved again. In prayer this morning, I wondered if we might be non-resident missionaries who could teach MasterLife *in China and India and other Asian countries.*

In Deuteronomy 3, before handing leadership over to Joshua, Moses recounted God's history with the Israelites and His directives for the people as they prepared to enter the land. Avery came to verses 23–26, where Moses pleaded with God to "let me go over and see the good land beyond the Jordan" and the Lord's response, "That is enough. Do not speak to Me any more about this matter."

Avery wrote:

Lord, it seems so sad that Moses did not get to the Promised Land. Yet You knew the people needed to trust You instead of Moses. Lord, I'll keep asking for the opportunity to serve You in other countries/missions until You tell me to stop. Maybe I don't plead enough. No, I believe I'm in Your will. But I still keep thinking that I'll get back in missions before I get too old. I also wait in faith for revival in the U.S.A. Lord, I take hands off my direction and way. Show me Your way and I will walk there.

A Crack in the Door

In March of 1992, Keith Parks, president of the Foreign Mission Board (FMB), met with the trustees; and although they unanimously begged him not to, he concluded that there were sufficient tensions that he would retire the following October.

March 21, 1992

I have really not known how to react. This has opened a small crack in what I have thought God might have in mind for me for a long time, but that I had determined was not possible: that I might lead the FMB.

Since early on in my mission call and when I heard [former FMB president] *Baker James Cauthen speak, I'd said, "Some day God may want me to be the one to lead SBC in missions." It no doubt intensified with the mission strategy Cal Guy taught me. I didn't tell anyone and even now have only mentioned it to Shirley and Henry Blackaby.*

When the last opening came, I felt with the deepest conviction Keith was God's man for the job. I believe he will go down in history as the greatest leader in mission strategy we've ever had. And I knew when Keith raised the question of going three more years that if he did so, it would forever shut the door to any role I might have. But I'd sincerely prayed he would stay three more years as originally planned.

I know the likelihood that I'd be chosen to lead are less than a million to one humanly speaking because I'm 58 years old and they want someone who could give them 10–20 years; I'm no longer associated with missions directly in most people's minds after 14 years at the BSSB; I'm not one of the conservative insiders and not well enough known in some circles; and I may not be the best qualified administratively.

I realize this is one job I <u>want</u>. With the exception of being eager to pastor Sunset Heights and going to Indonesia, I've really never asked for the jobs I've gotten. God always seems to lead me in unexpected directions. I do believe that He has led me to every job I've had and once I realized that, it was fine and right. So in the midst of one dream coming *true—God's people being discipled and equipped for ministry and missions, LIFE support groups reaching the lost in the U.S., and being an instrument for revival, I can't help but ask God about this one more time.*

I need a word from God. Whatever He wants, I will gladly do it, even staying in my present position. My feeling has been to do all I can for God's glory by His power in the place I find myself and leave the results and next steps to Him. We still haven't had revival and spiritual awakening on a large scale and that may yet be what God wants me to concentrate on.

It could be Henry Blackaby who'd be chosen FMB head. God's hand is obviously on him. I'd already thought a little about that and about Tom Elliff being the one. It could be God's will for me to help one of them. Lord, I'm available to wash feet if it will get the gospel out and bring Your people to do it. Wouldn't it be interesting if Henry, T.W, and I ended up at the FMB and we could lead them and the SBC to follow God?

Speak to me, Lord, lest I veer to the right or left or respond too slowly or run ahead of You.

March 22, 1992

Lord, You have humbled me and shown me my sin. I was looking at the FMB from my perspective—what I wanted or would like to do— even though I was motivated by reaching the world for Christ. I looked at the trustee's viewpoint, too: There is likely someone better equipped for the job. I only have the heart. My experience is 14 years old except for interest and annual trips to other parts of the world. I'm not gifted enough in management but more in leadership. Others are more charismatic speakers than me. I am behind in mission strategy—the FMB is now ahead of me. My goal was to get indigenous missions as the method. Someone else would logically have more years and could bring about long range change more easily.

Neither viewpoint was looking at it from Your perspective. Therefore, I leave this to You. You will have to bring it up if You want to talk to me about it. In all candor, I can't ignore it. Help me know whom I should pray for that You will be leading to this position.

April 18, 1992

Every day I think about the FMB and my role in foreign missions. I have a hard time telling whether it is fleshly (personal) speculation or the Spirit preparing me to talk with the Search Committee (if they ask). In trying to sort out my feelings, I have considered several things:

- *Missions is my heart. It is the thing that makes my life sing. I leap to be involved in any kind of foreign missions.*
- *This desire to lead missions in SBC is contrary to the way I have gotten any other job because those jobs led me further away from direct missions, especially evangelism (i.e. going to the seminary in Indonesia and here to the BSSB.) I've had this idea in the back of my mind for at least 30 years. I thought I might get back to missions in 1983 after* MasterLife *was written, in 1988 after* LIFE *was established, and even now with revival, lay involvement in ministry, and support groups on the way.*
- *What is missing are the circumstances and the confirmation of the Body—that is, the call by the trustees and the affirmation of God's people. Of course, this is where I was last time with Elliff's nomination of me for BSSB president and for it they never came. I really didn't want that job and was afraid God might be leading me there—although I would have accepted. Even then I prayed God would not let me get in over my head or pre-empt any plans He had for me in missions.*
- *I am not looking for position or "power." God has been teaching me humility and how to fight spiritual battles by depending totally on Him.*
- *Would the other ministries I am caught up in right now get done if I left them to go to the FMB or even another position in the upcoming BSSB reorganization? I really think someone else could do them if God moves me away.*

April 24, 1992

I talked to Tom Elliff last night. Both of us danced around the FMB issue. He said he told someone that though it would be a big shift for me that I had the heart to fill the position. I told him I'd said the same about him. We left it there and we will talk more when I spend the night at his house on May 5th—a week after spending the weekend with Bonnie Westbrook who is on the search committee.

On that Friday, when Avery stayed in the home of Bonnie Westbrook, FMB trustee and ex officio on the search committee, Bonnie never broached the subject of Avery becoming president. Instead, he asked Avery to give him a profile of a future president.

The Lord spoke to Avery not to worry but that he should submit a complete profile for a potential president based on the person of Joshua. So Avery listed as necessary qualifications the following: experience, vision, leadership, catalyst, reliance on the Word of God, and administrative integrity.

Shared Vision

In May, Avery and Tom spent the evening together. Tom was the first to broach the uncomfortable issue of how they each felt God might be opening a door for them to head up the FMB. As best friends, they decided to be completely honest with each other. They knelt and confessed their tentativeness to God. Both felt they could be the man God had ordained and were excited by the idea, but both would accept God's will if they weren't selected. Both men were committed to prayer and revival as the key to radical changes. They were both gifted visionaries and communicators and had prominent positions of influence.

Seeking God

May 16, 1992

I realize I have been hedging psychologically to protect myself if I am not selected. I'm taking a passive role because I want God to do it rather than promoting myself. I have had many Bible promises and several could be applied to this situation but they could also apply to where God has already placed me. I need fresh direction. I do not want to go through the waiting period without a clear word from God. I know that I must have the Word, prayer, circumstances, and the affirmation of the Body all lined up.

I spent the drive to Tulsa talking with God and asking Him to reveal what He had chosen to do. Psalm 71:17–18 was the key passage God used to affirm me. "Even when I am old and gray, do not forsake me, O God, till I declare Your power to the next generation, Your might to all who are to come." I was gray in my 20's when I first received this word but now I am old and gray proclaiming His wondrous works. I plan to do it until I die. The sign I ask is that the trustees ask me to do it. In the meantime, I will study what You want me to do and get ready to do it.

While Avery was in Tulsa to baptize his grandson Kyle, he talked with his mother at length about all the ramifications. He began to feel the tremendous weight of the position and the sticky issues he would need to face if selected: the schism with the Cooperative Baptist Fellowship; finances; the desire of the laity for freedom to go anywhere at any time, separate from the FMB; pressure from the trustees; the cries and needs of the missionaries; and more. God gave him Matthew 11:30, "My yoke is easy and my burden is light."

Avery sent his resume to Dan O'Reagan and Bill Tanner, who had each expressed their desire to officially recommend him to the FMB search committee. On the same day, God spoke clearly to him through Joshua 1.

May 20, 1992

Lord, I hear this as Your mandate to me to lead SBC to world evangelization and missions to disciple the nations into your kingdom through Your Body the church. Here are the Bible promises I claim:

1. *I have commanded you to arise and lead these people.*
2. *"I'll give you every place you set your foot." (I must lead missionaries to claim this.)*
3. *"I will be with you as I was with Moses." (What else could I ask for? Nothing!)*
4. *"You will be successful wherever you go" (as long as you obey my commands and keep my law)*
5. *The people will do what you command. (aligns with my previous Bible promise in 1 Chronicles 28:20–21)*

After the annual Southern Baptist Convention, the *Baptist Press* reported that the FMB search committee had thirty-one names (mostly current or former missionaries) on their list. They were to narrow the list by late summer or early fall. Despite rumors, they said they had no predetermined candidates. This news informed Avery that it would likely be the first of the year before a new president was instated. He would remain at the BSSB through the process of reorganization, so he had time to launch the *LIFE Support* series, get things in order, and focus on the call to revival.

Waiting on God

June 15, 1992
God said to me:
Avery, the question is not you but Me! I am God and there is no other. I take the initiative. This is the story of My history and My world and My plans that I will accomplish. You are wrong to focus on yourself, your history, your experience, your knowledge, your ability, your friends, etc. You must get beyond thinking of yourself.

Yes, I have chosen you, refined you, led and used you. However, it is I who put one down and lift up another. It not your "age" but Mine, the Ancient One. It is not the committee's wisdom but Mine. I will bring about all I have said. What I have planned, I will do.

You are to be a prophet to the nations. You are also a prophet to this nation. Learn to see ALL my work and not compartments or divisions of it. It will take everything to accomplish My plans for the world. I have been teaching you for a long time that "the battle is the Lord's." Challenge those who are My chosen to go to battle in the strength of the Lord. You are entering an era in which the past is not adequate to explain or exploit. You must watch and wait for Me and then obey immediately to stay in step with Me.

June 20, 1992
A question on the FMB profile that bothers me is the one about an "active soul-winner." This has been a pattern of my life I have let slip. I do witness but it has been some time since I actually led someone to

Christ. I say this to my shame. I've gotten so caught up in LIFE Support to eventually win thousands that I've let my personal witness slide. One problem is I am not in contact with enough lost people and I've let my responsibilities and priorities crowd out opportunities with strangers. I feel a twinge of guilt when I share the story of promising God to do all I can to get the gospel to everyone by 2000 A.D.

The only solution is to repent and focus on it. I know I must demonstrate a witnessing lifestyle. Help me, Lord to do it, beginning now: to pray for opportunities, to initiate witnessing experiences, and to lead people to Christ—not just for a few weeks, or for a committee—but for life. For I am wasting the suffering and blood of Jesus when I don't share it with every man.

On June 24, 1992, Avery read Isaiah 54:2, "Enlarge the place of your tent, stretch your tent curtains wide, do not hold back, lengthen your cords, strengthen your stakes, for you will spread out to the right and to the left; your descendants will dispossess the nations and settle in desolate cities," and wrote:

This is the time to move forward. The only way to enlarge the tent is to lengthen the cords that hold it up. We must extend the cords to enlarge our SBC missions tent to include volunteers, more career missionaries, and people outside of our own churches—other mission agencies and other denominations—in specific concerted actions to new nations and people, to all lost persons, through new means. We cannot hold back in any area if we are to see what God is doing in the world and our nation today.

When the tent is enlarged and cords lengthened, it will put much more pressure on the stakes. The stakes represent the values that hold us together. But currently, our discipleship is weak, our commitment divided, our priorities confused. These are the very stakes that are now being pulled up in the storm of controversy that threatens to shrink the tent. If we are to survive as a denomination, we must strengthen our relationship to our Lord, our commitment to God's word and Biblical values, and our resolve as a missions people through the dedication of our lives and stewardship of our resources.

Everything God does is in abundance. We have made it a scarcity. In Russia, there is not actually a shortage of food but a problem with the transportation infrastructure. We need a massive rebuilding of the infrastructure of the gospel to take it to each starving person who is dying from gospel malnutrition.

Based on the Bible promises he was receiving as he prayed, the possibility of leading the FMB was often at the forefront of Avery's thoughts. He began to write out vision and strategy and ways to implement it. He sought counsel from those he trusted on each of four topics posed by the search committee. He then prepared his own responses.

July 18, 1992
I really haven't had much interest in the BSSB reorganization because I feel I won't be there. However, I need to help shape it, learn how it works, and see if there are implications for the FMB. Jerry Rankin and others have indicated the FMB needs reorganization. There are too many levels of administration and everything is top down directives. I think we need an entrepreneurial spirit to reinvent the culture with basic principles to guide us but without so many policies to bind us.

On October 31, 1992, Avery and Shirley interviewed with the search committee. Avery wrote:

The session went well. Earlier I had felt dissonance because I think I was trying to absorb the advice of my friends, meet expectations, and also really be myself. I finally put that aside and concentrated on God leading me. I spent the first hour answering the four questions they had raised. They then asked Shirley about her call, conversion, and role in our partnership. She answered all well. They had 21 additional questions from the Board of Trustees.

In November, while Avery was reading in Scripture and thinking about the structure of the FMB, God said:

Realize that My plan covers a lot more time than your lifespan. My promises and plans are much bigger than you. Allow Me to speak to you in My time. You are anxious over a few months of waiting. Abraham waited 25 years for Isaac. Moses got anxious to deliver the Hebrews but then had to wait 40 years to be truly ready. Trust me. I am teaching you. Realize you are just a piece of the chessboard. You see everything from your viewpoint, i.e. the kind of piece you are (bishop, pawn, etc.) and your present location on the board. This is just one chess game in a series and in just part of my kingdom. Let Me call the shots and I will use you to defeat the forces of Satan.

Avery waited ten weeks without word from the FMB search committee. In December, he wondered if Jerry Rankin, Don Kammerdeiner, or Tom Elliff had heard a specific word from the Lord for themselves. He had not heard them say so. The committee was to meet on January 7–9, 1993, to seek the Lord in prayer and then meet with the trustees on January 21. On January 14, Shirley called Avery to say that the *Baptist Press* stated the search committee had reached a decision, but that it was a secret. She said her "woman's intuition" led her to believe they had chosen Jerry Rankin.

Confusion

That was a surprise. The fact that they haven't contacted me is not encouraging. I went to bed early just worn out and couldn't help thinking about this each time I awoke. Of course, that leads to doubt and saying if it doesn't happen after all the Lord has spoken to me, how can I be sure of other things I believe He is saying? Could I also misinterpret them? I remember in May asking God for a sure word after talking with Tom so I could believe Him regardless of how the circumstances looked. Therefore, this is the time for faith, not fear or doubt.

Avery was headed to a meeting in Atlanta in which he expected to see Tom Elliff. When Tom wasn't there, Avery called him and learned that the committee had agreed "unanimously—after prayer individually and as a group" to nominate Tom for the FMB presidency. Tom had spent hours since Friday night talking with committee members but had not made a decision. He was struggling since he had already relinquished any intention for the position. Now they wanted a decision by the following Friday.

Tom was very sensitive to my feelings and said he had planned to call me. We talked for an hour. He says it is not over yet but my gut feeling is that he can't turn it down unless the Lord clearly tells him no. Even then there is no assurance the committee would come back to me, even if he recommended me again. I told him not to let my situation get in the way of his decision.

He said maybe I could still do all God wanted to do through me if I went with him. I didn't tell him about my Bible promises. Until God or the FMB show me otherwise, I think I need to hold on to my Bible promises and my convictions.

I know I am going through the grief process even as I am trying to keep faith in the face of insurmountable odds. Yet, with Tom's not having made a decision, it is like my wife or I being terminally ill and having only hours or days left. I can't deal sufficiently with "the death of a vision" until it is dead. I still have hope. I'm not sure that it is faith.

I admit it really hurts. For 7 months I've been envisioning what I'd do in every situation if God put me in that position. As I remember, I want to cry. Isaiah 49:4–7 expresses how I feel: "But I said, 'I have labored to no purpose; I have spent my strength in vain and for nothing. Yet what is due me is in the Lord's hand, and my reward is with my God.' And now the Lord says—he who formed me in the womb to be his servant . . . I will also make you a light to the Gentiles that you may bring my salvation to the ends of the earth."

I feel a bit like Joseph in prison for 13 years and the butler hasn't kept his promise to tell Pharoah. But like Joseph, I must keep doing my job and depend on the Lord in due time. If Tom takes the position, I will need to face several decisions about what I will do next: stay at BSSB? Go with Tom to the FMB? Focus more on revival? Or does God have something else for me for this next decade?

Tom asked for my vision/question notes so I will send them to him. He was still "working on getting a word from God." He asked what my sense was that he should do. I told him to <u>get</u> that word from God—only He could truly give an answer. I shared the problems I felt he would have *if God led him there. He thanked me and asked where I saw myself if he became president. He shared his idea of 4 vice-presidents working together as equals on overseas, home front, nationals, and home office staff. I listed my strengths as either overseas with my missiology background or new laity involvement but I'd need to get a word from God on whether He wanted me there or not.*

January 24, 1993

Tom and I went to lunch and talked. He is to give his answer by Wednesday. He does not yet have a Bible promise, though his wife, Jeannie, expects him to get one today. I asked Tom how he handled Bible promises that don't come out like you expect. He said he had that problem about his parents never getting reconciled—to the point he laid Bible promises (one of his life messages) aside for three years. He has learned that we are not perfect and may misinterpret and sometimes God has a greater purpose that we only see later (as in his parents' case).

Avery began to get revelation from the Lord that he could do what God called him to do without being tied to a position. His influence had more to do with his obedience.

This morning I sensed I needed "faithfulness" more than "faith." I can't make things happen through faith. I can only receive what God wants to give. When I can't see or understand, I must keep walking with Him and be open to receiving whatever.

January 30, 1993

Tom called at 8:00 a.m. yesterday to say he told the committee that he did not have peace in his heart about accepting the position. He had prayed all Tuesday night and into Wednesday. He was twenty seconds from telling them "yes" but said he just didn't have the peace. He said one thing he had learned in this was "the will of God must be initiated by God." When the committee said "he was their sole candidate—what should they do?" Tom said, "Proceed with your work and find God's man."

The subsequent press release stated the committee would once again review its seventy-four candidates, which were grouped into tiers of eight by their level of consideration.

I find myself seeing double again. Tom's integrity is a mighty example that God still rules in some men's hearts and in the affairs of men. On the other hand, it may leave me out of the loop as an FMB vice-president if they select someone else. I am in a new place of peace. I do not feel I should get involved trying to relate to the FMB unless they call me again. I am going to proceed in doing all I can to get Fresh Encounter *and* The Mind of Christ *produced.*

Over the next weeks, Tom continued to pray as the committee asked him to reconsider and he and Avery discussed what they would do if they went together to the FMB—but once again, Tom felt compelled to decline the offer. Avery had mixed emotions: relief that perhaps he had not misinterpreted what he heard from God, fear that he may have lost his opportunity to lead the overseas mission force if the future president did not call on him, and some anticipation that he might yet be contacted as others were still recommending him for the position.

President Elect

On May 26, 1993, Dr. Jimmy Draper had lunch with Avery and informed him the committee had chosen Dr. Jerry Rankin as the next FMB president and it would be in the press soon. Jerry was to be elected June 14 and introduced at the Southern Baptist Convention. He also mentioned that Jerry had cited Avery's name as one of the top leaders he might choose alongside him.

Avery knew Jerry well from serving together as missionaries in Indonesia. In fact, Jerry and Bobbye Rankin had moved into the house the Willises vacated in Jember and continued the work there for nine more years. Jerry was currently serving as the area director for Southeast Asia.

May 28, 1993

Yesterday God continued to speak to me about the wilderness being preparation for what God was going to do in the life of Moses, Israel, and Jesus. I felt He was saying He loved me and was still guiding. It brought tears to my eyes.

Later I called Jerry Rankin to congratulate him and tell him what I had said in Indonesia to Shirley about how he would be used in high places and maybe even develop to be FMB president. I got emotional again. He said, "This is all I'm going to say now but I'm praying about your future. I think God has a special job for you to do."

The Door Closes

Avery and Shirley attended the FMB reception for the Rankins. That night he wrote:

This closes the chapter of my life related to the FMB presidency. I couldn't help but think of what I'd have been doing had I been elected. But I am at peace. Had I chosen someone, it would have been Jerry. I am relieved that Jerry hasn't asked to talk with me yet so that I can get past the emotions of this 14-month experience.

Coincidentally, this fourteen-month experience had been paralleled by another. Avery's mother, Grace, had suffered a heart attack that caused significant damage to her heart and kidneys near the time when the initial candidate search began. He had hoped she would live long enough for him to tell her that he had been elected president since she knew how deeply he longed for the missions door to reopen. During the long months that followed, she had become very ill and had been in and out of the hospital or specialized care, with a tenuous prognosis. It was almost as if her health mirrored Avery's process of waiting and hoping when circumstances looked bleak.

July 1, 1993

Mother has been in a life and death struggle all this time. It's almost as if she is a parable of my struggle and she is losing. However, she doesn't

*die and keeps coming back though weaker each time. It becomes a daily
stress factor as we try to manage her care.*

*Lord, there seems to be an ongoing sense of frustration and grief
that is shutting me off from our normal sense of intimacy. I know it is
from many of the same reasons I have listed before—my sense of missing
Your plan and my disappointment. Jerry seemed to indicate there might
still be a role for me but I haven't heard from him. I am going full-steam
ahead on what You have given me to do at BSSB, but it's almost like
I'm going through the motions without Your intimate touch on all I do.
I notice it most when I pray in my Quiet Time and all the* things *to pray
about come to mind instead of just fellowshipping with You. In the meetings, I seem to move on quicker and not be so dependent on You.*

July 17, 1993

*I must admit the opportunities and support in my present job indi-
cate Your blessings and opening of doors. It appears I can still do most
of the things You have given me as a vision and more than I have anticipated. If not on the front lines of missions, I can still influence missions
from BSSB. Jimmy Draper's plan is that we be a world-wide provider of
training through all of our literature. I have seen my role as a catalyst
for discipling, equipping, revival, and missions, even more so now that
we are adding to our curriculum base the whole new area of shaping
family life. Of course, the biggest thing I think You could have in mind if
You leave me here is to be a catalyst for revival and spiritual awakening
in America that would spread around the world. Help me rejoice in all
You want to do and follow You day by day in faith. Help me see Your hand
at work and to know when Your finger beckons me to follow You into a
situation or just to admire You at work.*

Another Door Opens

Dr. Jerry Rankin called Dr. Roy Edgemon and asked him to have
lunch. He asked Roy about his working relationship with Avery. Roy
said, "Avery is one of the finest men that I have ever known. We have a
great working relationship!"

Jerry said, "I am thinking of asking Avery to be a vice president at the FMB. Do you think he could handle the job?"

Roy answered, "Jerry, I wanted Avery to have *your* job! I believe you couldn't choose a more gifted and qualified person in all the world. Avery walks with God, and God leads Avery's life. He has the heart of a soul-winner and a missionary. He is loyal to his Lord and to his leader in that order. We have had the best relationship through these years together, and I will miss him, but I know his heartbeat is to reach the world. I believe he will accept your offer if the Lord tells him to go."

July 28, 1993

Jerry said he was ready to talk to me about my future—about a "significant place" at the FMB. He told me to be prayed up. As I prayed, I once again sensed I should ask the question:" What if he asks me what God has called me to do or shown me I should do?" Immediately I saw my life vision separated from its parts. My calling is to be the catalyst to get the gospel to all the lost people in the world, disciple them to follow Christ, help them to develop indigenous churches, equip them to minister and commission them to repeat the process until the world is reached.

August 1, 1993

Tonight Jerry asked me to become Executive Overseas Vice-President. He envisions it eventually covering everything overseas. Immediately, it would be to work with the ten area directors who live on the mission field and restructure the Missionary Learning Center. The present four vice-presidents would serve as consultants to me and the area directors and as a task force for new directions.

It is not all clear to me except that it is far more than I can comprehend: working with 168 countries now and responsible for the world, the spiritual life of missionaries, training of missionaries, etc. He made me a firm offer. This was not an exploratory meeting. He made the decision in prayer. I will share more of my philosophy, background information, and notes so he can defend his nomination.

He also said that I should spend half my time overseas. He thought I needed to keep my focus there and not get bogged down with the area associates in Richmond who could be under Don Kammerdiener. He wants himself, Don, and me to be a functioning leadership team without being tied to administrative areas.

The time frame is fluid from October 12-December 31 on moving. This gives me time to put some things in place. Now I must get Discipleship Training outlined before October 1 and pray for my replacement. And I need a fast learning curve and grace to better remember people and names to do this next job!

Lord, you are too good to me! You have entrusted me with more than I deserve or am capable of. You have refined my character and motives over the last 18 months. You have let me do what I wanted to do without all the overall administration of the presidency and dealing with the constituency—that part Jerry will do. You have given me time to shape the future direction of the Discipleship and Family Department. You do all things well in Your time. This timing is perfect—today is the fifteenth anniversary of my arrival at the Baptist Sunday School Board! I believe all my Bible promises fit what You are doing!

October 25, 1993

Today begins my last week of work at BSSB. Over fifteen years, God, You have led me and protected me and used me in ways only You could work.

Help me in the remaining time to lay out the design and desire of Your heart. Help the decision-makers to know the man You have chosen to take the position I hold, but even more, help him to be a disciple who knows You, Your ways, and Your leadership.

CHAPTER 28
Redesigning the Plan

Since the Spirit wrote the Word, who knows
if He is not continuing to write
the book of Acts in heaven and one day it will be read there.

—Avery

The profile for the Senior Vice President of Overseas Operations could not have defined Avery any better. Its qualifications were as follows:

- Extensive field experience and leadership, thorough understanding and support for FMB global strategies
- Unequivocal commitment to the FMB vision and passion for our task of reaching all peoples
- Proven spiritual leader who exhibits a disciplined walk with God
- Strategic thinker who is able to grasp a big-picture perspective, analyze alternatives, and determine appropriate and productive courses of action
- Communication and pulpit skills
- Proven abilities in business and organizational skills of financial management, budgeting, personnel management, and information technology
- Good relationship skills, well-known and respected by staff and missionaries; someone who would elicit confidence and trust in the FMB administrative team
- Commitment to relate to the president in a supportive role and willing to challenge and confront issues and positions

The President Search Committee's "Dream Team." Photo taken
in Atlanta by Bob Oxford
(From left) Trustee Bob Oxford, Don Kammerdiener,
Avery Willis, Tom Elliff, Jerry Rankin
All had been considered for the position. Jerry had told
Tom when he accepted the position "If you were wrong, we
are both in trouble." At this meeting, Tom turned to Jerry
before he got up to speak and said, "I was right!"

The Team

When Avery arrived at the Foreign Mission Board in Richmond,
Virginia, in December of 1993, he joined President Dr. Jerry Rankin
and Executive Vice President Dr. Don Kammerdiener, who adminis-
trated all the home office departments and staff. Avery's new position as Senior Vice President of Overseas Operation replaced the five
regional vice presidents who had previously supervised the ten area
directors and all overseas work.

All three leaders were highly qualified for their position, but they
were gifted very differently. Don was the pragmatic one, very realistic
with an in-depth and historical understanding of people and the organization, having served under Keith Parks and as interim president. Avery

was the visionary, "spinning off-the-wall initiatives and strategies at every meeting" and resistant to merely maintaining or managing the status quo. Jerry, as the leader and communicator of vision and purpose, had the challenge of setting a balance in all planning and decision-making.

Preparation

Avery spent the first four months learning all he could about leadership and how to successfully implement change. In January, Avery attended leadership training with Bob Agee, president of OBU, and others. He was learning much about communicating vision, planning, and setting goals and objectives. Dr. Agee believed it would take a minimum of eighteen to twenty-four months of planning to produce an initial strategy and three to five years of implementation to invoke serious change *if* it was given priority in prayer, time, and work. Avery was encouraged to move people and money to the places of impact.

November 3, 1993

The Lord is telling me in every way possible that I must receive the vision for me, FMB, and SBC in the world; clarify it for myself; get missionaries involved in stating it; and then implement it. I can't get bogged down in individual projects and lose the big picture. Experiencing God has taught me the basic motivations are glorifying God and working with Him on mission—to preach the gospel to all persons. It is not what we can do for God in America or around the world. It is what God wants to do through us for His glory among the nations. We need to give Bold Mission Thrust back to God. He is the author of the Great Commission. He needs to be the architect of how to accomplish it.

December 8, 1993

God said to me, "Look at Proverbs 24:5 as My word to you: 'A wise man has great power and a man of knowledge increases strength. For waging war, you need guidance; for victory, many advisors.' You have been given great power, but you must increase your knowledge to increase your strength. You need to surround yourself with advisors for victory. Use all the people I put at your disposal.

Avery, you don't have a strategy, and don't try to 'get' one. One reason you have not felt adequate is because you are trying to be adequate, even excellent. When you speak to the strategy committee of the trustees, you are to talk about My strategy. It is My strategy that causes these words: awe, wonder, amazement, surprise, astonishment. Even Jesus did not have a 'strategy.' He came to do the will of Him who sent Him. This is not a copout, it is reality. You must lead our missionaries and My people to follow Me and My voice. Your job is to help My people spiritually: to know Me and My ways—and strategically: to learn to discern and follow My leadership. You are to set up processes, people, relationships that will bring this to pass. Strategy is not made in the board room but discerned in the prayer room. That is why Jesus was always praying. He was hearing the voice of the Father. He was watching to see what the Father was doing."

December 28. 1993

How the church grew in Acts appears spontaneous but in fact God was overseeing His strategy. The disciples' strategy was to be obedient to the Lord who was building His church and spreading His kingdom.

Prayer Support

In this new venue, Avery also changed his plan for intercessors. Knowing that people might not have the same motivation to pray for him in an administrative role in the US as when he was actively on the mission field, but also knowing that he needed the prayer just as much, he cultivated a smaller group of prayer warriors who knew him well enough to pray for him daily and specifically. To these, he took time to write monthly prayer letters describing his activities, what they could pray for, and how God had answered the prayers from the previous letters. He kept it strategically small to be able to share openly and to "depend on them for maximum prayer support."

Collaborating

Jerry, Don, and Avery immediately began examining and redefining all operations. The three met regularly as SET—the Strategic

Executive Team—to pray and strategize. It wasn't long before major systemic problems in the organization were revealed.

January 6, 1994

I feel uneasy about the way we have organized overseas. Yesterday as I met with the Overseas Vice President advisory group, I realized we have a crippled organization. The normal chain of command runs through Area Directors. I have no means of two-way communication with them most of the year. The Associate Area Directors are conveyors of information but not makers of decisions. We must set up systems that involve participatory management and so far we don't have it.

I've prayed long enough this morning to be open to your decisions, Lord. Help me wrestle with this until we get a workable solution. Help me do what You want. Help me LEAD! I have strong convictions but I've usually worked through consultation and persuasion to bring people along with me. I can't do that at this point because I don't exercise leadership or communicate with Associate Area Directors and missionaries directly.

While the FMB had experienced successive years of record missionary appointments, there was a sense that they were not keeping up with global events, such as the breakup of the Soviet Union, which was opening doors to Central Asia and Eastern Europe, nor with the growth of the global church. They were receiving reports of phenomenal church growth in China and were participating in a new global awareness of the massive numbers of unreached people groups. While God was opening doors throughout the world, the FMB was plodding along with minimal church growth and meager progress toward unreached people groups.

It seemed the board had lost some of its pioneering spirit and that the time had come to reignite it. The SET team believed the time had come to decide whether their assignment was to hold ground or to take ground. They believed they needed to be more aggressive in reaching into areas with little or no access to the gospel.

Avery was instrumental in leading the team to formulate a renewed mission and vision statement and identify core values, but the SET team contested his effort to set goals and objectives. It had become evident that a new system was needed to decentralize ownership and allow the initiatives to come from the field and be reflective of each area's needs, culture, and responsiveness to the gospel rather than from the top down.

New Directions

In February 1997, the Strategic Executive Team pulled away for a time of prayer, brainstorming, and seeking the Lord together, away from the administrative matters that constantly competed for their attention. Jerry recalled, "The first night we prayed and just bared our hearts and began to focus on the question: We have three years to the year 2000 and a new millennium. What should the Foreign Mission Board look like and what should we be doing when we arrive in the 21st century? We recognized such a large, bureaucratic organization could not be changed overnight, but if we had a vision for where we wanted to be, what we should be doing, and what our organization would look like in three years, that vision would inform our decisions and drive our planning toward those goals. This was an anointed time. The Lord gave vision and insight through a phenomenal synergy of discussion."[1]

Several problems inherent in the structure and processes in overseas work were identified:

- The FMB was locked into existing churches, conventions, and institutions overseas, which repeatedly requested personnel and financial resources to sustain established work. A large proportion of the missionary force were in assignments serving the mission organization while very few were actually planting new churches.
- Field leaders were managers overwhelmed by budgets, personnel issues, national relations, and troubleshooting instead of projecting strategic vision. Because field leadership was organized to administrate areas where missionaries were working, no one was advocating for the unreached and unengaged in areas where there were no current missionaries.

- Decision-making was slow since it required consensus in annual meetings on the field. This group decision-making squelched innovation resulting in the loss of creative and visionary missionaries.
- Developing tensions led the SET team to recommend that Cooperative Services International (CSI) be brought under the umbrella of the larger mission strategy. CSI personnel used education and humanitarian work to gain access to restricted countries and engage unreached peoples, emerging as an elite structure of "real, cutting-edge missions" that appealed to new candidates. Much of their work was effective and creative but with limited accountability in regard to finances and policies, creating a dichotomy between the two mission structures.

It was clear change was needed in the Foreign Mission Board's ideology and practice. Following the retreat, the SET team formulated a rough draft of what they envisioned and their rationale and presented it to the trustees. These basic recommendations altered the FMB culture and philosophy:

1. Develop a new leadership profile for the field leader to free them from administrative tasks and thus enable them to give visionary, strategic leadership to the missionaries.
2. Release missionaries from subjugation to national conventions and partners under which they had to work.
3. Disband and redefine geographic areas. Missionaries would no longer function as a nationwide mission but would be reconfigured into smaller teams and clusters of teams, with shared ownership of the task, mutual accountability, and more freedom to directly implement the strategies they felt were most effective for their targeted people group. Regional leaders would provide vision and resources to engage and reach every people group within the region.
4. Dissolve CSI as an entity and incorporate it into the new regional structure in an attempt to infuse all of the FMB with its passion, vision, and innovative strategy.

Leadership convened the area directors to explain the new plan and process and asked their help to reconfigure the regions, focusing on the "reach every people group" objective. When the new regional structure was approved, interviews began for eleven regional leadership positions plus administrative and strategy associates. These leaders were elected at the July board meeting with the understanding that implementation of the New Directions strategy was to be in place by the end of the year.

The trustees simultaneously approved the new strategy and the FMB/CSI merger into the newly renamed International Mission Board (IMB).

Leading through Change

Change is always difficult, and these changes would not come easily. Avery's vision and creativity had much to do with formulating the New Directions strategy and its acceptance among field personnel. Avery felt strongly that the vision and fundamental commitment to "go to the lost by all means available" was the higher good and encouraged faithfulness to the vision, even though the process to get there was difficult.

Agnes Loyall, Avery's administrative assistant, said, "It was a difficult transition for him personally. So many of the area directors were moved out of their positions and others elected in their place. It was hard on him because he loved them all. It was a time of low morale for both missionaries and home office. Avery had to bear the brunt of the negativity and questions since most of the reorganization was in the overseas office structure and the structure of the missionaries on the field."

In the midst of stressful changes at the IMB, Avery went through two knee replacement surgeries. His first was in January 1997, during the rollout of the New Directions. He named that knee "new directions" and sent a picture of his knee with its stitches to the missionaries saying, "It really hurts now, but we're going to walk a whole lot better when we get through this!" The second occurred in 2002 during the time when missionaries were being requested to sign the 2000 Baptist Faith and Message (SBC denominational statement of faith) as a tenet of employment. He named that knee "BF&M" as a war wound of the intense times of struggle and prayer, compassion and negotiation. Someone later told him, "I hope you don't have any more knees!"

Avery communicated his vision and personal concern to those he led and served, face-to-face and in writing. In a letter to the regional leaders, dated November 26, 1997, he wrote:

Thank you for a good three weeks together. It was stimulating to be with you and to share the vision God has given us. I praise Him for you and the opportunity to work with you. Let me take this opportunity to state again what I said at the closing banquet in New Orleans.

I am committed to our overseas team being family oriented. Your spouse is a very important part of the team. Our wives can minister in ways that we can't and have many spiritual gifts that are needed by the Body and team. I would encourage your wife to take whatever role you and she feel she should take in your region and decide how much she travels with you in your role.

We will continue to cut the bureaucratic "kudzu" of the old paradigm in the overseas area and advocate it be cut in other areas of the Board. We have not come this far to back up. This is not a template over the old paradigm. We must press on to flesh out the new paradigm and kill the old one. Help us when you see it cropping up. Have patience with us as we work with other IMB components to do the same.

We are committed to pushing toward the edge of lostness in World A [David B. Barrett's classification of people groups of whom fewer than 50 percent have had the opportunity to hear of Jesus Christ]. *Our highest priority is to be "on mission with God" and doing His will. The next highest priority is the redemption of people for whom Christ died. The priority needs to be to those who have not had the opportunity to hear and respond to the gospel. Alongside that is the priority of seeing where God is evidently working and bringing in a harvest. We make a mistake to say a country is a harvest field. There are pockets of harvest in most fields and pockets where the gospel has not penetrated. We must discern the leading of God so we know how to best invest the resources He has made available. God is the real Prioritizer! That means we can't just operate by neat formulas and follow them alone. We follow Him to the ends of the earth and to the harvest fields as the Holy Spirit guides us as He did Paul in Acts 16.*

We intend for you to lead. We will try to dialogue about the vision and the principles and let you make the decisions. If our people understand the vision, they will be able to make the proper decisions without you or us having to prescribe them in most cases. That means we expect you to set up ways of accountability closest to the action. The one thing we can't do is not have accountability both ways.

If anything is not clear, let me know. I love you and praise God for you. Feel free to call me any time.

Avery

Responding to Backlash

Nevertheless, over a three- to four-year period, there was a good bit of upheaval and misunderstanding, resulting in some missionaries resigning or retiring from the IMB. An assessment three years later reflected 95 percent of personnel affirmed the changes, though 40 percent indicated that they did not agree with the process and resented that they were not given sufficient ownership of the changes. Nevertheless, the leaders realized that slowing down and seeking to give five thousand missionaries ownership of the decisions would have sabotaged or diluted the necessary changes.

The policy changes also created a strong negative reaction among national convention leaders when their countries lost missionary resources for their programs and financial resources for their institutions. They disagreed with the focus on people groups, and resented that they were not consulted before the changes were made. It was nearly deja vú of the missionary-national struggle in Indonesia, but this time on a global scale.

Realizing the extent of misunderstanding, Jerry, Avery, and Don traveled the world gathering representatives from national convention partners into what they called AWE (Accelerating World Evangelization) conferences. These were held in Mexico, Chile, South Africa, Kenya, Togo, Germany, Hong Kong, and Malaysia with at least

120 conventions represented. The IMB leaders apologized for any lack of communication and sought to clarify misunderstandings. They affirmed their commitment to a continuing partnership and support of the national convention work, while explaining that the rationale for the restructuring of their mission strategy was to make the reaching of unreached people groups their basic missionary task. The hope for these AWE conferences was that local national conventions would partner with the IMB in taking the gospel to the unreached in their respective areas. The IMB would continue to support initial church development and leadership training, with the nationals taking the responsibility for future developments.

We assured them we were not abandoning them but will limit the number of missionaries performing convention tasks. We offered to partner with them in local people groups teams and to welcome their missionaries to unreached people groups in other countries. Frank exchanges of past, present, and future relationships marked all the dialogues. Most wanted to relate as equals in the mission task. Leaders from each of the participating conventions expressed renewed commitment to reaching the unreached in their own countries. Several asked for missionaries to help them in mobilizing and training their people to become missionaries.[2]

Though there were strained relationships on the field, and some further backlash, overall these meetings were positive, deeply spiritual gatherings in which there was reconciliation. Many local, indigenous, missionary-sending efforts emerged from the AWE conferences.

Results of Reprioritizing

Some of the ensuing developments as a result of the organizational, strategic changes and the change in the mission ethos were the following:

1. Unreached people groups became the priority. There was a massive redeployment of missionaries from traditional fields to the unengaged. An average of more than one hundred unreached people groups were engaged for the first time

each year for the next ten years; one year, as many as 192 unreached people groups were engaged.

2. Mission institutions (hospitals, publishing centers, etc.) were nationalized and significant financial resources were redirected to missionary support for the unprecedented growth in candidates the board was experiencing.

3. Mobilizing stateside church partners to multiply the impact and resources became a growing pattern.

4. A more indigenous strategy began to produce church planting movements. The number of new churches started grew annually from four thousand in 1999 to more than twenty-four thousand in 2007.

5. Rather than working exclusively, partnership with other Great Commission agencies became the norm.

Positive Changes . . .

In 1998, over seven hundred new missionaries were appointed—a 38 percent increase and a record number of appointments for a single year. Offerings were increasing from all sources. The Missionary Learning Center doubled its space to train all the missionaries being sent out in a twenty-three-million-dollar expansion.

Vision trips for pastors became a venue to increase mission involvement in churches. At the Summit for the New Millennium in Nashville, Tennessee, 170 strategy coordinators (SCs) met with representatives of 230 churches to set up vision trips in 2000–2001 so churches could get a closer look at their adopted people group.

Pastors caught a vision of how businessmen could engage in missions when many remarkable connections were made. One couple was ready to go to the field as soon as there was a request. The request came in during the summit. One SC needed a museum curator as a door opener to his people group. A pastor at the table immediately phoned a member of his church and announced, "We have your curator!" A pastor had been asked to write a grant to get Bibles printed and translated for a people group. A man at the summit identified grant-writing as his profession and volunteered to fly to New York to help the pastor get the grant written. An SC who sought training for Chinese house church leaders sat beside a Chinese pastor who specialized in winning Chinese and helping them return to China to start house churches.[3]

The pastors could also see the impact in terms of harvest. Avery took forty-three pastors on a vision trip to China to visit several teams working with unreached people groups and to teach Chronological Bible Storying in an "underground" Chinese missionary training school. He interviewed the leader of a house church network that had grown from five to eight million people.[4]

As the twenty-first century dawned, the Bold Mission Thrust overseas goals were evaluated. In January 2000, Southern Baptists recorded unprecedented growth for that year: 10.5 percent increase in churches, 11.7 percent increase in new churches, 4.3 percent increase in baptisms, and a 95 percent increase in church membership. It meant that thirteen churches had been born and one thousand people baptized every day the past year.[5]

In March of 2001, Avery reported the following results to the trustees, demonstrating the impact of the new strategies toward the Bold Mission Thrust goals overseas:[6]

Number of:	1975 total	BMT goal	2000 Actual	+/- from 1975
International Missionaries	2,667	5,000	4,946	+ 185.5%
Countries Served	82	125	153	+186%
Annual Volunteers	1,200		30,362 with a total of 250,000 from 1995–2000	
Overseas Churches	7,584	X 10 =75,840	60,988	+ 804%
Overseas Church Membership	896,063	X 10 = 8,960,630	5,624,018	+ 627%
Annual Baptisms	80,747	X10 = 807,470	451,301	+ 558%

He added that due to church planting movements, incremental growth was changing to exponential growth. Where the average growth rate of new churches had been 15.3 percent over the last decade; in 2000, the growth rate was 37.4 percent. The ten-year rate of baptisms had been 4.8 percent but had increased in the last year to

24.1 percent. The growth rate of church membership had doubled to 14.4 percent.[7]

... Outrun Finances

After seven straight years of record appointments, the 1999 financial gifts failed for the first time to keep up with the accelerated number of missionaries being appointed—postponing some missionaries who were prepared to leave. In 2003, the IMB experienced four of the ten highest appointment services in the 157 history of the IMB, but they were forced to cut their budget by ten million dollars, delete sixty-one Richmond staff positions and curtail the number of noncareer missionaries to five hundred due to fund shortfall. It wasn't that people were giving less, but the increased number of appointments and the declining investment market meant that the IMB was obliged to slow appointments for the first time since the Depression.

In 2004, Avery praised God when the Lottie Moon Christmas offering increased almost 21.2 million dollars, allowing for two hundred new missionaries.

Church Planting Movements

As a result of these changes, church planting movements increased around the world. The results below were recorded by David Garrison of the IMB and sent to Avery, who posted them on his Caring Bridge in 2010:

Here are [some] cases of phenomenal growth in places where the IMB is involved as a primary partner helping nationals rapidly multiply churches and new believers. Of course, once we have started and taught them how to do it, the nationals have taken the lead and done most of the work. I have been to a majority of these places and we have had assessment teams go in to verify what has happened. You should feel confident sharing these.

The Home Mission Board started work in Cuba and when they turned it over [to the IMB] in the early 1990s, Cuban Baptists reported

235 churches. Strategy coordinators had to live outside the country and go in and train and advise. By 2000, the number had grown to more than 4,000 churches. By 2010 evangelicals across Cuba are on track to see 100,000 house churches with one million baptized believers.

In a closed North African country, a Strategy Coordinator began working with a people group. The church has grown from 22,000 baptized believers in 2003 to more than 160,000 in 2009.

In a South Asian country, a church planting movement started in 1996 with national initiative. At their request we came alongside of them to help and to learn what they were doing. An assessment team went in and verified more than 125,000 baptized Muslim-background believers in 2002. Unverified reports say now there are over 400,000.

A church planting movement (CPM) in a northern Chinese province had 20,000 new believers and 500 new churches planted in less than five years.

In southern China, a church planting movement produced more than 90,000 baptized believers in 920 house churches in eight years' time.

A church planting movement among Bhojpuri-speaking people in India was started by a strategy coordinator and resulted in more than 11,000 new churches and a reported one million new believers. This is the best assessment we could come up with but it is real.

A movement which began in China in 2001 has produced the fastest growing church planting movement in the world to date. They have already seen nearly two million baptisms and more than 80,000 new church starts in less than a decade.

More Iranians have come to Christ since 1979 than in the thousand years that preceded it.

Across the continent of Africa, Christianity has exploded from less than nine million in 1900 to more than 470 million in 2010.

These answers to prayer caused Avery's heart to sing. He was so pleased to be an instrument of God's mission in the world. He was seeing the fulfillment of years of preparation, promise, prayer, and praise. But life at the IMB was much more than statistics; it had a very personal side.

CHAPTER 29
A Glimpse into His Office

Your vision determines your mission in life.
Your mission determines your decisions in life.

—Avery

Avery in his office at IMB
(Photo courtesy of the International Mission Board)

A very's office was on the first floor of the International Mission Board. The room was clearly used for work. The conference table and chairs were bookended by an enormous map of the world on one end and a whiteboard to work out strategy on the other. Bookcases laden with books lined one wall. A large painting of Mount Salak, the scene from the Willises' Bogor house, filled the wall above them. The right side of the office consisted of long windows and a deep windowsill on which rested souvenirs from around the world. A picture of Shirley sat on the credenza behind his desk, and family pictures were scattered through the room. A large antique globe stood beside the desk.

A few papers he was currently working on would be found on his desk, but no messy piles. An in/out box was on the corner of the desk along with the trip folders Agnes prepared for him. A separate folder was created for each travel/speaking engagement complete with airline tickets and all necessary information. Sometimes it was a single folder, but Avery often traveled to multiple countries before returning home, so a stack of folders might greet him; then the walls of his virtual office would extend as far as airplanes could fly and jeeps could maneuver.[1]

Before his desk were a couple of chairs for people to meet with him. He kept his door open most of the time, and people dropped by. The information technology (IT) people knew the office well because Avery tasked his computer(s) so heavily that the hard drives had a higher-than-average incidence of crashing. Focused time to complete a major project, or confidential and extended meetings, earned a closed door. Personal time with the Lord or Bible reading had already occurred at six o'clock that morning as he knelt daily before his quiet-time chair with his Bible open so that when he arrived in the office, he was prepared for the day.

Working with Avery

During the BSSB reorganization, and when he was still waiting to hear about the FMB presidency, Avery was evaluated on his management style and his managerial, interpersonal, communication, and analytical skills to ensure his fit for the new position. The report claimed:

> Mr. Avery Willis is very, very mentally alert. He is stronger verbally than numerically although he is significantly above average in both. He is a self-starter but not so "type A" as to have stress-related problems. He has no problem making decisions, but some might be made on insufficient data due to

impulsivity. He is a risk-taker. He has the capacity to take the initiative and assume responsibility. He is not so dominant as to be autocratic, but Avery definitely wants to be in charge. He is very stable and will remain calm in a crisis. He is above average in sociability but even higher in reflective thinking. He much prefers working on analytical problems rather than practical ones. He enjoys working alone in addition to working with and through people.

In his present position, he said he works as an entrepreneur to get the mission of his department accomplished. In our discussion of management styles, Mr. Willis views his role with subordinates as that of a compatriot, as part of the team to accomplish the goal. His style with superiors is to accept their authority and respect their position.

Avery sees his strengths as being competitive, having an unusual spiritual relationship giving him special insights, and his excellent speaking skills. He is a good planner and has the tenacity to follow through. His weakness is delegation—if he has the expertise, he would rather do it than delegate. But he doesn't like to get involved with the details of day-to-day management and prefers to turn those responsibilities over to someone else.[2]

Those who worked with Avery found this description to be eerily accurate.

John White, cofounder of LIFESHAPE, a philanthropic ministry of Chick-fil-A, worked alongside Avery at the IMB for eight years, first as his associate and then as executive vice president. He tells what it was like to work for Avery:

Avery was one of the most creative persons I've known. When I went to work for him I thought he wanted me to follow through on every idea he discussed in a meeting. In a 15-minute meeting Avery could come up with 15 different ideas that needed to be implemented, and all of them sounded great. It took me several years to figure out that these were just ideas Avery was thinking about and he did not intend for me to kick them all into activation. Finally, after almost putting myself under trying to keep up, I went into his office one day and told him that I couldn't do everything he was suggesting. I learned then that if I didn't hear him make a suggestion three or four times over a period of days, I would not begin to implement it.

There are numerous examples of how Avery developed leaders above and below him in the organization. However, the most memorable for me was the first time we met for a performance review after I was named as the Executive Vice President of the International Mission Board.

Can you imagine how awkward it was for me to be giving a performance review for my mentor and former "boss"? But Avery smiled and said, 'This is not the first time someone I've led has become my boss.' That helped relieve the tension, but it also demonstrated Avery's humility through his entire ministry as he developed those around him. He was not concerned with his own position or power. His personal power came from his intimate walk with the Lord. It would be inaccurate to say that Avery had a daily walk with the Lord. His walk was moment by moment.

Leading from Below

Avery had learned long before that it was possible to lead—even from the middle. It required faithfulness to God, respect for those in charge, and the ability to know when to speak and when to remain quiet. He laid it out once in his journal:

Playing second fiddle, or second in leadership, is not bad. God smiles on those who serve in associate positions. Look at what God was able to do through Joseph, Daniel, and Esther. Paul was mentored by Barnabas. Jesus voluntarily took the role of a servant.

Sometimes, though, you have to be smart—and you always have to be faithful to God. This is what I mean:

- *Treat your leaders as you want to be treated.*
- *Be faithful to what God reveals to you.*
- *Be faithful in prayer so you can advise your leader and also make good decisions so God is glorified. As Nehemiah did, be ready to give an answer when asked.*
- *Be faithful to be as bold to speak as God wants you to be but in an appropriate way. Like Esther, be prayed up and then know what to ask and when. Depend on God to bring about the results.*
- *Be faithful to carry out your job as one of God's people because you could end up as the leader.*
- *If you get a chance to help someone do more than you can do, do it.*

Mutuality

Avery cared personally for those he worked with and saw them not as employees but as colaborers in Christ and dearly loved friends. Excerpts of a letter to the regional leaders dated May 12, 1998, affirmed his value for the whole person.

Dear Friends in the Fray!

By now most of you are back in your region and the May Regional Leaders' meeting is far back in the rearview mirror! Before it disappears completely I'd like to reflect on a couple things we talked about and what happened.

I enjoyed the personal time with each of you. At your personal conference in November, I would like to spend some time talking about how you see yourself, your Regional Leadership Team, and your region. I would also like for us to talk about your personal spiritual disciplines, physical health, family situation, and intellectual growth relative to your work. I will be glad to share the same with you. Right now I don't feel we need to set any arbitrary goals or measurements but I do believe we should be accountable as brothers in our walk together.

Let's pray for each other every day as I do for you. We are all facing tremendous challenges and need all the grace and strength God will give us. I believe we are a global team and want the best for each person even if it costs us personally.

—Avery

Indeed, he was serious about mutual prayer. John Brady, one of the regional leaders (RLs), shared about a time when he had not been faithful with sending prayer needs to the board. One day, he received a call from Avery, who was traveling between countries in Africa. He said, "John, this is the day I pray for you and you haven't sent me any recent prayer requests. You need to do a better job of keeping me up-to-date so I'll know how to pray for you specifically."

John also remembers the occasional Iron-on-Iron Sessions Avery had with the regional leaders as a group, so named for Proverbs 27:17, "As iron sharpens iron, so one person sharpens another." In preparation for one such gathering, Avery had sent out an e-mail alerting those who worked with him to get prepared for the upcoming session. Gordon Fort, one of the RLs, responded by sending a joking e-mail to his fellow RLs, suggesting that the session may be less like "iron-on-iron" and perhaps more like "iron-on-clay pots." What he didn't realize was that Avery's name was on the group recipient list. When John noticed it, he said to a fellow RL, "We're about to see a wonderful train wreck."

Forty-five minutes later, Avery fired back a direct response: "If we didn't have iron, it was going to be difficult to get anything sharpened."

When Avery retired from the IMB several years later, Gordon Fort became his replacement. The RLs presented Gordon with an iron rod while they all held up their clay pots!

Impact of Passion

Being positioned to steward God's redemptive mission world-wide would intimidate most people. Rather than causing sleepless nights, however, the level of responsibility energized Avery. There were unquestionably times when the Lord awoke him to pray and listen in the wee hours of the morning, but God's voice enabled Avery to obey, trust, and risk.

Avery's passion for the lost drove him. He took to heart the scripture in Ephesians 5:15, "Be very careful, then, how you live—not as unwise, but as wise, making the most of every opportunity, because the days are evil." To him, that meant every day should be purposefully spent. Whether planning, writing, or praying, he lived out his belief that the lives of a lost world were at stake. It didn't mean he didn't like to recreate—he certainly knew how to play—but he hated to waste productive moments.

Once, when he and Sherrie were coauthoring their book, she called him, woeful that the chapter she had been working on had "suddenly disappeared" from the screen and she hadn't saved it yet. She asked if he could send her the last version she had sent him because she was going to have to redo it. The chapter was later recovered, but Avery told her then, "I set my computer to autosave every five minutes. I have too much to do to waste more than five minutes redoing what I've already done."

His intensity had a downside as well. Jerry Rankin noted:

> God used him effectively to challenge Southern Baptists to a higher vision of global missions, but sometimes we had to do damage control due to his unbridled enthusiasm and charisma. Avery was so passionate and visionary that he could be insensitive to the perceptions of others and the impact of his ideas and proposals. Sometimes his Office of Overseas Operations became the essence of the IMB and other departments such as finance, personnel, communication, public relations, etc. felt they were peripheral step-children and existed to serve Avery and his team.

He set off several landmines with Southern Baptists and churches who did not understand nor support partnering with non-Baptist mission agencies or his mandate that church buildings overseas would no longer be built with mission funds.

When the emphasis on church planting movements emerged, Avery repeatedly brought it to the forefront so that missionaries and fields who were not seeing church planting movements felt less important and even like failures.

Passion and creativity also meant that Avery often left items behind. After a conference, his mind would be racing with ideas of how to streamline or advance the mission task, or he would engage in conversations to the point that he would forget to retrieve his suit jacket or phone or Bible. His associates, John White and later Randy Pegues, became caretakers of his things. They would scope the room, collect any stranded articles, and return them to the office until it became a game of what he had left and where. Unfortunately, phones left in the seat pocket of airplanes were goners.

Identity Switch
(Told by David Garrison at Avery's Retirement Roast)

David Garrison, global strategist at the International Mission Board, worked closely with Avery and traveled with him on many occasions. Once, he joined up with Avery and Shirley at the airport. Avery's connecting flight had been canceled, and he had been bumped to a later flight. He really needed to get to a board meeting. David was going to the same meeting and was scheduled on an earlier flight. So Avery thought it would be a great idea to switch tickets and David could follow on the later flight with Shirley. (Obviously this took place before September 11, 2001!)

Shirley thought this could be great fun and was going along with the scheme. She teased David, "Should I call you sweetheart?"

Avery quickly retorted, "No! You can't call him sweetheart! You don't call me sweetheart, why should you call him sweetheart!"

From Highs to Lows

Certainly, both privileges and struggles were imbedded in Avery's position as senior vice president of overseas operations. As he was leading meetings, making presentations, and meeting with missionaries, he traveled to six continents and 125 countries of the world. He embraced opportunities to hang glide in Slovenia, fly around Mt. Everest, and go on safari in Kenya. He and Shirley viewed men's achievements such as the pyramids of Egypt, the Taj Mahal, Petra, and the Great Wall of China and gazed on God's achievement in the beautiful Victoria and Iguazu Falls. They also witnessed devastation when they visited Sarajevo soon after the war and the Goma refugee camp not long after the massacre in Rwanda.

It's A Simple Question, Really...
(Story Told to Wade's Sunday School Class by Avery)

Avery spoke of meeting a student in South Africa at a bus stop. He introduced himself and engaged the man in conversation. He asked him about his life and what he planned to do.
"What are you going to do after this?
"Well, I plan to finish college."
"Oh, and then what will you do?"
"Then I plan to get a job."
"And then what will you do?"
The young man thought that then he would marry.
"What will you do after that?"
"We'll have children."
"Then what will you do?"
"Probably retire."
"And then what will you do?"
"Then... I guess I will die..."
"Then what will you do?"
Avery said the young man was saved after he heard the gospel.

Seeding Mission Hearts

One of the greatest blessings Avery and Shirley had was to transfer a mindset of missions to their children and grandchildren. Their own children had been raised overseas and had already seen the world and its need and the honor of sharing Jesus.

Willis family including spouses and 16 grandchildren, 2007

Avery and Shirley extended that to the next generation. They made it a priority to invite one grandchild per year on one of their trips overseas. It served two purposes: they got one-on-one time to develop their relationships with each grandchild, and it afforded that child a vision for the cultures of the world and for what God was doing there. They attempted to take as many of the sixteen grandchildren as they could before they retired. As a result, many of the grandchildren continued to go on mission trips or serve overseas in humanitarian ways.

When granddaughter Kara was asked what she had learned from her trip to Taiwan, she replied, "There are a lot of people in the world—so many more than I had realized—who have never known or heard of Jesus Christ. I grew more spiritually in the last five weeks than in all my life. I learned that God is my strength and that I can do a lot more than I thought I could. If God calls me to be a missionary overseas, I will be glad and willing to accept the call. Before this trip, I don't think I could have said that. I saw how much joy and fulfillment these missionaries had."

On Christmas Day 2007, after other gifts had been exchanged, Avery and Shirley announced they had one final gift. Cliff and Krista were serving in Indonesia at the time, and Krista was really struggling with missing family. In order to meet that need, Avery and Shirley offered to pay for each family's round-trip visit to Indonesia (one family per year) and to give Cliff and Krista a trip home for Christmas. It was a special blessing, met with much joyful and incredulous shouting, especially for the ones who had been raised in Indonesia, to take their families back to the "home of their heart."

The Difficulties

At times, there was pain. Avery and Shirley knew sacrifice when they released Krista's family to serve as missionaries in Indonesia.

We are experiencing how it feels from the parents' side now as they take three of our small grandchildren halfway around the world!

Avery, like all pastors and spiritual leaders, had to minister to people in all types of situations. Being missionaries does not preclude families from dealing with issues such as chronic illness, death, divorce, sexual abuse, adultery, loss of possessions, or rebellious teenagers in trouble. It simply makes those problems more difficult because the missionaries are away from family support.

The extended Mission family and cluster teams were an important part of each missionary's support group, but pain in one part of the Body always extended to the rest of the Body. In his role, Avery, along with the regional leaders and area directors, provided outside pastoral care and counseling. In some situations, he had to enact discipline, even to calling missionaries back from the field, and then do damage control with the affected parties, both missionary and national.

The Dangers

Sometimes the job involved personal danger.

Disease

As he traveled, Avery sometimes had to fight through illness and infection. On one occasion, he picked up a viral infection in Africa. For two weeks, he experienced reoccurring urinary infections, but the E. coli bacteria was resistant to normal medication, and he was allergic to others. He finally returned to Africa with the promise that they could give him injections of the one medicine he could tolerate. Nine shots later, it finally cleared up.

Mugging

Avery had experienced nearly being pickpocketed on several occasions. Once in Indonesia and twice in South Africa, he had fended off culprits with an instinctive blocking maneuver left over from his days of playing football.

In February 1996, just after their fortieth wedding anniversary, Avery and Shirley were in Antigua, Guatemala, for an annual Mission Meeting. Having had too many meetings and too many meals, Avery and Shirley decided they needed to walk more than eat dinner. There was a large cross up the hill overlooking the city, so Avery chose to walk there. The missionaries later claimed there were signs in the hotel warning against going up that road, but the Willises had not noticed them. They got up to the top of the hill at dusk, just as a car containing a courting couple left.

Avery stepped to one side to look out over the city, and Shirley continued toward the top. She suddenly cried out as two young Guatemalan men jumped out of the bushes. One of the men grabbed her arm and swung her around to take her watch. The man then asked for money. Shirley turned her pockets inside out to show she had no money. Holding a carpet knife next to her finger, he demanded her wedding ring. She wanted to tell him that he didn't really want that ring—it was forty years old and had only cost $35, but she didn't speak Spanish.

By then, Avery had run up and said, "Shirley, don't argue with him. Just give it to him." But her fingers were a bit swelled, and she couldn't get the ring off. The man stuck his fingers in his own mouth to indicate that she could moisten the ring with saliva and get it off, which she did.

Then the thieves turned to Avery to see what they could get from him. He gave them his wedding ring, dropping his billfold in the process. Shirley stooped to pick it up and hand it back, and one of the men struck her on the backside and knocked her to the ground. Avery willingly gave over his cash, but insisted he needed to keep his billfold and his credit cards and somehow convinced them to let him do so. Since the men were no longer paying attention to her, Shirley got herself up and told Avery she was going back down. He later accused her of deserting him, but her intention was to make a report of where he was and what was happening. He caught up with her a few minutes later.

When they got back to the hotel, no one but the treasurer was back from supper. When Shirley told him they had just been mugged, he said dismissively, "Welcome to Guatemala!" He came back later and apologized profusely for his flippancy. A missionary couple invited them over for a game of 42 (dominoes) to help settle their adrenaline so they could sleep that night.

When they got back to the US, Avery and Shirley bought themselves new matching wedding bands for Valentine's Day, which served them well for fifteen more years.

Persecution

Other threats were not to himself, but to others (some of whom he was responsible for). Avery often enlisted his prayer partners to engage in intercession and spiritual warfare on their behalf.

- *Pray for the 100 top leaders of a huge church planting movement in South Asia who have been targeted by militant Muslims for martyrdom. Last week one was beheaded and another killed.*

We are to go to this country to teach their leaders more about Chronological Bible storying.

- *Pray for a Solemn Assembly I will lead in Myanmar for the leadership of several denominations and mission agencies. I have never led a solemn assembly in another country where I was not familiar with the situation. This is not a free country. Christians there are living under one of the most oppressive and cruel governments in the world. Many are paying with their lives. There is rampant liberalism and crushing apathy in the churches there. Pray for deep repentance and a mighty outpouring of the Holy Spirit.*

- *"Abdul", a South Asian Muslim who turned to Christ has helped spark a movement in his homeland that has changed thousands of lives for Jesus Christ. Despite persecution, the ministry has 400,000 followers and nine thousand churches at this time. Sixty-three church planters involved in the ministry were recently arrested. In the past, when people were imprisoned, Christians would scramble to raise money to get them out. This time, it is different. Instead of paying for lawyers or court fees, the money is being given to their families for food. "We think God has placed all of these men in jail for a purpose. We feel confident that incredible things are taking place inside the jails. When the men get out, we will hear their stories."[3] Pray that those imprisoned will endure the beatings and harsh conditions and that the prison guards and other prisoners will be open to the gospel through their witness.*

- *We have just completed one of the most demanding, fabulous six-week trips of our lives. I spoke eight hours a day for most of the trip. Almost every country we were in had a major crisis during this time. Yet, in each place God protected us and we felt no fear.*

- *We had a fabulous Lead Like Jesus workshop with forty-five participants from Jordan and Iraq. Some pastors did not come from Baghdad because of the massacre of others who had come to training in Jordan earlier. Two flew in and testified how God was multiplying their church in the midst of the war. We left just four days before the bombing in Amman.*

- *I just finished a conference call with leaders from around the world who are on the steering committee for the Bill Bright Initiative to see five million churches started and one billion people reached for Christ in the next ten years. We all sensed that we each need at least twelve intercessors that will pray for us each day because the enemy [Satan] will not be pleased with this effort and will attack us. Would you would be willing to be one of the twelve who pray for me daily?*
- Even after retiring from the IMB: *Pray for the nearly 200,000 killed and five million homeless in Banda Aceh due to the earthquake and tsunami which occurred only a hundred miles from Sumatra, Indonesia. It was different for me from past disasters at Christmas time since I was not responsible for the IMB's response this year. However, we are trying to mobilize people to pray, give, and go to respond to this unimaginable need.*

(Avery's son Randy and grandson Kyle traveled to Banda Aceh on separate occasions to help.)

Martyrdom

Avery was deeply impacted when any of the missionaries made the ultimate sacrifice.

On December 30, 2002, during Christmas celebration with the family, Avery answered his phone. He quickly excused himself and left the room. Word had just arrived that three missionaries in Yemen had been martyred.

A man had entered the complex of Jibla Baptist Hospital in Yemen, hiding a semiautomatic rifle under his jacket, wrapped up to resemble a child. The eighty-bed hospital treated more than forty thousand patients annually, with free care for those who could not afford it. Its missionaries also taught English and clinical skills at a nearby nursing school.

The gunman walked to a room where hospital administrator William Koehn was holding a meeting and opened fire. Koehn, physician Martha Myers, and purchasing agent Kathy Gariety died from shots to the head. The gunman then headed to the hospital's pharmacy and shot and wounded the pharmacist, Donald W. Caswell.

Ironically, this was the next-to-the-last day the Baptists were seeing patients. The hospital, targeted by the Muslim gunman as an "affront to Islam," was to be turned over to the Muslim-led government on January 1. The transfer was part of the New Directions strategy to release institutions such as hospitals and schools to focus on church planting movements. In fact, the meeting the gunman interrupted was to prepare for the transfer.

Avery preached the memorial service:

The deaths of Martha Myers, Bill Koehn, and Kathleen Gariety were horrible in our eyes but God made them beautiful. Their acts of kindness stand out against the dark background of their murders. Bill gave food to the orphanage, put pipes in a prison so the prisoners could have clean water, and the day before he was killed he had 102 donkeys loaded with food to be delivered to the widows and divorcees of Yemen. Hundreds of Yemenis wept at their funeral, lining the streets in their honor.

They could not preach on the streets but they could let their lights shine in a dark place to glorify their Father who is in heaven. They could not proselytize but they could minister to 40,000 Yemenis a year and bring healing to hurting bodies and hope to failing hearts. They did what they could.

We don't determine the time or place of our death but we do choose the time and place of our service. They did not waste their lives. They planted them in the soil of Yemen and it has become an oasis in the desert.

A year later, missionary Bill Hyde was killed by a terrorist bomb in the airport in Manila in March 2003, while picking up the Stephens family, fellow missionaries, some of whom were wounded in the attack.

On March 15, 2004, in the area of Mosul, northern Iraq, six terrorists surrounded the vehicle and opened fire on four missionaries delivering relief supplies. Larry and Jean Elliot and Karen Watson were killed on the spot. David McDonnall lived only long enough to get his newlywed wife of two months to the hospital. Carrie survived her wounds. Avery wrote in a special March issue of his prayer letter:

Several have asked if we are still going to Iraq since our missionaries were killed there last week. Yes, I believe a leader never asks people to do what he is unwilling to do. We counted the cost of following Jesus a long time ago and we believe it is worth the price whatever the cost. The missionaries and nationals there need our encouragement more than ever! Please hold the ropes for us in prayer.

(To Avery's disappointment but resignation, the trip was, in fact, cancelled in light of the escalation of kidnappings of foreigners from their homes even with security guards.)

All the joys and all the sacrifices were accepted because of the greater calling of the ministry of reconciliation of the world to Christ. "Since, then, we know what it is to fear the Lord, we try to persuade men ... For Christ's love compels us ... He died for all, that those who live should no longer live for themselves but for Him who died for them and was raised again" (1 Corinthians 5:11, 14, 15 NIV). But it was a global task and required global partnership.

Spiritual Marker #12

God orchestrated the partnership
of multiple global ministries
for unreached people groups.

There before me was a great multitude that no one could count,
from every nation, tribe, people, and language,
standing before the throne and in front of the Lamb.
—Revelation 7:9 (NIV)

CHAPTER 30
Building a Global Partnership

Continue with unceasing prayer in every direction until God substitutes
people as his instrument to the nations.

—Avery

The increasing role of specific, targeted prayer toward people groups was demonstrating remarkable results.

On January 21, 1993, three hundred prayer leaders from a variety of denominations met in Colorado Springs, Colorado, for the National Consultation of United Prayer to share the current prayer plans of their denominations. Prayer walks, multichurch and interdenominational concerts of prayer were being conducted, and twenty-four-hour prayer rooms were being established. Methodist pastor Terry Teykl declared, "Denominational pride builds walls between our churches but no single denomination can evangelize the world. We must humble ourselves, and repent of competitiveness and exclusive attitudes."[1]

Avery was privileged to be in the midst of seeing God bring about that reality.

Sharing Resources

In May 1995, the Global Consultation on World Evangelization (GCOWE) was held in Seoul, South Korea. Hundreds of volunteers from the Korean church had organized, prayed, and invested thousands of hours of labor for the event, as well as given millions of dollars to cover the cost of food and housing, all so four thousand delegates from 186 countries could focus on establishing a church planting movement among the unreached people of the world by the year 2000. It was an extraordinary gathering since 70 percent of the participants were under the age of fifty, a quarter were women; and for most, it was their first global-level meeting. More than two-thirds of the delegates came not from Europe or North America but from Africa, Asia, Latin America, and the Middle East.[2]

As representative of the International Mission Board, Avery was asked to present a case study of what Southern Baptists were now doing to carry out the Great Commission. After over 150 years as an agency, they had been willing to look afresh at what God was doing and ask, "What needs to change about our organization and culture to make that possible?"

Instead of presenting the resulting changes, Avery surprised all in attendance with his confession. *I don't want to talk about what we've done but what we've learned.* With tears, Avery continued:

I also want to apologize on behalf of Southern Baptists because we have tried to do what only the <u>whole</u> body of Christ can do. We have been too isolationist and too independent in trying to reach the world. We had a goal to get the Gospel to everybody in the world by the year 2000 but learned that, rather than setting man-made goals, we should have been setting God-given goals.

Avery went on to say that Southern Baptists needed to, and would begin to, intentionally work together with other Christian groups to carry out the Great Commission. He then put the International Mission Board contact information on the screen behind him and offered to all mission organizations in attendance all the resources of Southern Baptists.

Planning

On November 28 of that year, 262 Christian leaders representing 140 mission agencies, denominations, and educational centers in seventy-seven countries met in Colorado Springs to consider the future thrust of pioneer missionary outreach through the AD 2000 & Beyond Movement. Much of the early discussion at this meeting stemmed from the Joshua Project 2000 plan to spread the gospel through existing mission networks in 160 nations.

Focusing on ethnicity, the Joshua Project synthesized data produced by the International Mission Board, Wycliffe Bible Translators, Adopt-a-People Clearinghouse and Operation World to create a database, by country and language, of "unreached peoples." They compiled a list of 1,700 cultures residing in 123 countries of the world with the least access to the Christian message. The goal was to see "as a minimum, a pioneer church planting movement resulting in one hundred or more Christians in one or more reproducing churches within every ethno-linguistic people of over 10,000 individuals by December 31, 2000." Under the plan, churches and agencies would send research and prayer teams to each of the listed people groups to lay preliminary groundwork for evangelism and church planting.[3]

Partnering

In June 1997, Avery traveled to Pretoria, South Africa, to consult with five hundred mission executives of the Global Council on World Evangelization.

Executive leadership from significant mission organizations, both Western and non-Western, were invited to ensure greater cross-fertilization and cooperation. Also included were representatives of churches large enough to be their own sending agency. These leaders were invited because they could commit personnel and resources to unreached people groups as well as go back to their constituencies and bring specific focus to the task. Ralph Winter, founder of the US Center for World Mission, said, "Let's don't just have popular meetings about completing the missionary task; let's get together the people who have the resources, the authority, and the position to follow through on specific suggestions and initiatives."

Avery listed the primary objectives:

We wanted to get the missions executives into an arena where we could discuss what God is doing. We wanted these mission agency leaders to share what they were doing, especially among unreached people groups.

A major objective was asking agencies to take responsibility for engaging the 700 of 1,739 unreached people groups on the Joshua Project list thus far unassigned and attempt to answer the question: "How can we strategically work to get to these peoples?"

We also wanted time for the mission groups from the newer sending countries to have an opportunity to interface with those agencies with more experience. Conversely, the older sending countries wanted to learn from the newer ones with more innovative strategies.

Thirdly, we emphasized "How do you establish a church planting movement among an unreached people?" because that is really what we are looking for when we are looking at these unassigned 700 unreached groups.[4]

Table 71[5]

On July 29 to August 6, 2000, the Billy Graham Evangelistic Association invited ten thousand participants from around the world, many from Third World nations, to the Netherlands for "Amsterdam 2000."

Three hundred of the world's most prominent Christian leaders, teachers, and evangelists were invited to speak. Among them were Billy Kim, Bill Bright, Chuck Colson, J. I. Packer, and Luis Palau. The event was translated into over twenty-five languages.

Billy Graham had asked Paul Eschleman, then director of the Jesus Film Project and president of Finishing the Task, to bring together six hundred mission strategists from around the world. They were to take one segment of the Amsterdam 2000 schedule and meet in a room around seventy-five tables, eight to a table, to discuss everything necessary to complete the Great Commission.

On the third day of meeting, Paul Eschleman went to the platform to talk specifically about the 230 people groups of the world that had never even been targeted. Bruce Wilkinson, founder of Walk Thru the Bible, challenged the participants, "There shouldn't *be* any untargeted people groups in the world. Just the idea that there *are* means we are not doing our job. We, the leaders gathered in this room, lead the vast majority of today's Christian army. We could decide, together, today: let's finish it."

Roy Peterson, former president of Wycliffe Bible Translators and president of the Seed Company, recalled, "There was a growing sense in the room that this was deeply on God's heart and that He had given the Body of Christ everything it needed to reach these people groups."

Wilkinson went on to challenge the leaders to get the people sitting at their table to take a serious look at the people groups listed on sheets of paper at each table. He asked them to pray about which ones God was calling them to take ownership of, and when they had decided, they were to go to the platform and tell Paul which groups they were committing themselves to reach.

One representative said, "We'll take one." Another said, "We'll take three." Another, "We'll take ten," and on it went. Bruce Wilkinson stood back and watched as God tapped people's hearts all across that room. Some wept as they came forward. Others embraced each other as they put their names next to the people groups they were committing themselves to reach. Mark Anderson, international director of Youth With A Mission (YWAM) and president of Call2All, said it was one of the most electrifying moments he had ever experienced. Bruce could almost picture the celebration in heaven as the blood of Christ was being applied to these groups that had yet to hear He had died for them.

But then it suddenly stopped. When they reached 141, no one else came. It was as if the participants were saying, "We're all done."

Bruce Wilkinson again invited men and women to consider coming forward to make additional commitments, but only a few came. It was over—or so it seemed.

Paul Eschleman remembers how quiet the room got. "As exciting as the euphoria over adopting untargeted people groups was, there was now a sense of discouragement. No one moved. Just silence."

Bruce Wilkinson remembers stepping back from the podium and praying, "Lord, every time I've ever watched You do something, You've never done it halfway. You've always completed it. Whatever You want, *please* complete it!"

Steve Douglass, who had just become the new president of Campus Crusade (CRU), leaned over to Mark Anderson of YWAM, who was sitting at his table, and asked, "Why don't our two organizations take the remaining groups?"

Bruce Wilkinson, watching from the platform, soon noticed that the table where he had been seated suddenly began to buzz. While most of the people around the other tables were sitting in silence, praying, this table had come to life. They were very animated, talking excitedly to one another. They began to nod in consensus, and then someone from the table walked to the front, took Paul's hand, and said, "Table 71 takes the rest!"

Table 71 takes the rest!?

Bruce Wilkinson reminisced, "There must have been shouting in heaven! I can't imagine what the angels sounded like as the sons of men stepped to the plate in such a way that the agenda Christ has been waiting to see completed was finally becoming our most important finish line!"

Meanwhile, back at Table 71, Mark Anderson's head was spinning as he looked at the list of the untargeted people groups that were left. He was thinking, "What did we just do? We took responsibility for 120–130 people groups, and these are the hardest ones to reach! You might be able to get in to these people, but you might not come back out!"

Realizing the immensity of the task ahead, Steve Douglass, moderator of Table 71, and the others started working overtime. They worked during the breaks; they worked past the time the group was supposed to end. Now that they were committed to reach these groups, what did "reach" mean? How were they going to do it? What would be the strategy? Where would they begin? They soon agreed that one of the goals must be the planting of churches.

Meanwhile, David Garrison, who was on Avery's staff as global strategist for the International Mission Board, overheard what was going on at Table 71. At one of the breaks, he said to Avery, who was seated with him at another table, "You've got to get over to Table 71 because something's happening."

As Avery approached Table 71, Mark Anderson, knowing that indigenous church planting was one of Avery's passions, remarked, "Avery, we need you to help us with church planting." His immediate response as he pulled up a chair was, "I'm in."

They knew they were going to need someone to spearhead the translating of Scripture into these native languages; and not coincidently, seated at an adjacent table was Roy Peterson, who was at that time president of Wycliffe Bible Translators. At a break time, someone from Table 71 called him over and said, "You've got to hear what we've been thinking about." Roy pulled over his chair and joined the conversation. Another need was met. Eventually, one by one, sitting at Table 71, were leaders of the Christian world representing a combined ministry to millions.

Avery reported,

Every session we were building, one category upon another, until we came to the point of writing up a contract that each of us signed—a commitment to each other, and to the untargeted people groups, to begin partnering in an effort to reach all of the remaining unreached people groups of the world—to evangelize, make disciples, and to nurture indigenous church planting movements.

After signing the contract, they sat there, looking at each other until someone asked, "Is this what we are committed to?" And in unison, everyone responded, "YES!"

Steve Douglass, president of Campus Crusade, summed it up: "We have committed ourselves to the number '0,' meaning that someday people who do research will look throughout the earth and find *zero* unengaged, unreached people groups."

Avery left "Amsterdam 2000" and "Table 71" (which would continue to work together), full of vision and already strategizing his role to make the new commitment a reality.

SECTION 7
Engaging the Oral Learners

Spiritual Marker #13

God led Avery to a new mission strategy
of oral-based discipleship.

*Everyone who calls on the name of the Lord will be saved.
How, then, can they call on the name of the
one they have not believed in?
And how can they believe in the one of whom they have not heard?
And how can they hear without someone preaching to them?*
—Romans 10:13–14 (NIV)

CHAPTER 31
Making Disciples of Oral Learners

Until we have made salvation at least an
option for every person in the world,
we can't afford as God's people to make it optional
that we are involved in God's mission.

—Avery

It was at the Amsterdam 2000 Billy Graham Conference for Evangelists, in the midst of all of the Table 71 buzz, that Avery was asked a question that changed the trajectory of the rest of his life.

"Avery, how do you make disciples of oral learners?" questioned his friend Marcus Vegh. Conference participants had just been reminded that two-thirds of the world's population did not read or write and would not be reached through literate means.

"I don't know," Avery replied with a shrug. "People have been asking me that question for twenty years. I don't work with illiterates. If you do, you need to figure it out."

Marcus was the founder and director of Progressive Vision, an organization that had identified 639 people groups with a population over one hundred thousand who had no written language. Marcus kept pushing, "Twenty years and no one has done it? Seventy percent of the unreached people groups in the world are oral learners. You know discipleship, Avery, it's your job."

Avery wrote,

I heard this as if it were the voice of God. I am not sure why this question hit me so hard. I was leading the five thousand IMB missionaries to focus on reaching the unreached. I was aware of oral learners but had never considered them my responsibility. Now God was telling me otherwise.[1]

EE-Taow: The Power of Story

As Avery mulled this over, he flashbacked to a visit with Tom Elliff eight years earlier. Tom had been excited to show him a documentary, called *EE-taow*, about how the gospel had penetrated an unreached tribe in Papua New Guinea.

Mark and Gloria Zook, missionaries with New Tribes Missions, had entered the world of the Mouk people in 1983. After months of culture and language study, they were ready to communicate God's Word. But how? They knew that the Mouk people had no previous exposure to the Scriptures, so they decided to tell Bible stories in chronological order to the entire tribe of 310 people.

As the tribe members gathered each morning and evening, Mark and Gloria began with Genesis and orally shared the stories of Scripture. Over the next several weeks, they observed the Mouk developing a sincere reverence for God as well as a fear that He might destroy them because of their sin. After storying the Old Testament for two months, they finally introduced Jesus Christ as the Savior, born as a baby in Bethlehem. The whole tribe fell in love with Him. Jesus became the Mouk's hero. Mark said, "They loved Him and they idolized Him. There were times when they became so intent on listening to the stories that they stopped eating and sometimes would not even sleep." The Mouk people spent hours discussing and listening over and over to the stories recorded daily on cassettes.

As the story of Jesus unfolded, they became very upset when they heard how Judas had betrayed Jesus, leading to the trial before Pilate. They had faith, however, that Jesus would somehow escape. Mark told them that he would finish the story the next day.

Early the next morning, Mark told them the story of the crucifixion and resurrection; then, without a break, he went back and briefly recounted the Old Testament stories, starting with Abel and his sacrifice that was accepted by God. When he got to the story of Abraham and Isaac, Mark explained that, just as a ram was substituted for Isaac, Jesus's death and the blood He shed was a substitution for the Mouk's sin.

At that point, Mark and Gloria could tell that the Holy Spirit was opening their hearts and minds. As the people talked among themselves, they began exclaiming, "EE-Taow! EE-Taow!" (It's true [or good]! It's true!) Then the rhythm of the truth built to shouting. Spontaneous celebration broke out as the people began to jump up and down en masse for two and a half hours, shouting "EE-Taow! EE-Taow!" and "I believe! I believe!" That day nearly the entire tribe believed in Jesus and His sacrifice to purify them from their sin.

Later, Mark asked some of the men, "When will you tell the other villages this good news?"

At first, they stood silent. Then one man said, "Yes, we will go, but we don't know how to do it."

Mark replied, "I will show you how." Celebration broke out once more.

Mark began to train the men, and a few days later, they assisted Mark as he shared the stories in the next village. In the third village, the men told the stories, and Mark aided them. The Word of God continued to be spread to twelve surrounding tribes, some of them with different languages.

Until that moment, the Zook's story had been a sermon illustration for me. Now I realized it was the key to reaching the nations. I repented and vowed to help believers learn to tell the stories of Jesus.[2]

Taking Up the New Challenge

Avery returned to his position at the International Mission Board a changed and challenged man. Despite all of his work and influence in the area of discipleship, he had neglected 70 percent of the world and set about immediately to address it.

He called together eight "storying" practitioners from around the world who had already refined the chronological Bible storying approach with great effectiveness. Among them was Jim Slack, an IMB missionary who had learned the New Tribes Mission approach in the Philippines and began developing chronological Bible storying. Jim and J. O. Terry had already begun teaching the process to missionaries in other parts of the world. Over the next three years, this group developed an oral approach to discipling, using Bible stories, including audio recordings of over four hundred stories. The CDs of the stories, *Following Jesus: Making Disciples of Oral Learners*, were published by Progressive Vision, led by Marcus Vegh.

Avery and Paul Eshleman, founder of the Jesus Film Project, called together a consultation group, formulating the Oral Bible Network. At the Lausanne Committee for World Evangelization in Pattaya, Thailand, Avery was among a group assigned to explore the topic of "Making Disciples of Oral Learners." This group merged with the Oral Bible Network to form the International Orality Network (ION) with the expressed purpose to "radically influence the way oral preference communicators are evangelized and discipled in every people group." Avery was named International Director. In 2004, Avery and Steve Evans produced a book from the group's paper, entitled *Making Disciples of Oral Learners*. A portion of that book reads:

> By "oral learners" we mean those people who learn best and whose lives are most likely to be transformed when instruction comes in oral forms . . . by means of stories, proverbs, poetry, chants, music, dances, ceremonies, and rites of passage . . . art forms highly regarded among their people. To effectively communicate with them, we must defer to their oral communication style. Our presentations must match their oral learning styles and preferences. Are we willing to seek God to become better stewards of the Great Commission and address these issues in serving Him in these last days? (p. 3–5)
>
> A "storying" approach to ministry involves selecting and crafting stories that convey the essential biblical message in a way that is sensitive to the worldview of the receptor society. The stories are faithful to the biblical text, and at the same time are told in a natural, compelling manner in the heart language . . . normally involving some sort of discussion

about or interaction with the story. (p. 11) The Word becomes readily available to them. They enter the stories and the stories enter them. (p. 16) Because it is in their own language, it captivates them and they want to hear more. It is easily memorized and retold to others. (p. 28) So those who respond can reproduce it—share it themselves with others who can, in turn, share it—with this pattern being repeated many times over. (p. 11)

The results of storying the Bible were dramatic.

In Nigeria, missionaries had preached to the Tiv tribe for 25 years in the manner they had been trained in Bible school—and only baptized 25 believers. "Then some young Tiv Christians set the gospel story to musical chants, the indigenous medium of communication. Almost immediately the gospel began to spread like wildfire and soon a quarter million Tivs were worshipping Jesus. The Tivs were not as resistant as the missionaries had thought. Prior to this, the gospel had been 'proclaimed', but it had not been heard!" (p. 13)

In south Asia, when storying accompanied agricultural training, the average number of new churches planted grew from one per year to one *per day*. (p. 47)[3]

Similar results of the power of storying were collected from J. O Terry.[4] (For security reasons, some of the regions and source names have been omitted.)

From Bob Creson, president of Wycliffe, on why the gospel is best heard in one's heart language:

At a Good Friday service in 1980, Leonard Bolioki stepped to the front of the church he attended in Cameroon and began to read the story of Jesus' crucifixion. Always before, this passage from John's gospel had been read in French, but this time the priest had asked Leonard to read it in the local language, Yambetta.

As he read, he became aware of a growing stillness; then some of the older women began to weep. At the end of the service they rushed up to Leonard and asked, "Where did you find this story? We have never heard anything like it before! We didn't know there was someone who loved us so much that he was willing to suffer and die like that—to be crucified on a cross to save us!"

Leonard pulled out his French New Testament and showed them that the story was in the Bible. "We listen to this Passion Story every year during Holy Week," he told them. But they insisted that they'd never heard it before. That is what motivated Leonard to translate the Scriptures into the only language his people could really understand—Yambetta!

Southeast Asia

A former Buddhist monk helped make a DVD of the Creation to Eternal Life story in "monk" style. He chants the story just like a Buddhist monk would do, and that attracts the desired audience. They now have ears to hear.

Name and Location Withheld

The security situation in this city was so tight that our team had to secretly conduct the first Bible storying training in a very dusty basement that did not have windows or air-conditioning. The trainees were new believers—nationals who wanted to win their people to Christ by telling Bible stories. They were committed Christians that knew little about their faith, except that they had been dramatically transformed. Now they were zealous to win their friends to Christ by telling stories from the Bible and then train them to do the same with their friends!

Training started with Old Testament stories. They learned to effectively engage a listener with stories about how Abraham was called by God, who promised to make his descendants into a great nation. This is common ground for Christians and this predominant faith because both recognize and honor Abraham and the Old Testament. They learned to share the story of how Abraham was willing to offer God his own son. They quickly and enthusiastically learned stories about sacrifice for disobedience to God and stories that pointed to the perfect once-and-for-all sacrifice and the coming Promised Savior. The day ended with a practical assignment: "Go now and tell some of these stories to your family or closest friends."

The next morning, the group gathered in the basement to relay what happened. One young man had instead gone to the main house of prayer! He said, "I told these stories to the religious leaders and they loved them. They had never heard such things and asked me to come back to tell them more!"

One of the trainees went to the house of his relatives. None were believers, and all were hostile to Christians. They were all watching television, a common luxury even in illiterate areas. He began to tell a Bible story to one person about the demon-possessed man found in Mark 5. The rest of the family turned off the TV to listen and then discuss the story for more than two hours! They asked him to come back to tell them more!

"People are coming to Christ every day through the stories. Over a few months we had 45 receive Christ and be baptized. We are also conducting Seeker Conferences where people come to learn about Jesus and hear the stories. Hundreds are coming! About 80 to 90 percent who attend are coming to Christ. Trained workers are sharing many experiences and exciting reports every day! The strategy is helping give birth to many new believers, who then lead others to Christ, just by repeating the stories they have heard."

Southeast Asia—Told to Cliff, Avery's Son-in-Law

> Mr. Cliff, after reading the story that you gave me to share last week (the Creation to Christ story), I

couldn't wait to share it. So I prayed in my heart, "Oh, God, please bring somebody to me so that I can share Your story!" Well, that next day we received word that one of my husband's relatives had died and we were expected to go to the Muslim funeral service.

When we got there, I pulled two of my relatives inside the door and began telling them the story. As I continued sharing, more and more people began to come in, listen, and then sit down. The more that came in, the more nervous I became! Before I was through, I had a room full. I was very fearful because there were two Muslim priests who came in to listen as well, but even they were nodding their heads and clicking their tongues in agreement! I prayed, 'Oh, God, give me boldness'—and He did!

When I got through, some of my relatives asked to hear more stories. Can you believe it? I can't wait to go back and tell them more. Pray for me that He will give me strength and that they will trust in Jesus as their Savior.

Told by Satish

I am pastoring a good church, but it is a long way from my own village. I was concerned because my parents were not strong in their faith. Whenever I would go back to our village, there was never enough time to teach them the stories. And I could not stay to disciple them in the gospel. So for a long time, I was thinking and worrying about how to share the gospel with them.

But I thank God because the last time I went home after the Bible storytelling training, my parents were interested in the storytelling assignment sheet that had been given to me. My father used to tell me Hindu stories when I was growing up. So I made three photocopies of my storytelling sheet and showed my father how to look the stories up in the Bible I had given him in our language.

Early every day, before morning tea, my father started reading these stories from the Bible. And every evening when all the farm laborers who work in our fields came to our home, my father would tell them the story that he had read that morning.

My mother is the head of the women's society. When Papa read those stories every morning and when he shared the stories to the workers in the evening, my mother also listened. So when my mother went to see the other women in her job as head of the Women's Institute, she would tell them the story that she had heard from her husband that day.

I thank God for this. Even though I was not able to share the word of God to my family, now through my mother and father, my whole village—and the surrounding villages—are all learning the word of God!

And in my own congregation also, every believer is telling the stories.

Romania—from IMB Missionaries to the Deaf People Group

A group of Deaf Romanian pastors my husband and I had discipled through stories were visited by a Deaf pastor from the United States. They were eager to welcome him and invited him to speak. His topic was "The Biblical Role of a Pastor." He provided a list of primary responsibilities and then, as if spinning a web, introduced verse after verse in support.

The Deaf Romanians waited for a story. Finally, one of them stood and said, "You state one of the roles of a pastor is to dedicate babies. We can recall two stories from His message where a baby was dedicated. Please tell us a story where one of the apostles or disciples or Jesus or the leaders of the early church dedicated a baby."

Another pastor stood and said, "Yes, please. Also, could you tell a scripture story that substantiates your claim that it is the role of a pastor to marry and bury. We know no such stories."

And then a third stood and said, "Yes, and please provide us a scripture story that states only pastors can baptize. This is most puzzling for us, for we are familiar with a set of seven stories about baptism, and we do not see any validity for what you exhort."

They all waited expectantly for the stories, but none came.

Even though this Deaf American pastor had a wealth of verses, he did not know stories (the verses in context), and he was stumped. I was so proud of the Deaf Romanians. The stories upon which they based both practice and faith had protected them.

What Avery was discovering was merely the tip of the iceberg. He had often quoted Romans 10:13–14, "Everyone who calls on the name of the Lord will be saved. How, then, can they call on the name of the one they have not believed in? And how can they believe in the one of whom they have not heard? And how can they hear without someone preaching to them?"

He now understood that preaching can take many forms, but must take the form of the hearer—which meant learning how people hear. This would be his learning curve for the remainder of his life and a new wineskin for disciple-making.

CHAPTER 32
Refirement

Whatever is ahead, I know God is leading.
I am amazed at how good God is to me.
I never will understand it.

—Avery

When the IMB trustees honored Avery at his retirement celebration, they called him both "a visionary servant leader" and "an ordinary man whose heart belongs to God." Jerry Rankin reflected,

> We could not overstate the significance of Avery's leadership as Senior Vice-President of Overseas Operations. When Avery came to the position ten years ago, we had just reported 2,000 new churches started around the world; this past year we reported 16,000 new churches. Ten years ago, we rejoiced in baptizing 251,000 new believers, but this past year the reports exceeded half a million new believers. In 1993, [when Avery joined the IMB], only about 1.3 percent of church members overseas were in discipleship training; today it is 13 percent—900,000 believers. During his tenure, the board has sent out, trained, equipped and nurtured more than 7,600 new missionaries.
>
> Avery would be the first to admit those accomplishments are God's, not his. But we all know that as he walked with the Lord, he provided vision, passion, and strategic leadership, nurtured the leader-

ship of others, and modeled servant leadership and a walk with the Lord for all of us.[1]

As Avery stood to speak to a standing ovation, he simply bowed his head and pointed heavenward. "Whatever has been done and whatever has been said is God's work. It isn't mine. Any accomplishments—and all glory—go to Him." He went on to say, "This isn't retirement, it's refirement. I'm just quitting my day job so I can go serve the Lord in ministry."

Avery's sisters and the whole Willis family at his
IMB retirement celebration, 2004

Change of Setting but Not Task

Avery's official retirement from the International Mission Board in February 2004 coincided with his seventieth birthday and his fiftieth anniversary of ministry. He had fulfilled many of his dreams; and by then, he had sixteen grandchildren to enjoy. For many, that would be reason enough to rest and enjoy retirement years.

Such was not the case for Avery. He received a special dispensation from the IMB to continue for two more years as pastoral counsel to the missionaries. For approximately twenty-five weeks per year, Avery and Shirley were given an allowance to travel and spend time with missionaries worldwide.

I prayed the prayer of Jabez and, as hard as it seems to believe, the Lord seems to be enlarging my circles of influence. I have already scheduled five month-long overseas trips to equip and mentor leaders, missionaries, and nationals. I must decide which writing and speaking requests the Lord wants me to do. I need your prayers even more.[3]

Avery and Shirley were gone so often that when people asked Wade where his dad was this month, he would answer, "I don't know where he is. But God does, and that's what's important."

When Avery and Shirley were in the US, they were acclimating to their new home in Bella Vista, in northwest Arkansas, first established as a summer resort town that quickly evolved into a retirement community. Ron and Patricia Owens, their good friends, had built a home there and invited Avery and Shirley to check it out. It was somewhat central to the four states their five children's families were living in and had relatively mild winters. Avery's initial response to Shirley's recommendation of choosing a central location was "No way! That would be Arkansas!"

However, the Willises held two family Christmas vacations in Bella Vista before retiring, and when the lakefront property next door to the Owens became available for sale, the Willises bought it. Shirley loved drawing floor plans, so she designed their dream home with the architectural help of her cousin's husband. They chose a Christian builder in town and work began in January 2004. The Willises moved into their new home in July.

Builder Billy Witcofski added a special gift for Avery: he built a gazebo down on the bluff overlooking the lake for Avery "to pray and write in." Extended prayer times in his office, on the back deck, or in the gazebo became a favorite part of Avery's daily time with the Lord.

The prayer gazebo

Learning to Soar

Avery used his time to write. Colleague Johnny Norwood would chuckle, "Avery could write more than any one human could read."

When asked if he liked to write, Avery emphatically said, *No, I don't enjoy writing. But I like "having written."* He sought to learn and expand his abilities because he believed it was an essential means of broader influence.

His eldest grandson, Matt, approached him about writing a book together on Avery's longtime sermon, "On Eagle's Wings." The message paralleled how a mother eagle stirs the nest, making her babies uncomfortable, in order to teach them to fly as a parable of God "stirring the nest" of the Israelites in order to create a new nation from them—His chosen nation. The resulting book, *Learning to Soar*, was published in 2009. It was a source book for small groups to learn how God was working in their lives.

Avery later received the following e-mail from a bishop in Uganda:

In Uganda Samuel Chiang blessed me with a book called *Learning to Soar*. I have preached and used your book with very great impact. [I] had been invited to speak in a conference of pastors in one of our towns and quoted how God stirs our nest as the eagle does. During the altar call three quarters of [the] pastors and leaders came for prayers and [gave] their testimonies that they [were] almost giving up their churches and families, because they were asking "where was God in their stirring?" Now they learned that God was giving them an experience through transition and growth. This is the kind of life that we experience and therefore the book was probably meant for no other people but us. God bless you abundantly and may you live to impact the whole world.

Authorship

Ultimately, Avery authored or coauthored over sixteen books in his lifetime and instigated the writing of others, such as *The Survival Kit: A Guide for New Christians*, *Experiencing God*, and *Story Thru the Bible*.

His *MasterLife* Discipleship series sold nearly sixty million copies and has been translated into seventy-two languages and adapted in 129 countries.

The following books bear his name:

- ➤ *Indonesian Revival: Why Two Million Came to Christ* ©1977
- ➤ *The Biblical Basis of Missions* © 1979
- ➤ *MasterLife: Discipleship Training, Vol. I and II* © 1980
- ➤ *MasterBuilder: Multiplying Leaders* © 1985
- ➤ *Disciple's Study Bible* (associate editor and developer/writer) ©1988
- ➤ *LifeGuide to Discipleship and Doctrine* ©1989
- ➤ *Masterlife* Series (four-book set) © 1997

> *MasterLife: Developing a Personal Relationship with the Master* tradebook © 1998
> *On Mission with God* © 2002
> *Following Jesus* CDs © 2002–2003
> *Lead Like Jesus Study Guide* © 2003
> *Making Disciples of Oral Learners* © 2005
> *Following Jesus Together* © 2008–2009 Real Life Ministries Story Set CDs and Workbook
> *Learning to Soar* © 2009
> *Real Life Discipleship Manual* © 2010
> *Truth That Sticks* © 2010, the first box of which arrived in his hospital room two days before he died

Avery and Shirley with books and CDs he authored, 2004

Avery continued to lead conferences on many of these materials. He and Henry Blackaby led an *On Mission with God* conference in

Manila because *nearly a million Filipinos go overseas to work every year and we want to equip them to be missionaries in the 217 countries in which they work.* They led a Spiritual Leadership conference for what they originally thought would be a small group of business leaders and were overwhelmed when 8,900 business, political, and church leaders filled the basketball arena. They were invited to return for a *Lead Like Jesus Encounter* the following year.[2]

GO Center

In 2005, OBU established the *Avery T. Willis Center for Global Outreach* (GO Center) to provide mission education and training and to link practical mission experience with academic excellence. Avery taught several courses as the scholar-in-residence for their new offerings of a cross-cultural ministry major and minor in missions, including one in orality. He was very pleased as well when his grandson Matt was asked to direct the efforts at the GO Center during its initial two years.

After he retired from the IMB, he bequeathed "the rock" to the Center. Avery had picked up a forty-pound red quartz rock at Glorieta in 1978 when he was seeking God about his part in Bold Mission Thrust. After his prayer time, he said to the Lord, *This rock will be my "Ebenezer," my altar of promise, that I will do everything in my ability to find and reach the peoples of the earth with Your gospel.* He brought the rock back with him. Over the decade at the IMB, Shirley and Avery hosted approximately a thousand new missionaries as they came through missionary orientation at the International Learning Center. One of the traditions was for each missionary to sign the name of the people group to which they had been appointed on the rock.

The "people groups rock"

After moving to Arkansas, Shirley continued this hosting practice and organized quarterly meetings of the Northwest Arkansas IMB missionary fellowship for former IMB personnel.

International Orality Network

Avery remained the executive director of the International Orality Network. Billy Witcofski introduced Avery to Rick Brekelbaum, a kingdom-oriented retired executive for Exxon. After a luncheon meeting, Avery asked Rick to serve as his operations manager. After reviewing the job description, Rick countered, "What you really need, Avery, is an executive assistant. I had them when I worked at Exxon, so I know what you need most at this stage." Avery agreed, and Rick served in that role for sixteen months, organizing interviews, appointments, and conferences. He also prayed regularly with Avery. He recalled how, during one trip to Missouri, Avery stopped to have lunch with a young struggling pastor in the St. Louis area "just to encourage him."

Avery also served as chairman of Epic Partners, later renamed OneStory, a coalition of global missionary organizations, including the IMB, Wycliffe Bible Translators, Campus Crusade for Christ, and Youth With A Mission. This organization trained two-year personnel to translate and record 50–60 Bible stories in the languages of unreached people groups—most of which had no Bible translation work among them—in order to launch a church planting movement among these people in their native tongue.

As such, Avery had ample opportunity to learn about the resulting powerful experiences and unparalleled successes overseas. Missionaries and friends e-mailed him regularly about what God was doing. As he read, saw, and listened, Avery began wondering if God wanted to use the same method to communicate with modern American audiences. Or was "storying the gospel" just a Third World methodology? Avery was soon to conclude that God had equipped *everyone* for stories. *God wired us for stories. We like stories. We remember stories. They penetrate beyond our heads and get down into our hearts.*[3]

In a December 15, 2005, article entitled "Storying Going Mainstream," Avery wrote,

The problem before us is that 90% of our current preaching, Bible studies, evangelism, and discipleship is reader-oriented. So how do we change? That is the question of the hour. We must do something before this wave engulfs us and before we lose a whole generation for the cause of Christ.

Presidential Nomination

In 2008, Avery was one of the six men nominated to serve as the president of the Southern Baptist Convention. When he was first approached, he declined, until the Lord reminded him he had yet to pray about it. When the denomination reported declines in the number of baptisms for the third consecutive year, and because of his yet unfulfilled desire to see renewal in the denomination, Avery allowed his name to be submitted.

It wasn't a huge decline but it's indicative of the fact that churches are very content doing what they are doing. But they are out of touch with so much of the world that needs help. We have not been going to the places Jesus would—to the poor, the depressed, the prisons, the broken-hearted. We've become comfortable communicating with people on our own social level.[4]

He believed the church needed to find a better way to share the gospel, specifically through oral means.

Real Life Ministries

It was in 2008 at a Finishing the Task conference when Avery first met Jim Putman. Jim and his associate pastor, Brandon Guidon, were discussing how strongly they disagreed with a conference speaker who had claimed that the American Church was dying and should focus on "casting her seed to the nations." Avery joined in on the conversation and would soon become intrigued by what was happening in their church.

In 1998, two families in Post Falls, Idaho, had convinced Jim Putman, a former wrestler and coach, and his family to help them plant a church. This resulted in the birth of a church called *Real Life Ministries* (RLM). Putman based his discipleship model for the church on the insights he gained from his coaching years, coming alongside people and moving them off the bench and into the game. The surprise was the impact of this strategy in America's northwest, an area usually resistant to an evangelical church.

In this small town of twenty-six thousand, Real Life Ministries church grew to the point that by 2008, their average weekend attendance was 8,500 people. Of those, approximately seven thousand met weekly in one of six hundred small groups where they were intentionally discipled by trained leaders to become reproducing disciples. Small group members commonly "did life together" outside their weekly meetings, strengthening relationships and connections throughout the church body. Most of the pastoring in this large congregation was carried out by small group leaders under the coaching of a large network of community pastors drawn from group leaders with demonstrated leadership gifting. It was a church where disciples were made and leaders were developed. RLM had planted several additional churches.[5]

It was not long before Avery paid a visit to Post Falls to see first-hand what God was doing. He found a church discipling people in a way that was church-based, relational, and incredibly effective. They had built a church that was succeeding at the most important level of doing church: they were making disciples who were making disciples.

But Avery could see how Real Life Ministries could be even more effective. What if they added Bible-storying within their small groups? He shared his thoughts with Jim and Brandon. Although skeptical at the outset, it would not be long before Jim caught the vision and storying the gospel would become part of Real Life Ministry's small group life. In fact, Avery joined with their staff to produce the *Real-Life Discipleship Training Manual: Equipping Disciples Who Make Disciples*, published by NavPress in 2010, to accompany Jim's *Real-Life Discipleship* book. The change to a storying format greatly strengthened RLM's small group life.

DNA-21: Biblical Orality in America

Seeing a church live out discipleship at its core and teach the Bible through storying was the impetus Avery needed to launch "DNA-21: A Discipleship Revolution" for the church in America. He realized that many young people in America were "oral-preference learners." It wasn't that they couldn't read, but that they preferred to get their information through nonliterate means. Video, blogs, websites, and smart phones gave them instant information with a touch of their finger. Widespread communication of news and personal opinion was available through social media. They were social learners who learned best through discussion and stories.

The means by which the Scripture was being communicated around the world might be the very means through which God would communicate His Word to this generation. Perhaps this would be part of the spiritual revival he had long prayed for in America.

In the summer of 2009, Avery traveled to Colorado Springs, Colorado, to meet with several of the Navigators' leadership team at their Glen Eyrie headquarters. Avery was there to lay the groundwork for what he passionately hoped would be a major change in the way the American Church thought about and carried out discipleship. It was a change he earnestly felt was needed to keep the American Church from falling under the judgment of God.

He communicated his understanding of how Jesus made disciples in the first century and his vision of incorporating that DNA of discipleship into twenty-first-century churches (DNA-21), encompassing all the tools and technology of this generation. He envisioned a revitalization and multiplication of churches focused on the Great Commission mandate of making disciples. He described the transformation that would occur in disciples of Jesus when the Holy Spirit applied the Word of God to their hearts and they responded in obedience. He was convinced that process was best achieved in relational, accountable small groups. He explained its four basic components:

1. small group transparency
2. intentional discipling
3. Bible storytelling
4. multiplication

In Avery's final book, *Truth that Sticks: How to Communicate Velcro Truth in a Teflon World*, coauthored with Mark Snowden, Avery described that stories are the "hooks" that help people remember God's truths, much like the hooks that give Velcro® its ability to adhere to itself so tightly. This is increasingly powerful in a world in which information can slip from minds much like food from a Teflon® skillet. The book explains the power and process of using storying for discipleship.

Storying is the process of accurately retelling and rebuilding the stories of the Bible so that the listeners learn them. Then a set of discussion questions lead the learners to notice God's truths and its application to their own life. The final question is "How will you obey what the Holy Spirit has revealed to you?" Those in accountable relationships can encourage one another in being "doers of the Word, and not hearers only," growing regularly in their knowledge and application of the Word to their everyday lives. The process imbeds the Bible in their hearts and minds so they can easily pass on the stories to those around them. The advantages are that deep truths can be communicated in a short time, persons new to a group can fully participate, and leaders are developed naturally in the group. Most of all, the process is reproducible.

On the DNA-21 website, Avery challenged his audience.

We've divided the Great Commission into four things: it's evangelism... or discipleship... or education... or missions. But it is one command— make disciples of all nations! That's revolutionary. A revolution is costly. It will cost you much. It's dangerous. You don't know what is going to happen once you sign up to be a disciple of the Lord Jesus Christ and do exactly what He tells you to do. It takes commitment, long-term commitment, in the same direction. But if you do, you can be a part of changing the 21st century. I invite you, I challenge you, to begin a disciple-making revolution in your sphere of influence.[6]

Sponsored by NavPress, Avery and staff members from Real Life Ministries held the first DNA-21 conference at the New Orleans Baptist Theological Seminary on April 22–24, 2010. More than a hundred people attended, and others in Atlanta, Little Rock, and Orlando participated via the Internet. The participants were gathered to learn about Bible storying and relational small groups as a discipleship method. "Our churches should be a place where everyone is a growing disciple," Putman said. "When that happens, a movement starts."

The official DNA-21 launch conference was scheduled for August 2010. Avery had been profoundly moved by David Platt's book, *Radical*, and his deep passion to move the American Church into global missions, so he invited David to come speak.

But death would keep Avery himself from attending.

SECTION 8
Leaving a Legacy

Spiritual Marker #14

Avery would make disciples
through his suffering and death,
even as he had in life.

*For I am already being poured out like a drink offering,
and the time has come for my departure. I have fought
the good fight, I have finished the race, I have kept the faith.*
—2 Timothy 4:6–7 (NIV)

CHAPTER 33
Leukemia

God may reveal Himself by your weakness
and the mark He has left on you.

—Avery

It was May 2009 when Avery first felt pain. He and Shirley had recently returned to the US from visiting their daughter Krista's family who were living in Indonesia. Avery thought the pain in his chest was muscle strain from his daily exercises.

A few months later, he began experiencing double-vision. The doctor had no explanation but prescribed special glasses. More doctor visits and tests did not yield answers for increasing symptoms. By Christmas of that year, Avery had so much pain in his hips that he spent a great deal of time sleeping under a blanket in his recliner, even while the children and grandchildren were home for the holidays.

It was a special Christmas for the whole family to be home together. Randy and Denyce's family were in from Tulsa, with the exception of their eldest son, Matt, and his wife, Allison, who were serving as missionaries in South Asia. Sherrie and her family were in from Missouri; Wade's family came from Tennessee; Krista's family was stateside from Indonesia—making use of Avery and Shirley's gift of a family trip; and Brett's family drove in from Colorado.

Sherrie and Brett accompanied their dad on a doctor visit for results of blood and bone marrow tests. Returning to the waiting room, Avery sat down across from them, looked up, and then his shoulders began to shake with sobs. Dreading the news they might hear, they immediately moved to his side. As Avery composed himself, Brett asked, "What did he tell you?"

Avery shrugged helplessly. "He said he doesn't know!"

Avery spent most of New Year's Eve Day receiving blood transfusions. By the time he returned in the afternoon, he was feeling so much better that he was determined to join the revelries of the evening before everyone returned home. Some of the family members joked about "wanting some of that blood" if it could make that much difference!

Diagnosis

On January 5, a few days before Cliff and Krista were scheduled to return overseas, Cliff went with Avery and Shirley to hear the results of the second bone marrow test. There was a sense of trepidation for all of them because it was not like Avery to be "down for the count" as he had been.

The diagnosis was suddenly and painfully clear. Avery had chronic myelomonocytic leukemia (CMML). At his age, the prognosis was bleak. He was informed that most people lived only six to eighteen months from the onset of symptoms.

As the word spread through the family, dismay and grief intermingled with information-gathering and problem-solving. Upcoming events became target goals. Avery was to be honored at Oklahoma Baptist University in March; the New Orleans DNA-21 launch was in April; an Indonesian missionary reunion was in July; and the Third Lausanne Conference for World Evangelization was in Cape Town, South Africa, in October. Those were highlights of a fully scheduled year.

Crisis

Within a few days, Avery's health deteriorated rapidly. His white blood cells, which had been low for months, were suddenly ten times the normal level. On January 10, he was taken by ambulance to the hospital with a massive infection.

Friends immediately began to intervene on his behalf. In less than a week, Dr. Bob Agee, former OBU president, contacted Dr. Susan O'Brien at M. D. Anderson in Houston, Texas. As a specialist in leukemia, specifically CMML, she agreed to receive Avery. Michael Kostner flew the Willises there in his private jet. Krista sent her family on home overseas and joined Avery and Shirley in Houston to help for three weeks. Sherrie hitched a ride with her daughter and son-in-law, who were moving to their new home in Houston that weekend.

It seemed that at every one of the many sites a needle was injected, the infection erupted and swelling occurred. The response of Avery's body was so dramatic that Krista wasn't sure he would survive the admission process. Avery sat weakly in his hospital chair and commented, "I am about to decide I am actually sick."

It wasn't long before the doctor arrived to give the latest results. Avery's blast cell numbers had increased to twenty-one, so his diagnosis was changed to acute myeloid leukemia (AML). Reminding Avery that it would not be a cure, the doctors offered to enroll him in a research trial therapy that might extend his life. It would not be as much for his sake as potential treatment for others. It would mean he would need to remain in Houston to ensure the protocols were met. As family members debated the pros and cons, the doctor mentioned that a possible side effect of the treatment was that Avery would be sleepier and his thinking might be increasingly cloudy or confused.

A quick glance at one another around the room made the decision unanimous, but it was quickly articulated by Avery as soon as the doctor left the room. "My mind is all I have going for me right now. I won't let them take away my ability to think."

It would be two months of chemotherapy and transfusions before Avery and Shirley could return home. Longtime friends Matt and Betty Bristol, who were at M. D. Anderson for her cancer treatment, helped the Willises get an apartment and groceries. Two churches in Houston provided recliners.

Redeeming the Time

Embracing new technology and social media to serve God's purposes, Avery began to respond to the many calls and e-mails by sending out daily Twitter tweets, Facebook posts, and blog entries on Caring Bridge.

Linda Beemis, director of prayer for ION, wrote of his Caring Bridge entries:

> The journal gives us a wonderful 'kingdom perspective' as Avery shows us daily relationships God put in place for the work of the kingdom! Avery's life has always been an 'open book;' but much more of it has been seen by those who came along for the ride as God launched Avery into this new season of life. God is showing us through these entries a glimpse into how to move day to day in life, of how to focus on HIM, rather than on our circumstances. God used Avery to be intentional, even into the final days of his life, teaching each of us alongside him how to walk into glory.

Avery Willis's Prayer Letter: February 2010

I like change but not so drastically or as quickly as it has begun to happen. I am undergoing treatment at M. D. Anderson Hospital in Houston for the foreseeable future. I have cancelled all travel for the immediate future. I will be involved in most of the listed prayer requests through electronic media.

We are dependent on your intercession to God for remission, which happens about 40% of the time with the treatments I'm on. We are depending on God, not percentages.

Before I give you God's remarkable answers and requests for the month I will answer a question several have asked. The question is, "How are you dealing with all this?" Some add, "... especially with 2010 being the year you think will be pivotal in launching a discipleship revolution, participating in historic missions advances, and powerful prayer movements."

Godly Perspective

When something like this happens everyone asks the question, "Why me? Why now?" especially if they feel that they are being used more than ever.

Some ask it selfishly feeling they don't deserve the illness, but I ask it in relationship to the Lord and what He has in mind. I believe none of this is a surprise to God. I told Him when we went as missionaries 46 years ago that if I were worth more to Him and the Kingdom dead than alive, then I was ready to go any time. Of course, I was thinking about something like martyrdom instead of leukemia but my commitment still stands. So here are some of my possible answers to, "Why me? Why now?"

- *God has given me a much larger platform to speak to His causes that He has laid on my heart and people are paying more attention.*
- *God is giving room for other leaders in the movements in which I am involved to lead and grow. It also is preparing my successors for their future service.*
- *God is calling out new people to get involved in making disciples of all nations and reaching the four billion oral learners.*
- *God is teaching many more people how to pray.*
- *God has been pushing me the last few years to use more electronic means to communicate and this gives me a chance to develop the skills for a much larger audience.*
- *God has much more to teach me about "the power of His resurrection and participation in His sufferings, becoming like Him in his death." (Phil. 3:10)*
- *God will use all this to change lives, churches, and peoples and help bring about a new resurgence of the Great Commission.*
- *It is wonderful to see that the advance of God's Kingdom is not missing a beat with my going through this experience. I am ready to stay or go and the decision is His. (Phil. 1:21–26)*

Thursday, January 21

This first day out of the hospital has been like letting a bird out of the cage . . . But I am not a flying bird right now, just a walking one. I got my new wheelchair, walked several blocks and Krista pushed me a couple of hours in Houston's 73-degree weather. I have experienced soaring on wings of eagles and have run and not grown weary but now I am trying to walk without fainting. (Isaiah 40:31) However, the key verses are verses 28–29:

"The Lord, the everlasting God, the Creator of the ends of the earth—He will not grow tired or weary and His understanding no one can fathom. He gives strength to the weary and increases the power of the weak."

Uplifted through Intercession

Friday, January 29

Yesterday I felt better than I have in two weeks. The test showed some progress but a decrease in hemoglobin so I got a transfusion. I had to spend all day at the hospital. That usually gives me more energy, but it must have been an old man's blood. Today, my energy is like the Energizer bunny whose battery ran out! I may need a platelet transfusion when I return tomorrow. I am overwhelmed by your love and care expressed through phone calls, emails, messages on Caring Bridge, and visits. I received this encouraging note today from Brother Mafdy in Egypt where I spoke at their annual prayer conference:

Hello Beloved man of God Brother Avery. We are in much prayers for you trusting the Lord to add another chapter to your life to finish the task that He has given you. The prayer group for the Streams movement were on their knees for the last 4 days fasting and praying for your health and for your commitment to the Lord. We have sent a note to many other prayer worriers in other parts of the world to pray with us.

Tuesday, February 2

I felt well enough to attend the Table 71 meeting in Orlando by video all day. This group of fifteen leaders of the largest mission organizations began when we committed ourselves to the goal of zero unengaged unreached people groups (UUPGs) in the next fifteen years or at least by 2020. We started with the 639 UUPGs with populations over 100,000. Of those, we and our overseas partners have fulltime workers in all but 166 of them and many of them have been adopted by churches although the workers are not "boots on the ground" yet. Praise the Lord—We are about to move down to the ones over 50,000!

Table 71 is one of my favorite groups of friends. We've met thirty times in the last ten years and this is the first time I have missed being there in person. We always get as much as we give as we hear marvelous testimonies. God has blessed me by letting me work with some of His choicest servants around the world. One told me today that he told some Indian brothers and 2,000 are praying daily for me.

Friday, February 5
God knows my days and it has been my prayer for more than fifty-five years for Him to help me to number my days and "apply my heart unto wisdom." In my early thirties, I had a premonition that I would die at age thirty-seven. So I have always lived with the urgency to use every day for the Lord. Obviously, I didn't die then but I have continued to work as if I don't know I have another day (and we never do). Some would dub me a workaholic but I am just living with a passion to reach the world and glorify God. That is not work. I do have hobbies but I don't let them take more time than I think I should give. At best, our days are few on the earth and I still believe in getting ready to serve forever in heaven. Every day is a precious gift from our Loving Father.

Remission

Thursday, February 11
HALLELUJAH! My leukemia is in remission! Already! They didn't expect this until the second or third cycle of chemotherapy at best! The bone marrow is producing healthy white blood cells and platelets. My blasts count (measurement unit for unhealthy cells being produced) has reduced from 21 to 1. Normal is 0–5. Praise God for answering the prayers of so many of you. Don't stop praying. My hemoglobin and sodium are still low and need to recover. What I say to you all, I say REJOICE!

Through Avery's remission, God showed him a parable of the illness facing the church.

Monday, February 15
Leukemia is exactly what the church has. Normally, bone marrow in the human body produces red blood cells to carry oxygen, white blood

cells to fight viruses and bacteria, and platelets to help the blood coagulate. What happens in leukemia is an abnormal development in the DNA so that the body produces large numbers of immature cells that do not perform their function.

I think that's almost a direct parallel to the church today. We produce a lot of members but they are not carrying out their functions because we have an overabundance of abnormal immature cells.

It is interesting to know that enough bacteria and viruses are in each of our bodies to kill us many times over. But God put immunity in the white blood cells to prevent that. However, if they don't work then everything is a threat. How like spiritual warfare that is! Satan and his forces are always present and looking for an opening to attack. No wonder the Lord tells us to always have on the full armor to stand against all the wiles of the devil. Without Him we are so vulnerable. With Him we are invincible!

Friday, February 19

The doctor told me yesterday that they might continue the chemo treatments six to twelve more months or indefinitely to keep the cancer in remission. That was a little disconcerting for me since I thought that six months was the max and I could get on with my life. So I am asking you to pray for a cure. Sometimes that happens, though not usually, with this kind of leukemia. But if God cured it then I would have more opportunity to serve Him and not go through monthly chemo treatments for the rest of my life.

Living in Gratitude

Avery spent his seventy-sixth birthday listing all that he was grateful for in his life.

Friday, February 21

The joy of the Lord is my strength. The best way to keep that going I have discovered is to express gratitude and thanksgiving for what He has done and is doing. So, on this my seventy-sixth birthday, I want to just thank God—and you are invited to go along for the ride if you want to see the things that cause thanksgiving to rise in my heart.

- *Thank you, God, that I am alive. I was surprised yesterday to learn that J. Paul Williams, a college classmate, was diagnosed with leukemia about the same time I was and he has already died. So it is not lightly said. "Thank you that I am alive." Every day is a gift from God.*
- *Thank you for my leukemia already being in remission. Although remission is not a cure it does mean that it has stopped manufacturing immature cells that can't fulfill their function and is generating good amounts of white and red blood cells and platelets. So, although we are praying for a full cure, remission is a great first step toward health.*
- *Thank God for my family. My wife, Shirley, has been a helpful helpmate for fifty-five years and God blessed us with five children, all married to Christian mates, sixteen grandchildren, and two great grandchildren. All are following the Lord and are such a source of strength. I also thank God for my heritage of godly grandparents, parents and siblings.*
- *Thank God for using me to advance the Kingdom. I preached my first sermon the day after my eighteenth birthday so I have been preaching the glorious gospel for fifty-eight years and served fifty-six years as pastor, missionary, disciple-maker, denominational servant and missions leader, including the opportunity to lead the 5,600 IMB missionaries in overseas operations for ten years. Then the last five years He has given me a much wider sphere of influence among the Body of Christ. All I have ever wanted was to be used of God and when I am no longer useful I am ready to go "Home."*
- *Thank God for manifesting Himself in my life and ministry since I don't have anything to offer except a willing vessel. The filling of the Holy Spirit from the first time fifty-seven years ago has been the abiding power, and He continues to fill me for each day.*
- *Thank God for all the wonderful people that He has allowed me to work with. Many of them have had the exact gifts to supplement*

my weaknesses. That goes right up to the moment. In the last few years He has brought Samuel Chiang and Rick Brekelbaum who are my right and left hands. That is why nothing has fallen through the cracks and my sickness has not slowed the progress down, especially for the International Orality Network and the DNA-21 Discipleship Revolution. All through my ministry God has put people smarter, more dedicated and more successful around me to accomplish the vision He has given me.

- *Thank God for seventy-five years of good health. Up until now no health issue has stopped me from going all out for God. Of course, I have had health problems but He has given me the physical strength, stamina and passion to keep going and He is my Healer.*

- *Thank God that even in my present physical condition He has kept my mind sharp, forward-looking and creative. I see no difference except others have to be the hands and feet to carry the ideas out.*

- *Thank God for this season of life when I am seeing the most productivity in writing. (I have never liked to write nor been very good at it but God has helped me, often because I have written on my knees.) Thank God for NavPress and President Mike Miller who believed in the vision I have shared and spared nothing to get the resources available.*

- *Thank God for all the disciples He has helped me make under His direction. Only God knows how many but I believe that the years ahead will surpass those numbers.*

- *Thank God for His Word and the belief that He gives us Bible Promises to direct us, give us faith, and pull us on toward His purpose for us.*

- *First and foremost, Thank God for His love, His salvation, His using sinful vessels as a part of His Family.*

- *Thank God for the Body of Christ in the 125 countries I have visited and immediately recognized these were brothers and sisters in Christ. What a fellowship!*

- *Thank God for prayer and direct access to Him through Jesus Christ.*

- *Thank God for what He is going to do the next five to ten years through the resources He has helped me create, the people He has let me influence and the leaders He has helped me train. I believe we are going to see a discipleship revolution that will change the church from the inside out and bring untold persons to Christ in America and around the world.*

Tuesday, February 23

Home at last! There really is no place like home. M. D. Anderson assured me they will manage the process to keep my treatments here in Arkansas the same.

Michael Kostner, pilot, owns the plane he flew us home in and uses it for ministry. He truly was used of God. He has been flying Johnny Hunt, SBC president, to his many speaking engagements. Johnny volunteered for him to take me to Houston. That was the MERCY flight. I took him up on it before I was attacked by the massive infection. I didn't realize how sick I was and how much I needed that flight.

It is like when we come to the Lord the first time and know that we need MERCY but we just don't know how much we need it. Only afterwards do we begin to comprehend what God has done for us.

Another thing I didn't know was that Michael left the plane in Houston the whole 7 weeks we were there. We at first thought it would be a few days or less than a week. We were so long getting clearance from the doctor to come home. So I realize this was the GRACE flight. I did not deserve it and had no reason to expect it but it meant Michael and Johnny did not have access to the plane all that time. That is GRACE out of the goodness of their hearts! So all the way home I was reflecting on the GRACE of God—He does so much more for us than MERCY. He does give us God's Resources At Christ's Expense—GRACE. I never deserved this kind of treatment nor could have afforded it but "in Christ all things are yours, and you are of Christ and Christ is of God." (1 Corinthians 3:22) So thanks, Michael and Johnny, for giving me another glimpse into both the MERCY and GRACE of God.

Between, and sometimes through, the hours of treatment while in the hospital, Avery made use of every opportunity to keep working.

He proofread and revised the book *Truth that Sticks*, even when he had to hold his hand over one eye to compensate for the double vision. He attended the meetings he had planned by conference call. He learned how to use his new Mac Pro computer to write and communicate. He spoke with publishers and friends, and mentored those who were filling in for him. He got the website for DNA-21 up and running and began taking registrations for the upcoming launch conference in New Orleans. He was simultaneously working on restructuring the ION organization, Table 71 matters, Call2All in several countries, the DNA-21 Launch, and Immersion Training at the Real Life Ministries church for thirty-six SBC state executives. He was also working on a new orality book and video for Lausanne, the program for the Lausanne conference in October, and a new electronic version of *MasterLife*.

Friday, February 26

I spent twelve hours in the doctor's office and hospital getting two transfusions.

I did some email, talked to several on the phone, revised Week 12 of Real Life Discipleship Manual *and started writing the monthly prayer letter. One of you mentioned that I was my full productive self. No, only about 25% of what I normally did before leukemia. But it keeps my mind occupied even when I don't have much energy.*

Milestones

Oklahoma Baptist University held a special event entitled Avery T. Willis: Tribute to a Vision on Thursday, March 4. Following a reception and banquet, Dr. Jerry Rankin and Dr. Tom Elliff spoke. Among the tributes given, what meant the most to Avery was Tom's simple declaration: "Avery has really simplified life. He's got it down to two words: *making disciples.*"

A video of Avery's impact on missions was shown, and then Avery himself spoke. He began jokingly with, "I hope the Lord doesn't take too seriously what you all just said about 'the world not being worthy of me'—at least for a little while. I hope to continue this journey of faith and continue joining God in His work." Though his weakness was evident, the longer he spoke, the stronger his voice became. After pictures and interviews, a special prayer time for Avery touched him deeply.

Thursday's "Tribute to a Vision" was a great time to see friends that I haven't seen in a long time. I was amazed at who was there and the distances people came. It was a very special time for me because of friends. I was able to talk over 20 minutes and share the up-to-date vision, including one for America: DNA-21.

Peril

However, the evening took its toll. The infection Avery had had since January 10, which initially put him in the hospital, was raging in his neck. He had hidden the abscesses with bandages for the tribute evening. By the next day, when the family returned to Bella Vista, he felt so poorly that he chose to go directly to the doctor's office and was immediately put in the hospital. An infection specialist inspected him on Saturday and scheduled surgery for early the next morning to clean out the infection. Six incisions were required to drain the abscesses.

The doctor informed him how life-threatening his situation was when he arrived. Had the infection spread another millimeter, it would have entered the throat, and it would have required scraping all of the skin from his throat to expose it.

Sunday, March 7
The surgery linked all six abscesses under my chin together and when they unpacked the gauze today it was 6 feet long. Gross! But we are making progress! I am glad they really got serious and found an infectious disease doctor. Since I have been to over 125 countries they can't rule out anything as to its source.

The doctor was on his way home when he kept thinking "I know that name. Avery T. Willis has been a patient of mine." But his computer search failed to turn one up. That is when he remembered MasterLife *which he studied in medical school! You never know whom you are going to bless today who will in turn bless you some day.*

Tuesday, March 9

I woke up long enough to visit with Ronnie Floyd and Andy Wilson from First Baptist Church, Springdale and Pinnacle Hills Church. They want me to come explain DNA-21, orality and church planting to their whole staff. It has been the first priority on my agenda for a while; I just have to get better first. I also had a good meeting with Mike, the CEO of Walmart, who is leading his small group to study Learning to Soar.

Tuesday, March 16

My case has become a dilemma. The infection wound, a gaping hole below my jaw, must get better before they can start leukemia treatments again. Today they said that even with a wound vacuum, it might take twelve weeks to get the infection completely healed (instead of the four they predicted last week). We cannot wait that long. Pray for the doctors making the decisions and that God will use this opportunity to cure me of leukemia.

The two are working against each other. The leukemia allowed the infection to catch on but my body's natural means are unable to stop it now in its weakened condition. If we treat the leukemia [and kill the white blood cells] it gives the infection an open door to grow.

Meanwhile, I feel caught in the middle of spiritual and physical warfare. I know that Satan wants me out of the picture but I believe that "He that began a good work in you will carry it on to completion until the day of Jesus Christ." (Philippians 1:6) So pray Hebrews. 10:36 for me. I need a lot of patience now since this is not going to be a "quick fix." Also James 1:2–8.

About that time, Avery received good news from Indonesia that the Indonesian Baptist churches had chosen Chronological Bible Storying as their discipleship curriculum for the next year. He also learned that his book on the revival in Indonesia, *The Indonesian Revival: Why Two Million Came to Christ*, was being translated into Indonesian.

Support in Suffering

Thursday, March 25

Because [son] *Wade is here and could take me to the doctor, it gave time off for Shirley who has been my chief caregiver. She was able to go to a well-deserved lunch with her college roommate from Springdale. She has done a wonderful job of taking care of me, being a nurse, dispensing medicine, etc. I don't know what I would do without her. Thanks for all of your prayers for her also. God has been so good to surround me with family and friends who uphold me and bless me. Praise the Lord.*

Sunday, March 28

Several years ago Marcus Vegh challenged me to discover how to make disciples of oral learners. We worked together with seven others to record over four hundred Bible stories called Following Jesus*. Then, at age forty-five, Marcus got cancer of the larynx and was given four months to live. I felt the "fist-shaped cancer" was a direct attack on his orality passion and led the prayer charge. He seemed to especially lean on me since I had mentored him. I found myself calling him five or six evenings a week to encourage him and pray for him. I had never given that much attention to one person in a supportive role and often wondered about it. Marcus lived for twenty months and faced many trials before he went home to the Lord. Now so many of you are giving me the support, love and concern I need. "If you sow bountifully, you will reap bountifully." (2 Corinthians 9:6)*

Monday, April 12

The presentation to Ronnie Floyd's church staff of forty-five persons went wonderfully. I was sustained through it all by the strength of the Lord for three hours. They are very interested in Bible Storying in small groups and Ronnie wants to start churches for the sixty-seven Unreached People Groups in Northwest Arkansas! Praise The Lord! They really want to reinvent their churches to go after the people. I am very encouraged and pleased.

Thursday, April 15

Good news! My white blood count is NORMAL for the first time since I contracted leukemia three and half months ago. I do get two transfusions for hemoglobin tomorrow so I can get the red count up before the DNA-21 conference. That takes between six and eight hours in the outpatient clinic. I found myself singing a song this evening as I watched the sunset. That is the first time I have done that spontaneously in at least four months. So I am feeling better and my spirit is stronger—even though my flesh is weak.

Suffering is one of the biggest challenges to our faith. God's Word is clear: all suffering is purposeful. The imagery of the jar of clay reveals this deeper truth as Paul described: ". . . though our outer self is wasting away, our inner self is being renewed day by day" (2 Corinthians 4:16b ESV). How can this be? Paul was always amazed that God would put a priceless treasure in a jar of clay. What is this treasure? It is Christ in us. It's the Holy Spirit's refining, empowering and sanctifying work in us.

One of the most encouraging Scripture passages given to us clay-pot believers also encompasses God's promises for us: "But we have this treasure in jars of clay, to show that the surpassing power belongs to God and not to us. We are afflicted in every way, but not crushed; perplexed, but not driven to despair; persecuted, but not forsaken; struck down, but not destroyed; always carrying in the body the death of Jesus, so that the life of Jesus may also be manifested in our bodies. For we who live are always being given over to death for Jesus' sake, so that the life of Jesus also may be manifested in our mortal flesh." (2 Corinthians 4:7–11 ESV)

Monday, April 19

Ronnie Floyd invited me to the "closed" meeting of sixty-one mega-metro pastors gathering in Northwest Arkansas today and tomorrow. Great to see friends. I was asked to address "lostness" and tell them about DNA-21 and Bible Storying.

Dr. Floyd had asked Avery prior to this conference, "What, at the end of the conference, would you be heartbroken if we did not address?" Avery responded in a letter that demonstrated the passion of his heart for the "lostness" of the world.

Dear Ronnie,

The last question you asked on the Great Commission Resurgence conference call the other day has continued to haunt me, "If you were sitting in the audience when the GCR Task Force made their recommendations to the SBC, what would disappoint you if it were not addressed properly?"

The other night as I went to sleep I asked the Lord to help me dream about Him instead of the random things I usually dream of. He brought the issue back to me again when a man in the dream asked me, "Why should we be so concerned about the lost of the world when there are so many lost persons here?"

I answered him and then woke up and realized I had to write you.

My answer is: the lostness of the world!

I know that it is foremost on your heart and the hearts of the task force, but it is so easy to get concerned for the lostness nearby that we neglect the utter, total lostness of more than five billion people in the world without Christ. I hear things from the North American Mission Board about the U.S. being the fourth largest nation of lostness in the world, by which they mean there are numerically more lost people here than in all but three other countries. And that is true, but it does not factor in the critical element of how much light the lost here have and how many ways they can find Christ in 350,000 U.S. churches (44,000+ of them SBC) and with probably more than a hundred million born again believers here whose responsibility it is to reach them. So let me say emphatically, yes, we must address the lostness of North America whom we have been given the responsibility to reach. No question! And our churches and members have to have that laid on their hearts.

However, when I compare that to the task of the Great Commission, it in no way compares with the lostness of the world in depth of the darkness or the multitudes of people. The U.S. is 6% of the world's population and 90% of the world is lost. At least 1.5 billion people in the world have NEVER even heard about Christ and the Good News. How easily that number slides off our lips with little comprehension of what it means!

One of the problems is that we are myopic and see what is close to us. That is why 97.5% of the money in the offering plates stays at home and only 2½% gets to the rest of the world. That is why less than one tenth of one percent of Southern Baptists becomes missionaries. This is not right. This is not just. This is sin.

Think of it this way. Suppose there is a disaster in a mine and thousands of people are trapped in darkness facing imminent death. You are among those on the rescue team. Suppose you clear out enough debris for a man who is only 100 feet from the mouth of the mine to get out. You call him numerous times. You shine powerful lights to show him the way out but he ignores you. You increase your efforts and get more on the rescue team to try to persuade him to come out but although he is alert and well, he rejects all efforts. However, there are thousands trapped in the mine hundreds of feet below the surface. It will take a lot more effort, people, funds and time to reach them but you know that at most they only have 24 hours to live. They have no light; it is totally dark. They hear no calls; it is silent. They have no hope; there is no escape—unless the people on the outside care enough and determine that these thousands will not die without every effort to save them. And you realize that many of these people will welcome the good news and be saved and many will respond when they see the light and hear the call. The question you face, "Where are you going to put your priority?"

We forget how dark it is without Christ for those who have never heard, who have no hope, who don't even know that there is a Hope. If the GCR Task Force and the Southern Baptist Convention don't address the lostness of the world both in depth of darkness and the multitudes lost in the valley of decision, I will be broken-hearted. I am praying that God helps you to sound the call and send the light.

Gazing on God's Glory and
Telling His Story,
Avery

Avery attained another milestone when the doctors took off the wound vac and gave clearance for him to attend the initial DNA-21 launch in New Orleans. His son-in-law, Steve Brown, went along as his caregiver. The response was all Avery had hoped for.

Saturday, April 24

The first night of the DNA-21 Launch was fabulous with people from nineteen states and Canada. We had a great twelve-hour day. A lot of people are buying into the discipleship revolution. It could hardly have gone better. I did well with one nap after lunch. God has been good to give me the energy and passion to do my parts on the program.

Respite

Tuesday, May 18

Hallelujah, the doctors discharged me from this infection I have had for four and a half months! God delivered me from the shadow of death. Now we can concentrate on fighting the leukemia. I had five chemotherapy treatments last week. I don't have a lot of energy but this is a good time with my two sisters. The three of us have not been all together in six years. So the tales are flying.

Ralph and Roseane Speas, friends for over thirty-five years, drove over from Tulsa to tell us about all they are doing in India and Africa in multiplying Bible Storying trainers in evangelism, discipleship and church planting. They are seeing amazing results and multiplication. They were in the original MasterLife *group at Eastwood, Tulsa. We were able to talk about what else they could do to take it to the next level and train leaders better. Ralph reported that he was invited to Liberia to do Bible Storying training. Soon the locals asked how they could reach five unreached people groups. But by the time the plan developed, they had expanded it to all of West Africa with a goal to reach 117 unreached people groups with the Bible stories. Pray for his second trip later this year to train trainers for all these people groups.*

Thursday, May 27 - On the return checkup in Houston

Dr. O'Brien at M.D. Anderson said that I was doing well and that she planned to keep me on these Dacogen treatments for two years, maybe spaced out a little more. She said that she hated to mess with success (remission) by going to more radical chemo which would lower the quality of life. I am too old for a bone marrow transplant which she would do if I were younger. We'll monitor the progress and return in three months.

So how am I responding to this? I am taking it in stride and knowing that Our Father will lead the doctors and us to make any different decisions along the way. I don't really believe I'll be on this medicine for two years.

Increasingly, as Avery wrote on his Caring Bridge, and read the daily responses, he realized God had given him a new platform to give spiritual encouragement and make disciples. His posts were less about updates on his physical condition and more about what God was doing around the world. The posts became longer and were filled with links to videos, stories, and opportunities to participate in the kingdom: to pray, to disciple others online, to call others to repentance, to learn, and again, to pray. He began to include training from *MasterLife* on issues like spiritual warfare and putting on spiritual armor. He also shared what God was teaching him through his own suffering—both physically and in being limited to his recliner when he wanted so badly to be on the front lines of God's activity.

Flow from Crushing

Monday, May 31

I felt better today and took my first walk in three weeks. I walked a mile very slooowly.

I have had some awesome worship times the last two mornings.

One of the things God spoke to me about is oil. Oil is one of the analogies of the Spirit especially in anointing, empowering, lighting a lamp, healing and flowing in the Spirit. The Bible references speak of olive oil but you can't get the oil without crushing the olive. It is also true that you can't be filled with the Spirit and flow in the Spirit unless you are crushed/broken first.

I know this was true the first time I was consciously filled with the Spirit and as I reflect on my life, I see the crushing and the flowing go together when we respond to God's Spirit. I think of so many instances when I felt crushed by something only to see the Spirit flow from that crushing to bless others. Some of the crushings were "circumstantial" or "spiritual" disappointments. Most of them came in spiritual struggles over where God was leading me that I did not want to go. However, in retrospect the oil flowed more readily after the experiences.

One of my crushing experiences was when God led us away from front line evangelism and church planting in an area of millions of unreached peoples to teach and later lead the Indonesian seminary. It took a while but I later realized this was part of God's plan to pour out His Spirit through me on many more people than I could have reached where I wanted to serve. Personal crushing meant multiplied blessings through the Spirit.

Later, God led us back to the U.S.A. (kicking and screaming) to lead MasterLife and discipleship training. It was crushing for me to leave the goal of my life—to be a career missionary—but I see the Spirit using that to spread His work much farther than I could have done without my going through this disappointment. Personal crushing meant multiplied blessings through the Spirit.

Now I am living with a crushing unlike any I have experienced in seventy-six years. It is physical. I went from very, very active service a year ago spending about half time overseas to the last six months not being able to leave my doctors. So if I accept this crushing as like others in my life when I was disappointed but which resulted in the flow of the Spirit, what should I be expecting now? That the oil would run out or flow? As I turn to the Spirit I know that He has ways to flow through me to people I have not touched and places that were unavailable to me in the past.

My task is to accept the crushing as the hand of God so He can flow His Holy Spirit through me to help others. Each time I have gone through this crushing/filling experience the results have been different but productive far beyond what I could have imagined.

The end of ourselves is the beginning of the Spirit's work. So when you are being crushed, don't give up; God has just shown you that He wants to use you in a different way as you allow the Spirit to teach and guide you. Are you going through a crushing time right now? It is not the end of the trail but the beginning of a new flow of the Spirit through you if you let Him fill you and lead you.

Reproducing

Thursday, June 3

Have you noticed that God expects everything and everyone to reproduce? Note in the creation story that He made seed bearing plants and trees so He would not have to re-create them over and over again. He expects multiplication. He did the same with all the animals, including mankind. He built in reproductive systems that would work and continue His creation. What does that say to you about spiritual reproduction and multiplication? God is looking for fruit from you. John 15:16 says, "You did not choose me, but I chose you and appointed you to go and bear fruit, fruit that will last."

Celebrating Victories

Friday, June 11

Lon Vining felt called to plant churches in Montreal, Canada. I have done some mentoring through email. Here is an email he sent this week telling me of their progress.

I am going about making disciples in a way very much like *Truth That Sticks* and DNA-21 envisions—by basing our church completely on holistic small groups that multiply (a pure cell church structure) and the use of storying as a means of discipleship. Our church does not have programs and committees. We are focused on making leaders and disciples. Instead, I pour into ten cell group leaders, specifically meeting with them each Monday night, and they in turn are pouring into the group members they have been given to lead. We began last year with two groups, and in the fall, we expect to be at six groups. We will begin a nine-month walk through the Bible from Genesis to Jesus in our cell groups. I am excited about this.

I wanted to share a couple of things with you I thought you might like, and maybe even want to use.

Chronological Bible Storying Is . . .

Getting God's Word off the page

And Into Our Hearts

So it can Flow Out of our Lives

And off of our Tongues
To Reach a Lost World and Disciple the Nations.

I find that explaining it this way helps literates get it a lot faster. In response to the expository preaching adherents, I say that I agree whole-heartedly. I just use "exposi-story" teaching—revealing God's Word one truth at a time, while hiding it in one's heart one story at a time.

Tuesday, June 15 - at the Southern Baptist Convention

Hallelujah! Southern Baptists agreed to focus on fulfilling the Great Commission! Pray for the implementation of the Great Commission Resurgence over the next several years.

After sixty-one years of going to the SBC, I am so happy to live to see this day and emphasis come. As with any monumental change in a huge organization it will take years for implementation by the respective boards to turn everything around. Persevere in prayer.

Thanks for your prayers for my strength. One more day and then two days of Table 71. We are seeing so many good friends that this is a wonderful time.

Saturday, June 19

God gave me unusual strength all week for the SBC and Table 71 and two Advisory Board meetings.

The report on the 639 UUPGs with population of 100,000 or more was thrilling. So far 414 now have workers living on the ground evangelizing and starting churches; 151 are adopted but as yet have been sent no cross cultural workers, and 27 are still unengaged and unadopted. If you know how to shout; now is the time! Join heaven in HALLELUJAH! It is also time to pray for the 178 UUPG's over 100,000 still unengaged without workers on the ground.

So far 43,429 baptisms have been reported, 7,591 small groups started, and 7,167 churches started. There has been so much progress that we are expanding the new list to include those with populations of 50,000 which makes a new total of 632 unengaged, unreached people groups (including those 178 from the first list that are still unengaged).

I have noticed that "unreached" has a red underline on my computer as not being in the dictionary. It tries to substitute "unrelated" or "unre-

acted." I guess that is a pretty good description of the unreached. They are not related to any Christian or to Christ and they can't react to a message they have never heard.

Avery continued to feel stronger in June than any time since he had become ill. Though he had lost forty-five pounds and moved slower, he felt well enough to want to go down the hill to his gazebo again. The hill was incredibly steep, but he had purchased a golf cart that barely fit on the narrow concrete path. He invited different family members to ride up or down with him. It turned out to be such a terrifying experience for the passengers, however, that it prompted a need for a T-shirt claiming, "I survived the trip to the gazebo!"

Wednesday, June 30

The family members visiting us went home today. What a blessing from God to have such a godly family from the youngest to oldest. God is so good. "I have no greater joy than that my children [and grandchildren and little great grandchildren who are still young] are walking in truth." 3 John 4

Relapse

On Sunday, July 4, Avery was readmitted to the hospital due to a 103-degree fever Shirley discovered when she kissed him good night. Upon admission, the fever reduced, but later spiked again.

We are still waiting until tomorrow on results from the tests and cultures but my lungs seem to be filling up. I am short of breath and my whole rib cage is aching which could indicate pneumonia. So I'm not feeling good on July 4th. I asked the hospital nurse to put me in a hospital room across from Pinnacle Hills church so I could watch the fireworks.

Thursday, July 8

My doctors have decided that I am dealing with more than just pneumonia, so are doing cat scans, cultures etc. to find the infection that is causing the fever. They have called in Dr. Bandy, the infectious disease doctor who treated my last infection. I may not get to go home this weekend.

Saturday, July 10

I have had no fever for three days but I don't feel well with the pneumonia which is being very resistant. I am getting a transfusion tonight until about midnight. I'll have to cancel going to Richmond for Dr. Jerry Rankin's retirement, celebrating his accomplishments through these seventeen years. Mostly I'll miss getting to go to Richmond for the first time in about four years and seeing so many friends on the IMB trustees and staff.

It has been difficult for me to deal with missing out on participating in several historic and many personal relationship events that I had planned on for several months and some for years. So this is a really disappointing year to me but I just have to deal with each health challenge that comes and make decisions accordingly. It is so different than when I could reach back on reserves and do whatever needed to be done.

However, it has been my philosophy since high school days that whatever the present time is, that is the best time of my life. I can't say that from a human perspective right now but if I look at the eternal perspective God may use this time far more than if I had been healthy. At least He is planning to work all things together for good for me for I love God and am called to His purpose.

I won't make it to church tomorrow but two couples from my Sunday School class brought brownies and chocolates. They know I am a chocoholic.

Sunday, July 11

Good news! I am better and making progress. Chest not hurting as bad. Back pain practically gone. No fever. Praise the Lord and thank you for your prayers.

Yesterday in my physical condition I had a hard time connecting with the Lord. I did all the disciplines of reading my Bible, praying, listening to Christian music, and thanking God for things, but I still did not feel the close relationship I usually do. So what do you do when you know the Lord is always near you and Christ is abiding in you but you don't feel His presence?

I heeded Paul's words in Philippians 3:13–15: "But this one thing I do, forgetting what is behind and straining toward what is ahead, I press on toward the goal to win the prize for which God has called me heavenward in Christ Jesus. All of us who are mature should take such a view of things." He had just said in verse 10, "I want to know Christ and the power of His resurrection and the fellowship of sharing in His sufferings, becoming like Him in his death, and so somehow to attain the resurrection from the dead."

So today I pressed on. I hate to admit that my physical situation yesterday kept me from feeling a close connection/relationship with God and that my feeling better helped that today. Yet, If I am going to accept one, I should accept the other. But I can't live long without that fellowship with God so I pressed on.

Today I invite you to listen to a short YouTube video by T. D. Jakes "Yes, Lord"[2] to understand what to do when trouble comes, or a feeling of not being connected with God or not being able to do what you want to do. I don't forward many things but this expresses where I am. Keep pressing on and saying "Yes, Lord!"

Tuesday, July 13

The videotaping of my testimony for LifeWay discipleship week at Ridgecrest went well this morning. It is four minutes long but took thirty minutes of standing to get it right and several hours of taping, counting the rests in between due to weakness. I am feeling pretty good and hopefully will be able to go home tomorrow after thirteen days in the hospital.

Wednesday, July 14

Praise the Lord! Home sweet home. I'm still taking medicine but plan to go to Jerry Rankin's retirement this weekend.

As I thought about the closed door to going last Sunday I asked the Lord to let me go on the basis of a Bible Promise: Psalms 37:4–5. "Delight yourself in the Lord and He will give you the desires of your heart. Commit your way to the Lord, trust in Him and He will do this." I felt that I had been too passive in my asking. God loves to answer prayers that come from those who delight themselves in the Lord. That way it is His initiative and our response. When you believe <u>before</u> it happens He gets the glory. Otherwise, afterward, you can say "Praise the Lord," but it does not carry the same weight of glory.

Monday, July 19

The trip to Richmond went as well as could be expected. But after I rested, I awoke with a fever. Sunday night my fever spiked to 102.8 so I went to the St. Mary's hospital in Richmond. Here is what they discovered: My leukemia is back and no longer in remission. They suspect the pick line I've had for six months caused infection and atrial fibrillation so my heartbeat has been all over the chart. They drew a pint of fluid from around my left lung.

I missed the staff luncheon today honoring Jerry Rankin and probably will miss the trustee banquet on Tuesday. The doctors say they hope to get me back home in a couple of days and in the hands of my regular doctors.

With the total medical workup in the last twenty-four hours, St. Mary's might have been the place to be because they have given more tests than I could have imagined and found more than I imagined (Romans 8:28). So, now you know how to pray.

The joy of the Lord is my strength.

My grandmother had a glittering motto on her wall that has really stuck with me: "Only one life, 'twill soon be past. Only what's done for Christ will last."

When I went to LifeWay, I determined I wanted us to produce discipleship material that would last beyond the normal book life of one to five years. I wanted it to last twenty-five years at least. So I put my life message in MasterLife, *Henry Blackaby put his life message in* Experiencing God *and T. W. Hunt poured himself into the* The Mind of Christ *and* PrayerLife.

Thirty years after MasterLife, *twenty years after* Experiencing God *and seventeen after* The Mind of Christ, *God is still using them. I am reminded almost daily how God is still using* MasterLife.

Thursday, July 22

PTL! Doctors dismissed me from the hospital. A friend is providing a plane home to Bella Vista tomorrow—with the oxygen I need. Pray that my doctors will know what to do next.

I got the word today that Truth That Sticks: How to Communicate Velcro Truth in a Teflon World *has been released by NavPress. God was gracious to give me six months to work on it before the leukemia broke out big time.*

It was just in time.

CHAPTER 34
Final Days

(Through the eyes of the family—and told in first person by Sherrie)

May it be said of me as it was of David in Acts 13:36,
"Now when David had served God's purpose in
his own generation, he fell asleep."

—Avery

The intensity began with Friday's Caring Bridge entry. As I was falling asleep on the couch at ten thirty Friday night, Steve said, "I think you'll want to read this." I had him read it to me:

The private plane was a blessing from God. I have taken a turn for the worse. I did not make it home but went directly to the doctor's office and ER and hospital in Northwest Arkansas. My leukemia has returned aggressively. My heart is weakened now and faces the problem of congestive heart failure. Fluid is on lungs with pneumonia. I gained 15 Lbs. in two days, mostly fluid. They took another 750 ccs off my right lung today. My kidneys are not working properly. As you know when you get more major organs in crisis you have greater risk. Please PRAY for this crisis I am facing to our God. We only want His will done, not ours . . . I dreamed the other night that two friends shot me in the back. My response was, "I didn't expect that but 'Hooray' I am about to meet Jesus." I lifted my hands up to receive Him. I can't imagine what it will be like. Just look at creation! This is the new Creation that I look forward to experiencing and all He has been preparing for all these years. PTL. (Friday, July 23, 2010)

I was instantly awake and deeply concerned. This was an entirely different tone from most of his posts.

Apparently, it had the same impact on all of us because Krista e-mailed me first thing in the morning to ask if she should return to the US. By 8:00 a.m., I was on the phone with Brett and Gretchen in Colorado who were already packing. I then called Randy, who told me his son, Kyle, had called to tell "Grandad" that he and Megan were coming up in a couple of weeks to which Dad replied, "If you wait two weeks, Kyle, I won't be here."

Mom couldn't give me a clear sense of "imminent," so I asked Dad directly if, knowing the travel time involved, Krista should go ahead and book her plane ticket from Indonesia. He said, "Tell her to come." Compelled by the same sense of urgency, we all prepared to go to Bella Vista with food and clothes to stay a while—possibly to the end.

After reading the Friday update, Randy, Denyce, and daughter Kara decided to make a quick trip from Tulsa to Bella Vista on Saturday and return for church on Sunday. So when Dad phoned Tom Elliff and asked him to preach the funeral, Randy was in the room. Randy was rather stunned to hear him say it—and so matter-of-factly. Only able to hear one side of the conversation, he was even more surprised to hear Dad say, "Well, you pray about it." Was it possible Tom had turned him down? (Later, Tom would say that he was just taken aback to be asked and did not know how to respond.)

Randy planned to teach a lesson Sunday morning that involved storying David and Goliath. He thought Dad would enjoy hearing it, so he practiced on him in the hospital room. Dad said, "Just ask them questions—they'll get the point."

Before leaving Bella Vista that Sunday morning, Randy and Denyce talked about what they should tell their son, Matt, and wife, Allison, knowing they were scheduled to return as missionaries to South Asia the following Saturday. Randy recounted a story Dad told about coming back from Indonesia for the first furlough and visiting his mother's family in Jackson, Tennessee. An uncle had passed away during their first term. Even though Dad knew it intellectually, he had not processed the loss emotionally until he walked into the house in Jackson expecting to see him. So Randy encouraged Matt and Allison to return to Bella Vista even though their whole family had been there three weeks before. Matt and Allison came to spend the day with Grandad the next day.

On their way back to Tulsa, Randy, Denyce, and Kara stopped again at the hospital. They were only there about thirty minutes. Mom was with them. Dad was not feeling well; Randy knew there was a possibility he would not see him alive again. He asked Dad if there were some Scripture he would like to read. Dad asked for two passages: Psalm 139 and Psalm 71. Randy knew immediately Dad's life verse was in the middle of Psalm 71 and that reading it was going to be very tough. He choked and wept his way through the first few verses: "In you, O Lord, I have taken refuge (v.1)... Rescue me and deliver me in your righteousness; turn your ear to me and save me (v.2) ... Be my rock of refuge to which I can always go (v. 3) ... For you have been my hope, O Sovereign Lord, my confidence since my youth (v. 5)" but somehow was able to regain enough composure to clearly read the remainder, including Dad's life verse: "Since my youth, O God, you have taught me, and to this day I declare your marvelous deeds. Even when I am old and gray, do not forsake me, O God, until I declare your power to the next generation, Your might to all who are to come" (vv. 17–18). It was a cherished father-son moment.

After a "frank talk" with the doctor, it was clear Dad was preparing to die and making arrangements. He and Mom discussed funeral plans. He wrote:

My major systems are working against each other and kidneys will probably shut down. Heart weakened. Praise strengthened. The time that God ordained for me will happen. He has prepared for me a place and will receive me. Glorious. (Saturday, July 24, 2010)

The first few days of his last week, we took shifts spending time with him at the hospital so as not to wear him out. There were special moments. As soon as Matt and Allison walked in, he said, "Come here. I want to bless that little one." He laid his hand on Allison's pregnant belly and prayed for unborn Ethan, his third great-grandchild.

A box of his newly published *Truth that Sticks* book arrived at the hospital, and he signed a few for us. He actually enjoyed the Baskin-Robbins ice cream brought in and the beautiful "edible arrangement" fruit basket (or maybe that was all of us enjoying his fruit). He had a long conversation with his cousin Mike, who was dying of bone cancer and encouraged him. He dictated his Caring Bridge entries and taught us his three-step sequence for updating his audience on Twitter, Facebook, and Caring Bridge.

Leukemia is back, and the doctors feel treating it will push me over the edge. I may go home Wednesday to die at home rather than at the hospital. Krista arrived from Indonesia today so she is here along with all the other children. We're having a great time. Pray this will be a glorious week. (Tuesday, July 27, 2010)

Dad received two particularly poignant e-mails. One from Sid Schmidt read, "The woman with bleeding in Scripture said, 'Oh, if only I could touch the hem of his garment, I would be healed.' You have not only touched the hem, you have been wrapped in His garment; the garment of suffering, pain, agony and VICTORY. Avery, memories of assisting you in *MasterLife* Workshops in SE Asia allowed me see the 'cloth from which you were cut.'"

Johnny Norwood, missionary friend from Indonesia, sent a quote from the book *The Match* by Mark Frost:

> "Life is not a journey to the grave with the intention of arriving safely in a pretty and well-preserved body, but rather to skid in broadside in a cloud of smoke, thoroughly used up, totally worn out, and loudly proclaiming . . . 'Wow! What a ride!'"[1]
>
> Thank you, Avery, for showing us how to *skid* into heaven.

We thought Dad was scheduled to be dismissed to come home on hospice on Wednesday, so most of the family stayed home to prepare, make banners, etc. He really wanted to get away from the hospital and back to his recliner. When I went to the hospital, there was very little activity that looked like preparing for dismissal. It turned out to be a very quiet day.

That afternoon, I was at the foot of his bed, rubbing his swollen feet. He opened his eyes, looked at me, and smiled. I asked him if he preferred to sleep or talk. He said, "I'll talk if you will. It keeps my mind off things." I shared the first two paragraphs of "The Chair," which I had written for him. I wish I had asked him who the friends were who shot him in his dream and what he thought it meant. Instead, knowing how he liked to think and talk vision, I referred back to an earlier discussion and asked him about his conversation with Tom Elliff. The more he talked, the more the energy returned to his voice. Suddenly, in the midst of it, he said, "Hand me my phone."

He dialed up Rick Brekelbaum and began to instruct him to keep connected with Tom and make sure that he stayed in the DNA-21 loop—that Tom would be a powerful spokesperson because he "understood groups and discipleship."

My discharge from the hospital was delayed because of transfusions. Hopefully, I can go home Thursday. God and family are very precious right now. God is leading each step of the way as we follow Him. I especially appreciate all of your encouraging words. (Wednesday, July 28, 2010 – his final post)

Thursday morning, as he waited to be dismissed, he was about to show me the video of his testimony that LifeWay had filmed the week before. Just then, the nurses came in with discharge papers, so I told him we would watch it at the house with everyone.

At noon, he came home via ambulance, brushing his head against the welcome banner as he was rolled in on the gurney. He admired the artwork the kids had done on the window and the freshly made brownies waiting on the table. His equipment was set up, and some of the family sat on the carpet near the recliner, played games, and talked to him. The girls massaged his feet as he watched the baseball game.

At one point, Mom suggested that we be a little quieter, but Randy reminded her that this was why he wanted to come home. Mom, Gretchen, Randy, Krista, and I sat and visited with the hospice nurse for about three hours, signing forms, going over medications, and learning what to expect. Had we known these were his final hours, we would have "chosen the better thing."

Before she left, the hospice nurse asked Dad if he had any questions. He looked up and asked simply, "I am just wondering what it will be like . . ." She told him he would begin to sleep more and more until one day he would drift away—that it could be days, maybe even weeks—that he looked like he still had more to do. His face lit up, and he said, "Well, I do!" A short time later, Claude King called. Dad told him cheerily, "Well, the nurse just gave us a little more time." Claude prayed for him and hung up.

At suppertime, I made him a grilled turkey and cheese sandwich. He only ate one or two bites. The brownie he decided to save for later, and we put a sticky note on it: "Granddad's brownie. Do not eat."

About 7:00 p.m., he decided to take a nap. He started out walking toward the bedroom, got about a third of the way there, then sat in his walker chair and scooted himself the rest of the way. He slept in his clothes. The Hendricks, longtime friends from St. Louis, arrived at the Owens' house next door and asked to come visit. I told them he had just gone to bed and was pretty tired—that tomorrow would probably be better.

Granddaughter Lauren needed to leave for Kansas City, so she and Steve woke Grandad up around 9:00 p.m. so she could say goodbye and tell him she loved him. He gave her a great smile. After she left, Steve went back in to help him use the restroom. Dad asked Steve to sing the "Yes, Lord" song—meaning the version by T. D. Jakes he had seen on YouTube and which had really ministered to him. Not knowing that, Steve sang the only "Yes, Lord" song he knew, "Trading My Sorrows" with the "Yes, Lord" chorus (words still totally appropriate). I asked him later what Dad did.

Steve smiled and shrugged sheepishly, "He sang along."

When it was clear that Dad wasn't getting back up that night, we debated whether to write a Caring Bridge in his voice or ours. We opted for the former, and Randy wrote:

It has been a tiring day, so this will be short. God is so good to allow me to make it home from the hospital around noon and have been visiting with family and friends. Will update more tomorrow.

We went to bed around eleven o'clock that night. Mom and I slept in the bedroom with Dad. Around 2:00 a.m., Dad woke up and moaned loudly. He began muttering. I got up and sat by his bed, holding his hand. His pulse was very rapid. The only clear thing I understood was,

"I may not make it."

I answered with, "But's it's okay, Dad."

"Yeah, it is."

"Because if you don't make it here, it means you made it there."

About three thirty in the morning, when his pulse continued to be rapid and weak, it was becoming clearer to me that we might be close to the end, and I woke Mom up. By 4:00 a.m., he was having trouble breathing. He wanted to sit up.

After gathering Brett and Krista and calling Randy and the hospice nurse, we sat with him. Dad was sitting weakly on the edge of the bed as we supported him. Suddenly, his body slumped, and he exhaled. Then he gave a small gasp, and then there was no more. Brett said, "That's it. He's gone." I looked at the digital clock on the dresser, and it clicked to 5:01. I kissed Dad on the back of the neck, Mom kissed him on the lips, and we laid him back. It was all very surreal.

When Randy arrived moments later, he looked in for a moment and then went into Dad's office, and on his computer wrote the beautiful Caring Bridge entry which was often quoted in the news releases about Dad's death:

> My dad graduated to Glory early this morning, July 30. He died peacefully, without pain or anxiety. My mom, sisters, and brother were with him. I thank each of you that have visited, called, written, and prayed over his past seven months. Your words of encouragement meant so much to him and to all of us. What a privilege to hear of the lives he impacted during his 76 years. May that influence extend through the generations...
>
> My dad's life verse was Ps. 71:17–18, "Since my youth, O God, you have taught me and to this day I declare your marvelous deeds. Even when I am old

463

and gray, do not forsake me, O God, till I declare Your power to the next generation and Your might to all who are to come." And so he did.

This is the time to celebrate a life. Do we not know the God who spoke the world into existence? Do we not know the only God who provides true forgiveness of sin? Do we not know the God of the ages, who knows the end from the beginning?

This is not the time to mourn as those who have no hope. If my dad were still here, he would say we should be mourning for those that have no hope—those that do not know the Creator of the universe, the Forgiver of sin, the Eternal God—for the billions of people in the world that do not know the power of the name of Jesus.

The hospice nurse came, and while she washed the body, Gretchen, Kristine, Megan, Krista, and I sat out on the deck and watched the sunrise. I called Wade, who had returned to Tennessee two days earlier. Mom woke the Hendricks, who came to see the body. I felt badly that we had held them off the night before.

Later that morning, we all watched the testimony video at the kitchen counter... and cried. What a powerful way for him to still speak to us. When it was played at his funeral, Brett quipped, "Leave it to Avery and the Holy Spirit to find a way to preach at his own funeral!"

I look back now and think about how calmly we took care of business that day—letting people know, making funeral service arrangements, holding each other up; there was a deep peace. As surprised as we were that he only lived one night at home, I remember being so grateful that he had died so peacefully, without lingering, and that it meant we were all there. It was such a miracle that our family members who lived overseas: Krista, Kent, Matt, and Allison were all in the US and were able to be with him right before his death. We had not needed to make the difficult decisions of how long to stay and when to return home as so many do in hospice times. We were able to stay together through the funeral and part of the next week.

Because a reunion of the Indonesian missionaries was being held that very weekend in nearby Branson, Missouri, it even meant that many of the Indonesian mission family could come to the funeral. For me, that was a great gift from the Lord.

Tom Elliff said he "googled" *Avery Willis* the next morning as he prepared for the funeral, and the first thing that popped up was "Avery T. Willis, Jr: *Learning to Soar . . .*"

Tom chuckled as he thought, "You have no idea how true that is!"

It wasn't until several days after the funeral that we had the heart to throw away Dad's brownie.

For Dad, during his leukemia...

The Chair

He sighed and laid back in his recliner, closing the computer for now. He was tired again and needed sleep. He missed the twelve-hour days of active work. His mind could remember the dialogue and the stunts but his body could no longer follow.

He had a new role now, with more authority and effectiveness. He had a vision for the whole piece, not just his part. His responsibility was to envision the best way to produce the show, crafting the plot, arranging the players, and designing the best way to communicate the message. No longer the actor, he had become the director.

Then came the day, he rose from that chair and joined the audience, taking his seat in the grandstands among a great clouds of witnesses to watch the full story unfold.

By Sherrie Willis Brown
Final Verse Completed July 30, 2010

Postlude

Final Tributes

"Willis embodied the 'faithful servant' with his passionate pursuit of reaching the lost and teaching the saved. His lasting legacy will not be just the orality strategy of storytelling the gospel that he championed abroad and at home, or the *MasterLife* resources found in church classrooms. His enduring heritage will be the lives changed because his love for Christ stirred his heart to reach one more soul."

—Morris H. Chapman,
President of the SBC Executive Committee

"Because of his discipleship materials, Avery would be as close to a household name among Southern Baptists as any other figure. A loss of a man like this would leave a crater in Southern Baptist life were it not for the fact that he has so effectively filled his own crater with the thousands that he has discipled."

—Paige Patterson,
President of Southwestern Seminary

"He envisioned every born-again believer becoming a true disciple of Jesus Christ. He saw the church being on fire for reaching the lost and functioning as a God-glorifying Body of Christ. And he never wavered in his vision of people from every tribe, language, and nation gathered around the throne of God."

—Dr. Jerry Rankin, IMB President

Personal Charge

Avery Willis Jr. was only one piece on God's chessboard, one soldier in God's army, one committed disciple who chose to live his life as obediently as he could. You are another—equally important to the overall strategy God has for bringing the world to Himself.

Will you commit your life to follow Jesus wholeheartedly, walk in the power of the Holy Spirit, make disciples of all nations, and live for God's glory?

If you feel God leading you to continue Avery's vision to reach the lost people of the world, the unreached people groups, those without access to the gospel, or to learn more about Bible storying, please contact:

The International Mission Board: www.imb.org

International Orality Network: https://orality.net

DNA-21: www.dna-21.org

Appendix

God's Story of Reaching
Manuel Noriega

(Told by Anthony Ponceti in a personal
phone interview, April 16, 2016)

D r. Clift Brannon Sr., a lawyer who had presented cases before the
United States Supreme Court, had a phenomenal gift for reaching
leaders in foreign nations. As soon as a national leader of any country
was elected, Clift would send him/her a Soulwinner's New Testament.
In January 1990, when Dr. Clift heard the news that Manuel Noriega
had been captured, he took a New Testament from his inventory,
wrote in the front "Jesus loves you and so do I," and mailed it to the
Metropolitan Correctional Center in Miami, Florida, where Noriega
was being held. Reminded that Manuel would not speak English, he
brought out a Spanish New Testament, asked Rudy Hernandez to
translate his message in Spanish, and mailed it off as well.

Anthony "Tony" Ponceti was involved with Texas Baptist Men. He
had been trained in *MasterLife* and had worked with Avery on some
MasterLife training weekends and joined him at several Texas Baptist
Men's Cedars Conferences in Mt. Lebanon, Texas. When Tony saw the
newscast that General Manuel Noriega had been caught, he leaned over
to his wife and said, "Why didn't we blow his brains out in Panama?"
He hated Noriega and everything Noriega represented. Tony's brother
had died of an overdose of heroin, and his own daughter was involved
in drugs.

The following week, Tony attended a Bible study led by Don
Gibson, from Lay Renewal Ministries, on "What the Holy Spirit Is Saying

to the Churches" (a study written by Henry Blackaby, a forerunner to *Experiencing God*). Don told the group what Clift had done and asked them to pray for Noriega. Before he could pray, Tony first had to confess to the group and repent for what he had said to his wife. When he got home, he called Clift to inform him he was moving back to Miami to care for his aging parents and that he spoke Spanish. He asked if he could be of any service.

With their belongings packed and the car loaded for the move to Miami, Tony called Clift hoping to meet with him, but filled schedules prevented it. As it turned out, their scheduled event was the same—the Lay Renewal Coordinator's Conference in Dallas, Texas. They shared several meals together and began a long-term friendship and partnership to reach Noriega with the gospel.

Clift heard from Manuel Noriega's lawyer that Manuel had received both New Testaments and wanted to know the God who loved him— now! Tony's job was to get into the prison to witness to Noriega. Tony visited multiple Spanish churches trying to find a pastor who would be willing to go in to the prison. However, most Hispanics hated Noriega and wanted no part of it.

With hopes of making an inroad, Tony joined Glenview Baptist Church in Miami where the pastor was a chaplain. At that small church, Tony began teaching *MasterLife* under a tree on Tuesday mornings. One Tuesday, he asked the men to kneel around that tree and pray that God would open doors to the prison. He felt peace and knew the prayer would be answered.

On May 13, the prison warden sent word to Clift that if they could come on May 15, the men would be allowed to see Noriega. Rev. Billy Graham had telephoned former president Carter, who contacted President Clinton, who, in turn, had authorized their admittance. So on May 13, Clift traveled to Miami to find Tony.

On May 14, Clift, Tony, and Rudy Hernandez, a Texan of Mexican descent, who had interpreted for Billy Graham and would interpret for Clift, met in the hotel room, prayed diligently, and laid hands on the Bibles. On May 15, Tony drove the car, opened doors, carried bags, and most importantly, sat in the car and prayed while Clift and Rudy went in to see Noriega. At that time, they were the only ones—besides lawyers—allowed to speak to him. Though Manuel was in solitary confinement in a six-by-six-foot cell, Clift preached to him with the same voice and vehemence he used to preach in a stadium.

When Clift laid out God's plan for salvation, Noriega replied, "The king can do no wrong." He was unwilling to admit his own sin and seek forgiveness. However, when they returned the next day, his heart had changed; and on May 16, 1990, Manuel Noriega gave his life to Jesus.

Clift and Rudy continued monthly visits to the Miami prison cell, spending over ninety hours in personal time with him. When the travel became too expensive, Clift turned the role over to Tony, dictating to Tony (in lawyer-speak) the letter he needed to write to the warden to ask permission for weekly visits. Clift instructed Tony to have his pastor and the Director of Missions write similar letters of referral.

The following day, Tony took his three letters and went to see Noriega with Clift and Rudy. While Clift and Rudy were ushered in, the guards laughed at the letters, denying entrance to Tony. Filled with boldness, Tony said to them, "You might be laughing today, but God has called me to go in, and I will go in someday." He went back to his car and prayed for over five hours.

The next day, all seven of the heavy metal security doors were opened to him, and he found himself standing face-to-face with Manuel Noriega. Tony's first action was to ask Noriega for forgiveness for what he had spoken against him months earlier. They both wept as brothers in the Lord.

Within a few weeks, Tony was arriving weekly to teach *MasterLife* to Noriega. When the request for *MasterLife* was granted, it was contingent upon two FBI agents and a chaplain listening to everything that was said. Around the second or third week, the topic of study was forgiveness. Noriega needed to forgive former president George H. Bush, who had been his mentor when Noriega served as an undercover cop during the war on drugs, and by whom he felt betrayed. Through many tears, he chose to forgive, and in that action, he demonstrated his walk as a disciple and that Christ was the center of his life.

MasterLife Discipleship Training was followed by studying *Experiencing God* together. Tony and Manuel would spend six hours together each Wednesday and four more hours on Saturdays. At times,

Tony would call Avery to seek his counsel. Tony claimed, "I discipled Manuel Noriega for three years, and then Noriega discipled me for the next six years" (since Noriega had all day every day to spend in the Scriptures).

Noriega wrote his family, urging them to know Christ. At his request, Rudy Hernandez flew to the Dominican Republic to witness to his wife and three daughters. In a phone call from his prison cell, Manuel told them Rudy wouldn't leave till he received an answer. Clift and Tony were privileged to be with Manuel in his cell to witness the day his family accepted Christ.

The men agreed not to share this story until after Noriega's trial. They did not want publicity. They only wanted to be ministers. Noriega had two public interviews. In the nationally televised interview with Diane Sawyer in August of 1993, he gave an impressive testimony. The interview was rebroadcast at the Southern Baptist Convention.

At the completion of his trial in 1992, Noriega was convicted and sentenced to eight five-year sentences to be served consecutively. Manuel never expressed bitterness about his conviction.

In October of that year, General Manuel Noriega was baptized in a portable baptistery in the Federal Courthouse in Miami by Dr. Clift Brannon Sr., assisted by Pastor David Wideman of University Baptist Church of Coral Gables, the church into which he was being baptized. Several prior requests to do so had been denied because the warden at the prison would not allow it. He said, "When a man has that much bounty on his head, no way am I going to let you hold him under water!" However, after Noriega's conviction, it was permitted. Following the baptism, those present took communion together.

On April 20, 1993, Clift wrote a letter to President Clinton asking for a passport for Noriega's wife, who had not seen him for three years. Later, Rudy, Tony, and Bill White officiated at the wedding of one of Noriega's daughters. To the whole family's surprise, they arranged it so that Manuel Noriega would be allowed to speak by phone over a public address system to give his daughter away and give a charge to the bride and groom. Two senators from Panama who sat on the front row began to weep.

Manuel was later allowed to be under house arrest, but returned to the prison hospital when he became ill with cancer. His US prison sentence ended in September 2007. Both France and Panama requested he be extradited to them for crimes again their countries. He was extradited to France in 2010 for money laundering, found guilty, and sentenced to seven years. He was then conditionally released back to Panama in 2011 to serve twenty years for murder. But his heart was free.

Notes

Introduction
1. Jerry Rankin, "Missions Leader Avery Willis Dies at 76," *Baptist Press*, July 30, 2010.
2. Avery T. Willis Jr. and Sherrie Willis Brown, *MasterLife: Developing a Rich Personal Relationship with the Master* (Nashville: Broadman & Holman, 1998), 7. Reprinted and used by permission of LifeWay Christian Resources.

Section 1 Heading:
1. Henry Blackaby and Claude King, *Experiencing God: Knowing and Doing the Will of God* (Nashville: LifeWay, 1990), 103.

Chapter 1: Legacy
Information in this chapter from AT's journals, home video of Grace Willis and Avery Willis Jr. retelling stories, and Avery's background information in his application to the Foreign Mission Board.
1. August 16, 1993 (loose paper).
2. Story also recounted in: Avery T. Willis Jr. and Sherrie Willis Brown, *MasterLife: Developing a Rich Personal Relationship with the Master* (Nashville: Broadman & Holman, 1998), 48–49.

Chapter 2: Finding the Power
1. Phone interview with Bill Richardson.
2. Mark Fackler, "The World Has Yet to See," *Christianity Today*, no. 25 (1990).
3. This story is originally in Avery's written testimony in *PRAY* newsletter, February 1965, and told in his testimony video produced by LifeWay. It is also found in Avery T. Willis Jr. and Matt Willis, *Learning to Soar: How to Grow through Transitions and Trials* (Colorado Springs: NavPress, 2009), 31–32 (used by permission of NavPress, represented by Tyndale House Publishers, Inc.) and in Avery T. Willis Jr. and Sherrie Willis Brown, *MasterLife: Developing a Rich Personal Relationship with the Master* (Nashville: Broadman & Holman, 1998), 1–2 (used by permission).
4. Written testimony, *PRAY* newsletter, February 1965.
5. Recounted in *MasterLife: Developing a Rich Personal Relationship with the Master*, pp. 105–106 and in *Learning to Soar: How to Grow through Transitions and Trials*, 111–112.

6. Directly quoted from Avery T. Willis Jr. and Sherrie Willis Brown, *MasterLife: Developing a Rich Personal Relationship with the Master* (Nashville: Broadman & Holman, 1998), 106–107. Reprinted and used by permission of LifeWay Christian Resources.

Chapter 3: First Loves
Information in this chapter is from an interview with Shirley and her written testimony in *PRAY*, June 1965.
1. Story also found in *Masterlife: Developing a Rich Personal Relationship with the Master*, 3–4.

Chapter 4: Growing Churches, Growing Family
1. "Extension of Connell Forms a New Church," Tarrant Baptist Challenge, Fort Worth, Texas, May 15, 1959.
2. Questions found in an outline for a *MasterLife* presentation.
3. "Born to Reproduce - Early History of The Navigators," YouTube, https://www.youtube.com/watch?v=VQ_dVYTjLb0.
4. Avery's application to Foreign Mission Board.
5. "Inglewood Baptist Grows from 10 to 541 Members," *News Texan*, March 27, 1964.
6. Excerpt from sermon: "Pathway to God's Presence," Avery Willis, May 13, 1990.
7. Story also recorded in *Learning to Soar: How to Grow through Transitions and Trials*, 90–91.
8. Newspaper article from *Grand Prairie News* 54, no. 109.
9. Avery T. Willis Jr., "Memories of New Life Movement, Japan, 1963," journal booklet.

Chapter 5: Headed to the Mission Field
1. C. L. Culpepper, *The Gospel Truth: The Shantung Revival*, gospeltruth.net/shantung.html.

Chapter 6: Uncertain First Days
1. Avery T. Willis Jr., *Indonesian Revival: Why Two Million Came to Christ* (Pasadena: Carey, 1978), 68–70.
2. This paragraph from *PRAY* newsletter, April 1965, inserted into journal entry.
3. Journal, January 22, 1965.
4. Journal, January 7, 1965.
5. Journal, January 12, 1965.
6. Journal, February 25, 1965.

Chapter 7: Preparing to Sow
1. Journal, April 18, 1965.
2. *PRAY* (Willis's monthly newsletter to intercessors), September 1965.

Chapter 8: Revolution: The Indonesia Coup

1. Clarence W. Hall, "Indonesia: Dawn of Terror, Dawn of Hope," *Reader's Digest Special Feature*, October 1966, 277–278.
2. Avery T. Willis, *Indonesian Revival*, 68–70.
3. Clarence W. Hall, "Indonesia: Dawn of Terror, Dawn of Hope," 294.
4. Clarence W. Hall, "Indonesia: Dawn of Terror, Dawn of Hope," 296.
5. Recorded in *Indonesian Revival*, p. 85, quoting John Hughes, *Indonesian Upheaval* (New York: David McKay Co., 1967), 198.

Chapter 10: Breakthrough

1. *PRAY*, September 1966.
2. For more information on how to win victory over temptation and how to surrender to the Holy Spirit, readers can study the "The Disciple's Personality" or "The Disciple's Victory" chapters of *MasterLife: Developing a Rich Personal Relationship with the Master.*
3. *PRAY*, October 1966.

Chapter 11: Church Planting Expansion

1. Information from *PRAY* newsletter and May 1, 1967, extended journal entry enhanced from Avery's article "Tickets for Revival" in *The Commission Magazine*.

Chapter 12: Furlough

1. *PRAY*, May 1968.
2. E-mail from Johnny Norwood, January 16, 2016.
3. *PRAY*, November 1968.
4. *PRAY*, July 1969.
5. *PRAY*, June 1969.

Chapter 13: Jember: Church Planting amid Opposition

1. *PRAY*, October 1969.
2. *PRAY*, November and December 1969.
3. *PRAY*, May 1970.
4. *PRAY*, June 1970.
5. *PRAY*, July 1970.

Chapter 14: Semarang

1. Taped diary, May 8, 1971.

Chapter 15: Collision Course

1. *PRAY*, April 1971 records the spiritual renewal at the Central Java Prayer Retreat.
2. Quote from "Spiritual Breakthrough in Indonesia" 1A (see below).
3. *PRAY*, June 1971.

4. *PRAY*, May 1971.
5. Taped diary, June 1971.
6. *PRAY*, July 1971.

Chapter 16: Spiritual Breakthrough

1. "Spiritual Breakthrough in Indonesia," two cassette audio version written and narrated by Avery Willis Jr. and created by the Portable Recording Ministries Inc., 681 Windcrest Drive, Holland, Michigan, 49423.
2. "Spontaneous Spiritual Revival Continues in Indonesia Mission," prepared for release to the *Baptist Press* by William E. McElrath (recorded in *PRAY*, August 1971).

Chapter 17: Backlash and Turmoil

1. "Spiritual Breakthrough" tape.
2. Letter to Musjawarah attendees from Dr. Catherine Walker, August 7, 1971.
3. "Spiritual Breakthrough," 2B.
4. Letter from Keith Parks, read aloud in Avery's taped diary.
5. *PRAY*, January 1972.
6. Diary, December 12, 1971.

Chapter 18: Seminary Development

1. Avery quoted by Ione Gray in an article in December 1975 issue of *Baptist Program*.
2. Letter to AT and Grace Willis, August 7, 1971.
3. *PRAY*, February 1972.
4. *PRAY*, March, 1972.
5. *PRAY*, February 1972.
6. *PRAY*, May 1972.
7. *PRAY*, June 1972.
8. *PRAY*, March 1973.
9. *PRAY*, January 1973.
10. *PRAY*, May 1973.
11. *PRAY*, June 1973.
12. Cassette tape to Keith, December 21, 1972.
13. *PRAY*, November 1973.

Chapter 19: Stirring the Nest

1. Taped diary, September 7–14, 1973.
2. "On Eagle's Wings" sermon, preached Sunday evening, March 4, 1974, at Royal Palms Baptist Church in Phoenix, Arizona.

NOTES

Chapter 20: Decentralized Theological Education Works!
All information is from a taped diary recorded in 1976 to summarize 1974–1975.
[1] Asian Perspective No. 8 (Taipei: Asia Theological Association, 1976).

Chapter 21: About-Face: Call to America
[1] These are excerpts of Shirley's testimony when she returned to Indonesia to share the journey that led them to resign from the FMB.
[2] Journal, February 27, 1978.
[3] Story from Roy Edgemon.

Chapter 22: Discipleship in America—and Beyond
[1] "FACES_NAME" video, produced by the International Mission Board, 2005.
[2] PowerPoint presentation for the Faith Task Force of the Bill Bright Initiative and Avery T. Willis Jr., *Biblical Basis of Missions* (Nashville: Baptist Sunday School Board, 1992), 86–90.
[3] Avery T. Willis Jr., *Biblical Basis of Missions*, 89–90.
[4] Roy Edgemon, *Church Training Magazine*, April 1985.
[5] Roy Edgemon, e-mail dated March 6, 2017.
[6] Told by Tony Ponceti, in phone interview, April 16, 2016.
[7] Reported by Claude King (e-mail dated March 15, 2017).
[8] Mike Creswell, "MasterLife: Tool for Worldwide Discipleship," *The Commission Magazine*, September 1983, 42–43.
[9] Ibid.
[10] Reported by Claude King (e-mail to Ron Owens dated November 26, 2013).
[11] "After the Walls Came Down," Avery's synthesis of his journal, April 1990.
[12] Letter to Discipleship Department personnel summarizing Avery's China Journal, September 1991.
[13] Roy Edgemon, e-mail dated March 6, 2017.

Chapter 23: Aligning the Leaders
Much of this chapter reported by Claude King and Roy Edgemon.
[1] Language used in *Experiencing God: Knowing and Doing the Will of God*.

Chapter 24: Call for Solemn Assembly and Spiritual Awakening
[1] Information from Claude King.
[2] "Solemn Assembly," *Spiritual Renewal Manual*, quote on p. 1 by P. Douglas Small and description by Dr. Robert E. Fisher, p. 8–9.
[3] Journal, March 1990.
[4] Willis, quoted in the *Baptist Press* by Terri Lackey, release date: September 25, 1989, and excerpt of "Call to Prayer" sermon, May 13, 1990.
[5] Excerpt of Avery's message at the National Prayer Conference on Solemn Assembly, held June 7–9, 1991, in New Orleans.

6. Journal, December 13, 1989.
7. Journal, February 21, 1990.

Chapter 25: Conviction of Pride
1. "Others May, You Cannot," *Silent Evangelist*, no. 76.

Chapter 26: Seeking God's Next Assignment
1. Journal, January 28, 1990.
2. Journal, March 15, 1990.
3. Journal, May 24, 1990, and June 26, 1990.
4. Journal, August 21, 1990.

Chapter 28: Redesigning the Plan
1. Quote and much of the material in this chapter is directly from Dr. Jerry Rankin (e-mail to Ron Owens dated January 9, 2014).
2. Prayer letter, May 2000.
3. Prayer letter, January 2000.
4. Prayer letter, December 2003.
5. Prayer letter, January 2000.
6. Information charted from Mark Wingfield, "Bold Mission Thrust Comes to an End with a Few of Many Goals Realized" (title referring to the US goals), *Baptist Standard*, June 25, 2001.
7. Results listed in April 2001 prayer letter.

Chapter 29: A Glimpse into His Office
1. Description from Agnes Loyall, Avery's administrative assistant.
2. Evaluation performed by Russel, Montgomery, and Associates and summarized in a report to Roy Edgemon, August 31, 1992.
3. Shawn Hendricks, "Abdul Update: Amazing Growth and Increased Opposition since SBC," *Baptist Press*, October 18, 2004.

Chapter 30: Building a Global Partnership
1. "Solemn Assembly," *Spiritual Renewal Manual*, 4.
2. Rick Wood, "GCOWE '95: A Major Step Forward in Building a Movement to the Frontiers," *Missions Frontier* (July–August 1995), missionsfrontier.org.
3. "The AD2000 and Beyond Movement Launches Joshua Project 2000 in Global Gathering," *Missions Frontier* (January–February 1996).
4. Avery Willis, "GCOWE '97 Mission Executives Consultation Praetoria, South Africa, June 30–July 5, 1997: What Do 500 Mission Executives Hope to Accomplish? An Interview with Avery Willis, Cochairman," *Missions Frontier* (March–April 1997).
5. From the Table 71 Vimeo: https://vimeo.com/38237609.

Chapter 31: Making Disciples of Oral Learners

1. Avery T. Willis and Mark Snowden, *Truth that Sticks: How to Communicate Velcro Truth in a Teflon World* (Colorado Springs: NavPress, 2010), 22. Used by permission of NavPress. All rights reserved. Represented by Tyndale House Publishers Inc.
2. Retold from Avery's account in *Truth that Sticks*, 31–34, referencing *EE-Taow!* video (Sanford: New Tribes Mission, 1989), excerpted from *On Mission with God* video (Nashville: LifeWay, 2002).
3. *Making Disciples of Oral Learners*, Lausanne Committee for World Evangelization and International Orality Network, 2005.
4. J. O. Terry, *Story by Story to Empower Every Person Oral or Literate for Witness and Discipling Their Own* 17, no. 2 (April 2010).

Chapter 32: Refirement

1. Mark Kelly, "Avery Willis Honored for Vision, Passion, Obedience in Mission," *Baptist Press*, February 16, 2004 (at Avery's retirement from IMB), www.bpnews.net/17651.
2. Prayer letter, August 2004.
3. Gary D. Myers, "Avery Willis: Bible-Storying Not Just for the Mission Field Anymore," *Baptist Press*, March 23, 2010.
4. *Arkansas Democrat-Gazette*, religion section, June 7, 2008.
5. Lisa Sells, "Avery Willis' Last Dream," *Missions Frontier* (January–February 2011), Discipleship Revolution.
6. www.dna-21.org.

Chapter 33: Leukemia

1. Caringbridge.org/averywillis (no longer active).
2. https://www.youtube.com/watch?v=6_PfDRZpUKs

Chapter 34: Final Days

1. This quote is also attributed to Hunter S. Thompson, *The Proud Highway: Saga of a Desperate Southern Gentleman*, 1955–1967.

Postlude

1. "Missions Leader Avery Willis Dies at 76," *Baptist Press*, July 30, 2010.

About the Author

Sherrie Willis Brown is the daughter of Avery Willis Jr. and thus has an inside look into his life, personal connections with his friends, and access to his private journals. Growing up overseas on the mission field allowed her firsthand experience of the accounts in this book. She was personally discipled by Avery and has coauthored another book with him: *MasterLife: Developing a Rich, Personal Relationship with the Master.*

Sherrie is currently a reading specialist for elementary students in the North Kansas City School District. She has a BS in special and elementary education from Peabody-Vanderbilt and a master's degree in Learning Disabilities from the University of Missouri, Kansas City.

She and her husband, Steve, reside in Kansas City, Missouri. They serve as leaders and teachers in their church, lead an outreach children's ministry, and continue the DNA-21 ministry of discipling through Bible storying.

Sherrie is both a mother and a grandmother. She loves long walks, spending time with family and friends, and working with youth. As time allows, she also enjoys playing games, refinishing wood, reading, and writing.

CPSIA information can be obtained
at www.ICGtesting.com
Printed in the USA
FSHW02n2309240718
50664FS

9 781642 998528